About the author

Vanessa Donnelly is a software designer and Ease of Use consultant within the IBM Ease of Use group in Warwick, UK, where she specializes in the definition and design of computer user interfaces. More recently, she has concentrated her efforts on website analysis and development processes to improve how websites are defined, designed and developed in order to make them easier to use. She also acts as a consultant to businesses advising them on how to improve their websites and in addition provides input to IBM software groups and website teams about different analysis techniques, website design, information modelling and content management.

Vanessa joined IBM as a software developer in 1989 after graduating with a BSc in Computer Science. Since that time, she has worked on many different software products, and worked with human factors and graphic design experts to create software specifications. Vanessa has practical experience of all the main stages within the web development cycle, from writing code, creating high and low level design specifications and defining requirements from different types of analysis.

She now spends most of her time defining reusable models that can be used by web publishing systems. The goal is to help aid the process of creating, publishing and maintaining content on a site, the assumption being that well defined common models, templates and task flows can be reused to speed up, but also improve the web development process, and the website design that is created. As with all the research work undertaken by the IBM Ease of Use group, the focus and primary objective of this work is to make life easier for users.

For Tom, Max and Oscar

Designing easy-to-use websites

Designing easy-to-use websites

A hands-on approach to structuring successful websites

Vanessa Donnelly

 Addison-Wesley

An imprint of **Pearson Education**

Harlow, England · London · New York · Reading, Massachusetts · San Francisco
Toronto · Don Mills, Ontario · Sydney · Tokyo · Singapore · Hong Kong · Seoul
Taipei · Cape Town · Madrid · Mexico City · Amsterdam · Munich · Paris · Milan

PEARSON EDUCATION LIMITED

Head Office:
Edinburgh Gate
Harlow CM20 2JE
Tel: +44 (0)1279 623623
Fax: +44 (0)1279 431059

London Office:
128 Long Acre
London WC2E 9AN
Tel: +44 (0)20 7447 2000
Fax: +44 (0)20 7240 5771

Website: www.aw.com/cseng/

First published in Great Britain in 2001

© Vanessa Donnelly Limited 2001

The right of Vanessa Donnelly to be identified as Author of this Work has been asserted by her in accordance with the Copyright, Designs and Patents Act 1988.

ISBN 0-201-67468-8

British Library Cataloguing in Publication Data
A CIP catalogue record for this book can be obtained from the British Library.

Library of Congress Cataloging in Publication Data
Applied for.

10 9 8 7 6 5 4 3 2 1

Typeset by Pantek Arts Ltd, Maidstone, Kent.
Printed and bound in Great Britain by Biddles Ltd, Guildford and Kings Lynn.

The Publishers' policy is to use paper manufactured from sustainable forests.

Contents

Background and justification for a structured web development process

Introduction

My introduction to web usability

A few years ago I was asked to review one of the first designs for our Ease of Use website, a site created under the huge www.ibm.com umbrella at www.ibm.com/easy and one which has since been replaced numerous times by newer and more up-to-date versions. The goal of this site is to provide resources to an external community interested in ease of use issues and the area of human-computer interaction. Quite understandably, it was felt that such a site that offers guidance on how to make user interfaces easier to use should at least be fairly usable itself, and should undergo a level of usability review and evaluation.

In line with nearly all website development projects past and present, nobody wanted to hang about too long for this to happen. Due to the fact that this early version involved little user interaction, it was felt that an informal exercise could be undertaken to highlight any potential usability problems. I was asked to perform a simple walkthrough of the site, making notes of any usability problems that I encountered. At the end of the review I was also required to present my findings to the team who had put the site together.

The reason why they chose me to do this job was quite simple. Admittedly I had a background in designing and developing software user interfaces and had been involved in research into improving software ease of use for a number of years. Also, I used the internet regularly as a consumer, being quite vocal in criticizing the awful usability of many of the web interfaces that I had encountered.

But the overriding reason why I was chosen over perhaps more senior members of the team was the fact that I had not been involved in any of the design and development decisions that had been made to create the site. I was the most independent person available at the shortest notice and, in addition, in the unique position of being completely unaware of whom I was going to praise, or whom I was going to offend.

I sometimes look back at this turning point and reflect upon a piece of impeccable timing. This exercise was my first foray into examining the subject of website usability, and it was to be the start of a long process researching this topic, looking at current web development methods and trying to understand and define how a development team should approach a website development project.

The importance of a structured approach

Performing a usability evaluation and feeding back the results to a development group can be a daunting experience. Usability problems encountered on a personal level without any supporting evidence from usability tests or current usability research can often be dismissed out of hand by developers who have a healthy disrespect for anyone who has not contributed to the code. Their suspicions are usually well founded. It is almost always the case, in any walk of life, that opinions are never in short supply from those who will not have to do the work. It is always very easy for someone to offer opinions and criticisms about software interfaces, but it is not nearly so easy to change the system as a result of whims and fancies that may easily vary from one week to the next. Therefore the developers' age-old comment 'well that's just your opinion' is, in most cases, a justifiable reaction. Having spent time on both sides of the development fence, I soon learned that everyone has an opinion about the way a user interface should look and work, usually based on their individual preferences and experience. Therefore, any 'expert' evaluation of a website needs to be backed up by evidence that supports the argument, evidence such as findings from independent and credible usability studies.

Luckily, most of the problems that I had found and reported back had already been recognized. Many were a result of organizational and content management problems rather than real design disasters. This was an interesting finding for someone who had come from a software development background. It became apparent that there was another dimension to website development that needed to be taken into account – that of the publishing environment that exists behind the site. In addition, while preparing for this website usability review, there were other complications.

● Firstly, there was very little usability information available at the time about how to make websites easy to use.

● Secondly, the criteria for whether a website was usable were not necessarily the same criteria that were used to evaluate software.

It was obvious that if I were asked to do the same exercise again with another website, much more information on web usability issues would be needed.

I started building up a set of web usability heuristics that I could refer to in order to help design web user interfaces and to evaluate existing websites. Today, there seem to be as many internet surveys as there are days in the year, and many useful web usability studies have been carried out. This is great news for those of us whose job it is to design websites. However, it is still a fact that there are very many unusable sites on the web from companies which should know better. One can merely guess that the only people reading these reports are the same usability experts who are writing them – experts who for the most part are being ignored by development teams creating the websites.

From my years working as a software developer, I have seen some of the reasons why usability experts unfortunately alienate themselves from the very people they wish to influence. Developers are usually placed in an impossible situation. They are handed ideas, concepts, screen shots, and maybe a few loose requirements, but they very rarely receive a clear and complete specification of what they are to produce. Often development projects are date driven, with a strict set of deadlines that the developers have hanging over their heads. When a time limit applies only to one group within the organization, that group can understandably have very little patience with those who have time to pontificate, opinionate, and provide woolly theories about how things should work.

Developers need specifics and they also need them at the right time within the project. Having usability experts coming in right at the end and criticizing the way something works is usually a pointless exercise. By that time the screens have been designed, the code has been written, and any significant change will mean a major rewrite. Therefore, developers have in the past seen usability experts as annoying people whose job it is to slow down the development process by identifying problems, usually right at the end of the project. In other words, a role that is one rung lower than a tester who at least identifies problems that are quantifiable and reproducible.

To be effective, web usability experts need to be involved at the very start of a development project and they need to provide enough detailed information during the design process to help steer and define a design specification before any serious development effort is expended. Coming in at the end and waving a stick at all the usability problems they find is too late, and it is up to usability experts to learn how to work within a development team and to be seen as a positive force rather than as a negative one. It is also up to the development team to establish a process that enables usability input at an appropriate stage.

As I found out, it is very easy to criticize other people's websites and to find usability faults with other people's website designs, but to actually develop usable web solutions is another matter entirely. This is why any serious web development team should be looking to follow a structured development process rather than leaving it to luck that everything will fall into place.

Trying to put it into practice

As a consequence of reviewing the Ease of Use website and making recommendations on how it could be improved, in the best management style I was then given the job of improving it. The target was to increase the independently tested user satisfaction rating for the website to more than 80 per cent – double the amount that it was currently at.

One of the problems that had been identified within the usability review was that of the quality of content and content style being inconsistent across the whole site and also inconsistent within the different related sections. Part of the problem was the environment in which the content was being created. Secondly, there were organizational problems, with content providers unsure about who was responsible for reviewing content and the correct procedures they should be following to create content and move it on to the site.

In the same way that there was very little information available on web usability issues, there was even less on content management and the best ways to structure and define content destined for a site. Therefore, the next exercise I engaged in was to analyze the different types of content within the Ease of Use site and then to compare these content types with similar content types used by other external websites. This was achieved by performing a large-scale content analysis. The purpose of this exercise was to first create a list of the document types that we would need to create templates for, such as news articles and feature stories, and then to analyze how other websites had defined these types within their web interfaces. By analyzing the makeup and variations used by different companies to present the same types of information, it was hoped that common templates could be created that captured all the best features, ideas and common themes identified. It was also hoped that by performing such an analysis, common information models could be created to capture the attributes, behaviours and strategies that would make the content more flexible, maintainable and easier to manage in the future.

While performing this exercise, it soon became apparent that a content analysis for a website cannot be carried out in isolation. It was evident that certain content structuring and design decisions had been made based on other factors, such as the type of business or the types of users coming to the site. There was also a feeling that the way a site had been developed or the way that an organization generated the content also had a strong influence over how that content appeared on a site. Therefore, to really understand whether an information modelling approach was useful within the web development process, it was necessary to understand the web development process as a whole.

This book is about that process, and it concentrates in particular on the information that should be available before any website design work actually starts. The analysis stage of any development project is perhaps the most challenging part of the process. This is the stage where design decisions are influenced and business directions are set. It is also the stage that many web development projects ignore, and it is for this reason that many websites fail.

While researching the content of this book it was necessary to try to understand the relationship between content analysis and other types of analysis used to develop websites. It became clear during this exercise that although there are some excellent sources of information on parts of the web development process, such as defining an information architecture (Louis Rosenfield and Peter Morville, *Information Architecture for the World Wide Web*) and the papers on current issues in web usability (*www.useit.com/alertbox* – Jakob Neilson), there is very little information that covers the process as a whole.

I can only guess at the reasons for this. Perhaps the most likely is that everyone is still learning, and although most internet analysts agree that the potential for business on the web is enormous, they are not necessarily agreed on how that potential can be realized. Another reason may be that those working in this area are spending all their time just trying to keep up with the speed of change, and are caught up in the quick iterative development cycles that are required to keep apace with the latest, greatest, new interface designs and web technology.

This book does not attempt to talk about the technology. If it did, it would be out of date before it was published. Instead, it concentrates on the fundamentals of getting a website development project to succeed. It is of no consequence how a website is developed if the business model is flawed. It is of no consequence how a website is designed if there is no understanding of the users and their expectations of the site. These are the fundamental analysis stages that need to be understood before any development work starts, and especially before anyone starts designing and laying out web pages.

For a company to have any chance of establishing a successful website, the necessary hard work needs to be done. It will never be enough to look at a competitor's site or any successful site and try to copy what they have done. Designing and implementing an attractive interface is important but on its own will not produce a good website. A website has to:

- address the needs of the business;
- be easy to use by those who are supposed to be using it;
- deliver content that is correct, complete and current;
- be created in such a way that it is able to grow, change, be analyzed, managed and maintained.

To be sure of making an improvement in the usability of the Ease of Use site, our team had to go back and work through some of these fundamental analysis stages. However, after doing this ground work it was designed and developed with increased confidence that this new version would address the expectations of the users coming to the site, and be usable by those users. In addition, by creating a publishing environment behind the scenes, there was an additional confidence that the quality of the site could be maintained. It took five months to create this new version, and two more months to test the satisfaction rating, which easily beat the 80 per cent target.

This book looks in detail at these analysis stages and in particular at the kinds of information that should be available before the web design and development work starts. It looks at how business analysts and usability experts can really be part of the development process and how their expertise should influence the way that a solution is delivered. Most importantly, it provides a way in which an organization can set up an environment where everyone within the wider development team contributes to the overall success of the web solution, and therefore an environment where there exists ownership, responsibility and accountability.

Theory, experience and avoiding analysis paralysis

The audiences for this work are those who are making the decisions on how their websites should be developed and those who will design or develop the solution. The material that I have included here has been built up as a result of the experiences I have gained from researching web usability and design issues in order to redesign websites to make them easier to use. I have taken much of this knowledge and used it to provide consultancy to IBM customers on ways to improve the usability of their current websites. I have also worked with internet start-up companies to undertake various levels of content analysis and information modelling. This has proved invaluable in testing out the usefulness of these techniques, and has also made me realize why a book such as this is needed.

Many non-computer businesses want to get online. They understand their business, they understand their users and the information that they wish to deliver, but they do not know how to use that knowledge to create a successful website, or how a site should go about integrating with existing processes. On the other hand, web developers and designers know the latest web technology, they know how to set up the web servers and e-mail, and they know how to write queries and updates to existing databases. They can create beautiful graphics and layouts and can measure page impressions and site usage, but they cannot necessarily create a successful website for the business.

What is needed is a process that captures the business knowledge and understanding of the user requirements and delivers a clear specification that can be used to create a design. In trying to define such a process I have talked to people inside and outside IBM about their experiences, their ideas on how best to approach certain problems, and their successes and failures.

The books I have included in the bibliography are those that I feel are well worth reading or referring to and are worth the investment in time. I believe that in most cases busy people in industry would prefer a list of ten excellent books than a list of 100, some of which are truly applicable and others of which are solely for academic background or intellectual stimulation. Sometimes, these long book lists are there for the benefit and credibility of the author, rather than being of use to the reader.

Developing good websites is a very difficult job, and one can underestimate the task if one reads only the theory behind doing it. Even though this material goes to great lengths to emphasize the importance of the proper amount of research and analysis, practitioners know that one can become good at a job only by actually getting one's hands dirty. The worst case is to find yourself in an 'analysis paralysis' state where nothing actually gets churned out at the other end except piles of papers, design guidelines and best practice process documents. If you have not found yourself in the middle of a website development project, you will probably not appreciate how easy it is to get in a mess. Hopefully, this book will provide some pointers on how these problems can be avoided.

About this book

The book is structured into four main sections.

Background and justification for a structured web development process

The first section provides some background information about how the web has evolved and how this evolution has affected the way that websites have been developed. It provides an argument for why ease of use should be a primary goal of any web development project and looks at the justification for a more formalized and structured web development approach as a way of achieving it.

Web site development overview and analysis techniques

The second section looks at a simple model for web development that encompasses analysis, design, implementation and roll-out and then covers in detail each analysis stage that should provide the foundation and information required for the complete web development project. The analysis stages are covered in varying detail, but include the business analysis, the user analysis and the content analysis. This section also includes chapters that look at design considerations to do with web user interfaces and content structuring and delivery.

Analyzing the requirements of the different contributors to the site

The third section looks at the individual requirements of those people within an organization who will need to interact with a system that is set up to deliver a website. It provides an overview of the advantages of a content management approach and then looks at the way that an environment could be provided to make it easier to deliver a site that contains quality content and is both manageable and maintainable.

Translating requirements into information models

The final chapters look at how information models can be used to translate requirements into a formalized website and content management design specification. This section also provides an extensive number of common information models that have been derived from studying many different kinds of websites and that also include and combine common requirements for website content management.

Information modelling and the use of UML

Throughout the later parts of the book, information models are shown within diagrams that use the Unified Modelling Language (UML). This should not put off those who have no experience of UML or indeed of object-oriented modelling techniques. Models that define the structure of information tend to be simpler and somewhat self-explanatory compared with other types of analysis models. Where complexity starts to creep in, the explanations provided should be sufficient to cover the important aspects that the model is trying to convey. For an explanation of the small subset of UML notation that is used within this book please refer to Appendix B. If a more detailed understanding is required, *The Unified Modeling Language Reference Manual* by James Rumbaugh, Ivar Jacobson and Grady Booch is highly recommended.

Although I have endeavoured to make the UML models correct, this is not a book about how to model websites using UML. The emphasis is firmly on the ideas and concepts of using information models to help analyze and design websites. If there are any UML notation errors, it is hoped that the underlying concepts that the models are trying to convey will still be clear, valid, meaningful and hopefully useful.

A quick note for those who are experienced in object-oriented analysis techniques. Many of the UML models that are used to show the design concepts use inheritance rather than aggregation. Even though I prefer the aggregation method to inheritance and have found in my experience that it is far easier to build up content types within a content management solution using a bolt-on approach of common useful little parts, I believe the models 'read' more clearly using the inheritance semantic. For example 'A document *is a* content item within a content management system' makes more sense than saying 'A document is within a content management system and *has a* content item'. The person responsible for delivering a content management system using information models should be adept enough to be able to decide where aggregation can be used more effectively with the tools that are available.

Acknowledgements

There are a number of people who have made a significant contribution to this book, whom I would like to acknowledge.

Tom Donnelly
Vice-president of e-commerce at CityWire (*CityWire.co.uk*), Tom provided invaluable and insightful information on the business aspects and opportunities on the web. Tom introduced internet technology into businesses around the world while working at IBM, and now sits on an internet venture capital board that advises internet start-ups while also running the CityWire financial website. His contribution has been invaluable in validating much of the content of this book, especially in the areas of business priorities and internet trends.

Denise Burton
Denise used to be an information designer within the IBM Ease of Use group in Austin, Texas (*www.ibm.com/easy*) and now works for frog design (*www.frodesign.com*). Denise provided support, encouragement and practical help in formulating many of the ideas presented in this book. Her belief in the applicability of this work was based on conversations with people involved with website development within IBM and outside with customers, finding out about their experiences, best practices and the ways that they would like to work in the future. Many of the ideas and thoughts generated have been incorporated into this book.

Alan Capel
Alan used to be head of image information at Getty Images where he helped set up the classification system to run the process of categorizing the Getty digital library. He now works for an internet start-up that delivers photographic art to consumers (*www.eyestorm.com*). Alan provided excellent firsthand knowledge about classification systems and designing vocabularies. Classification is a subject about which I previously knew very little, but I have since become quite an evangelist with respect to its applicability to the web information architecture and design process.

Millicent Cooley
Millicent is a customer experience architect and user researcher with Scient (*www.scient.com*). Her experience includes visual and interaction design with IBM's Ease of Use group in Austin, graduate studies in interaction design at Carnegie Mellon University, and design and production consultation with the magazine industry in New York and Los Angeles. With this background she provided invaluable

information on publishing processes and how these techniques could be incorporated into developing websites. Millicent also worked on the content analysis for the IBM Ease of Use website, the results of which are incorporated into this book.

Mark Frost

As head of BBC Online (*www.bbc.co.uk*), Mark provided information pertinent to content management and issues that are applicable to a site such as the BBC that is very heavily content based. He also validated the user-centred design approach by explaining the BBC's approach to user analysis and how successful the BBC site has been as a result.

Carolyn Bjerke

Carolyn is an interface and information designer within the IBM Ease of Use group in Austin. Carolyn provided invaluable information on content licensing, content ownership and the requirements for content approval. Much of this knowledge has been incorporated within the book.

Peter Hsu and Scott Morgan

Two developers from the IBM Ease of Use group in Austin, Peter and Scott based much of the current Ease of Use website (*www.ibm.com/easy*) on the information models described within this book. The process of translating the designs into real production code provided a way of validating the usefulness of the approach within a real web development project. As a result of this exercise, the models have improved through design iterations by the valuable contributions made by both Peter and Scott.

Rhydian Lewis and Yatin Patel

Rhydian and Yatin are two computer science students from the UK who developed an external conference website using the information model approach for the IBM Make IT Easy '99 Conference held in New York. This piece of work not only covered the development of the website but also the underlying content management system that handled conference registration, hotel bookings and the approval process for agenda items and published papers. This provided a validation for the types of workflows needed to move content from creation, through approval and publication to a site. It also looked at the issues of extending a model to incorporate different document types.

Dave Clark

A software development expert at IBM in Warwick, UK, Dave provided invaluable input on both the writing and the content of this book. Dave reviewed the information models from a technical perspective and spent many hours reviewing and rewording initial drafts of the book. He is also the person responsible for suggesting that this work should be made available to a wider external audience.

Dr Elizabeth de Mello

Elizabeth's PhD was on the mental models engendered by user interfaces and she is an expert in ergonomics/human factors and cognitive psychology. She has many years' practical experience of designing and evaluating the user interface of computer software. After spending several years working within research and development at Rank Xerox, and on software development at IBM, Elizabeth now runs UserData (*www.UserData.co.uk*), a company which offers ergonomics expertise in such areas as user interface design and also in assessing industrial environments that cause injuries within the workplace. During the review stages of this book, she has made comments that have resulted in improvements to the areas covering human factors engineering and provided much-appreciated validation of the level of usability information that can realistically be included in a book such as this.

Adrian Cowderoy

Adrian, of NexusWorld.net and The Multimedia House of Quality, is an expert in helping to improve the quality of websites and multimedia. He provided many useful comments as a result of ploughing through the initial drafts of the book, many of which have been incorporated into the final version.

Tony Temple and John Peters

Both Tony, vice-president of Ease of Use for IBM Corporation, and John, the Ease of Use strategy and design development manager at IBM Warwick, have fostered an environment that enables time to be given to advancing ease of use issues both inside IBM and within the wider usability community. Without this support, the work that is presented here would not have been advanced to the degree it has, and it would not now be presented externally within a book.

Information model technical reviewers

Throughout this project a number of people within IBM have taken time to technically review the information models presented here. During these review sessions many useful and valuable comments have been given, and as a consequence design changes have been made. Those who have been involved from IBM in Warwick, UK, are: Ray Trainer, Dave Clark, Paul Englefield, Mark Tibbits, Roland Merrick, Dave Roberts, Chris Gallagher and John Peters. Those who have contributed from IBM in Austin, Texas, are: Denise Burton, Dick Berry, Carolyn Bjerke, Peter Hsu, Scott Morgan, Millicent Cooley and Linda Lisle.

In addition, I received help from Justina Gilbert, Rob Lawrence and a special thank you to Marilyn Myers from IBM Canada who was instrumental in organizing the CD that is included with this book.

I would also like to extend a special thank you to everyone at Addison Wesley, especially Steve Temblett, the commissioning editor.

Background and justification for a structured web development process

This first section provides some background information on how the web has evolved and how this evolution has affected the way that websites have been developed. It provides an argument for why ease of use should be a primary goal of any web development project and looks at the justification for a more formalized and structured web development approach as a way of achieving it.

Why ease of use should be important to company websites

In his Alertbox column 'Failure of Corporate Web Sites',[1] Jakob Neilson provides some interesting statistics that relate to the consequence of having a badly designed company website. Being 'badly designed' in this context does not relate to graphic design issues such as colour schemes, fonts and backgrounds, but rather to the bigger picture pertaining to whether those who are trying to use the site to achieve some specified goal can actually accomplish what they are trying to do.

The overall usability of many of these business websites is deemed to be so bad that the Forrester report 'Why Most Web Sites Fail'[2] warns that failure to act and correct these problems will have a 'measurable impact on revenue, expense, customer retention, and brand recognition'.

These are strong words that should be heeded. Historically, companies invest an inordinate amount of time and money in building a strong company image through marketing and promoting a strong brand with strong brand messages. In addition, companies have been falling over themselves in the rush to introduce loyalty schemes that offer incentives and rewards to their regular shoppers. Why, then, are these same companies not investing the same amount of time and consideration in their company websites? It seems that in the clamour to get a web presence, many organizations have ignored the negative aspects of having a poor website. It also seems that these organizations have little understanding of the importance of making electronic interfaces easy to use, and if they do, not much idea about how to go about it.

Measuring the usability of a site

A simple way to assess whether a company website is usable or not is to try to interact with it *in the way it is expected to be used*. This seems such an obvious statement that you might be tempted not to read on. The plain fact is that many of us whose job it is to develop websites do not judge websites in this way. We look at sites for design pointers such as how the content is arranged, what categories are supported, how effective their search engine is, how their navigation system works, or how they have designed their pages. Although this is all useful information, it will not provide any real indication as to whether the site is usable or not. To understand this, you have to be either a real user of the site who has a goal to achieve and then try to achieve it, or you have to analyze the types of people who will be using the site, understand what their goals are, discover how they would approach the problem, and test the site to see if these user goals can be achieved in the way that is expected.

If a site is easy to use, a user will be able to achieve their goal quickly and efficiently. As a result, they will feel positive about the site and may bookmark it to return another time; they are also likely to recommend the site to others. A personal recommendation of a website is a common way for people to find out about good sites.[3]

By comparison, an unusable site will cause frustration, irritation and annoyance. A really unusable site will result in the user abandoning the task and looking for an alternative that offers the same service. A bad site is unlikely to get bookmarked or recommended to others. In fact, depending on the level of competition within the same service domain, this kind of site may be unlikely ever to be visited again.

A serious consequence of presenting an unusable website alluded to by the Forrester report[2] is that the user will view the company negatively if they experience problems on the website, and this negative feeling can influence their shopping behaviour in other traditional channels. In other words, if the user gives up trying to use a website because it is too difficult or confusing, they might also assume that the company is going to be just as bad to deal with in other environments such as the high street store or mail order service. This suggests that there may be significant hidden costs associated with website usability problems that many companies might not have even considered.

My own experience of this kind of negative feeling relates to online food shopping. Currently, if I wish to shop for my groceries online, I have only one choice of store that will deliver to my area. I have struggled through its site valiantly to try to achieve this feat – sometimes I have managed it, and sometimes I have not and have given up in frustration. If as a result I am forced to buy my shopping by visiting a store, I never choose to go to this supermarket. Perhaps irrationally, I see this as my protest against the website that has forced me out of my comfortable house! The company in question of course has no idea about my behaviour, and indeed probably has no idea of my existence. However, when it starts to annoy a significant percentage of its customers who respond as I do, it might start to wonder why sales are falling off.

An important fact that needs to be understood is that the expectation levels of web users have shifted considerably and will continue to change and become more demanding. In the early days, users were excited if they could just browse the web to find what they were looking for, let alone buy anything useful. But the phenomenal take-up of websites by companies offering all kinds of services and products means that now the user is in a far more powerful position to decide which company website they wish to use.

An environment that provides so much choice to the user creates a competitive market where the user can be very choosy. No longer do they have to rely on the corner store mentality with its limited and expensive product range and idiosyncratic customer service. On the internet, users have access to a huge shiny mall where they can transport themselves from store to store, and service to service, by the click of a mouse. The mere fact that it is so quick and easy to give up and go elsewhere means that the shopping behaviour of the web user is very different to shopping behaviours seen elsewhere. In addition, the incentive to struggle through a bad user interface is not as strong as it might be if the user had bought and installed a software package on their machine. The online shopper has to some degree adopted the television 'channel-hopping' behaviour, and the online user usually sees little benefit in having to learn how to use a particular website.

In this kind of environment, where the audience is not captive or particularly loyal, a company needs to understand what its differentiators are. More importantly, it needs to focus on how its website can not only attract users to the site in this very crowded global marketplace but also how it can keep them. The best way to succeed in keeping users is to make it as easy as possible for them to achieve their goals.

The result of competing in an environment that makes it so simple for users to switch to a competitor means that businesses need to focus on adding value and competitive levels of service. They also need a trustworthy brand and strong marketing to get users to their sites and for them to feel safe providing credit card details and personal information about themselves. These are all important aspects of a good website. However, although brand recognition may help attract users to a site, it is the expectation that their goals will be satisfied that will keep them there and how easy the site makes it to achieve these goals that will encourage them to return[4]. A user might not even get far enough to judge whether the pricing is competitive if they cannot find the price of the product in the first place.

Time for a design shift

A radical shift needs to occur in the way that most companies think about and develop their websites. It is similar in some ways to the shift that was needed when the personal computer was introduced to the marketplace in the early 1980s. Before this, computing had been defined by mainframe computers which were large and highly functional number-crunching machines that required expert training to understand how to switch them on, let alone to use one. By contrast, the personal computer or PC was targeted at a far wider user population and therefore had to be designed to be easier to use. Much of the design emphasis shifted away from performance and functionality to concentrate on the user interface. Graphical user interfaces (GUIs) were introduced so that users did not have to remember long cryptic text commands. The new PC operating systems attempted to hide as much of the internal computer environment through the use of friendly icons and movable windows. This design shift was essential in order for companies to sell the idea of a computer to the large targeted user population. They recognized that if people could not use the PC or understand what it was capable of, they were hardly likely to buy one.

In most cases, company websites are targeting the same audience as the PC. However, there is a big difference: websites need to be even easier to use than PCs and easier to use than the application software that runs on them. This is because a web user will not invest time in learning how to use a website. When you buy a computer or a piece of software there is a feeling that you must at least try to get it to work. The amount you try is usually directly related to the amount you have paid or how easy it is to exchange the goods for something else. There is no cost in going to a website, and no investment to deter you from leaving.

The internet is now at that stage where consumers expect to be able to use it. Web users are not the most patient of people, and they are unlikely to keep popping back to a site to see if it has improved the way it does things. There are millions of potential people who are very keen to use this new sales and marketing channel, so it would be a disaster to drive these customers away by making them work too hard at your site.

Therefore the design shift that many websites have to face today is exactly the same as the design shift that was needed to create the PC. The emphasis for designing and developing websites needs to move from capability to usability. In other words, once a site understands how to do something it needs to concentrate on how to make it easier for users to do it; it needs to adopt a user-centred design approach. Many companies are still at the capability stage and have been seduced along the way by technology fads and fashions. Understanding what these fashions have been, and where companies have focused their efforts in the past, will provide some clues as to why many websites need to make this shift as a matter of urgency.

Understanding how websites have evolved

A house will not be safe or solid if it is built on shaky foundations. Many problems that company websites face can be traced back to one fundamental problem: they have not evolved successfully. In the past few years the internet has changed out of all recognition, from being a repository for information sharing to a significant commercial channel for purchasing products and services aimed at a global mass market.

As the web has become more significant to businesses around the world, businesses have jumped on to the bandwagon at different stages of its development. Understanding these different stages provides some insight into why these companies are now facing real problems with their sites. It is also worth considering a significant contributory factor to this problem. In their rush to put up their sites, development teams have taken shortcuts in order to quickly get the site up and running. Little consideration has been given to how a site can be designed to be manageable and maintainable in the future. Content has been generated and added to sites in such a random and disorganized fashion that to unravel the mess means major development surgery.

Therefore, many sites have adopted a strategy where new functions and information are bolted on to the existing site structure when what in fact is needed is to let the site, not the URLs (universal resource locators), die and to re-evaluate what the site is trying to achieve from both a business and user perspective. Only when this is clearly understood can anyone realistically assess whether the content that is being published on the site, and the navigation system that is in place to access this information, actually help achieve both the business and user goals.

Unfortunately, human nature is such that deleting existing work and starting from scratch is psychologically very difficult. Therefore what has happened, and is still happening, is that many company sites build upon seriously faulty structures and enshrine design principles that were established when the internet was a completely different proposition.

Understanding the different web evolutionary stages can throw some light on why some websites are designed the way they are, and why the technology has tended to dominate the way solutions have been conceived. In addition, by looking at the history of web development and website design from a human factors and user interface perspective, it is possible to trace how technology fashions and, more recently, business priorities have evolved the interface and consequently how these iterations have affected the user experience of the web.

Web presence

In the early days, the typical types of content that were found on the web were white papers and research material, and the typical users were firmly housed in the world of academia, research and computer science. It provided an easy mechanism to share information and ideas and built upon the success of e-mail as a communication tool between universities and research institutions.

The culture of sharing information was the initial driving force for the web, and there existed only a very small group of people who understood what the world wide web was, or understood how to use and access it. It was usually the same kind of individuals within companies who convinced their management that the web was a significant technology that their company should at least understand. In most cases, the extent to which a company invested in the web amounted to registering the company domain name, creating a simple home page that was accessible from a search engine, and displaying the traditional company contact information. The web was seen as a fairly passive information service where a company could place its standard company marketing literature.

Web technology

With more and more companies registering their sites on the web, and the number of users starting to become significant, predictions from business analysts began to frighten executives into action. Consequently, company marketing machines started to become interested in, and take control of, the management of the company website.

Still seen as primarily an advertising and marketing tool, companies hired the same kind of organizations to design their sites as they had used to create their marketing campaigns and publishing material. The design thinking behind this new stage was to create a virtual shop window using the latest eye-catching technology. The reasons why some companies did not adopt this style of site were that they were technologically behind the times, did not want to invest the money, or did not have the necessary web skills to build these kinds of sites.

This stage saw the introduction of graphical animations and 'best website' competitions, where the winning interfaces could be seen as entries within a technology fashion show. In other words, winning sites displayed a variety of unusual and maybe stimulating arty designs that were neither particularly practical nor easy to use. Graphic designers from a print or advertising background usually created these designs – individuals with very strong visual skills but little or no experience of user interaction or usability issues. The design was still hinged around the individual web page rather than the website as a whole.

Web experts were considering websites as the new media, more related to the publishing environment, with the predominant emphasis on advertising and marketing messages rather than that of the traditional software application development process. Graphic designers from publishing backgrounds and new-style media companies started to make money from companies wanting 'glossy'-style websites, all with their subsequent performance and usability problems. Such sites thrived on displaying large promotional graphics that took a long time to download and using fonts that looked good but were not particularly easy to read. To make money, these new companies had to excite their business sponsors by creating stylish, brand-driven graphical layouts that looked professional. It was quite common for these designs to be presented using the standard print medium of a storyboard, and for the business sponsors to sign up as a result of liking the style of the artwork. At the time, the usability or interaction design of these interfaces was something that was not considered particularly important.

Also at this time, web developers were beginning to experiment with new programming languages for the web such as Java and JavaScript. These languages provided the capabilities for web designers to create more interactive and graphical interfaces and gave scope for designers to introduce spinning animations, non-standard navigation mechanisms and even more problematic page load performance times. This stage was defined by the attention given to the graphic design included within a page and the inclusion of non-standard web interfaces through the use of new interactive web technology.

Web commerce

The ability to introduce programming logic on to a web page meant that there now existed a way of introducing more complex user interaction. Up to this stage, the level of user involvement had been fairly passive. The only real interaction a website expected from the user was the selection of navigation links to move between various parts of a site. Through the use of online forms, a company could take advantage of a completely new opportunity: electronic commerce.

To capitalize on this, a website now needed to design for interaction. If a site expected a web user to find a product, select the product to buy and then provide credit card and delivery details, the site needed to become user goal oriented and concentrate on the tasks that the user would need to accomplish in order to achieve the desired goal. The intention of such sites was to make buying on the web easier, quicker, cheaper and more convenient than conventional shopping channels.

In addition to those sites selling products, other business models were introduced. Online forms meant that online subscriptions could be taken. Information providers such as newspapers and magazines could reproduce their content on the web and accept electronic subscriptions from web users. And if a website could attract a large number of users through the usefulness and popularity of its content, it could also attract advertising revenue. In the same way that traditional publications release circulation figures to attract potential advertisers, a popular website could offer advertisers an attractive alternative by making available the number of users coming to the site. By capturing page impressions, a company could devise electronic advertising rate cards. And by supporting advertising banner technology within the most popular pages, a company could start to display adverts on the site.

This stage was a parting of the ways between those sites which did not want to lose out on their initial investment and those that recognized the need to undergo a thorough redesign and restructuring exercise in order to react to the change in business goals or new business opportunities. This second kind of site was more likely to do a better job of being user oriented and supporting the primary user tasks, merely because at the start of the website development process the goals and objectives of the site were very clearly defined. In contrast, the kind of site which was reluctant to ditch the existing site structure started to use a bolt-on strategy to accommodate the new content being created as a result of any business or organizational requirements. In most cases, company websites have adopted the first and more flawed approach.

By adopting the bolt-on strategy, company websites have tended to grow exponentially due to a proliferation of sub-sites. This has proved the point that it is far easier to create content and add it on than to invest in strict review and maintenance processes to keep the site relevant and useful. Consequently, these kinds of sites have become large, disorganized spider webs of information where the site content has no overall owner, where the structure is more organizational than user oriented, and where the information quality degrades due to the fact that content is rarely updated, reviewed or deleted.

Back-office integration

One of the stages that commerce websites are tackling currently is the process of connecting their web client interface into their back-end systems. Many sites have seen this process as being to some extent one-way. For example, a customer orders a product through an online form, the order is transferred back into a back-end order database and is fulfilled in the same way as if the order had been taken over the phone. However, to make the commerce experience better for web users, the system needs to be able to provide the level of communication that they would hope to receive within a traditional shopping environment.

For instance, a commerce site should allow users to purchase goods only if they are in stock, or if the user has been made aware of a delay and is still prepared to go ahead with the order. Orders should not be accepted if delivery cannot be made to the address given, and the system should provide the customer with information regarding the progress of their order and any confirmation of payment received.

To achieve this level of service, a commerce website needs not only to integrate into back-end systems such as stock control, purchasing, distribution and invoicing but also to provide the appropriate level of feedback and status information back to the web user at the appropriate time. A web commerce system has the means of delivering accurate and timely information to its web customers, and it also has the means of offering expert assistance and alternative product information and advice if a product is out of stock. The goal of the designer responsible for defining the purchasing task flow within a commerce site should be to provide an interface that is more helpful, more informative and provides a better all-round service than the traditional shopping channels.

Not only can the successful integration to back-end systems help the end user, it can also provide the business with important information about how the site is being used. Reports can be generated that show accurate data about which products are selling and which products are not, or which delivery options are popular and which ones are never used. The web designer can be provided with information about which links the customers are taking, the terms that are being used within a search function, and where in the site they are ultimately leaving to go elsewhere.

Intranets and extranets

Companies have recognized that the web interface is more than just a good way to conduct external business on the web. It is starting to make more sense to use the same medium to publish internal company information and provide internal services such as company telephone lists through a web browser. The usability of intranets has an obvious cost implication. Such a mundane task as an employee looking up an internal telephone number takes time and therefore costs money. Reducing the time it takes to complete this task for every employee within a company, will save a significant amount of money over time. Suprisingly, this kind of service is often not thought of as particularly important, and the amount of time put aside for the design and delivery of company information and services does not reflect the potential savings that could be made by streamlining common employee tasks.

Extranets are those parts of an external website reserved for special users, and are normally password protected. They are usually set up as communication channels between businesses and provide additional information pertinent to a business relationship. So far, much of the design of website interfaces has concentrated on 'business-to-consumer' relationships; however, in order to support the supply and delivery requirements generated by consumers, there is a growing demand for better 'business-to-business' sites that are able to support the very different goals and tasks needed to support the business relationship.

In order to provide different levels of access to information through various kinds of sites, a level of classification needs to be assigned to the content that is being published. The only other way is to rely on someone putting the right files on to the right server, or into the right directory structure – something that is almost always likely to go wrong. Therefore, company sites that do not want to go down the disorganized 'spider's web' route are opting for data-driven content management solutions that deal with issues such as workflow and classification. Any reasonably sized site needs to be created and designed with change in mind. The more content there is and the more manual that process is to update the content on a site, the more expensive and time-consuming a site will be to maintain. When something becomes difficult to manage, maintenance suffers, and when a site is badly maintained it eventually becomes unusable.

Standardizing on the web client

As companies adopt the web as their main publishing vehicle, systems will need to be created that integrate web publishing with company processes and organizations. Systems will also need to provide for the different publishing roles of content creators, web authors, visual designers and, of course, end users. As it becomes more important for a site to have up-to-date and accurate information, so an integrated system that makes publishing that information as seamless as possible becomes increasingly necessary.

Creating and maintaining any reasonably sized website requires a disciplined approach, with roles and responsibilities clearly defined. Whatever the initial good intentions and design principles of a site, if the business procedures are not in place to support a structured website development and content publication process, things are likely to go dramatically wrong.

Devices and gadgets

One of the latest advances in web development circles is the ability to create web pages that can be downloaded on to a mobile phone. It has been predicted for some time that smaller specialized devices will start to be developed that enable users to perform certain information tasks away from their PC. Companies that have not yet managed to create usable websites for large computer screens are gearing themselves up to make even more unusable interfaces for mobile phones! However, as with any development project, just because the technology is there to do it does not necessarily mean it is a good thing to do.

What is needed is the same process that should be employed with any software project, which is an evaluation of the business reasons for undertaking the project and then a rigorous analysis of the user goals and tasks. Due to the obvious interface limitations of a mobile phone display, there has to be a very clear understanding of the likely user scenarios that will lead anyone to try to use a web page from a mobile phone and what their goals and expectations are. It can be seen that even with the newest technology there is a great need for the proven techniques of user-centred design.

Summary

The shift from seeing the internet as a simplistic marketing vehicle to the main way that companies do business has been as dramatic as it has been fast. It is not surprising then that development groups have been struggling to keep up with the speed of change.

The main problem that companies face today is that they have been reluctant to completely redesign and redefine their site to match their changing business goals. Those less generous might suggest that some companies have not really defined any business goals in the first place – the core information that should be driving the purpose of their sites. They also have not gone back to their target audience and performed any validation to see if the site is usable by the kinds of people they want to use it.

The majority of companies that publish sites on the web are not computer software companies and therefore have no background in good user interface design. Many of these companies do not even develop their own solutions but contract out the work to external web development shops without much idea of how to assess whether these companies have done a good job or not. It is small wonder then that many have been seduced by the 'more graphics the better' design approach.

Problems with HTML authored sites

The importance of the website over the web page

When the internet was first used to communicate information, the typical types of content published were information and academic papers. As such, originators of this type of content created single web pages using HTML (hypertext mark-up language), the basic formatting language that makes it possible to lay out information and publish a formatted page to the web. Each individual web page has a unique network address called a URL (universal resource locator) and a web page can contain hypertext links to other related pages that allow users to browse (or 'surf') the web down predefined information chains.

The fact that HTML was so easy to write allowed almost anyone to create a web page and publish that page for anyone else to see. The web would never have taken off to the extent it has if it had required a high level of technical expertise to create and display web pages. By making the process of publishing information to the web easy, it fostered an environment where the emphasis could firmly be placed on the writing, creating and sharing of information, rather than one in which content creators needed to understand the technical ins and outs of how the web worked. It needed a relatively low technical entry level to encourage the multitude of contributors to create the remarkable information store it has become.

However, the web has diversified. No longer is it just a passive information store, but an interactive environment for whole communities to shop, chat, sell and exchange goods, book holidays, research topics, find out about events and generally provide support in all aspects of a global market-driven life. The way that people use the web has changed and their expectations have become increasingly more demanding and sophisticated. Reading a set of information papers and selecting links to other web pages is fairly passive and these are easy tasks for users to perform. By contrast, ordering goods, searching for airline flights and writing an online book review can be quite complex operations for a web interface to deal with and to get right.

To meet the additional complexity of guiding users through complex task flows, companies have moved to creating websites that contain a multitude of web pages. A website needs to organize individual pages in a way that enables the user to find the information they are looking for and also to perform any interaction necessary to successfully complete a set of user tasks. In this kind of environment, the idea of the individual page being the most important unit on the web is no longer valid. When a site needs to concentrate on designing interfaces for users to perform complex operations, the individual pages are only cogs in a wheel to help the user to achieve their goals. It is the website as a whole that needs to be carefully designed, and in particular the relationships between pages or between page elements.

When the emphasis changes to the website being of primary importance, allowing content creators to carry on generating individual HTML files can lead to a number of problems.

The writer becomes the designer

The fact that the creator of an HTML file provides content in terms of a page layout language means they also have to provide information on the presentation of that content within a web page. Putting this responsibility in the hands of someone who potentially has no skill or interest in visual or interface design will result in a web page that does not look as if it has been put together in a professional way.

When the web was used initially, it was common to use HTML to format the text into headings and paragraphs in exactly the same style as one would use a word processor to format a document. This kind of minimalist presentation of information is still quite common on the web, but unfortunately is not at all easy for people to read. This is because reading text on a computer screen is far more difficult than reading text on hard copy. Information that is presented on a screen needs to be designed and formatted for a screen. A writer is unlikely to consider these visual and usability aspects when inserting a few HTML tags around paragraph after paragraph of information.

The other extreme is where a writer uses a web page design product that makes it easy to add all sorts of visual accoutrements on to the page. With a few clicks of a mouse, the writer can introduce clip art, animations, loud backgrounds and repeating textures. Any useful information being displayed will be directly competing for visibility with everything else on the page, and most likely losing the battle. Users find it very difficult to read information when they are being actively distracted by stronger visual images, in particular by anything that is actually moving on the page. Users who encounter these kinds of distracting or badly designed web interfaces will rarely read the contents, and will probably quickly leave the site.

The last thing that a company should want or encourage is for pages to start appearing on an external company site that have not been designed by someone who knows what they are doing. A website should be aiming at presenting a consistent visual style that backs up the company brand image. Users do get lost on the web. If an organization can reinforce a 'sense of place' within the user's mind by presenting a cohesive visual and professional-looking interface, it will increase the user's confidence and trust with the site and with the business as a whole. It is worth remembering that users will not pass on personal and credit card information to sites they do not trust or sites they deem to be unprofessional.

User interface design is as much of a skill as writing good articles. It is important for a company to recognize both the skills of writing and the skills of user interface design, and not assume that just because someone is good at one they will necessarily be any good at the other.

Ad hoc content relationships

In any size of website, users rely on links to find the information they are looking for. A website typically organizes pages into a hierarchical structure, with a single homepage at the top that contains a number of links to a set of secondary pages. These secondary pages then contain further links to the next level of pages and so on. Contextual relationships provide additional support to a hierarchy by providing links that span the main hierarchical organization of the site. One of the most powerful aspects of the web is the way that users can easily link to other pieces of information. It is also one of the most positive aspects from a web user experience point of view. Users like to surf, especially if by surfing they feel they are uncovering useful information along the way, information they would not otherwise have come across.

Allowing content creators to define their own content relationships within HTML files can lead to problems on a site. There is a likelihood that:

- there will be inconsistencies between the level and detail of contextual relationships provided by different content creators;
- any links that are provided will not add value to the user;
- collections of links will become incomplete and out of date or even incorrect;
- some of the links will not exist any more and therefore will be broken;
- the new page will not be accessible from contextual links in other pages within the site.

When a website is created by manually linking a collection of hand-crafted HTML files, every HTML file needs to contain the hypertext links that define the relationship of the page to other pages within the site. This means that every time a new page is added, someone needs to look at the current structure of the site and add the necessary new links to the right files. As this is an arduous and time-consuming task, what tends to happen is that a new page is bolted on to an existing page and becomes a new node on the site hierarchy. By adopting this strategy, the task of creating the links in existing files that will provide access to the new page will take considerably less time.

However, while this might save time for the development team, it is not likely to produce the best information design for the user. What should happen in this situation is that an information architect should go through all the existing pages to see if the new page is applicable to the page contents of any other files. If it is, the relationship should be added as a related link. This would then ensure that the content is supporting the best level of contextual information through hypertext linking rather than the user being forced through a hierarchical navigation scheme in order to find all the related content.

Although a hierarchical structure is the common way to define a primary navigation mechanism, the information architect should always be looking at ways of complementing it with secondary contextual navigation paths. It can be a long way up for the user to return to the homepage, only to have to traverse all the way down another branch of the tree to find the related information they are looking for.

Because the manual process of looking for contextual relationships rarely happens, due to the cost in time and the tedious nature of the task, contextual navigation is rarely supported well in this kind of environment. Users rely heavily on links to find the information on a site. When links are missing or incomplete, this causes one of the main usability problems on the web, where users cannot find the information they are looking for.[5]

Another major usability problem is where links are broken. When link creation and deletion is a manual process, there is more likelihood that not all the files are checked to see if they contain links to pages that no longer exist. This is the sort of problem that becomes worse over time, and really requires an automated process to be run that checks and removes broken links from the HTML files that make up the site.

Ad hoc content structure

Developing content by creating individual HTML pages means that potentially every page has a content structure that is defined by the person creating the page. There will be no enforceable rules defining the levels of required content or indeed any validation that certain pieces of information have been included

within that content. When a site has a collection of heterogeneous information, i.e. each page has a different type of content within a different type of
layout, this is not so much of an issue. But in the case of an online news site
that displays homogeneous content such as news articles or feature stories,
defining a required structure for a piece of information has many advantages. It
could be argued that such a site has to rely on some sort of database or content
management-style approach to have any chance of ensuring content quality
and meeting publication deadlines.

The approach to providing content to a site by defining a common information template is a strategy that can be employed by many kinds of sites. Creating
guidelines documents for content providers is one approach to try to improve
content quality, but everyone knows that these documents are never read on a
regular basis, or even read at all by some people. Therefore, a strategy that can
succeed is to embed the content creation guidelines and rules into the same
system that the writers use to create that content, thereby ensuring a level of
quality and inclusion of certain pieces of information at the time of writing
rather than as a result of a review or, at worst, a complaint from a user of the site.

Lack of support for meta-data and content classification

Meta-data is information that describes information. In the case of a web page,
the most common example of meta-data is the information that describes the
contents of the information within a page. The obvious advantage of providing
this information is the ability to be found correctly by global search engines such
as Yahoo! (*www.yahoo.com*) and Alta vista (*www.altavista.com*). However, there is
scope for providing all sorts of different kinds of meta-data that can be used in a
variety of ways, such as for the automatic generation of contextual relationships
or to help provide a better search facility within a site.

In the same way that creating content without using any templates allows
the content creator the freedom to define the structure and level of information
they supply, it also gives them the freedom to provide (or not provide as is the
usual case) any meta-data or classification information.

Classification schemes that use structured vocabularies are one way to help
content creators add meta-data that describes the information they are providing. Being able to classify content correctly at creation time will decrease the time
it will take someone else to review and add content classification at a later stage.
There are certain sites that provide access to large digital libraries of books, CDs
or images. These kinds of sites rely heavily on classification schemes to support
the levels of search and indexing that are needed within this environment to
make the site usable.

It is easy to understand why digital libraries need a classification system; it is
perhaps not so obvious to see why it might be worth investing in classification

schemes for other kinds of sites. However, every medium to large company site consists of a considerable amount of information. Providing a better way for this information to be indexed, cross-referenced and searched can only be advantageous to the user of the site. Also, being able to generate related links between content items and to automatically generate navigation paths and summary views across the site content are further benefits that could be achieved by adopting a controlled strategy for content classification.

The importance of managing a website

When the web was initially used to share information between small groups of people, there was not too much thought given to how this information would be maintained in the future. This was because:

- relatively speaking, there was not much information to maintain;
- the information being shared was normally complete and unlikely to change;
- the information being published to the web was usually owned, written and published by the same individual;
- the number of people assessing and reading the information was very small.

There was also not too much to worry about controlling how new content ended up on these sites. Individuals who were publishing information on the web were also the ones who were likely to have set up the server, defined the directory structures and set up any file-transfer mechanisms that were needed.

Having a web-publishing environment that relies on individuals manually transferring the right files in the right directories on to a web server is fine for some sites, such as those

- that have a relatively small number of files;
- where the files do not change very often;
- where the access to the web server is tightly controlled;
- where the small group of people responsible are competent, careful and know what they are doing.

However, medium to large-scale company websites do not usually fit into this picture. Most companies have sites that are ever expanding and changing, where the content is not created centrally and where the number of people working on the site is more than a handful who have varying degrees of experience and knowledge. For this kind of site, an organization really should be thinking of using a content management system instead of relying on a small number of developers to try to manage a changeable site and contain the problems caused by non-technical content contributors.

An organization that tries to manage a changeable, content-heavy website outside of any controlled content management environment will eventually suffer problems at every stage within its web development process. The seriousness of these problems will be directly related to certain characteristics of the site and the characteristics of those involved in the development and maintenance of a site. Site maintenance may become a problem as a result of content characteristics such as the number of supported web pages, how changeable or dynamic the content is within those pages, and how often new content is added and removed. Site quality may become a problem as a result of resourcing characteristics such as the number of people who have access to update both the design and the content of the site and whether the process involved takes account of the skill levels of the people trying to do the job.

Many of the content quality problems that are encountered within medium to large-scale websites result from a lack of any controlled approach to the creation and management of site content and any prior consideration as to how that content will be managed and maintained once the website is up and running. To appreciate the issues involved in designing a site for change, the content life cycle really needs to be considered before any design work is undertaken.

Content life cycle

It is a common mistake when any group embarks upon creating and setting up a new website to only consider how they are going to create their web pages and to ignore how those pages will be maintained. In many cases the cost of site maintenance can far outweigh any web page creation costs, especially if the site hopes to offer up-to-date quality content. In the haste to get a site up and running, another common short-sighted approach is to allow content creators the freedom to handcraft their own HTML files, as this will have further implications on the potential cost of site maintenance. Although there are some types of pages and some kinds of sites where this approach works, a site architect or project leader should be aware of the negative aspects of going down this path before making the decision.

Content has a life cycle that involves three main stages, as shown in Fig. 2.1.

Figure 2.1   The content life cycle

Content creation

When most people think of publishing information to a website, they think in terms of creating pages by either writing HTML or by using a web page designer product. Both of these approaches create a single static HTML file to represent a single web page. The HTML file contains the contents of the page, the page layout information for that content, and any navigation elements such as hypertext links that appear within the page. But there are a number of negative aspects to creating content in this way.

Knowledge of HTML a prerequisite

In this environment, anyone who wishes to contribute content to a website needs to either understand HTML or know how to use an HTML designer tool. In some cases it might even be more complicated than this if the organization has defined house styles for visual presentation or has provided templates to be used to create HTML layouts.

As an HTML file has to contain layout information and will almost certainly require some navigational controls, the writer is almost always likely to be drawn into providing additional information over and above the content to be written. This is not a good environment for getting the best out of an organization's resources. Writers have a skill to write. It can be a costly exercise to slow professionals down by surrounding them by technology that they have no need or desire to understand or learn.

If the requirement is for a writer to create and edit textual information, there should be no need for them to have HTML experience. It should be enough for them to provide this information by using the common tools for the job, in other words through a text editor that provides basic formatting capabilities.

Ad hoc review procedures

When content is created and published outside of any controlled content management system, there will always exist an ad hoc review procedure. Maybe the person creating the content will use a spell checker to remove any silly typos and spelling mistakes. Maybe they will test all the links on the page to see if the link goes to the right place and is not broken. Maybe they will ask a colleague to cast an eye over the page to make sure it looks all right and makes sense. But without any formal workflows being in place, it is up to the person creating the page, or the one moving the page on to the server, to take the trouble to ensure that it is of the right quality to appear on the website.

A more conscientious management team might define roles and responsibilities for reviewing new content destined for the site. Written processes might exist defining how new content should be reviewed and who should do the reviewing. This is obviously an improvement and might catch the majority of problems, but it is still an ad hoc process depending on individuals within the organization understanding what the process is and then following it correctly. Just having a written process is no guarantee that anyone will follow it.

There is another problem with ad hoc review procedures outside of a content management system, in that there is no associated edit history attached to the HTML file. It may be difficult to find out who owns the source of the material, who has created the graphics, who has defined the meta-data or who has reviewed, approved or rejected the publication. It will also rely on other ad hoc methods to see related history information that may provide reasons or background information as to why certain decisions have been made.

Having a log of events can be useful and may save a significant amount of time. For instance, if a page had been rejected for missing a single piece of information, second time around a reviewer may only need to check that this missing field has been provided. This will be far quicker than ploughing through the whole file again. A flat HTML file that is passed around for review will not automatically hold this level of supporting edit history information.

Ad hoc file editing

Access and version control is always a problem when source files are being handed around to different people to work on or review. Determining who has the latest copy and deciding which are the latest changes are the most common problems experienced by development groups. Additional problems include scheduling updates and changes, files waiting in in-baskets while people are away on holiday, files waiting in in-baskets of people who have more important things to do, or files just waiting for someone to approve them before they can be moved to the server to be published.

Using a content management system for content creation

A content management system can provide not only a mechanism for version control but also information about who is editing a file and details about any changes that have been made. This means that it can prevent content providers updating the same file and overwriting any changes that are being made by locking out files when someone else is using them. Overwriting changes is a classic problem within the software development environment where a version control system is not used. Exactly the same problems can arise with website content source files when more than one person has access to edit and update the same file, and is unaware that the file is being worked on by somebody else.

Another advantage of adopting a content management system is the support provided for defining and maintaining a status for a particular document or file. An HTML file might have been rejected through some sort of review process, but there is likely to be no indication of this within the file itself. If the file is then moved to the server by mistake by some well-meaning individual, the page will end up being published anyway. In the absence of any defined control variable that an automated publishing system can check, the mere fact that a file has appeared in the right directory structure on a publishing server may cause it to be published to the website, irrespective of the fact that it contains rubbish. No safeguard will exist to prevent this from happening.

What is needed is a system that defines a current state for a content item and carefully controls the processes that allow this state to be changed. This will enable an organization to set up a publishing environment that only adds pages to a website that have been reviewed and accepted as being of the required standard.

Content publication

The way that content is moved to a place where it is added to a website can be viewed as a publication process. The level of support for content providers can range dramatically depending on the publication environment that has been set up.

Technical knowledge needed to publish

When a site publication process necessitates the person creating the content having to physically move the file to a directory on a web server in order for it to be published, this requires a certain level of technical expertise.

Firstly, they need to be set up with the right level of access to the right server, and these network corrections need to be created and maintained. Secondly, they need to be aware of the directory structure of the operating system they are working on, and the directory structure of the server used to publish the site in order to move the file from their system to the correct place. Thirdly, they need to know how to use a file-transfer mechanism. This may be a simple file copy, but it is more likely to be something like ftp (file transfer protocol), which is not necessarily straightforward to use. Lastly, they need to understand how the server is set up to refresh the site in order to know whether the web page that they have just moved is publishing successfully. They will also at this point need to check that the new page works and looks acceptable.

For someone who is reasonably computer literate, these tasks can be pretty straightforward. However, people who have a skill in writing content or laying out web pages are not necessarily the kinds of people who understand ftp commands or directory structures within operating systems. This kind of environment is the

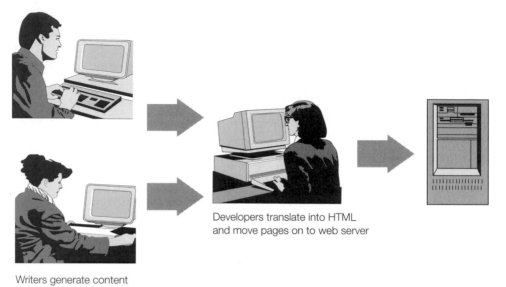

Writers generate content

Developers translate into HTML
and move pages on to web server

Figure 2.2   Usual content generation bottleneck

historical environment set up by the technical hobbyist and is not the approach that should be used for creating sites that have contributors who are non technical – which covers the majority if not all of company internet and intranet sites.

What usually happens in this kind of technical environment is that a bottleneck develops where the content creators are dependent on developers checking that their HTML files will format correctly and then moving these files on to the publishing server. This can be frustrating for content providers, but unavoidable if the environment has been set up to be understandable only to the technically astute (*see* Fig. 2.2).

In an ideal environment, the content contributors should not have to go cap in hand to technical experts to move their content on to the web server. Neither should they have to have any knowledge of how their content is published to a site, or knowledge of how the files and directories are organized on the web server. The responsibility of the content provider should be to provide content that is complete and correct. How that content is published should be the responsibility of others or, even better, a publishing workflow within a content management system.

Content maintenance

Setting up a website for the first time is simple compared with the ongoing maintenance of a site that grows daily. The level of difficulty and costs of doing site maintenance are of course directly related to the number of changes that need to be made. But the ease in which content creators can generate HTML means that in most company internet and intranet sites new content is always arriving on the doorstep and existing content is being corrected, changed, moved and deleted on a regular basis.

Difficulties in managing content outside of a database

One of the problems with not holding content within any content management system or database is that there exists no automatic way of analyzing the content that exists on a site. Site feedback might suggest that users are always searching for a particular topic, but without any query facility, or structured support for keywords and synonyms, it will be very difficult to find out how much of the content of a site really does support the requested subject matter. It might be the case that the information exists but has just not been labelled correctly. Without any way of analyzing the site content, it will be difficult to judge.

Secondly, there exists no support for project or resource management reporting. A site may be in a position where marketing literature needs to be published on a certain date to support other marketing programmes or product announcements that are to coincide. Separate systems can be set up to track the progress and status of content, but when they are separate to that content they will always rely on someone keeping the data up to date for anyone else to have any confidence that the information is correct. Far better for this kind of tracking to be built into the files themselves so that it is easy for someone to see status information that is automatically associated and generated by the edit history of the file.

Implications of site redesign

Having HTML files that contain content information, navigation information, layout information and classification information means that a redesign of a site will usually require every single HTML source file to be updated manually. And as we know, manual processes are prone to error. Therefore a site design can not only be time-consuming and costly, it can also introduce errors and therefore impact the quality of the site.

The best way to manage site content is to break it apart into manageable chunks. One very useful approach is to separate out navigational relationships from the underlying content. By doing this, it is then possible to change and add to any navigation scheme, without having to edit any content files. Secondly, by separating out the content from the presentation of that content, changes can be made to individual page layouts and site look and feel without disturbing the files that contain the underlying information.

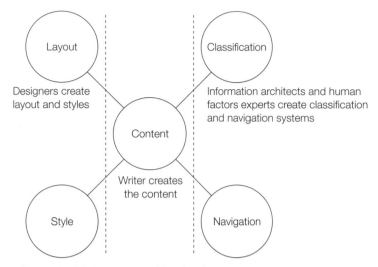

Figure 2.3   Separating site content into manageable chunks

It should also be possible to separate out some of the categorization information from the content, such as additional information for keywords. This can save
an enormous amount of time, for instance if you need to add a new synonym
that should be supported by a site search function. Far better to make this change
in a central classification scheme than to go into each HTML file and add the new
synonym into the relevant meta-data field (*see* Fig. 2.3).

Ad hoc change control

When content is held outside of a database or content management system, there
exists a possibility for major problems in managing changes and checking that
these changes have been applied correctly. One person may notice that there is an
error on a page, and in the time that it takes for the file to be edited and corrected
someone else may be editing and correcting another part of the file. Outside of
any version control system, it is easy to be unaware that someone else is currently
changing a file. Whoever completes the change and returns the file first will end
up losing their work, due to the fact that the file will be subsequently overwritten
by the second person copying their updated version over the top of it.

Sometimes groups try to work around this problem in a number of ad hoc
ways. A team may use a white board where people record the files that they are
working on, or teams adopt an even more casual approach by relying on the act
of shouting out to anyone in earshot to find out if someone is working on a particular file. These approaches are never foolproof, even within small development
groups that sit close together. There will always be times when a change gets lost
and recriminations abound and accusations are made about who didn't check
first that someone else was editing a file.

Ad hoc processes for archiving and deletion

Another problem that can arise is when a web page needs to be moved, archived or deleted. This is a maintenance problem that affects the linking and navigation between pages. Outside of any automated system that checks for broken links, it will be up to the individual moving the page to check each HTML file that is published to the site to see if a link exists to the page that will be removed.

We can guess from the number of broken links that exist on the web today that relying on a manual process to do this is less than successful. Broken links are especially annoying to users and also a serious usability problem. It shows a level of sloppiness and an inattention to detail that will affect the way that the user perceives how professional a site is, and ultimately how professional and trustworthy the organization is which is responsible for the site.

A user might reasonably ask the question: 'If a company cannot be bothered to check the links on a site, can they honestly be trusted to check that my personal details and credit card details are secure?'

3 The need for a process

When you mention processes or controls to some people involved in website development, they shudder. To them, the web still has an image that conjures up creativity, impulsiveness, smart young individuals hanging out in garages, eating pizza and writing clever search algorithms through the night.

This was the web, but it is not how businesses see the web today. Companies invest in developing websites because they perceive some value in it. The value is never to play with the technology, or very rarely to create visual interfaces in order to win awards. Value is in enhancing the company brand, in advertising company services and products, and ultimately in making money, whether directly through a commerce website and advertising or indirectly through the marketing and promotion of the company products and services that are available through more traditional channels.

Achieving a quality website

The website is an important external face of the company to its potential customer set. Therefore the quality of that interface and the way that web users perceive it should be of paramount importance to the organization responsible for the management and development of the site.

To achieve a quality website, an organization needs to provide the necessary level of controls to ensure that:

- web pages do not just turn up unexpectedly on the site without the necessary validation being in place;

- the quality of the information being presented is of the required style, uses required terminology, is written at the right level, and is correct and complete;

- new content will enhance the user experience and help users achieve their tasks;

- the layout and the visual design of pages is consistent and of the required quality;

- information is classified correctly and fits into an overall information architecture;

- the site reflects and enhances the company brand, supports the business goals, and fulfils the user goals and expectations of its targeted audience.

Developing good and maintainable websites is difficult. It has nearly all of the problems and pitfalls of developing software, plus the headaches and work-flow requirements of a publishing environment. The good news is that creating a usable website has very little to do with technology and everything to do with designing a solution that people can use. It is also possible to put in place good practices that will help ensure that any solution that is created will be usable.

Within the software development process there are many useful techniques that have been researched and developed to try to make software products easier to use. Many of these techniques are just as applicable for developing websites as they are for developing usable software interfaces. However, simply adapting the software development process to web development is not enough. Websites have this extra facet of evolving after they have been developed and delivered on to the internet. They evolve through the ongoing additions and maintenance of the information that they present. Software products do not have to consider this phase. A software product changes when the development group releases a new version. The changes are tightly controlled, and the different versions are made available only when the product has been through a planned development cycle.

To overcome this extra hurdle, a web development process needs to consider how a publication process can be successfully implemented within the organiza-tion. It also has to consider designing processes that can be used by those within the organization that will be creating and maintaining the site content. Fortunately, there are many publishing companies that have perfected publica-tion processes. Within the publication world, there are also many proven techniques that are just as applicable to delivering and maintaining content on a website as they are for delivering news articles to a newspaper.

Therefore there needs to be a consideration of both of these disciplines before it is possible to define a workable web development process. When one considers only the software development aspects in creating a web site, there will be little regard for how information is published to the site or how the site will evolve. When one considers only the publication aspects of a website, the design, usability and implementation of the site will suffer. Approaching the design of a website in the same way as one designs published material is fundamentally flawed due to the fact that task flows and design requirements for user interaction are not considered. This is the main reason why many of the early websites that were created by publishing companies had very high-quality visual interfaces and very bad usability problems.

For any medium- to large-scale company website, the development project should have at least two main usability goals:

- to create an easy-to-use website that delivers up-to-date content of a high quality. Such a site is often referred to as a content-driven site;
- to create an easy-to-use system that allows content to be created, published, managed and maintained on the site. Such a system is often referred to as a content management system.

Content-driven website development projects have two types of users to consider:

- the end users of the site;
- the end users of the system that delivers the content to the site.

Making the website easy to use will involve designing interfaces that are usable by the target audience. Making a content management system easy to use involves designing a system that can be used by those within the organization who will be creating and maintaining the content that is published to the site. Techniques from the software development process and the publishing process can be adapted to achieve both of these goals.

Learning from the software development process

There are a number of documented software development processes that attempt to define approaches that bring an engineering discipline to the way that software is developed. Many of these processes build upon the traditional waterfall methodology that defines the main stages of analysis, design, development, testing and delivery. Variations to this main theme include the idea of iterative development where the process stops being sequential and prototypes are used to iterate between each stage to validate that any analysis and design decisions will work. In addition there is a philosophy, a design approach and a methodology called user-centred design, which attempts to place the end users of the system at the core of the design process.

Essentially, the main ideas remain the same – usually it is only the extent to which an organization attempts to implement a disciplined process that determines how well the methodology is applied and how successful the end result will be. An important success factor in the equation is whether the necessary skills are available within the project teams and whether an organization is able to manage a multidisciplinary team effectively. These software development issues will be exactly the same for web development teams. It is fine for a process to define a level of user analysis and validation, but if the organization does not have the necessary level of human factors skill, or is not prepared to buy these skills in, this stage is unlikely to be done well.

Why software development processes are needed

Software development houses have adopted academic methodologies for the fundamental business reasons that:

- any reasonably sized software product is very expensive to develop;
- high-quality software is difficult to create.

These factors have contributed to the fact that software projects are notorious for costing more than was originally planned, running over time and not being of a high enough quality. Therefore, over the years, many approaches, methodologies and disciplines have been developed to try to bring these costs down while increasing the quality of the code that is created and decreasing the time it takes to create it.

The steps involved to delivering a software product

In an ideal software development project where all the required skills are available, the following stages occur.

Defining the market

Because software applications are so expensive to create, software houses recognize that there really needs to be a marketplace for a proposed product before investing so much money into the development process. Business analysts identify the business opportunities and market segmentation and create requirement definitions to provide the scope and functionality that the product must support. They also perform a level of competitive analysis to understand who the competition is and where their strengths and weaknesses lie.

Defining the usability requirements

Human factors experts define the user tasks that must be supported within the product, including design features that the software should comply with. By working closely with and performing a user analysis of the defined intended audience, design ideas and assumptions can be validated before the expensive software design and development process starts.

Defining the system

System architects define the overall structure of the software, translating the business and user requirements into high-level functional specifications. The role of the architect is to oversee the whole software development process and to understand how all the pieces will work together.

Defining the visual designs

Visual interface designers work with human factors engineers and system architects to define the user interface designs for the product. This process is difficult as trade-offs and compromises often need to be made. Developers need to consider the implications of performance, development schedules and whether the technology is available, while human factors engineers are intent on concentrating on enabling the user to achieve their goals in an efficient, effective and enjoyable way. On the other hand, the visual designer wishes to create something that is both memorable and aesthetically pleasing. It is up to the team to try to define a design that somehow accomplishes all three goals.

Developing the code

The job of translating both functional and interface designs to code is usually a highly skilled and specialized one. The process is iterative, as a functional design specification is rarely complete; the programmer needs to make informed decisions along the way. Programmers need to design a technical solution that is structured to be easily maintainable and in some cases reusable. There will also be a need to consider how the code can be optimized for performance.

Writing the help text

Professional technical writers write help text and support documentation for the product. The information developer needs to work closely with all members of the development team to ensure that the published material that the end user will read matches exactly the software product that they are using.

Building the product

The build process is usually run by a dedicated group who use tools to pull all the software modules from program libraries to generate a complete and clean compilation of the most up-to-date versions of the code.

Testing

The software is tested vigorously internally and externally within beta programs. Test programs and scripts are developed that are both manual and automatic to try to cover as many test paths through the software as possible.

Marketing the product

Finally, the marketing professionals provide the collateral that will publicize the product to generate sales. This will hopefully recoup all the development costs and make a healthy profit on top.

Usability testing the product

Throughout the development project, human factors experts perform user validation tests to see if the product will be usable. After the product has been released, further tests are conducted and usability questionnaires may be designed to gauge the overall acceptance of the product by those who have bought and used it. It will be up to the human factors engineer to recommend any changes that may be needed as a result of identified usability problems.

Relationship to the web development environment

It can be seen that all of these steps are in some part applicable to the web development process.

- All web development projects should define the business and usability requirements up front before any development work starts.

- Any web solution will need a high-level design that defines the overall structure and operation of the site.

- Visual interfaces will need to be created by visual designers, ideally with the help of human factors and development experts.

- Development groups will need to assemble the site and write any specialized software that is required.

- It may be applicable for certain parts of the site to offer some help or assistance.

- Someone will need to eventually test the site on the environments that are deemed important, for instance on different browsers and operating systems.

- Marketing a site is just as important as marketing a product, otherwise how will potential users know that the site exists?

There is one significant difference, however, between the web development process and traditional software development. In traditional software development environments, the technology has always been difficult enough to get in the way of enthusiasts getting involved with the code. By contrast, any enthusiast can have a go at creating a web page and without any controls being in place, add that page to the company website.

Learning from the publication process

There have been many documented approaches to defining publication processes that can be used within an organization. Outside of traditional publishing houses, these techniques have mostly been incorporated into document management systems that attempt to control the creation, revision and access to important information within a company.

However, the web publishing model is more aligned to the kind of publishing environment that is seen inside newspapers or magazines. It is the way that these organizations operate in order to meet the business models and objectives of the organization which is of special interest to the website publication process. Of particular interest is the definition of responsibilities within the publishing teams and how workflows are designed and implemented across the organization to allow content to be created, reviewed, modified, prioritized, classified and, most importantly, published in a final state to an overall body of information.

Why publishing processes are needed

Publication machines are set up at different speeds depending on how often a publication is printed. The daily publication of a newspaper has very tight time lines compared with the monthly periodical that can have a more relaxed attitude and can be more flexible about deadlines. Ultimately the fundamental process is the same, irrespective of the different timescales involved. Content intended for a print publication has to be available at a certain point in time in order for it to make the print run. It also has to be written to a defined format, in the required writing style, and be of the desired quality, which implies that some sort of content review process is in place.

In order for a scheduled print run to be achievable, there needs to be a very clearly defined process in place that those within the organization adhere to. The business reasons for this are:

● the success of a publication is dependent on the *quality* of its content and the applicability of that content to its target audience;

● in order for a print run to be scheduled and for the publication delivery to be achieved, there need to be strict *deadlines* that are adhered to by everyone involved in the process.

For these reasons, the creative processes of writing, providing images, editing and laying out pages are all controlled by strict time schedules. Missing these schedules is likely to have a serious implication on the business. Therefore the importance that is placed on content quality and timely delivery is very high within any organization that prides itself on delivering a professional publication.

The steps involved to delivering a professional publication

In an ideal publishing environment where all the required skills are available, the following stages occur.

Defining the market
Because the success of a publication is dependent on its circulation, irrespective of whether the business model is predominantly advertising or predominantly direct sales, business analysts clearly identify the business opportunities and market segmentation that they expect the publication to appeal to.

Defining the readership requirements
When the market has been identified, analysis of the readership requirements takes place and publishing guidelines are produced that define how the publication will satisfy its target audience. These guidelines are revised as a result of measuring the success of the publication or analyzing other successful publications within the same domain.

Defining the roles and workflows required
The content publishing process owned by the publication editor identifies who within the organization has responsibilities for commissioning new articles, accepting article proposals, editing content, laying out the page and deciding the information structure. Information structure defines such things as which articles are lead articles and where articles are placed within the overall layout. Responsibility will also be assigned to who owns the overall visual aspects of the publication.

Setting the publication priorities
Early within the publication cycle the priorities for that publication are set out to define which stories are likely to be lead stories and which are likely to appear within the special interest sections. Once these priorities have been set and the likely structure of the publication has been defined, articles and any photography may be commissioned to various individuals. At this point there will also be an indication of the number and size of adverts the publication will be printing and where within the publication these adverts will appear.

Creating articles
The type of publication will dictate the balance of in-house contributors to roaming journalists to external freelance feature writers who are commissioned to

write specialized articles. Irrespective of the source, articles are written and submitted to the publication house by a certain time to meet the publication deadline.

Editing and reviewing article content

Editors take these articles and review them for writing style, grammar, factual accuracy and legal issues, and may change the number of words, alter headings and rewrite any part of the content. There will also be a decision made on the classification of the content with respect to how it relates to other articles that have been published on the same subject. This will determine where the article will be archived after it has been published. Finally, the article will be proposed into a certain place within the publication such as a lead article on the front page or within a features section towards the back.

Deciding on the publication structure

Once articles have been submitted, there will be a decision made on the relative importance of each story, which in turn will directly relate to where in the publication the article will appear. This decision also takes into account any visual material that may be included with the article – extra visual material may need to be either found or created.

Providing the visual material

Visual interface designers work with edited articles within a rough page structure to add photographs, cartoons and diagrams as appropriate.

Reviewing the publication

Once all the rough pages have been laid out with both articles and accompanying visual material, a first review takes place of the proposed publication. Articles may get reprioritized or even taken out as others are deemed more important or current. Visual material might also get promoted, changed or removed. This iterative process will often cause editors and visual designers to make changes to the content as the information structure of the publication is changed. At some point near the print deadline the decision is made to go with the current version.

Setting out the page

The job of typesetting a page with the correct fonts, colours and column sizes is a specialized and time-consuming one. The typesetter takes the publication design and translates it into a format that can be used for a print run.

Printing and distributing the publication

The print process is run by a dedicated group within the organization who take the page type settings, load them into a machine and activate a run. The distribution team takes the publications and may distribute to retail outlets via air, rail or road.

Marketing the publication

Finally, the marketing professionals create and execute marketing plans that will publicize the publication to generate both sales and advertising revenue. This will hopefully recoup all the publication costs and make a healthy profit on top.

Relationship to the web development environment

There are remarkable similarities to the software development process, such as defining the business need, defining and analyzing the target audience to set some usability review criteria, performing a build of all the relevant parts, and distributing and marketing the final product. However, the main difference is the processes that go on in between that allow the content to enter and move around the organization in order for it to hopefully be published at the other end.

These workflows are the missing parts that need to be analyzed and adapted to suit website content generation. The way that information is managed and the different roles that need to be in place within the organization to automate workflow processes is an area that clearly needs to be understood before a web development process can be properly defined.

It can be seen that any organization that generates a large amount of information that is later stored within an archive will need to adopt some sort of classification system. It can also be assumed that if it is a strong requirement for users to find this information quickly, the classification system that is used will need to be carefully designed and applied consistently to the underlying data. This should be of particular interest to web information designers who struggle to come up with solutions that make it easy for users to find information on a website. It is all well and good designing an easy-to-use interface for a search query, but if the underlying classification system is not designed and applied correctly to the site content, the search results will not return the best matches to the user.

Other areas that are particularly relevant to web content generation include the use of layout templates, the definition of house writing styles, and the review cycle used to check proposed material against defined review criteria. It is also significant that the publication is reviewed as a whole and decisions are made about the relative importance of individual pieces of content within that whole. It seems inconceivable that in this world articles could start appearing within the finished product that have not been reviewed or indeed exactly positioned by someone who has overall responsibility for the job.

Why web development processes are needed

After the initial flush of creating a site with a simple navigation structure and information hierarchy, companies are now experiencing the pain of having a website that seems to grow in content size daily. There are common problems that many companies experience that in the end degrade the quality of the site, such as:

- new content that is easy to create and publish leads to a volatile and changeable site prone to errors;

- sub-sites are created that mirror the organizational structure rather than reflect the purpose of the site or any user tasks that the site should be supporting;

- redesigning the site and restructuring the information on the site is very expensive;

- content creators do not always understand any underlying information architecture that may exist, consequently inappropriate relationships are added on an ad hoc basis;

- content creators do not classify content consistently, leading to inadequate support for searching, cross-referencing and indexing;

- content creators do not create information with consistent structures or follow writing style guidelines, leading to different levels of information quality on the site;

- visual designers do not follow design guidelines, leading to inconsistent visual styles within the interface;

- review processes are ad hoc, which leads to inconsistencies in content quality;

- ownership of existing content is hard to manage, consequently content maintenance can be time-consuming or non-existent;

- no one owns the job of reviewing the site as a whole to ensure that the purpose and goals of the site are not getting lost;

- no one measures the success of user task flows to make sure that the site is usable. In fact, many web development teams do not involve users at any stage of the project or have anyone on the team who understands how to create usable interfaces.

These factors have contributed to the fact that many web development teams create websites that are not as usable as they should be, and are also costly to maintain once content is being added on a regular basis. Web projects that involve any maintenance, redesign or restructuring on an existing site are notorious for costing far more than was originally anticipated. It is for this reason that many websites degrade over time. This deterioration affects the usability of the site, the quality and therefore usefulness of the content, the visual consistency and design quality across the site, the levels of supported contextual relationships between related information, and how information on the site is classified and therefore accessible through a search engine.

It is for this reason that many companies are having to go through the painful and costly exercise of evaluating the content on their sites and setting up an environment that helps them manage that content in a more efficient way. At the same time, these companies should also be applying some human factors techniques to ensure that pages on the site have a valid justification for being there. Their existence should be measured by the amount they help a user to achieve some user goal or by the amount they support the business purpose of the site. For many, the time has come to introduce structure and control to the way that a site is created and managed in order for that site to be manageable in the future. How quickly a company website can react to change, add new features, offer new products, introduce new business models, and reach out to new customers could make a difference to who leads the internet market and who doesn't.

Summary

Many businesses have woken up to the fact that there is a whole new way of making money and a whole new global market waiting to be tapped into. The internet has significantly moved away from being just a geeky, technology-driven information dumping ground to potentially being the primary product sales and marketing channel for all major and minor business around the world. The number of users entering the web marketplace grows significantly every day. Users like the idea of sitting at home and buying goods and services without having to fight for car parking spaces, wait in queues and waste time walking between shops. For the same reasons that many people prefer to use a car rather than use public transport, many people prefer to shop online rather than visit a public shopping mall – it is more convenient and it is quicker.

Because of the history of the web and where we stand with its evolution, many companies know that they have to start applying some discipline to the way that their websites are developed. The gradual shift away from being just a backroom web enthusiast's hobby to a major shop front for a company's products and information means that the whole process of website development needs to be controlled and managed. It needs to become as disciplined, if not more disciplined, than the software development process, and as process oriented and quality conscious as the publication process.

Many businesses are becoming more aware that by having a website on the internet means that the potential audience is massive and global, and the impact on the business is potentially huge. It is also becoming evident that creating good websites is very difficult, and made more so by the lack of a disciplined environment for website development that successfully preserves the scope and goals of a site while preventing the flood of organizational 'shovel ware' by enthusiasts who have acquired some web page designer software and have discovered the publishing option. Without having any controls in place, a company can find itself in the embarrassing position of enabling anyone to add anything they like to a company site.

In the user's mind, the website 'is' the company. Users more and more will judge how reliable, how professional and how good a company is by the image it projects through its website and how easily that site allows them to achieve their tasks.

Website development overview and analysis techniques

This second section looks at a simple model for web development that encompasses analysis, design, implementation and roll-out and then looks in detail at each analysis stage that should provide the foundation and information required for the complete web development project. The analysis stages are covered in varying detail, but include the business analysis, the user analysis and the content analysis. This section also includes chapters that look at design considerations to do with web user interfaces and content structuring and delivery.

4 Website development overview

In any serious web development project that aims to deliver a content-driven site, it is impossible to consider a development process that does not take into account the development of the content management system that will support it. It would be like a newspaper company considering only the design, content, layout and production of the paper and ignoring how the articles are created, reviewed, classified, cross-referenced and archived. The more important the information, the more emphasis needs to be placed on the management of that information. It is also the case that the requirements placed on a content management system will be inextricably linked to the requirements placed on the website. In an ideal situation, the two should be created and set up at the same time.

The main stages to consider

In a simple model for developing a content-driven website with a supporting content management system there are some well-defined stages to be considered.

Analysis

Definition of the website requirements
Analyzing and defining the requirements for a website includes defining the market, creating the business models, performing a competitive analysis and defining the target audience. Most importantly, this phase should clearly outline the main purpose of the site and the primary user goals and tasks that the site must support.

Definition of the content management requirements

Analyzing and defining the requirements for the supporting content management system includes defining the organizational workflows that will move content from creation and review to publication, and the workflows applicable for the maintenance of site content. It will also include the definition of responsibilities, the specification of review criteria for new or changed content, and the organizational requirements for access and version control of the files that make up the site.

Design

Design of the website

The design phase of a website includes the definition of visual interfaces and the specification and design of the user interactions that will support the tasks identified during the analysis stage. It will also include the design of the site navigation, the specification of visual styles to be used across the site, the designs of view templates, and the design and layout of any site-wide views such as indexes and site maps.

Design of the content management system

The design phase of a content management system includes the definition of visual interfaces and the specification and design of the user interactions that will support the tasks identified in the analysis stage. In particular, designers of content management systems define the design and layout of forms for content providers to generate the information that will appear on the site.

The design of the content management system will be driven by the content management requirements, but also by the website designs that will specify the view templates that are required (*see* Fig. 4.1). Once these templates are defined, the forms within the content management system can be designed to give content providers the ability to create the information that will eventually appear on the site.

Delivery

Implementation

Once the website and supporting content management systems have been designed, there will be a dependency for both to be implemented and up and running together in order for them to be individually tested. For example, the

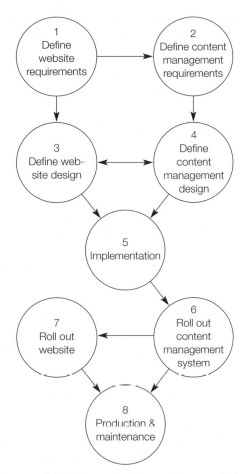

Figure 4.1 Simple model for creating a website delivered through a content management system

web pages that will be generated and displayed on the website through a view template will need the content management system to be in place so that the templated data can be translated through any stored view templates before being published to the site.

Content management system roll-out

The roll-out of the content management system will give content providers the ability to create and publish information to the site. It will also allow the management of that information to be controlled through review procedures, access controls, change management and automatic archival and deletion.

In an environment where the site content is generated from underlying structured data created by content providers, the content management system needs to be rolled out and successfully up and running before the website becomes available. This is so that the processes for creating, publishing and maintaining the site content are tested and established before the information is accessible to the outside world. The roll-out of the content management system provides a period of time when the quality of information being published to a site can be reviewed and the process for delivering that information can be modified without impacting any content delivery schedules.

Website roll-out

Once the content management system is up and running and the website has been tested, it can be released into the public domain.

Maintenance

Production and maintenance

Production is a term that can be used for the ongoing process of creating content, having that content reviewed, and publishing that content on to the site. It may also include the regular creation of site statistics that feed back such things as the number of visitors coming to the site, the queries that users are typing into search entry fields and, in particular on a commerce site, the number of orders being taken, the amount of money being made and which products are selling and which are not.

Maintenance includes the need to update, change or correct existing information that is being published. It will also include the archiving and deletion of old and out-of-date information, and updating, changing or correcting visual and layout attributes, navigation paths and any classification system that is in operation.

The need to control major changes

If any major changes are to be made to the website or the content management system, these changes should be validated and implemented by going back through the complete process from analysis to implementation. This is important because if this is not done, it is very easy for a site to gradually shift direction away from the organizational site goals and business purpose. As more and more content gets added, and more and more navigational links are made available to users, strict controls need to be in place to ensure that the primary user goals and tasks are not being lost in a mire of less important information.

Controlling major changes such as adding a completely new category of information to the homepage is not the same thing as iterative design and development, where in real life small changes to the design will occur throughout the development cycle. There are many valid reasons why changes occur and the web development process needs to be flexible enough to accommodate changes throughout the development life cycle. However, there is a difference between this kind of iteration and creating brand new versions or redesigns for a site. Major changes in design direction should be managed and controlled within a structured process and the analysis or requirement stage should always be at the beginning of any new development cycle.

As part of both the website and the content management system development cycles there should be an explicit exercise to involve users at every stage. These users need to be representative of the types of people who will eventually be using the systems so that they will be in a position to validate the usability of the interfaces and the validity of any design assumptions that have been made. Involving users early on can help ensure that usability problems are detected early and will hopefully lead to the system being understandable, usable, useful and hopefully an enjoyable experience for those who are intending to use them.

The importance of the analysis phase

As with the traditional software development process, the later any design problems are encountered within the website development cycle, the more expensive they will be to rectify. That is why it is imperative to ensure that the analysis stage of any development project is conducted thoroughly.

Requirements set the parameters for a design. The fewer the parameters, the more freedom the designers will have to design what they want. It is a wrong assumption to believe that most designers like being given this freedom. It is also a wrong assumption to believe that the more freedom a designer has, the better the site design will be. Usability is not graphic design. A website needs to have a very clear business model and a very clear user model. It also helps to have a clear content model. A content management system needs a clear organizational model and a clear user model and cannot be designed without a very clear content model. It is unlikely that a website or a content management system will be designed or implemented well without investing in the level of analysis that is required to understand what these models are.

Different types of analysis generate different types of requirements, and it is possible to have conflicting requirements from the different groups. Providing a level of prioritization can not only help decide the order in which things get developed, it can also help decide a strategy when there is a conflict in requirements.

A common example that illustrates this potential conflict is the placement within supermarkets of popular products such as milk and bread. From a shopper's perspective, it would be far easier and quicker if these goods were placed near the door. A significant percentage of users visit a supermarket with a very short list of things to buy, almost always including milk or bread; how much quicker for that shopper to grab those products near the door and quickly proceed to the checkout. However, this is not the sort of behaviour that the supermarket wants to encourage. Far better for them to force that shopper down as many aisles as possible with the hope that along the way they are either tempted by an impulse buy or see something that they have forgotten.

By the number of supermarkets that adopt the 'further the walk the better' strategy, the business requirement has taken precedence over the user requirement. However, the first supermarket to risk this strategy must have known – or if not took a gamble – that shoppers would not feel so frustrated by this product positioning that they would shop elsewhere. In fact, the original business model might have made a decision that their target audience were not those shoppers with short lists consisting of bread and milk.

The important message in this is that designs should be based on informed decisions with supporting evidence and background knowledge, not assumptions and guesswork. The analysis stage of the development process is the stage that provides that knowledge, and defines the foundations and framework for the system that is to be created, whether that system is a website, a content management solution or even a supermarket.

Defining the different requirements

There are four distinct groups of requirements that need to be considered:

- business requirements
- user requirements
- content requirements
- system requirements.

The analysis phase that generates these requirements can then be broken down into the same distinct areas and it is usual for different groups or individuals within an organization to generate them due to the different skills needed.

Business requirements

When a business plan or model is defined that justifies a business investing in a new website, this model will generate a number of requirements that will influence the design and content for a site. For instance, if the business model centres on a website generating revenue from online advertising, this will make very real demands on the navigational structure of the site and the layout of pages to include the ad banners that will be the vehicle to generate income. There will also be implications on where the most enticing content will appear in order to increase the number of page hits throughout the site.

In addition, some aspects of a business plan may generate activities during the development cycle that will need to be carried out at an appropriate time. An example of this is the need to register the site with search engines. The marketing and communications aspects of the business plan will directly drive the level of investment in this activity. The business analysis defines the business requirements into the system and provides the scope, directions and priorities of the solution that is to be provided to meet the defined business targets.

Requirements from the business surface as organizational requirements when related directly to the development of a content management system. The organization defines the roles and responsibilities for owning and reviewing information destined for the site. The organization is also likely to set requirements on who has access to the system and the processes that need to be in place to manage site content.

User requirements

There are two sets of users that need to be analyzed during the user analysis phase. The first is the target audience for the website that will be defined by the business model. The second will be those who will be responsible for the delivery and management of the website content.

The target audience for the website and the analysis of this user population should provide usability requirements on the design that will ensure that the website user interface makes it easy for users to achieve their tasks. The target audience for the content management system is likely to be people within the organization. The quality of a site is usually measured by the quality of its content. Thus it is of equal importance to ensure than the creation, publication and maintenance of the site content is designed to be usable by this second user population. The user analysis generates usability requirements into the system as a result of analyzing the factors that will influence the acceptance of a solution by the targeted audience.

Content requirements

A content analysis looks at the types, attributes and characteristics of information that will be published to a site, and defines the relationships that exist between different pieces of information and information types. A content analysis also defines requirements for the classification of keywords in order to support any required search tasks identified within the user analysis, and also to support any navigational and contextual relationship requirements that may exist.

Different types of content may have different requirements for creation, maintenance and quality assurance. As such this will generate requirements on a content management system to support the necessary levels of organizational workflows that will need to be in place. Other characteristics of content that will need to be considered within a content analysis are ownership and copyright issues. The content analysis phase should also define the organizational structure of a site and how content will be best arranged from a navigational point of view. This will always be in support of the primary user tasks identified within the user analysis stage.

System requirements

The two systems that are to be provided will need their own system analysis due to the fact that the business requirements and target audiences will almost always be different. For instance, the system analysis for the published website will need to analyze the type of content that will be delivered to the system to determine the requirements for static or dynamic pages, performance, security and site availability.

The system requirements for a content management system are likely to concentrate on issues regarding access and version control, document management, data storage or any automatic notification facilities that may be required. The system analysis will provide a set of requirements based on the level of system that will need to be in place to support both the site content within a content management system and the published website that will be developed and published to a web server.

Summary

A development process for content-driven websites can be defined that follows the software development waterfall methodology of analysis, design, delivery and maintenance, with the difference that there are two systems to create: the website with its own goals and target audience and the content management system that needs to be usable by those within the organization who will be creating and managing the information that will be published on the site. The requirements for the content management system are driven by the requirements of the website; however the success and quality of the information on the website will be dependent on the successful implementation and design of the content management system.

As with any development project it is the analysis stage, that is key to getting the right solution in the shortest amount of time. There are four analysis stages within a web development process: business analysis, user analysis, content analysis and system analysis. The first three are covered within this book, and the content analysis stage will be examined in some depth.

The fourth stage, the system analysis, is outside the scope of this book because that web technology and the tools available are topics that would fill many books several times over. It is also an area that moves so fast that there is a danger that the information that could be included here would have a much shorter shelf life than the rest of the book. The contents of this book attempt to define a structured approach to website development that includes analysis and design techniques that enable a web development team to design usable websites – techniques which are good practice irrespective of the changing technology that will eventually be used to implement the solution.

chapter 5 Business analysis

The business analysis stage of website development and delivery defines the scope, directions and priorities of a site. This chapter gives an overview of the sort of information that a business analysis phase should provide in order for the business requirements to be created that feed into the design of a website.

Information defined as part of a business analysis

Defining the business goals and objectives

Defining the site purpose means clearly stating what the business goals and objectives are, which will subsequently define what the primary user tasks should be in support of these goals. At the highest level, these goals and objectives define the scope of the site and underline how the site will be assessed from a business perspective. Site goals need to be both clearly communicated and actively maintained to ensure that the purpose of a site remains clear. Ideally, all site content should be formally reviewed and prioritized against these goals and primary tasks to clearly understand whether the content is relevant and meets the business objectives of the site.

Defining the business model

There are only three clearly different revenue-earning business models for the web:

● commerce: the marketing and sale of products and services through an online channel, including affiliate relationships;

- advertising: this can include the selling of advertising banner space on a web page, renting keywords out to return links, or adding sponsorship information to content or e-mail notifications;

- subscription: the collection of revenue on a regular basis from a registered user population for services provided by a website.

In addition, there are two other models that are non-revenue earning:

- promotional – the marketing and promotion of products and/or services;

- cost saving – typically a business to business type model where web-based transactions reduce operational costs including the costs of acquiring new customers.

A website can be a hybrid of different models and depending on which models are required determines how the site will be designed and what the relative priority of elements will be within the interface. It will also have a strong influence on any navigational structure that is provided.

Defining the value proposition

In a crowded marketplace on the web, a business should be able to clearly state why customers will choose this site over any others. It might be because the products are cheaper or of better quality. It might be because the site is first into the market or has the backing of authoritative professional organizations.

An internet start-up will have to supply this kind of information to any venture capital fund if it wants that company to invest money into the new business. However, it is something that every business should at least understand and communicate as part of the business plan, even if it is not dependent on any outside investment. Defining why a website will succeed will clarify and add weight to the business goals and objectives. It also provides valuable information to those who will be defining the marketing and communication plan for the site.

Analyzing an existing brand and defining the brand for the web

The company brand can play a very important part within a web interface as it can help to create trust and bring credibility to a site. Even though competitive sites may be only two mouse clicks away, accessibility is not the overriding reason why users choose one site over another. There exists a natural and justified wariness by users to provide credit card and personal details over the internet, especially to companies of which they have no previous knowledge. Therefore, bringing an existing trusted brand image on to the web can provide automatic advantages over other competitive sites that are created by companies users have never heard of.

When bringing an existing brand to the web environment, or developing a new brand image, there must be a clear definition of what that brand is and what it stands for. A brand image should be easily recognized within the interface. Most companies use logos, a recognizable colour scheme and consistent visual styles throughout the site. A brand can also be communicated through the kind of content being displayed and the style of writing being used. All these factors can reinforce the feeling for the user that they are in a site that is integrated and cohesive. When a user moves around such a site there is a 'sense of place', in other words there is a comforting feeling of knowing where they are. This should not be dismissed as unimportant. One of the most common complaints from web users is that they often feel lost and disoriented as they jump from one page to another.

Every brand should be supported by a small number of core brand messages. These brand messages should be clearly communicated as part of the design. An example of this might be a company's commitment to customer service through such things as a good returns policy. To reinforce this brand message, a business requirement may be to give prominence to a section on customer service from the homepage. The placement and visual prominence of elements within the interface will have a direct correlation on how the user perceives a website, and therefore perceives the company as a whole.

Target audience

The clear definition of which set of users the website is aimed at forms part of the business plan and is a vital piece of information for any marketing or advertising campaign. The target audience definition is the key piece of information that feeds into the user analysis and will usually identify primary and secondary audiences by gender, age, social and economic factors and behaviour patterns.

It is common for a business analyst to try to opt out of this definition when it comes to a website by defining that the site should appeal to everyone. This makes the job of user analysis and design very difficult, as it is impossible to please everyone. Even if the business objective is to target anyone who logs on to the internet, this definition needs to be refined by identifying and prioritizing the primary or most important users to attract. If the majority of CDs are bought by males between the ages of 18 and 25, this has to be a primary target audience for a non-specialized online music store, even if it would like to attract older and maybe more affluent buyers in future.

Compet evaluation

Most companies will have some competition on the web, as well as their historical competition in other traditional channels. It is imperative that these competitors are identified and a competitive evaluation undertaken to understand and compare strengths and weaknesses.

As the web opens up accessibility to sites in all countries, there needs to be some analysis carried out that understands the competition from both global competitors and local ones. There are many successful sites on the web that have made location a non-issue by pricing their products competitively and by setting up business relationships with distribution companies. This provides the user with the ability to specify delivery options when ordering products and having a single payment interface to cover the integrated service. In this environment, it hardly matters where the company is if the service is cheap enough and the delivery time is acceptable.

There also needs to be an understanding of the differences between the competition on the web and the historical competition in more traditional channels. The two sets of competitors might be totally different, and the level and type of services that are offered might be different as well. The web is a unique shopping experience and needs to be treated as such. Even though much can be learned from previous business models, sometimes bringing existing metaphors into the web environment will not work. A user analysis can provide an evaluation of these aspects and their applicability to a web environment.

The objective should always be to do things better, which means exploiting the strengths of the new web environment and leapfrogging the competition by reusing or applying their good ideas and working on better solutions to their problem areas. To complete the job and to fully appreciate what a competitor's strengths and weaknesses are, a competitive analysis needs to also involve users from the target audience to understand how they perceive the competition. This is normally done as part of a user analysis exercise.

Funding and business commitment

Business commitment and funding obviously have a direct effect on the scope of the web development project. It also has a clear relationship to the goals and objectives of the site, as it will further clarify any prioritization to high-level objectives as a result of any funding or planning constraints. The whole project management area of the web development cycle will need to take into account the development costs, the quality of the work, and the time that the required solution will take. As in most cases there will be trade-offs and negotiations between those funding the project, those managing the project, and those responsible for delivering the solution. The skill is always to get the best solution within the constraints of time and money. The arguments usually start over what the best solution is and whether anything less justifies more expenditure or an extension to a delivery date.

This is where defining the business success factors and targets becomes so important, and where the user analysis can provide invaluable indicators early on within the development cycle about what will constitute a successful site as defined by the targeted audience. The system analysis exercise will also provide an invaluable insight into what will be manageable within the development timescales and what might be problematic, providing another early warning to where the development time might be eaten up during the web development life cycle.

Success factors and targets

Defining the business success factors and targets emphasizes where the business priorities lie, but more importantly puts requirements on what needs to be measured when the site becomes 'live'. Targets are normally defined as part of a business plan, which projects such things as expected revenue and costs over time. Tracking the actual figures against the planned ones gives the analyst an indication as to whether the plan is realistic or whether it should be revised. Understanding whether a business is meeting its business targets is a standard business requirement and it is possible to design a content management system that provides this kind of information in a timely and accurate way – it will be a far cheaper exercise if requirements are known in advance.

The easiest kinds of success factors and targets to measure are those that are easily quantifiable. For instance, a site may set a target to generate so many user subscriptions within a month. This kind of measurement is a straightforward indicator for anyone to understand how well a site is performing against predefined business targets. More difficult to measure are those targets that require a level of user evaluation, for example if a company wishes to measure whether the site reflects a strong brand image or whether users understand how to navigate the site. To understand how well a site is performing against these kinds of targets, a business will need to invest in an amount of user analysis and perform user validation exercises. In order to successfully measure such criteria, a human factors engineer really needs to be involved to carefully design and undertake usability tests – tests that will result in some overall ratings that can be relied upon to present a reasonable representation of the views and opinions of the targeted audience. How this is done is covered in Chapter 6 within the user validation section of user analysis.

Cross-marketing and collaborative filtering

There is one thing that a website can do very well that previous channels could not: it can dynamically change the environment as a result of behaviour.

This effectively means that any user interface can be designed to automatically change as a result of the user doing something, or as a result of a change in the state of the system. Where this can have obvious advantages to a business is when there is a requirement to promote certain products or services, either as a direct response to an action that a user has performed or as a result of some business priority to push certain products and services irrespective of who the users are or what they are doing. For example, a shop may find itself in the unfortunate position of having a surfeit of perishable goods that really need to be sold quickly. In a more traditional shopping environment, these goods would be physically moved to a very noticeable part of the store and would be surrounded by brightly coloured messages announcing all sorts of tempting reasons why customers should buy this product: 'Reduced', 'Sale', 'This week's special offer' etc.

This kind of push marketing is a direct result of a business priority to shift something as quickly as possible and has no relationship to any previous user behaviour. In contrast, a gentler approach is where a business does take into account what the user is doing and pushes other products as a result.

This can be a very powerful feature to exploit in certain types of web interfaces, but it can be effective only if a level of analysis takes place to understand which relationships should be supported, and what their effect will be on the users of the site. There are five main relationship types to consider:

- the relationship between content to content;
- the relationship between an individual user and content ;
- the relationship between user types and content;
- the relationship between content and a business priority;
- the relationship between content and time.

In order to automatically adapt interfaces to support these relationships, there will need to exist a classification scheme that is applied consistently to the underlying content. Such a scheme would need to have a system that classifies content and users so that the different types of relationships can be created.

An example of a content-to-content type relationship is often seen in sites that sell books or CDs. When one type of product is selected, the interface offers a selection of additional products that the user might be interested in. For instance, on a website that sells CDs, a content relationship may have been defined between two artistes such as David Bowie and Lou Reed. When a web page is displaying details of a David Bowie CD as a result of a user selection, a list may be automatically generated that provides links to other CDs by David Bowie, but also links to CDs by Lou Reed. The aim of this approach is to provide the user with value-added information at the appropriate time. However, from the business perspective it is actively encouraging the user to look at more products that they might be interested in buying. If the relationship is useful to the user, it is a win-win situation.

In the majority of cases a business will have historical data or even just business knowledge that defines what these common content relationships are. If these relationships are known about and deemed strong enough to be useful, a classification system can be designed to support them.

Marketing push can be strengthened further and become more focused if a level of personalization is added. If the site keeps a track of the buying history of individual users, not only can the common behavioural relationships be validated and updated by data generated by actual user behaviour, but also the interface can be adapted to be applicable to the individual user at any particular time.

An example of an individual user-to-content relationship that extends the example given above might be to add links to those artistes that the user has previously purchased from the site.

The relationship between a user type and content can also be very powerful if it is possible to collect the necessary data about a user to successfully categorize them. In the situations where a user provides information about themselves, either through previously purchasing a product or through a registration mechanism, it can be possible to categorize the user into a predefined user classification group. For instance, a registration scheme may ask for information about a user's age, gender, education level, salary, lifestyle, hobbies, interests and so on. This is not nosiness on the side of the business but a marketing ploy that will enable the business to more successfully target products to different user sets. Of course, users may not wish to supply the amount of information that a company would ideally like to have, which is why some companies offer huge incentives to encourage them to fill in lengthy forms about themselves. For instance, to get access to a free online newspaper, users may have to complete a huge question-naire covering all sorts of personal questions in order to get the service. Many users are prepared to do this rather than pay a usage fee.

Why is this information so important? The two main reasons are:

- to target internal products and services when they are released; and
- to support targeted advertising as part of an advertising business model.

When new products are released – which can be frequently – a blanket mar-keting approach is not nearly as effective as one that is targeted. To continue with the example of an online music CD store, it might be the case that in any one week more than 20 new CDs are added to the site catalogue. The problem the website will have is how to successfully advertise all these new products without overloading the homepage or primary interfaces. In this instance the user type-to-content relationship can be employed to target particular products to the most likely types of users who will buy them. For instance, a female user over the age of 50 is more likely to take notice of an advert for a new Barry Manilow CD, than one for Blur or Oasis. Therefore it is possible for a company to design a home-page that has a single advertising space and insert different adverts into this area depending on the type of user who has come to the site.

Collecting information about the types of users who are coming to a site, along with the number of page impressions a site achieves, can help define advertising rate cards. A good example of where this information is used to attract advertising revenue is within the South China Morning Post. This site collects user data, groups it into meaningful user categories, and provides advertising rates based on usage and site audience. A prospective customer can very easily see enough information to understand if the site and audience profiles match their requirements.

Temporal relationships allow a system to adapt as a result of date and time. Many products have a seasonal relationship, in that they are more likely to be bought at a particular time of year or even a particular time in the day – Valentine cards in February, fireworks in July (US) or November (UK), lawn mowers in the spring. Seasonal and temporal classification schemes can be designed and associ-ated with underlying content if it is deemed a worthwhile exercise. If it can be seen early on that the business will wish to promote certain products at certain times of the year and will not want to go as far as manually redesigning the homepage or primary interfaces every time a promotion occurs, it may be worth making the investment early on to define these content relationships.

There is so much opportunity to explore and exploit cross-marketing and col-laborative filtering techniques within a web interface that the usefulness and

SCMP.com requires users to register with a brief questionnaire, providing us with information on their education, age, gender and more. Like the newspaper, our sites are sought out by well-educated, intelligent and influential readers who are curious, discriminating, Internet-savvy and responsive to Web-based advertising.

Registered Users
Total* 359,076

Distribution by Education		Distribution by Country	
Post Graduate	42%	Hong Kong	49%
College & University	43%	China & Taiwan	6%
Secondary	14%	USA	18%
Primary	1%	Canada	5%
		Europe	6%
Distribution by Gender		Australia & New Zealand	5%
Male	71%	Others	11%
Female	25%		
Not specified	4%	Distribution by Occupation	
		Professional/ Management/Executive	46%
Distribution by Age			
Below 21	6%	Student	27%
22-30	19%	Office Worker	12%
31-40	31%	Skilled Worker	3%
41-50	24%	Not specified	12%
Above 51	20%		

* As of March 28, 2000

Figure 5.1 Audience categories within the advertising rate card information from the South China Morning Post *www.scmp.com*

acceptability of any such proposal would need to be validated as part of the user analysis work.

Business partnerships

Depending on the business model and type of site, a company may wish or need to set up business partnerships to achieve the goals and objectives of the site. Many web retail sites have such relationships with distribution companies which take on the responsibility for delivering the products that have been bought on the site. When such a relationship is created it will inevitably place requirements on the design of a site and there may have to be trade-offs within the interface to accommodate any business agreements that are in place.

The business analysis will need to clarify what these arrangements are and what the requirements will be to support any business partnership agreements. Ideally, the business should be aiming to protect the user from these relationships. Most users want an integrated service and to feel they are dealing with one company. When a website starts to lose a sense of place – i.e. the user does not feel they are still in the same site or, even worse, is not sure whether they are dealing with the same company – they can become disoriented or suspicious. This can lead to a loss of trust and potentially a loss of a sale. It is far better for a site to offer a complete service under one umbrella and the business to negotiate these relationships so that they are transparent to the user.

Marketing and communication

The business analysis should define what the marketing and communication plan is to promote and advertise the site. This will cover such things as banner advertising, registration with search engines and marketing through non-web channels. This exercise may create business requirements on the design and it may generate actions or work items during the web development life cycle. Either way, it is a vital part of any website business analysis and therefore part of the web development process.

Business requirements

The business analysis stage will generate requirements into the system. Below are some of the most common.

Support the site objectives and goals

Business requirements that are created to support the site objectives and goals will fall into two categories: those that apply to the design of the site and those that apply to the design of the content.

A requirement that defines the need to bring the company brand successfully online may require a graphic designer to use certain colours within a palette and an existing company banner or logo. In contrast, a requirement that defines that any new products added to the online catalogue need to be classified according to their relationship to other products that appear on the site requires that the person creating the content uses a correct classification scheme, and furthermore that a controlled vocabulary is in place that allows such a classification. Such a requirement may necessitate a set of business review criteria being defined so that new content destined for the site meets the business goals and objectives. This requirement may also generate other related requirements such as the need to support a review cycle of new content before it is published externally.

Support the business model

A business model that revolves around selling goods on the web is likely to have many business requirements to do with the integration into existing back-end systems, such as stock control, invoicing and distribution. How products and services are found on the site will place requirements on the information architecture, covered below, and how the customer is able to buy the products online and have them delivered will also place requirements to support a customer database and set up business relationships with delivery firms.

Any business plan that involves selling goods in multiple countries will place heavy demands on any system that is put in place. Translation is an expensive business and the complications involved in different tax laws and currency conversions may require a good accountant on the team. It is usually wise to understand that the requirement is there, and to try to put in place a system that is able to be extended to other languages, currencies and tax laws, but to get a single site in a single language up and running first and then to gradually extend the site one country or one language at a time.

The advertising business model will place requirements on the definition of page views to include advertising banners. If a revenue stream can be identified for keyword rental, this will automatically place a requirement to have clearly defined keywords that can be associated with a primary customer link. It will also necessitate a classification system being in place and a search function that is capable of returning the link at the top of the search results list. The ability to offer sponsorship on content may put a requirement on the site to support a content newsletter, and in addition to support the active collection of opt-in e-mail subscribers to send the e-mail to, in order to make it an attractive proposition to those sponsoring the content.

If it is expected that users will pay for content delivered on a site, this will place demands on the quality and timeliness of that content. However, if the model is free subscription supported by revenue from advertising, this will place demands on putting in place services that will actively attract users to provide their e-mail information, for instance, mail a news story to a friend, write a book review, bulletin boards and chat services.

All business models are likely to place requirements on the delivery of ongoing site measurements in order to compare how well the website is performing against any targets that have been set within the business plan.

Deliver ongoing site measurements

For measurements to be useful they need to be relevant, measurable and accurate. The sort of ongoing web measurements an e-business is likely to require are:

- revenue: how much revenue is being generated by the site, either through online orders, advertising or subscriptions;
- costs: what the overall expenditure is to run the site. This might include such things as banner advertising, off-line promotions, keyword rental and the costs of using third-party content;
- asset usage: which content is receiving the most and the least interest, which products or services are being selected the most, what types of information are being read the most;
- customer behaviour: information about any registered users or customers of the site, the information they tell you they are interested in through feedback or registration information and what their behaviour tells you they are interested in – what they buy, what pages they visit and where they leave the site.

Information architecture

The analysis of the benefits of push marketing on a site is likely to place requirements on any classification system that is designed. There is also the likelihood
that a classification system already exists and will need to be implemented to
integrate and be consistent with existing systems and channels. Even though a
business analysis may place requirements and predefined rules on an underlying
information architecture, this does not necessarily mean that this classification
mechanism will be surfaced (made visible) to the user of the website. The job of
defining the most appropriate vocabulary and the most usable navigation structure for a site should be determined as part of the user analysis exercise.

Site goals

Problems

A major problem with website development projects is that the goals of the site
are either not defined or are not clearly communicated to the website contributors. In some cases, the goals are defined at the onset of a project but are not
maintained to reflect changes in the business or as a result of a better understanding of the users' behaviour or requirements.

When a company website starts to expand with sub-sites that define their own
goals, there is a danger that the purpose of the new sub-site has no relationship to
the overall goals of the site. Worse still are sub-sites that work against the site goals
either through ignorance or because they ignore or just misunderstand the business and user priorities of the main site. Often they assume that because their role
within the organization is important, the details of what they do must also be of
importance to the users of the website. This is usually a wrong assumption.

Websites that have no clear purpose are confusing to the user. Users tend to
be very task oriented and they will have a mental model about the structure and
facilities of a site even before they reach the homepage. If they take the trouble
to go to an airline website, there is probably a good chance that they are there to
look at flight schedules, availability and prices. Any other options that are presented fight for the user's attention. Any option that promises to be useful and is
not will waste the user's time and test their patience. The performance of downloading pages on the internet can be very slow, so the primary user tasks should
stand out plainly in the interface and should not be competing with secondary
options that are fighting for the limelight.

The importance of defining site goals

The definition of a set of site goals should ideally outline the highest levels of
user tasks that must be supported within the website interface. For example, a
primary goal for a theatre website may be to provide the facility to purchase the-

atre tickets by providing information on forthcoming performances, dates and prices. The sub-goals or business rationale for doing this may be to reduce the number of telephone bookings that are made to the theatre box office and to increase the number of bookings to overseas tourists.

These kinds of goals are critical to defining the set of user tasks that need to be analyzed, i.e. what kind of information the user requires to reach a decision to buy a set of theatre tickets and, more importantly, what would encourage them to buy their tickets online instead of through the traditional channels. Chapter 6 provides an overview of how these kinds of questions can be answered.

Site goals are also critical in deciding what the ultimate priorities are within the user interface. It may not always follow that the ultimate usable site meets the goals and objectives of the business. The skill is to get the balance right and to provide a solution that both meets the business goals and provides a pleasant, goal-oriented experience for the user.

The importance of maintaining site and sub-site goals

When the goals of a site get lost or are no longer applicable, this is when problems are likely to occur. Company websites are constantly evolving and growing, and when a site expands rapidly and becomes inundated with all sorts of content, users start to become lost in different information hierarchies, often feeling that they cannot find the information they are looking for. A search facility may return several pages of links that look promising, but after six or seven failed attempts to the right page, a user will give up and assume that the information is not available or for some reason has been removed. It is a sad fact that in most cases the page containing the information that the user is trying to find does exist on the site but has become buried under a mass of content clutter.

In a disciplined web development process, all the site and sub-site goals would be clearly defined, and their relationship to each other clearly documented. In addition, all the user tasks would be clearly analyzed and would have a clear relationship back to these defined site goals. If a publishing process were adapted to the web environment, there would exist some role that reviewed proposed new content against these user tasks and goals. Only when it had been agreed that the content was in support of these tasks and goals would the new content be allowed to appear on the site. In the situation where a new user task needed to be added to the site, or where new business goals were defined, there would exist a process that allowed for priorities and relationships to change. Any proposed major changes such as a redefinition of the business goals or the introduction of a new user task would need to kick off a new analysis stage to make sure that any design that is created still supports the main goals and objectives of the site, and the critical user tasks that enable the user to achieve their goals.

The goals and business objectives of a site, along with the user tasks that support these goals, should be the primary definition of what a company website needs to be.

chapter 6

User analysis

The purpose of a user analysis

There are two very clear business reasons why a company should want to invest in a user-centered design approach to their website development project.

- The first is to reduce website development and maintenance costs.
- The second, to increase the success of the website by making the user's experience of the site so positive that they return to use it again and again.

In *Software Engineering: A Practitioner's Approach*, Pressman makes the claim that for every dollar spent to resolve a problem during product design, $10 would be spent on the same problem during development, and $100 or more if the problem had to be solved after the product's release. In Jacob Neilson's report on a recent Danish e-commerce study[4], the overwhelming reasons why customers shop at websites is ease of use and convenience. Therefore, it is a very risky strategy to jump straight into designing a site without any consideration or analysis of the types of people who will be trying to use it.

Usability engineering can be broken down into two main areas, design and evaluation. The design part, is everything a development team can do to proactively influence how the eventual system will work. Evaluation covers the methods that can be used to validate ideas, assumptions, prototypes and the eventual solution to make sure that users are able to use it. The purpose of a user analysis stage, in simple terms, is to find out:

- what users would like to be able to do at the site;
- how they would like to do it.

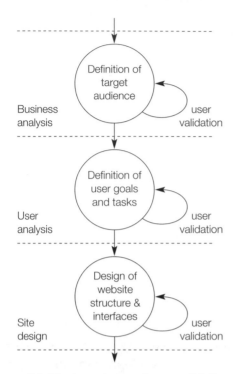

Figure 6.1 The importance of user validation during the development process

This information can then be used to guide how the site is designed and to provide enough background information to ensure that the interfaces created will be usable.

The business analysis phase produces the initial audience definition, which outlines the kind of people the site should be aiming at. The user analysis phase takes this definition and looks at the characteristics and behaviours of these users. By analyzing the user in detail, the usability expert can make recommendations to the designer about:

● the overall structure of the site;

● the structure and priority of different user tasks;

● the information that needs to be available for users to complete these tasks;

● how individual interfaces that support these tasks should work.

User validation is an exercise that needs to be done many times during the development process as it is always wise to keep checking with representative users when assertions and design decisions are being made (*see* Fig. 6.1). However, the job of designing the site will and should rest with the user interface designer. Users can validate ideas and test proposed solutions, but they cannot design interfaces. The job of website interface design should rest firmly with a user interface designer and be informed by a user analysis, thereby taking as much guesswork out of the design process as possible.

To design software that feels natural and intuitive, it is necessary to structure the interface around the way that users themselves think about the tasks supported by the system. To achieve this goal, the design needs to be supported by user profiles and task modelling. User profiles analyze the physical and cognitive abilities, constraints, and expectations of users. They also investigate the physical and social environment in which the system is to be deployed. Task modelling studies user goals, the associated task structure and task flow, and the conceptual objects that are of interest to the user.

What is a user analysis?

User analysis complements business analysis by concentrating on the people who are going to use the system. It takes the target audience information from the business analyst and attempts to define the characteristics of the user group that affect their behaviour and responses. This information can then be used to determine the acceptability of any proposed solution and test whether the goals and objectives of the site are valid and whether the information presented on the site will be acceptable. For instance, if a site goal is to sell online CDs, there are many factors that a user analysis should look at. Of primary interest would be whether the target audience would buy a CD from an online website in the first place and what would persuade them to buy a CD this way rather than from their local high street store.

An example of the kind of information that a user analysis will attempt to uncover is the internal and external factors that affect the decision-making process. External factors are those things that influence the user that lie outside the product domain, such as the influence that chart information or magazine reviews have on the decision to buy a music CD, or the influence that a fashion show may have on the decision to buy certain brands of clothes. Internal factors are within the product domain and include such things as product cost, available delivery options and payment methods.

How the user behaves, the way they understand how their world works and the influences that affect their decision making all should feed into the website design, so that the organization of information on a site and the layout of information within a page is not purely a graphic design exercise but a user interface and user interaction design based on the user being in a position to achieve their goals in an easy and efficient manner.

This is the essence of an easy-to-use interface – not one that is flashy and full of the latest technology, or one that has the most professional-looking graphical interfaces. Creating a usable site is about providing the easiest way for the user to achieve their goals while satisfying the business goals and objectives of the site. If it looks great, that is an added bonus.

What kind of information does a user analysis take into account?

Social and economic factors

There are some factors about the user's background which so influences their decision-making process that the business analyst and designer ignore them at their peril. Show-stoppers might include offering limited methods of payment that are unlikely to be available to the target audience, or ignoring the different attitudes to buying goods over the web across the social and economic groups with regards to the expectations of terms and conditions or the level of product information required before deciding to buy a product. The decision to buy is a complicated one, and there might be many reasons why the user starts to feel uneasy with a site or prefers one site to another.

Skill levels

The skill level of a user looks at previous experience both on the web and from other traditional channels. For instance, someone who is used to buying CDs from a high street store will already have a mental map about how CDs are classified, and how one would go about trying to find a CD and then buying it. Someone who has used the web extensively will have developed a mental model about how certain interface elements work, such as links, the back button, bookmarking and print. The usability of an interface becomes seriously threatened once the designer breaks away from the user's mental model on how things should work.

Environment

This covers the environment that the user has to work within when using the software and would include such things as the browser level, the screen size and network speed that they are using. If the target audience is likely to be accessing a site across a 28.8k modem, performance becomes a critical factor within the design. If access were through a kiosk, the interface would need to be designed completely differently to one that is intended to be used by a normal PC, keyboard and screen. A website that will be accessed through a kiosk situated in an open and public place may have to take into account such things as external noise levels, queues and the need to protect individual privacy by screening personal information from casual passers-by.

There has been much discussion recently on the introduction of new and different devices that can be used to view websites. From a technical viewpoint, much has been made about the ability to create a single design that can be shared by different networked tools, such as a PC, a telephone or a PDA. This may seem a laudable goal, but it is a dangerous starting position as far as a user analysis is concerned. When a business wishes to offer a service on markedly different devices, someone needs to define the situations where a user would use such a device and the kinds of tasks that they would expect to perform on them.

All devices have different capabilities and different constraints and users choose to work with one device over another for different reasons. They also have different expectations about how each device will operate and they will use the device to perform tasks in a different way. Therefore, there needs to be a great deal of analysis work undertaken to understand the different user goals for each device and the tasks that make sense in each environment. It is far safer to assume that the usability goals and tasks for each device will be fundamentally different and then be pleasantly surprised if they can technically come together at a later stage.

Vocabulary

The terminology that the user adopts, the understanding of what certain terms mean, and terms that the user identifies with to complete their goals and tasks are critical in designing a task-oriented interface. This becomes very important when designing a classification structure, a search capability, and a website navigation scheme.

The correct use of keywords can help make an interface quicker to scan and therefore easier to browse. When users can understand and find the terms that they are looking for they will be in a much better position to complete their tasks quickly. By contrast, when a user sees professional buzzwords, obscure terms or words that they do not understand, they have to start concentrating on getting to grips with the interface rather than concentrating on achieving the task in hand. This kind of interface has serious usability problems and has the effect of hiding information from the user. Presenting obscure category names and ambiguous navigation labels can lead the user into a hypertext hell by forcing them to make link after link to try to find the information they are looking for. Some sites are so successful at hiding useful information that they leave their users feeling it must be their fault that they cannot find the information they are looking for. When users see professional-looking graphics on the homepage, they assume that the site has been well designed. This, however, can be a completely misleading assumption.

Doing a good job of defining the user vocabulary will mean that the user will understand the purpose of the site and how to go about getting on with the job that they have come to the site to complete. It will also help in designing the main hierarchical navigation structure, ensuring that the labels that are used are the same terms that the user identifies with different information categories. Building up this vocabulary goes some way to understanding the mental model that the user already has of the problem domain.

The need to perform a user analysis for all targeted user groups

The great thing about the web is the immense opportunity it can offer a business to reach out to a potentially massive user population, which are all potential new customers to the business. For the user interface designer this can present insurmountable difficulties in trying to design an interface that will try to keep everyone happy. This is why the business targeting information is so vital within the whole process and where a level of user analysis can help narrow down the problem to concentrate on a finite number of user types.

The worst target audience definition to receive from a business requirement is that 'it should appeal to everyone'. This is an impossible task, for both the designer and the person responsible for setting up the user validation exercises. At the user analysis stage of the development cycle, it should be a primary goal to produce workable audience definitions, even if this means offering a helping hand to the business analyst to break down their target audience requirements into more distinct and meaningful user type definitions.

What are the interesting aspects to a user profile?

The investment that a company makes at the user analysis stage can be variable and greatly depends on how important a company perceives that information to be in determining the success of a site and how important the success of the site is to the success of the business. Some types of information may range from just being of intellectual interest, others may be critical factors. For instance, consider the scenario where an e-business site is regularly losing sales to a competitor, even though the product quality and the pricing models are the same. At some point a business may feel the need to question whether the website is at fault and try to understand if there are usability problems that are causing their customers to turn to a competitor site. To be in a position to answer this question, a user analysis will need to be undertaken before any user validation can take place. Usability tests can be designed only when it is known:

- what the user profiles are, so that the right people can be recruited for the tests;
- what the main user goals and tasks are so that task scenarios can be designed.

Building up a profile

A human factors engineer will take each target audience definition from the business requirements and create one or more user profiles. There are many types of analysis that can be combined to create a complete user profile. In Ben Schneiderman's excellent book *Designing the User Interface*, there is a whole chapter dedicated to human factors of Interactive software which talks in detail of the many factors that may need to be considered.

Pragmatically, there is usually not enough time to undergo a complete analysis of each individual user set. The skill is in doing enough to really understand the usability success factors for a site, and to be able to recognize and recruit sample users who match the profile in order to understand further the way they think and to gain knowledge from their experiences and behaviour. During any user validation stage, these profiles are again used to recruit test subjects to validate any significant assumptions that have been made and any designs or prototypes that have been created.

Building cultural models

Many businesses see the internet as a commercial channel capable of reaching into all sorts of countries to many different people of all nationalities. It can be a valid business requirement to ask for a site to be designed so that it can be translated into different languages and to provide services and products that can be purchased in different countries. This kind of requirement can open up a real can of worms for a designer as not only does there need to be a consideration of the legal and financial aspects of trading in each country, but there also needs to be a clear understanding of the cultural aspects of the different people who will be accessing the site.

Technology allows templates to be created that are translatable, but the headache is not really the process of translating existing content – although that in itself can be quite an expensive job – it is the process of checking that design assumptions that have been formed and tested in one culture are applicable in another. This includes testing to see whether the same tasks are valid, whether the content is meaningful or relevant, or whether the site is making assumptions about lifestyles, attitudes or social conventions that may not be applicable or may even be offensive to certain cultures.

Building cultural models is a specialized form of user profiling and is covered well in Chapter 3, Developing a Cultural Model, in *International User Interfaces* by Nancy L. Hoft.

Usability objectives

Part of the problem with many website designs is that priority is given to the aesthetic visual quality of the interface or page rather than whether the site as a whole can be used or is indeed useful. A graphic designer might grudgingly accept that a homepage has to have a number of useful links on it, but may be less inclined to accept that the easiest and quickest way that a user perceives a link is with standard link text, and that a straightforward piece of text might be better for certain types of users, especially those who might be in a hurry, than a wonderfully crafted image map that takes time to load.

Users are rarely in the game of comparing website designs or indeed basing their decisions to buy products or use services on the quality of graphics within a web page. There is definitely an argument for producing great visual designs, but this should never be at the expense of usability. In fact, the use of colours and fonts and the way that a page is laid out is ultimately a usability issue. If a user finds a product description hard to read and cannot find the price within the page, they are going to be less inclined to move to the next step of buying it.

Another common problem with websites is the mapping between the user's expectation of what a site should do and what it actually does, or the user's expectation of where information should be and where that information actually is. This is normally as a result of site designs being approved by the management who have funded the project, rather than being validated by the people who will be expected to use it. Often you can observe some strange levels of prioritization of information on a homepage or obscure links within the primary navigation structure that do not seem to have any relevance to the types of tasks that the user would expect the site to support. These anomalies are likely to relate directly to how an organization views the priority of information on a site rather than being prioritized according to the relevance of the information to the set of primary user tasks that the site should be supporting.

An example of this is when a company homepage is seemingly there to sell computer software, or hire out rental cars, or book hotel accommodation, but actually uses the first navigational link to take the user off to look at information about the company or its company results. One might guess that this information is much more important to the organization than it ever will be to any users who have come to the site with the intention of buying software, hiring a car or booking a hotel room.

In an ideal website development environment, trained human factors engineers and cognitive psychologists define what the usability objectives should be based on previous research papers, usability studies, and a level of user analysis applicable to the current problem domain. Too many website development projects leapfrog this phase and rush headlong into the design, relying on a level of usability testing at the end of the project to verify that the website does what it ought to do. Too often this is the time when problems are found. It is not only very expensive at this point to correct usability problems, it might also be impossible if a design has been based around totally wrong assumptions.

The most important part in creating usability objectives is that they are not a mirror of the design opinions of the person creating them. If possible, all the objectives should be backed up by sound human computer interaction principles that have been proven through usability studies. This will usually get around many of the objections of other people within the team or management who have an opposing view of how things should be done. It is far easier to document a usability objective and to argue the case if there are statistics to back it up.

The need to define clear usability objectives

Before any serious investment is made in the visual or system design of a site, enough of the user analysis work needs to be done so that very clear usability objectives can be set. There are essentially two areas that need to be well understood.

Understanding the service
This covers issues relating to the service that the website is trying to provide, for instance, the business of selling CDs or the process of publishing an online newspaper. Analyzing the service will usually involve looking at existing channels through which this service is offered. For instance, the high street CD store, mail order catalogues or traditional print media.

Understanding the environment
This covers issues to do with the web environment, such as consistency, accessibility, performance and web usability. There have been many studies undertaken to understand usability issues to do with the web, and there are fundamental core

tasks that web users perform on nearly all sites. Chapter 7 covers critical design features and specifically looks at these core tasks and provides some usability objectives that can be used as design guidelines for most websites.

Understanding the traditional environments and the new web environment is fundamental. The two need to be analyzed independently and in combination. For the CD shop example, it is imperative to understand the mental map of someone who is used to buying CDs in a conventional high street store, as this will be the most common model that the majority of users will come programmed with to the site. However, it is just as important to understand their experience of the web and how they would expect a web interface to work. It will then be possible to understand what the influences are that direct their thoughts on how they would like to buy CDs on the web in future. Someone who has no web experience but plenty of traditional shopping experience is likely to see the web interface working in exactly the same way as the high street store. Someone who has plenty of web experience and has experienced competitive sites is likely to make suggestions that form a model similar to those sites and recommend a site design that works in the same way. Every now and then, users provide brilliant new ideas and insights into better ways of doing things, usually as a result of some obscure but good experience that they have had in a completely different environment.

Simply copying how a traditional environment works and designing interfaces that mimic a traditional shopping environment is not usually a good move, especially if in doing so it breaks usability guidelines for the web.

There has been much debate over the usefulness and the usability of 3D shopping environments and strong metaphor designs within a web interface. Such designs are based on the idea that you can simulate a user walking around the aisles of a CD shop in order to find the CD they are looking for. In most cases, it is advisable not to go in this direction due to the fact that the technology and network performance is not yet up to it and secondly there are normally problems in maintaining the metaphor for all the kinds of services and functions that a site will need to offer to the user.

It is certainly true that users look for things that they understand and recognize. Offering interfaces which are obvious and familiar can in most cases get over any initial learning difficulties. The problem is that computers are not natural interfaces. A mouse, keyboard and rectangular windows on a screen are very unnatural environments – they become easier to use only with experience. The process of learning about this environment invariably means learning about the common 2D representations that are commonly used. This usually means that a consistent interface that uses strong visual affordances – i.e. a push button that looks as if you can push it, or a hypertext link that looks as if it can be selected – is often clearer and easier to use than one which attempts to simulate a 3D world through non-standard visual controls. A good explanation of affordances and why visibility is one of the most important principles of design is covered in *The Design of Everyday Things* by Donald A. Norman.

The aim for any website design should be to offer something better than before. To achieve this it will be necessary to understand the expectations, experiences and capabilities of the new web environment. The idea of copying the existing way of trying to find a CD within a store is unlikely to translate very well to a web interface and will probably have serious usability drawbacks; far better to offer a search capability that is the common and familiar web technique used for this task. Of course, offering such a boring shortcut immediately breaks the 3D store metaphor, but this might not deter some. Metaphors are successful only if they can work in a consistent way inside and outside the user interface. If they do not work the same way, this causes a different set of problems and can negate any initial advantages gained from offering a seemingly familiar and recognizable user experience. It is far safer to avoid going down this path altogether.

Therefore the goal when defining usability objectives is to guide the design towards an easy-to-use solution. By documenting what the user is trying to do (user goals) and how they are trying to do it (user tasks), usability goals can be defined that will emphasize how the goals can be most easily achieved by supporting task designs. Usability priorities will also need to be defined so that a visual designer will be in no doubt as to what the most important aspects are to get right and where usability should definitely not be compromised.

An example of usability objectives

Table 6.1 below shows a short extract from the usability objectives created for the redesign of the news section of the Ease of Use website.

Table 6.1

User goals	User tasks	Usability objectives
1 To look at how IBM designs easy-to-use web interfaces	Evaluation:	
	Evaluating a site would involve a user assessing the:	
1.1 To look at the writing style and vocabulary	a) site content	1.1.1 Interface should present good writing and familiar vocabulary
1.2 To look at the amount, size and quality of graphics used	b) site presentation	1.2.1 High-quality graphics
	c) graphic usage	
1.3 To look at navigation techniques	d) any navigation techniques	1.3.1 Familiar navigation concepts
1.4 To measure the performance	e) download performance	1.4.1 Performance targets need to be set

Table 6.1 Continued

User goals	User tasks	Usability objectives
2 To find out if the news section has anything of interest	Browsing:	
2.1 To scan article headings and lead paragraphs to see if anything is of interest	Defined as searching without a specific end, e.g. scanning a daily newspaper, paging through a magazine or flipping channels on a TV set	2.1.1 Interface should make good use of keywords, headings and lead paragraphs
2.2 To find interesting phrases or keywords on ease of use	Browsing is the act of identifying articles of interest by:	2.1.2 Interface needs to have a content structure and navigation model that the user understands
	a) noticing familiar terms b) being attracted to an interesting heading c) perceiving that a subject is important or relevant	2.2.1 There should be sufficient headings that contain relevant keywords on ease of use to make the user feel comfortable that they are in the right place for news on ease-of-use issues
	User tasks are: a) scanning an interface b) clicking to move on c) clicking on something interesting	

Involving users

It will be impossible to determine what users want to do and how they want to do it without actually asking them. A user analysis can be completed only if those performing the analysis can gain access to people who are representative of the types of users who are being targeted by the website. Once this access has been arranged, there are a number of useful techniques that the human factors engineer can employ to extract the relevant information.

Accessing expert knowledge

Any user that fits into a required audience profile is, by definition, an 'expert'. Either they have used existing systems and can provide information about what works and what doesn't, or they have no experience of an existing system but are very clear on what the process should be in an 'ideal' world.

Very importantly, they have a vocabulary and use familiar terms to describe the objects that exist within the problem space which can provide classification, categorizations and synonym information that will eventually help with a navigation design, the design and support for a site search facility, and the specification of any controlled vocabulary that is defined for classifying content.

In the online music website example, the problem space would refer to a music store and the objects that exist within that store would include CDs, tapes and maybe videos. When the analyst involves users to understand what their model of a music store is, the kinds of questions to ask would be:

- Why do you go to a music store?
- Why do you go to one music store over another?
- Have you ever needed to ask an assistant for help and if so what did you need to find out?
- How would you go about finding a CD if you knew the name of the artiste?
- Have you had any problems trying to find what you were looking for? If so, what were they?
- What would be a better way of finding CDs?

These are very open questions and are ideally suited to a focus group environment, where a small group of, say, six to eight people sit and answer questions in an informal and seemingly unstructured way. In fact, the analyst conducting the session has defined the structure beforehand by preparing a list of open questions that will hopefully stimulate conversation and encourage discussion around topics within the problem space domain. The session will almost always be recorded so that it can be analyzed and written up later.

Running focus groups can be expensive and time consuming, however, and can involve only a relatively small number of users, compared with sending out a questionnaire, for example. However, the power of such an exercise is in the way that it can uncover all sorts of information that the business or design teams may not previously have thought about. To design a questionnaire, the designer has to know almost all the answers beforehand. The skill of the person running the focus group is to make the users provide all the answers and to get involved only to steer the conversation back on track or on to a new subject.

Information from these sessions can sometimes produce surprising results. For instance, the answer to the question above that asks 'why do you go to a music store?' will inevitably get the obvious answer of 'to buy a CD, video, tape etc.' but may also get other answers such as 'to buy a present for my brother', 'to look at the charts' or even 'to meet my friends'. The business analyst may not have even considered a social aspect to an online music store. However, if during the user analysis it was found that providing such a feature would attract a significant number of users from the target audience, it may be decided that this feature should be included within the site.

Accessing expert knowledge also involves defining the clearest and most obvious terminology that should be used within the interface. These terms will almost certainly be used during a focus group discussion and it provides an opportunity to clarify and test the acceptability of one term over another, for example, the use of CD over compact disc or the use of tape over cassette. If the majority of users refer to compact discs as CDs, this needs to be the primary keyword that is used within the interface. However, the term compact disc may still be an important keyword to support as a synonym for CD within any classification design. Users may still type in this keyword from any search interface, including the major search engines such as Yahoo! and Alta Vista.

Creating affinity diagrams

Affinity diagrams are a method of grouping together problems and requirements into high-level groups. This process can also be described as pattern matching between the information gained from many different users. Grouping similar tasks, problems and workarounds can help gain an understanding of the functional priorities of the target audience, and should heavily influence how the site prioritizes its features within the website interface. Consider as an example the design of an online florist. If the majority of users from the target audience say that they would always want to provide a personal message with flowers that are being delivered, and only one person says they also want to provide their own graphics on the card, then a judgement can be made on the relative priorities of these two requirements.

An example of a common grouping is search. In the online music store, users may want to find CDs, tapes, or videos. They may have experienced problems trying to find different products and they may also provide recommendations on how things could be done better. These search experiences can all be grouped together to see if any commonality can be found, and also to understand if any differences exist. It may emerge that users have a completely different model for finding videos than they do for finding CDs or tapes. It could be that because the classification schemes are different and the fact that videos have a rating, the majority of users employ a completely different search strategy for finding videos than they do for finding music products. If this is the case, it may mean that two search interfaces will need to be designed in order to cope with these differences, rather than trying to create a single interface that attempts to bundle all the available options into one confusing interface.

Defining user scenarios

By interviewing users and gaining knowledge of their experiences, requirements, problems, desires and workarounds, it is possible to define some common user scenarios that capture how the eventual system will or should work. These scenarios build up a picture of the user's world and describe the reasons why they attempt the task and outline the way in which they try to achieve it. It is very useful to capture concrete examples of the circumstances under which a website will be used, when it is used, and what the desired results should be.

For instance, a user scenario for using an online florist might be:

'I got into work early on Monday morning as I had quite a few things to do before my 9am meeting. One of the first things I always do is pick up my telephone messages. Imagine my delight to receive a message from the husband of someone in our team who had left work to have a baby. He was phoning through to let us know that she had given birth to a baby boy on Saturday morning. After sending a note around the department, I realized that I had better send some flowers from all of us. The florist I would normally use doesn't open until 9am, so I thought I would try to find a florist online. I went to www.yahoo.co.uk and entered 'florist' in the entry field. Up came a whole list of links. I selected the link of a well-known floral delivery company that I recognized, but the homepage took an age to download, so I gave up and tried another link that I assumed was local as it had our city name next to it. This is the site that I used...'

It can be seen from the above example that these user scenarios can sometimes be longwinded. But users' decision-making processes are usually quite complex and may be influenced by many external factors. It is extremely useful to uncover these external influences and decision-making processes as they will add weight to the usability objectives that are being defined. From this scenario, the analyst can conclude that the reasons why this user chose an online florist over the traditional high street shop were:

- the user was in a hurry;
- the online delivery service was available at the time when the user wanted to place the order.

If this experience is backed up by further evidence from users that performance is a critical success factor, designing an online florist website that has a slow-loading image map for a homepage will have obvious usability problems.

During the interview that helps create these user scenarios, it is always beneficial to try to find out what makes a user select one link over another. Do they always pick the one at the top of the list, or are there other variables that influence the selection? Search engines are a major way that users find out about sites. In an overcrowded marketplace, it is useful to understand what will bring a user to a site and what makes a site get noticed.

The more concrete examples that are collected, the easier it becomes to identify the common ways that users find sites, access sites, navigate through sites, and buy goods and services. All these user scenarios can be used to later test initial interface prototypes. Can the user achieve the tasks described in the scenario with the proposed design? In the above scenario, the user would have had no opportunity to select the site if it had not been registered with Yahoo!

Collaborative user interface prototyping

Collaborative user interface prototyping involves working with users to define the easiest interface that enables them to perform their tasks. This can be achieved by following the user scenarios that have been defined and paper prototyping screen designs that the user can work with to follow their scenarios. These iterative design sessions should encourage the user to move things around on the prototype, add descriptions, and even add their own fields using sticky pieces of paper. This can be an incredibly helpful exercise and provide all sorts of useful information, from defining the level of help that is needed within the interface to agreeing the correct terminology and naming conventions that should be used.

The prototype should always encourage the user to feel happy about making changes. This is best achieved by using very basic tools such as paper, pens and sticky notes. The more professional the prototype, the more likely it is that the user will feel inhibited about making changes or voicing any criticisms about the design. This exercise is a very cheap way of understanding the critical parts of a website interface in the user's opinion, and invaluable in providing an insight into the user's model of how the system should work. However, this exercise should be used only as input into a design process. A user is not an interface designer and can provide only a certain level of useful information.

Card sorting

This is a technique that can be used to discover how users classify information, and can help create a navigation design. The idea is that a group of users from the target audience are presented with a range of different content items and asked to group them together and provide textual labels for the group. In some circumstances the test subjects will offer different groupings based on different criteria, which can be very useful information to capture as it identifies different search strategies that users may employ in various situations.

The skill of the person designing the test is to present a good sample of the types of content items that users will expect to find on the site and to present the content items without any existing categorizations being obvious. For example, a design for a card sort test for food within an online supermarket may present photographic images of the goods that are life-sized, due to the fact that food-shopping customers use a number of search and browsing techniques to find products that include both mental maps and visual cues.

This exercise identifies content relationships and the terms that users associate with a content group. This is very valuable information and can directly feed into the design of the site navigation and the labels that should be used within the design. The variance of terms that users come up with during the exercise can also feed into any classification system that is being created to support synonyms and common spelling mistakes. In addition, it can identify the content items that users find hard to classify. This is usually a very good indication that these are the same content items that will be difficult for users to find on a site if a single hierarchical navigation system is used that force-fits every content item into one place within the hierarchy. These are the content items that may need to be made available in more than one place and be supported through strong contextual relationships where appropriate.

Task analysis and creating task-flow diagrams

The goal of all of these methods is to gain enough information to clearly understand how the site should be designed so that it will be easy to use. In practical terms this information will be used to create a definition of the user goals that the site will need to support and the definition of the tasks that users need to perform in order to achieve these goals. Task analysis is the name given to this process and whole books have been written on it. Perhaps the simplest technique is Hierarchical Task Analysis (HTA), which is a very useful way of understanding the different priorities of user tasks and the relationship of tasks to each other.

The idea is that the analyst first uncovers the goal that the user comes to a site expecting to achieve, then systematically breaks down the goal into the tasks that the user must perform in order to achieve the goal.

An example goal for an online florist may be to order some flowers to be sent to a relative in hospital. The high-level tasks that may be identified during the user analysis to achieve this goal may be:

1. Find a florist that can deliver in the required area.
2. Select a bouquet of flowers to send.
3. Provide the details of where the flowers need to be sent to and when they should be delivered.
4. Add a personal message that can be sent with the flowers.
5. Pay for the service.

Once the high-level tasks have been identified, they can be broken down into sub-tasks. For instance, the first task of finding a florist may be broken down to:

1.1 Open a search engine such as Alta Vista.

1.2 Type in 'florist' and city name.

1.3 Select a link from the search list.

1.4 Find out if the florist will deliver to the hospital within the city.

Alternatively, a second strategy for someone who already has bookmarked a florist may be:

1.1 Open the bookmark file and select a florist.

1.2 Find out if the florist will deliver to the hospital within the city.

It can be safely assumed that the first task for the majority of users coming to the site to order some flowers is to find out whether the service can deliver to a certain location. This provides an indication as to how visible this query facility needs to be on the homepage. The logical order of tasks that users perform in order to achieve their goal is also a strong indication of the logical order of the primary navigation scheme that should be employed by the site.

An additional piece of information within a task definition is adding conditional routes. For instance in sub-task 1.4 Find out if the florist will deliver to the hospital within the city, if the answer is 'Yes' then the user will continue with the site, if it is 'No', the user task will be to leave the site and go elsewhere. If the failure of a sub-task causes the failure of the main task that also happens to be supporting a primary user goal – in this case the goal of ordering flowers to buy – it needs to be flagged and given a high priority. High-priority tasks need to be supported by critical design features and given a high visual precedence within the interface. They are also the ones that will need to be first in the queue to be usability tested.

Task-flow diagrams provide a way of capturing user requirements when they relate to a sequence of events or are time specific. For instance, it may be found that the majority of users will proceed with entering credit card or personal details about themselves only if certain pieces of information or confirmations have been made available beforehand. Using the example of the online florist, it may be discovered during the analysis phase that in the majority of cases users would not place an order for flowers if they had not first received a confirmation that the flowers could be delivered at their requested location at their requested time.

These kinds of task-oriented paths are very important to capture. They are especially important when they are related to important user tasks such as buying a product. Too many websites ask for personal and financial information before the user feels comfortable or ready to enter into a transaction or financial agreement. Consequently many users will back out of such a task until they feel comfortable that the site is trustworthy.

Defining the critical design features for a website

Once a task analysis has been completed, it will start to become clear that certain elements will need to be present within the interface that will allow the user to successfully and easily complete the task. For example, taking the task 'select a bouquet of flowers to send', it may be discovered during the user analysis phase that when users make a decision on which bouquet to order they base it on price, colour scheme, and the type of flowers within the bouquet. However, the most important criteria in most cases is price and its relationship to whether the bouquet looks good. From this kind of information, critical design features can start to be defined that will make it possible for the user to complete the task in an easy and efficient way. Critical design features for this task may include:

- the list of available bouquets should be sorted by price;
- the price of each bouquet needs to be clearly displayed next to each bouquet;
- a picture needs to be made available for each bouquet that can be ordered;
- more detail for each bouquet should be available that displays a clearer picture of the arrangement, plus the information of the types of flowers included;
- a feature should be available that allows the user to search for bouquets within a certain price range and that match a certain colour scheme;
- an action needs to be available that allows users to select the bouquet they are interested in ordering and this action should take them to where they can provide delivery details for the order.

Critical design features are so named because if they are not supported, some users will not be able to complete the task in hand. If a user is unable to select a bouquet to order, or finds the interface too difficult to use, the online florist will have lost a sale. Critical design features define:

- what information and actions need to be available to enable the user to complete the task;
- what information and actions will be needed to allow the user to move to the next stage of the task flow.

Task definitions and critical design features are quite abstract in as much as they do not define how the information is presented within the interface or how that information is broken up into different web pages. Tasks define what the user needs to be able to do and task flows define the logical order that the user does them in. Critical design features will provide a level of usability requirements for the design of the tasks and task flow by specifying the priority and availability of information and actions that will need to be in place in order for the user to complete the task easily. How the information and actions are visually represented within a web interface will be up to the visual designer of the site.

Summary

If the aim of a web development project is to create an easy-to-use website, some level of a user analysis will need to be carried out. Many development groups leapfrog this stage and jump straight into the fun job of designing website interfaces. Either the functions and task-flow design are copied from a successful site in the same domain or are generated from the ideas and opinions of the people within the team. Sometimes the site is designed to suit the opinions of the individual funding the project. Short term, this approach may keep the team on the right side of the boss, but it will almost always backfire when recriminations start to abound as the site is found to have usability problems.

A user analysis builds up a picture of the types of people who will be coming to a site, and defines their skill and knowledge levels and what they expect to be able to do at the site and how they expect to do it. It is a simple concept and there are many methods that can be used to access this information. Focus groups give users the freedom to talk about their experiences and how they would like to see things work; collaborative prototyping gives users the opportunity to design their ideal interfaces. Interviews can be used to create user scenarios that provide concrete examples that describe how users approach a particular problem and how they go about completing their tasks.

Many companies use expense as a reason not to bring in users at an early stage. A company that uses this excuse should try to measure the cost of having an unusable website and having to redesign and redevelop it as a result. If a company wishes its site to be usable, it will need to invest in some level of user analysis. Otherwise it will be more luck than judgement if the site ends up being easy to use – and no company should be relying on luck to stay in business.

7 Critical design features for common web tasks

Critical design features are those requirements that a website must support to allow a user to complete tasks in an enjoyable and efficient way.

Each website will have specialized task definitions that directly relate to the kind of service that is being offered. For instance, in the example of the online florist, one such task was the ability for a user to select the bouquet of flowers that they wished to send, and some of the critical design features that supported this task were:

- the ability to see the price clearly;
- being able to read a description of the types of flowers in the bouquet;
- the ability to see a picture of the bouquet and individual flowers on demand.

By defining critical design features, the analyst is making clear to the designer of the site that in order for the user to successfully complete the task, certain features need to be present within the interface. In the above example, the analyst had discovered that the majority of users would not select a bouquet of flowers without first being sure what the price was. This piece of information becomes critical in moving the user forward towards completing the task and on to the next task of providing the delivery details.

Therefore, critical design features specify what needs to be in place for the user to complete a given task. On the web there are sets of common tasks that web users perform every time they go to a website. They browse, they read, they navigate and they also seem to spend a long time waiting for things to happen. Changing a website design to incorporate the critical design features of these core tasks can significantly improve the usability of a website.

Waiting

Performance is one of the main usability problems on the web[6] and is normally associated with the user task of waiting for a page to download and display. Typically, during this time the user will be:

- making a judgement on the site;
- watching for navigation links to appear in order to click through to secondary levels;
- scanning the page contents as they appear;
- hitting the stop button and going elsewhere.

Considering the value proposition to the user vs. page loading time

Long delays cause stress, annoyance, frustration and impatience.[7] Users need to feel in control, and especially like to feel in control of the time they are spending on any particular task. This is why it is especially important to make a homepage quick to download. A user always comes to a site with a purpose. At the point when the homepage is loading, the user has not requested anything from the site, and in most cases the user has not built up enough of a demand to make them want to wait. The analogy is the amount of time and effort it takes for a person to physically enter a store. Many shoppers are put off going to particular shops if the car parking is difficult or they have to spend too long getting there. Not many store designers would make it a slow process to actually get into the building, and yet website designers seem to give little thought to how long it takes a user to get into a site.

The homepage has a very small value proposition to the user and therefore needs to be quick to load in order to present its value and generate the demand. In contrast, if a user requests a chart of the highest selling shares on the New York Stock Exchange, there will be expectation that this process will take time, especially if the site is polite enough to warn beforehand that this is likely to be the case.

Performance should be seen as a form of politeness. A site that performs well and is responsive to the user shows a level of consideration and recognizes that the user's time is important. There is no problem in offering services that take time within a web environment, as long as the user feels in control and perceives that the performance delay is an understandable consequence of the kind of task that they have requested.

Increasing perceived performance

Ways to increase perceived performance can significantly reduce the stress of waiting for tasks to complete. Graphical progress indicators not only let the user know that something is happening, they also provide some visual distraction that reduces the boredom of looking at the same things on the screen.[8] It is those interfaces that sit there and do nothing until a task is completed that cause the most problems. After a certain amount of time during which the screen does not change, users will assume that the site is broken or that their selection did not work.[9] Users will repeatedly click on the same thing until they or the server gives up.

Displaying value content first, fluff content last

A level of information priority should define every screen. Even if this definition is not categorically stated anywhere, the human factors engineer, the information architect or the designer should know which are the critical pieces of information or the critical actions that are needed by the user to perform the task in hand. When a user analysis has been performed, the important information and actions are defined within the critical design features created for each user task. These are the interface elements that should be loaded first. Any other kinds of decoration or backup information should wait their turn. This approach provides the expert user with the ability to complete their tasks in as short a time as possible.

In the example of the online florist, the user analysis had determined that the first logical task that the majority of users do is to find out whether the florist can deliver to the required location. This immediately creates a requirement on the homepage to display this feature as the first option that the user can interact with. The interface elements that should always display first on a homepage are the visual features that will create the site brand. It is always important for a site to quickly display enough of the brand for the user to feel comfortable that they have come to the right place. However, strict performance targets should govern the time it takes to display the site brand. It does not take the user long to form a first impression of the type of site they have come to.

In nearly all cases, graphics are not critical to completing a task, they simply backup associative text, and provide visual adornment that can enhance the interface and make it look professional. Because they slow down a page load, they need to be optimized for performance, used sparingly, and loaded at the right time.[10]

It is also not possible to make general rules or even site-wide rules about the best sequence for loading interface elements. The priority of elements for each page is likely to be different. For instance, the navigation links on a homepage are likely to be the most important elements to load first. By contrast, when someone links to a news article, the most important elements are likely to be the news article title and the lead paragraph. In most cases, a user will read 30–40 words of a news story before deciding whether to continue. Therefore, the interface has the time it takes to read those first 30 words before displaying the navigational elements that will allow the user to go elsewhere. In this case loading the navigation elements first will be distracting, because the user is not yet in a position to decide whether they are ready to go some place else.

Offering links as text before loading any graphics

Offering links as text first is a technique that solves the problem of including graphical links on a page. Because graphics are slower to load than HTML text, displaying a textual string first will give the user something to read and assimilate while the page-loading process is under way. Depending on how slow the page is to load, it also provides the experienced user with a quick way of jumping to another part of the site, or clicking through, without having to wait for the navigation graphics or the rest of the page to load.[10]

The purpose of navigational links is to provide the user with an overview of the services available on a site and provide the mechanism for the user to move to the part of the site which is of interest. The user task involves first identifying that something is of value, then performing a selection to move to the required part of the site. The textual hypertext link provides a quick mechanism for this. It comes back to being considerate towards the user. Offering a textual shortcut, ahead of the preferred graphical method, is a way of saying that the user's time is more important than the aesthetic design goals of the site.

Performance rules of thumb

Many usability studies were carried out in the 1980s looking at the effect that performance delays have on the stress levels of users, and how users react to various delays imposed on them. The first user interface guideline that came from this work was to try to react visually to a user request in less than one second. This means that if a user selects a link on a web page, something changes visually within that time frame. This does not mean that the task has to complete, only that a level of feedback is provided to let the user know that the action has been taken notice of.

The second guideline is to allow the user to carry on with the requested task within 8.5 seconds.[9] For instance, if the user has made a link to a news story, they should be in a position to start reading the title and lead paragraph within that time. This does not mean that the whole page has to be downloaded and all the graphics displaying, although it would be a good performance target to set, but the primary interface elements should be displayed that allow the user to move on.

This approach is really defined as a user task-oriented design, where the concentration is always firmly on allowing the user to complete their goals and consequently their tasks in as efficient and effective a way as possible.

Browsing

Browsing can be defined as the user task of searching without a specific end, for example, scanning a daily newspaper, paging through a magazine, or flipping channels on a television set. Typically, users scan an interface by:

- noticing familiar terms;
- being attracted to interesting headings;
- perceiving that a subject is relevant or important.

Using clear and consistent keywords, headings, lead paragraphs and bulleted lists

Web users scan web pages to see if the page has anything of interest or has the content they are looking for or expecting.[11] Busy pages with interface elements that compete for attention are as unscannable as large blocks of dense text unbroken by headings and paragraphs. White space plays a very important part in making a web page scannable and it will be the designer's ability to draw attention to those interface objects which are of primary importance that will ultimately make it easier for users to browse or scan the contents of a page.

The use of terminology is also important. When a user comes to a site in order to perform a task, there will be a vocabulary that the user associates with that task before they even get to the site. During the user analysis stage, this vocabulary needs to be captured and used within the interface. When there are differences in vocabulary use among the targeted audience of the site, good synonym support needs to be provided. The most common keywords need to be used consistently within the interface so that the majority of users will immediately feel comfortable that the site supports the service they are expecting and that they feel comfortable to move forward with their tasks.

Organizing blocks of text by having one idea per paragraph

This is related to web writing style, and recognizes that a user may have a strategy to scan a large amount of text on screen by reading a part of the first and last sentence of each paragraph, then making a judgement as to whether that block of text will contain the information they are looking for. Following the pattern of having one idea per paragraph and not embedding important points or new ideas in the same block of text allows users to effectively scan large pieces of text relatively quickly.

In order to succeed in finding the required information, the user relies on a level of page browsing. It is because of this that the designer needs to lay out information in a way that enables the user to use the strategy of scanning as a way of honing in on the information they are looking for.[12]

Having a clear navigation model

One of the most common complaints that users have with websites is that they cannot find what they are looking for.[6] The user analysis should be able to identify the types of items users are most commonly expecting to find and identify the strategies for achieving that task. Obviously there are search design considerations, which are considered later, but in most cases users do not rely on the search mechanism until they have at least had a go at scanning pages and using the primary navigation mechanism. There is an assumption that the site will provide an easy route to the most important parts of the site.

Designing the primary hierarchical navigation system relies on an easy-to-understand labelling system being used, and the site content being categorized according to these labels. A common guideline is to favour breadth over depth when designing hierarchies for websites, but it is also important to recognize and define the contextual relationships between different content instances and support these wherever possible. This topic is covered in more detail in Chapter 9.

Using graphics with care and avoiding animated graphics

This guideline further emphasizes the point that the use of graphics within a web page is usually there to support the primary information conveyed in textual form. Understanding the priority of the information should inform the design, to make sure that graphics do not distract the user's attention away from the main messages.[13]

Animation is the number one way to grab attention, which may be fine if the main message or the main way to move forward with a task is the thing that is animated. However, recent studies have suggested that users have become quite adept at ignoring and blanking out these irritating features, to such an extent that if any important information is placed in close proximity to an animated graphic, there is a good chance that it will not be seen.[14] This skill in blanking out animated graphics is probably the reserve of the experienced web user who associates a moving image with an advert and therefore studiously ignores it.

Other strategies that users employ for ignoring animations are reading web pages with one hand over the moving image or alternatively, if the animation has been conveniently placed at the top of the page, scrolling the page down far enough so that the animation disappears off the top of the screen.

Hunting

Hunting or searching a web page or site is defined as the action of looking for a specific kind of information about a specific topic and conducting a search, such as finding a book in a library. Users hunt for information by:

- scanning a page for specific keywords, product names or other tags;
- using a keyword search function;
- using a search interface to build a query.

Mapping the user's model of content to the interface

During the user analysis stage, the analyst should not only define the priority of the information that needs to be within the interface but also what that information needs to be for the user to move forward with the task. This is especially applicable to commerce websites, where there is a hope and expectation that the user will complete an online order to purchase goods. Many users will not complete such a task if the bottom line price of the goods is not made clear. Each user will have a mental model before they visit the website of how a task is performed, and what the stages of that task are likely to be. Usability problems emerge when a site breaks the user's task model, displays labels that are unfamiliar, or does not supply the level of information required in the expected place. This is what is meant by mapping the user's model to the interface.[15]

When a user hunts a page for information, they have already formed an opinion that at this point within their task model, certain information should be available. An example might be when a user has refined their product selection choice to the page that allows them to buy the product. At this point the user needs to receive the level of information that will make them comfortable enough to take the next step. It could be delivery options, it could be terms and conditions, it could be a policy statement on privacy. Whatever it is, if the information is unavailable – and user analysis has identified the need for this information to successfully complete the task – it is unlikely that the user will go ahead and purchase the product. The company has just lost a sale, and will probably not be sure of the reasons.

Avoiding specialized terminology and the need for prior knowledge

Those within a business are likely to use different terminology to those outside the business. If a website is being designed and reviewed inside a company, the use of specialized vocabulary might not be noticed or indeed might not be considered a problem.

The question of which vocabulary and terminology to use should always come back to who the target audience is and what wording they associate with a particular domain or task. Of course, it is never that easy to define what the single vocabulary should be, especially if a site is aiming at different levels of expertise and different types of users.

The user analysis stage and the user validation stages for validating designs and prototypes should be able to identify any wording that causes real problems or confusion, but it might not be able to supply the best alternatives.

A couple of techniques can be used to try to find these out. Probably the quickest way, and sometimes the most effective, is to find an expert user to help define the vocabulary that should be used. This type of person is someone who interfaces with the target audience on a regular basis, usually in the role of answering their questions and queries. Examples of these types of people are help desk staff, box office booking agents, hotel receptionists or customer service personnel. Because these people regularly deal with enquiries from outside the business, they are likely to have a very good mapping model between the vocabulary that the target audience uses and the equivalent terms used within the business.

Another technique, which can be very effective once a system is in place, is to analyze all the keyword search queries that the user enters on to a site. This will provide a clear indication of the terms and keywords within the user's vocabulary, with the understanding of course that not all users will resort to using a keyword search function. This technique will only be able to give an indication that one term may be better and more commonly used than another. A level of user validation will be needed before any decision is made to reword the whole navigation system.

Providing a search facility with synonym support

When trying to understand the common vocabulary that is used by the target audience, it is likely that there will be more than one term used to mean the same thing. When this is the case, the information architect has to make a decision about which label to use within the interface – hopefully it will be the one that is the most easily identified. However, the rejected alternatives should not be discarded. Instead, they should be incorporated as synonyms to the chosen label, ideally within a central site classification system.

An analysis of user queries can identify the need for new synonyms, but it can also show a pattern of common spelling mistakes. In some cases it is just as important to support a commonly misspelt word as it is to support commonly used synonyms. An example of where this is very useful is when users are searching for people's names. A site that supports authors, artistes or musicians should not refuse to help if the user cannot spell the name correctly. A good search facility should support a number of strategies for returning results to the user depending on the type of site and the characteristics of the content within the site.

Information that is gleaned from a query analysis can be used to enhance a classification system that supports the mapping between synonyms and keywords for a site search facility. This should at least improve the likelihood that the user will find what they are looking for if the user wording is recognized and mapped to a corresponding term within the defined vocabulary.

Using simple categorizations and good coverage of subject domain

A content analysis should determine the applicability and structure of existing content and the requirements for new content in order to be confident that the information available to the user will be both correct and complete.

However, a content analysis is not a one-time job – there should be continual assessment of the content within a site, resulting from usage measurements and direct user feedback. Usage data can ascertain the pages within the site that are getting the most visits; conversely, it can identify those areas that users never go to. This of course may not automatically mean that the subject is of no interest or relevance to the user. It could mean that the navigation labels are confusing or these items are buried too deep within the hierarchy structure. In some cases it might highlight pages that have become detached and are not actually accessible through hypertext linking. Whatever the reason, the measurement should invoke an investigation into the cause so that the necessary action can be taken. If the content is no longer needed, it should be removed or archived. Too many sites allow their sites to grow into enormous spider's webs of information clutter, because no one is responsible for making sure that the site content is current and relevant to users.

An analysis of user queries can determine the subjects that users are looking for, and the quality and number of results they receive within a search results list. More importantly, it can highlight those subjects that users are expecting to find that are not supported on the site. This will probably give more indication of the user requirements than supporting a user feedback mechanism. Although user feedback forms can, in some cases, provide a certain level of useful information, they cannot be relied upon solely to provide an indication that all is well. Users do not come to a site to fill out forms and will not see much benefit in letting you know that something is wrong with your site.

Providing advanced search and summary views that convey site scope and content classifications

It is widely accepted that for anyone to use a reference book successfully, the book has to support a table of contents and an index. These techniques provide two services: they quickly give the reader an indication of the scope of the information within the book and they provide the necessary information to go directly to the place where a piece of information can be found.

Although this is such a common and simple technique used for years as a way of searching for information, it is rarely adopted within websites. Many web interfaces rely on the keyword search as being a better way of achieving the same result. However, the keyword search does not offer the same service to the user. There is no doubt that if the user knows what they are looking for and knows how to word the search query so that the results will create the right matches, then a keyword search can be a fast path to finding the required content.

However, the difficulty users have with a keyword search is the process of defining the search parameters that gets them the results they are after.[16] In most cases, the user is presented with a small blank entry field that provides no clues as to what the user should enter. The size of the field is quite important, as the user perceives that the length of an input field is an indication of how many characters they should be entering. The smaller the field, the more the interface is saying to the user 'this query better be concise'. Consequently many users have problems defining search queries from scratch due to vocabulary, scope and terms which may be ambiguous, and this is exacerbated by search engines not providing enough support for synonyms, spelling mistakes and disambiguation (where there exists multiple meanings for the same word).

Many sites try to get around this problem by offering an advanced search interface that provides fields for the user to supply values against defined types. For instance, an advanced search for a CD may have a field for an artiste, a music label, a release date and a music category. These field definitions provide the user with a data model for the content type they are searching for, but on their own may still not be particularly helpful. Not many users will be able to remember the exact name of the recording label and may not know the exact spelling of the artiste's name. With this lack of clarity, the user will not feel particularly confident that they will find what they are looking for, unless there are lists showing the whole range of possible values.

If a site has enough content to require a navigation scheme, it has enough content for a classification scheme, and this will provide the best mechanism to allow users to find content on a site. The mechanisms and techniques for doing this are described in more detail within the content analysis chapter. The main points to understand are that it is imperative to capture the required searching strategies of the targeted users. It will then be possible to provide the necessary level of indexing information with the content that allows summary views, such as an index, to be created. Views that summarize the content of a site can provide the user with a familiar and comfortable way to search for information. They can also quickly convey the scope of information contained within the site if the design uses prompted indexing techniques that clearly convey the options available.

Reading

Reading can be defined as the action of identifying words and sentences as presented through an interface and understanding the content by using existing skill, knowledge and experience. There are three aspects to consider when designing a readable interface for the web:

- physical aspects, which deal with selection and navigation;
- perceptual aspects, which deal with the identification of words through an interface;
- cognitive aspects, which cover the understanding of the information.

Typically, when a user decides to read some text on a web page, they will do the following:

- navigate to the place within the page where they wish to start reading;
- scroll the page to continue reading when text is outside the current screen boundary;
- perceive the words and try to understand their meaning;
- form an opinion on whether the text is useful, interesting, well written and correct.

Keeping vertical scrolling to a minimum and avoiding horizontal scrolling wherever possible

There have been some studies that suggest that many users do not bother to scroll down a web page because they will make a judgement on how useful that page is by scanning and then reading the first few lines or labels at the top of the page.[14]

This has implications on how designers structure information and also how that structure is laid out within a page. Newspaper journalists are experts at grabbing the reader's attention, first with eye-catching and interesting headlines, then using a lead paragraph that provides a quick overview of the interesting parts of the column or article. In most cases, this style of writing needs to be adopted by websites. The writer must provide meaningful headings and very quickly give a summary of the information that is contained within the page. The details can then be displayed for those users who want to read on. With this model, all the important information will be in the top half of the screen and the user who isn't keen on scrolling will not miss anything that is tucked away at the bottom.

Another layout choice to avoid is having a vertical scroll bar that is detached from the window boundary. Some sites choose to format their pages by defining a column size and attaching the scroll bar to the side of the column instead of to the side of the window. This may make logical sense as the scrolling refers directly to the text within the column. Unfortunately, 99 per cent of sites have their vertical scroll bars in the same place, and this will be the first place that users will look when wishing to perform a vertical scroll. By being inconsistent, you will divert the user's concentration from the important task of reading the column to the unimportant task of scrolling the page. Physical tasks such as scrolling should be transparent to the user. Breaking the concentration to perform something as mundane as scrolling will increase the user's perception that the site is not very easy to use.

Horizontal scroll bars are a usability headache. Users hate them because they interfere too regularly with the primary task the user is engaged in, whether that is reading or entering text within an editable area. Best to avoid them.

Optimizing the design to make on-screen reading easier

Reading on a screen is not a comfortable experience for many users due to a number of factors, including screen resolution and the display characteristics of terminals. As such, users will rarely read large amounts of text on a screen, but will scan to home in on the parts of the page that are worth reading and read only those parts, or they may print out the page to read off-line.[17]

This is why it is important to try to make the important pieces of text within the website easy to read, and to look at reducing the need for the user to read heavy and long-winded blocks of text unnecessarily.

There are certain guidelines to help make text easier to read on a screen, including:

- using negative contrast (e.g. black text on white background);[18]
- using mixed case and a well-designed screen font;[18]
- having a good balance of text and white space;[18]
- formatting the text to have a comfortable line length of 10–12 words per line or 40–60 characters;[18]
- making the text left aligned;[18]
- using a sans serif typeface;[18]
- having non-justified text;[18]
- never having an animated graphic anywhere near the text that you wish the user to read.[14]

Concentrating on the writing style

It cannot be stressed enough that content needs to be considered in relation to the web experience, which really hinges on designing the best structure and using a writing style that will work in this environment. If people will not read long documents online, there is no point having them there; far better to create a new style of document that provides a summary of the information and then pointers to where all the relevant details can be found. If content creators and site designers understand that web users like linking, don't mind scanning and reading a few lines of text but don't want to work very hard at getting at the information, this might change the way a site structures and segments information and how a site organizes and presents these different levels of information within an interface.

Different writing styles exist for different audiences and it is important to understand what those styles are and which styles should be used when. A site may support many different styles of writing depending on the type of content and whom they expect will read it. A technical support document should be written in the style that is applicable for technical experts to understand, using terminology that is consistent with the technical area, being factual and complete. By contrast, a feature article marketing a product targeted at business managers must concentrate on highlighting key features and it may include opinions and reviews from industry-related press. It does not necessarily have to be entirely factual or complete, but only contain the information that will reflect favourably on the product, written in an upbeat and positive way.

Navigating through a site

Site navigation is the action of perceiving a structure or a contextual relationship through a series of links and selecting a link to move to another part of the site. Users navigate a site by:

- perceiving a site structure;
- perceiving a contextual relationship that is of interest;
- perceiving that a site supports a required task or provides the required information;
- perceiving that a link exists;
- understanding the nature of the link;
- making a selection.

Designing the site structure to map to the user's core tasks

How to capture the user model for a site is described in the Involving users section in Chapter 6. It basically should identify the user goals and tasks and outline the critical design features that need to be provided in order for the user to achieve these tasks. Most importantly it assigns priorities to tasks and defines the logical task sequence that users will follow in order to achieve their goal.

The primary navigation scheme needs to mirror the most common user model of the target audience, and provide a clear and simple route to the tasks that the user has come to the site to perform. It should not be a reflection of the organization or a mirror of the commonly performed tasks of the web development team. It should also not be polluted by add-on categories that content providers have invented because they are too idle to find the correct home for their content. Ideally, all site content should be funnelled through an information architect who understands the classification and categorizations employed by the site.

Using cross-referencing for related information internally and externally

One of the things that users enjoy the most about the web is the ability to link from information source to information source with the expectation that the information that they receive along the way will not only answer their original query but will provide additional information, ideas and avenues of investigation that they had not thought of. The best browsing experiences are those where the user learns along the way or finds answers to questions which they would have asked if they had managed to think of them in the first place.[21]

This browsing experience is best supported by the careful use of rich contextual and subjective relationships between content items. One example is the kind of value-added information you get at online bookstores when you reach a book that you are interested in and the site gives you a list of links to related books. How this list is generated is unimportant as long as it provides a useful service to the user. Experts within the domain may create it manually or it may be generated by dynamic queries against tables holding customer buying patterns. Either way, it returns the online shopper to the environment where people working within a store were interested and understood the product range, could help the shopper get the best product or service available, could offer alternatives, and could intelligently help the shopper find what they were looking for.

Exact classification schemes such as alphabetical lists are useful when users have a reasonable idea about what they want; however contextual schemes allow the user to browse a site according to some kind of expert knowledge, and if done well are obviously a superior mechanism.

Avoiding deep hierarchies and dead-end streets

The general consensus seems to be that a hierarchical navigation system for a website is better for a user if it is broad rather than deep. Users become disoriented within sites that have too many levels and would rather have more options visible at any one time than having to keep clicking to the areas they are interested in.

Dead-end streets are where the leaf pages at the bottom of a hierarchy offer the user no other browsing path except back to the page they have just come from. This is where secondary navigation schemes should be employed, such as contextual links (for example, related information) or in some website models a concept of sequence, such as the next article to read.[22]

Using default link properties

In the first instance a user needs to be aware that a link exists. This seems an obvious statement, but there are many sites that use all sorts of visual representations for depicting a link that provide few clues that selection will generate a link action. A persistent or patient user may click on graphics to see if they do anything, or may even sweep the mouse over a page to see if the mouse pointer changes to indicate a link. However, any user who is in a hurry or not inclined to investigate an interface will more than likely assume that a link does not exist and move on. There are very few reasons for deliberately hiding links within a web page or making the user work hard to find them. Games thrive on such techniques; websites fail by them.

In the second instance a link should support the notion of history.[23] Standard HTML links show the user that the link has been made previously, thus providing valuable feedback for the user. This kind of feedback is invaluable if the user has become lost within a hierarchy, or if they are trying to work their way through a site systematically for whatever reason. Many graphical representations for links do not support this visual feedback, and they are far less useful because of it.

Visual affordance is the term used to describe an interface element that clearly signifies what it can do for the user. The raised 3D representation of a standard push button indicates that it can be selected; the entry field with a flashing cursor indicates that the field can accept character input; and for most web users, a blue piece of text that is underlined indicates a link. The user can of course change some interface settings through the browser they are using, although this is usually the behaviour of an expert user. A website designer who uses non-standard links has just taken that control away, and introduced an inconsistency into the interface. In itself, such a design decision will not automatically make an interface unusable. There are a number of common visual metaphors that users will assume they can select to make things happen, such as tabs on a notebook, or entries within a hierarchy tree view. However, every time an inconsistency is used within a interface, the cognitive load on the user is increased, and when a user starts to feel that they are working too hard or having to think too much to complete a task, they may give up and go elsewhere.

Providing information about a link

The majority of web users are task oriented and care about the amount of time they spend trying to complete a task. Making a link to another page can be expensive in terms of time and distraction. Therefore there should be enough information about the link so that users can make an informed decision as to whether the link is worth taking.[24]

One-word labels can be useful to draw attention to a subject, but on their own they may not convey enough meaning for the user to be sure that the link will take them to the right place. A useful and common mechanism is to provide some contextual text in close proximity to the main label as back-up. This additional text can be static and always visible or can pop up as a result of a roll-over action by the mouse. Pop-up windows can be useful for providing additional backup information that, if included within the main window, would make it cluttered and confusing to read. However, this technique should never be used to display critical information – users should never have to experiment with an interface to get the understanding they require to move forward with a task.

It may be useful to think of a web page that is used to navigate to other parts of the site as a hierarchy structure in its own right. Users can quickly scan labels and headings to see if any of them match the goal they are trying to accomplish. When a label seems to match the desired goal, the user will require further information to ascertain whether the match is correct. With a page that clearly backs up headings and labels, this can be achieved quickly by scanning the associative text. When additional text is not provided, the user is forced to select the link and wait for a page to load to get the same information.

The first scheme has a much better chance of being more useful than the second but of course will always depend on the clarity of the backup text and whether the link page provides the level of service expected by the user. This will ultimately come back to understanding and designing to the user's model, rather than to the model defined by the content or how the designer thinks the navigation system should work.

Regularly running a dead-link checker to reduce the risk of broken links

One of the biggest annoyances that web users experience is broken links.[6] Not only has a site stopped the user in its tracks, many sites provide no other help than displaying a useless message and requiring the user to return to the page from which the link was taken. Sites that attempt to be more helpful try to provide a list of links that may be useful or applicable, but they have still broken the promise between the site and the user, and users will not have the same level of confidence that the site will deliver the information they require.

Tools exist to check the existence of dead links, and outside of any controlled content management system they are a necessity for tidying up sloppy maintenance. A site that has dead links will be seen as unprofessional. A company should not want to generate this perception about itself, especially if it wants to do business with users. Therefore any site that includes external links should be checking at least every week that these links are still working.[5]

Finding sites and printing web pages

One of the main problems that any website will have is to get noticed within the crowd and to attract users to the site. Surveys have proven that users find their way to sites in a number of ways.[3] The top three are:

- search engines
- links from other sites
- bookmark or favourites list.

Finding sites through a search engine

One of the most common ways that users find new sites is through a search engine. Therefore, a site that means to do business on the web should definitely be registered with the most popular engines, which typically include Yahoo!, Alta Vista, Lycos and Hotbot. To be most effective, an amount of work needs to be done to define the necessary level of meta-data information for each significant page within the site. The page title needs to succinctly describe the purpose of the page or section and the meta-tags need to contain descriptive labels and classifications that provide the scope of information. These meta-tags should be derived from any underlying classification and synonym support that has been defined.

In addition, if the marketing budget allows, it may be worth taking out banner ads, paying for keyword rental, or negotiating an affiliate program deal that provides a financial incentive for the search engine to direct as many users as possible to the site.

Finding sites by linking from other sites

Users like hypertext links[12] especially when they perceive that the new path presented to them will provide additional or related information on the subject that they are viewing. A site that offers these kinds of outbound links can also improve its credibility in the user's eyes and will be perceived as being more useful than sites that attempt to keep the users locked into the content on their site.

If a site has information that can usefully be backed up by the services of another, it makes sense for that site to link to it. This kind of relationship should be a win–win situation, whereby the second site gets users to its site, and the first site increases its value, credibility and usefulness in the eyes of the user. The first site will indirectly be given the credit if the link is useful and valuable. Conversely, if the link turns out to be a complete waste of time, the first site will also get the blame. Therefore, it is very important that the promise implied by an outbound link is justified, that the link is appropriate, useful and clearly sign-posted as to what its purpose and relationship is to the content within the current page.

Persuading other sites to link to you may be an uphill struggle, which is why affiliate programs have started to become an attractive proposition. These programs provide a mechanism whereby a site can offer a kind of commission to other sites that include their URL and send users their way. For instance, a site that sells CDs might set up an affiliate program for magazines that provide music reviews. Every time a user reads a review of a CD, a link is displayed that will take the user directly to the page that allows them to buy the CD from the online store. The CD store keeps a track of users who have come into the site via the music magazine, and if a sale is made as a result of the link, pays a commission of the sale to the music magazine.

This can be a beneficial relationship to both sides, as long as the site that signs up for the affiliate program actually does contain the kind of content that will be enhanced by the affiliate relationship, and the site that is being linked to can be trusted to live up to the recommendation promised by the link. Adding outbound links for the sake of it will clutter up the interface, confuse the user, degrade the user's trust, and all in all reflect negatively on the site as a whole.

Supporting bookmarking

Any company that wishes to make money from the web as a result of users coming to its site should have a primary goal of being bookmarked. Of course, there is a difference between getting users to the site for the first time and then looking at strategies for encouraging them to return. A company will have to rely on search engines, links from other sites, and traditional marketing mechanisms for the first-time visit. However, after that, a company should consider and provide for all the strategies that can be employed to encourage the user to come back.

Bookmarking is the best way to encourage users to return. This means that a site should concentrate on making all the primary and useful entry points on to a site bookmarkable and making sure that the page title for these points will be meaningful when placed in the bookmark file. This objective may influence the way that a site is set up, especially if there is a strong desire to use frames. Frames can disable bookmarking, which may be a good thing in some circumstances, for instance in cases where information is transitory or the page represents a stage within a task flow where the task cannot be started in the middle but needs to be started from a particular point. However, disabling bookmarking is definitely not a good thing if a user detects a useful point within a site and values it enough to want to return.

Framed sites that only allow bookmarking of their homepage, even though the action of bookmarking is enabled anywhere within the site through the browser, cause great confusion and irritation. Users will assume that the bookmark entry will represent the view they are currently looking at. When the bookmark returns them to a completely different view, and usually the entry page of the whole site, they have to somehow remember how to navigate back to where they were previously. Such a site cannot be judged usable if it is happy to make life difficult for the user, and this kind of scenario does just that.

Identifying and using URLs

A company should aim to support simple-to-remember URLs that closely match the company name. Some users who wish to go to a company site will have a go at forming the URL themselves by guessing the format to be *www.companyname. com* or *www.companyname.co.country*. For companies which jumped quickly to register their company name in this popular format, getting their customers to find their brand on the web has been a relatively easy task. Putting the company name in the forefront of a customer's mind is then just business as usual as far as marketing and advertising goes.

Less well-known brands, and companies that have had to settle with not quite so obvious associations, have to rely more on external marketing of their URL, building up the association between the web address and the company name through marketing collateral, and forming alliances and relationships on the web that will direct users to their site.

Supporting printing tasks

The browser offers a print action that results in the web page that is being viewed being printed in its entirety. A framed site can mess this up, which is another reason to carefully consider the consequences of using frames within a site. However, printing the whole contents of the current page may not be the task that best supports the user's needs. From the user analysis it should be clear where printing is a task that the user feels is important and which parts of the content the user wishes to see printed.

As we have said, users do not like reading a large amount of text on a screen, and in many cases would prefer to print off the contents to read off-line. If a site needs to make available long pieces of textual information to users, it should provide either a mechanism to download a document containing the information in a file format that can be easily printed, or offer printable versions of the page.

However, many sites do not bother offering such services on their content, they sit back and feel happy that a print function is available through the browser. But a simple generic web page print function does not have enough information to make decisions on which parts of a web page are important to the user. It will try to print everything on the page, including advertising banners, navigational elements, and controls such as push buttons and entry fields. In most cases, if a user wishes to print a page, it is because they wish to read the content of the page; the definition of which content they wish to read can be known only by the site itself as a result of user and content analysis. Therefore it is up to the site to decide the level of support needed for printing, what the user expectation is of the task, and to provide the level of support that is necessary.

Summary

There have been a number of web surveys such as the GVU WWW User Surveys (*www.gvu.gatech.edu/user_surveys/*) and usability tests and studies (*www.useit.com* – Jacob Neilson) that have found common usability problems and made recommendations to web designers on how they can improve the usability of websites. This chapter summarizes this research and organizes the recommendations into suggested critical design features for the core web tasks that users do every time they visit a web page. In summary, the main points are:

- increase user satisfaction of site performance[8] by providing:
    - visual response to user-initiated action < 1 second
    - enough of the page load for the user to continue working < 8.5 seconds
    - increased perceived performance, e.g. offer text links first, then graphics
    - warnings beforehand of possible long delays, i.e. keep the user in control;

- increase the speed of on-screen[18] reading by using:
    - black characters on a white background (or strong negative contrast)
    - mixed vs. single case and left aligned
    - type size (10–12pt with a well-designed screen font)
    - line length (80 characters or 10–12 words per line)
    - white spaced with margins
    - using a sans serif typeface
    - having non-justified text
    - short to medium-length paragraphs with first sentence indented;

- increase browsability[24] by using:
    - eye-catching conclusion within the first 30–40 words, followed by the detail
    - highlighted keywords
    - meaningful subheadings and bulleted lists
    - one idea per paragraph;

- increase readability by making the writing style:
    - short, to the point, and half the word count of conventional writing
    - factual, correct and objective, rather than using hype and promotional spin
    - professional, credible, using high-quality graphics, good writing backed up by outbound hypertext links;

- increase the usability[25] of navigating and linking by:
    - designing the site structure to map to the user's core tasks
    - regularly running a dead-link checker to reduce the risk of broken links
    - using default link properties as defined by the browser/user
    - providing information about a link, what it is, where it goes, will there be a performance hit?
    - avoiding deep hierarchies and dead-end streets
    - using cross-referencing for related information internally and externally
    - keeping pages short and not relying on the use of the scroll bar for any important information;

- increase the user's ability to find and return to your site/page by:
    - registering the site with all the major search engines
    - defining the keywords that will return the page from within a search engine
    - marketing the URL, online and through traditional channels
    - actively seeking opportunities for other companies to include a link to your site
    - supporting bookmarking
    - having a page title (and window title) that is meaningful when placed in a bookmark file
    - having a URL that can be easily remembered, typed and guessed by a user.

Content design considerations

There are a number of design issues that should be considered before a content analysis is undertaken. These issues will affect the process that looks at the existing content or proposed content and defines any new format, schemes, approaches and processes that will be used in the future. When taking this step it is important to appreciate when certain design techniques are useful and applicable so that an informed decision can be made at a later stage. For instance, there is no point in investing many months of effort in a complex classification system if it is not applicable to the site goals or will never be needed by the users coming to the site.

This section looks at the main design considerations when evaluating the definition and structuring of website content, and explains when it can be useful to invest time in various techniques.

Classification

Supporting search

Many users have problems trying to find the information they are looking for on a site.[6] There are a number of reasons why this may be the case. Firstly, the terminology that is presented may not match their vocabulary, secondly, the structure of the site may be confusing or incomplete, thirdly, the navigation system may be broken and littered with link errors.

A further impediment may be the search facility that is offered by the site. A common problem is when a search query results in too many hits that seem to have no relevance to the keywords that are entered; even worse for the user is the query that returns no matches without any clues or useful information on alternatives that may be applicable. This kind of negative interface is treating the user as if they are being deliberately stupid for entering keywords not supported by the site. In fact, it is the site that is being the awkward party by not offering a reasonable level of user assistance, whether that is within the search interface itself or as a result of the failed query.

Users need to be able to specify queries that they consider to be precise enough to return only those documents that match their model, and also to be presented with suggestions for other subjects that may be applicable.

A major problem with the whole area of search is that users are not good at defining the queries that will get them the results they are looking for. When presented with a simple search entry field, the user has no clue as to the scope of the site, or the vocabulary that is used, or the sorts of category names that can be added to a query so that the information can be filtered effectively. It would be very difficult to solve this problem with a generalized search engine that attempts to search the whole contents of the web; however, within an individual website, the content could be defined in such a way that a single information architecture is applied and made visible in some way to the user. If this were the case, it would then be possible to provide a far easier-to-use directed search interface that helps the user define a query based on the content available on the site.

For a search function to work well and be easy to use, the search interface has to be easy to understand and offer assistance with the kind of information that is available on the site and assistance to the user to build up a search query. Secondly, the content on the site needs to be classified consistently and correctly so that when the user generates a search query and runs it against the site content, the results of the search will also be correct and complete. Within any organization that publishes content on a regular basis to a website, this will be almost impossible to guarantee unless there is a centralized classification system and processes and controls in place. To ensure that content is being classified correctly, a system will need to be provided that:

- allows content providers the ability to classify the information they are creating;
- provides a way for content classifications to be reviewed before the content is published (*see* Fig. 8.1).

A good example of a directed search interface can be found at the Hermitage Museum, where the advanced search mechanism is treated as a task flow that allows the user to build up a query by only selecting terms that are within a controlled vocabulary (*see* Fig. 8.2). The interface also supports the notion of contextual indexes, so that a user can narrow the field of search first and then, within certain fields, choose a value from an alphabetical list that displays the whole range of values for that attribute.

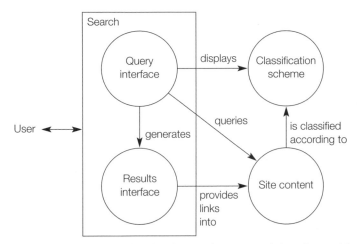

Figure 8.1 Classification scheme that binds together a search interface with the way that site content is classified

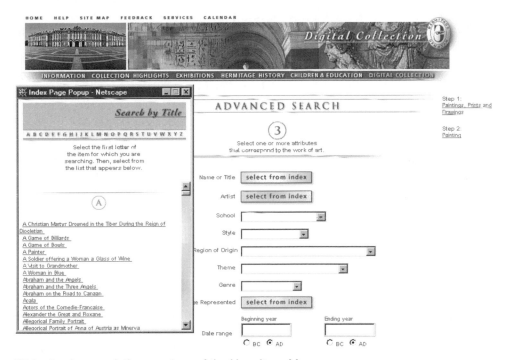

Figure 8.2 IBM e-business solution courtesy of the Hermitage Museum
www.hermitagemuseum.org/ html_En/index.html

Supporting different strategies for search and allowing the user to refine a query in a helpful way is essential when dealing with large information sources. It is also achievable only if a controlled classification vocabulary is in place and the content on the site is classified according to this scheme.

As well as the need to support search, there are a number of reasons why it can be worth defining a single information architecture for a website.

Providing a consistent terminology

The act of sitting down, defining and structuring a single classification system that will be applied to a whole site requires a certain amount of discipline, hard work and patience. A classification that attempts to be the single source for keywords for all the different types of content on a site is likely to go through many review cycles until agreement is reached. It will also need to evolve over time to capture the new areas of content that the website wishes to support. However, once a system is set up that allows content providers the ability to work with a content classification system, it can provide a very powerful way of standardizing the terminology used within a site.

The aim is to create a set of keywords that will be used consistently throughout the web interface and will be easily recognized by the intended audience. The idea is to avoid the common mistake of using professional jargon or buzzwords which may well be easily understood within an organization but have little meaning to the types of the users who will be visiting the site.

When a keyword vocabulary has been defined it needs to be tested and verified with users. This can be done within a collaborative UI (user interface) prototyping exercise, focus group or in a questionnaire. Once the keywords have been agreed, they need to be applied appropriately throughout the web interface, and used consistently to classify the site content (*see* Fig. 8.3).

Having 'user understandable' terminology within an interface makes the job of browsing, scanning and reading the content much faster. When users do not understand the terminology, or have to perform a mapping between an unfamiliar term and the definition they are used to, this stops them or slows them down. The badly designed interface will have forced them to switch concentration from the job they were in the middle of doing to the job of understanding what the site terminology means.

Using a term consistently and not interchanging different words to mean the same thing also makes an interface easier to learn and quicker to use.

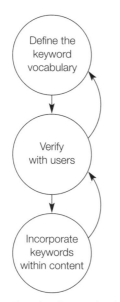

Figure 8.3 Creating, testing and using keyword vocabulary

Providing consistent support for synonyms and acronyms

Having one place of reference for a keyword gives one place of reference for any synonyms and common spelling mistakes that are associated with that keyword. This allows a search facility to be provided that automatically maps these supported attributes to the keyword before a search takes place against the site content and before a search results list is created. This means that if content providers use the keywords within the single classification system, they will automatically have the same level of synonym and common spelling mistake support as all the other pieces of content that use the same keywords.

This takes the difficult job of providing the necessary level of synonym support away from the content provider and places it firmly with the person maintaining the classification system. This will save a great deal of time in an environment where content providers provide and maintain information that describes the content that they are creating. However, in most cases, content providers do not bother with this level of meta-data support, and therefore in this environment it will provide a new and powerful mapping facility that can significantly improve the site search capability.

From the user's point of view, having consistent support for synonyms and common spelling mistakes associated with all the information on the site means that a user-defined search query is more likely to return the information that they are looking for. Improving the way that users find information on a site can only increase user satisfaction.

A good example of mapping important synonyms to keywords can be found on the IBM homepage, where a search for Laptop causes the search results to display links to the main IBM laptop product, ThinkPad (*see* Fig. 8.4). It would be very inconvenient to users if the search interface recognized only product names, and quite unusable if it did not recognize industry-standard terms and provide the correct mapping into the IBM product set.

Providing a central service where synonyms are mapped to keywords

An additional advantage of having a single central vocabulary is being able to add to that vocabulary without having to re-examine all the existing content in order to perform certain reclassification exercises.

All vocabularies and languages change over time, and during the life of a website the use of keywords and terminology is also likely to change. It is very likely that the classification system that is used by a site will be updated and changed, due to any number of factors including a change in business direction, a change in product focus, or support for new types of information, products and services. Therefore, any controlled vocabulary that is defined and any classification system that is created to support this vocabulary needs to be designed with the expectation that it will need to change over time.

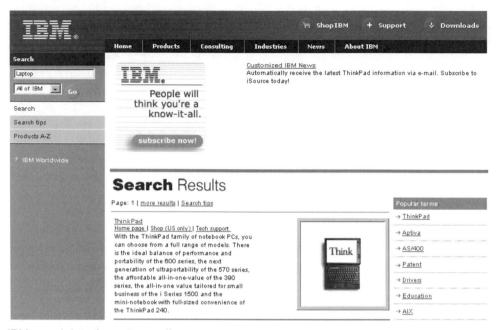

Figure 8.4   IBM search interface at *www.ibm.com*

Many company websites have pages and pages of content that are not classified in any controlled way. The content creator may include some meta-tags, and may even try to include keywords that will usefully describe the content and make it more likely to be found successfully within any search function, but this is not a controlled environment for classifying information. When the results of a query analysis find that a number of users are entering a term that does not seem to be supported by the content of the site, there will be no way for an organization to address this other than requesting its content providers to start using the term and to go back and look at the existing content to add the new keyword. This is not a very scientific way of ensuring that the search results will significantly improve as a result of the query analysis work.

By contrast, if the only way a content item can be classified is by selecting predefined keywords that are held within a central classification system, then all the synonym additions and mappings can be done in one place. There will also be room to add classifications and to provide ways for these new keywords to be mapped to existing meta-data by defining a method of associating keywords with a query.

For example, consider a classification system that contains animal keywords. A website that contains articles about animals may use a controlled vocabulary to classify the site content, so that an article about 'tigers' may be found if the user enters 'tiger', 'big cats', 'cats', 'wild animals', etc. If, after a query analysis, it was found that users were trying to find information about 'jungle animals' and were not getting any matches due to the fact that the term was not supported in the classification hierarchy, it should be possible for it to be added without totally redesigning the classification system, or going back over all the existing content to add the new term. By defining a new keyword with an associated query, a relationship can be made between the new keyword 'jungle animals' and the existing keywords of 'tiger', 'lion', 'snake' and 'monkey'.

It is unlikely that any system will totally remove the need for additional classification maintenance to be done on content. However, costs can be significantly reduced and controlled by adopting a structured classification strategy at the onset and providing mechanisms whereby content classification data is reviewed as rigorously as the content information itself.

Defining the accuracy of how content is classified

There are situations where the information architect would like to define the accuracy of the classification that is provided by the person classifying the content. When a site supports a mass of archived digital information, how well the search facility works can be a determining factor for whether the site will succeed or fail.

When the information source is vast, it is imperative to make it easy for the user to define an accurate enough search query to return a manageable number of search results. This is where an information architect may wish to create a classification system that goes further than just the support of keywords, and to look at a system that provides a method whereby keywords can be described in more detail.

For example, a website that supports a digital library of thousands or millions of greeting cards will need to design a way of describing a card and a way of distinguishing different types of cards in order for an effective search facility to be created. The main classification hierarchy is likely to be the event to which the card relates, i.e. birthday, anniversary, and congratulations, etc. A secondary hierarchy may be the style of the message, i.e. humorous, cute, sincere, rude, none, and so on. A third and more difficult one may try to classify any predominant graphical image displayed on the card. This is where a system that allows keywords to be further described may be required.

A classification system can be designed that recognizes keywords as objects and allows the definition of attributes or verbs to be defined against those objects. For instance, a card may contain a picture of a man playing golf. The keyword 'man' may allow the further definition of attributes such as 'young', 'old', 'healthy' and allow the definition of verbs such as 'walking', 'cycling' and 'running'. The example of 'playing golf' is even more complex as the verb 'playing' requires the additional information of 'golf'. This kind of classification system can be difficult and time consuming to design and manage. However, if the success of the site is dependent on the success of the search facility, the more accurately the information can be classified and indexed, the more likely it will be that the user will be able to:

- define the query that matches their requirements;
- find the content that matches their request.

There may also be a requirement to support disambiguation if the scope of the keywords within the classification is large. Disambiguation is where there exists multiple meanings for the same word, and a definition is provided to distinguish which meaning is required. For example the word 'orange' could mean the fruit or the colour. Keywords within a classification system that have more than one meaning will need to have this additional information associated with them, so that when information is classified using the ambiguous term it will be clear which classification term is applicable.

Controlling and analyzing the scope of a site

The act of defining a controlled vocabulary for classification can also be seen as defining the ideal scope of a site. It provides a heavy indicator to content providers of the type and range of information that is expected. Another advantage is that it can be used to help analyze the information available on a site.

For example, an online news site may have an information architecture hierarchy that includes foreign news broken down by continent and country. If a system can be assured that all foreign news items will contain a predefined country classification, a report could be generated to look across the content of a site to see what the content load is by country. Such an analysis may reveal that the site is delivering very little news from Japan or China and has a flurry of stories on Belgium. If the user analysis has identified that the most important countries to cover in terms of news stories include Japan and China, and Belgium is somewhere near the bottom of the list, obviously there is some mismatch between the user requirements of the site and what is actually being delivered in terms of foreign news articles.

Many sites are unable to perform effective content analysis because they have no way of determining the coverage of certain subject matters. Without a controlled classification scheme that is designed around an information architecture, the only option is to perform a full text search on the site content. This is not usually a very efficient or effective way of analyzing this kind of information.

An important aspect to designing a content classification system is to understand the kinds of content analysis reports that may be required. This will ensure that the site content will contain the necessary data to be effectively analyzed at a later date.

Separating out a process for information classification

For content to be classified correctly in a uniform way, it needs to contain keywords that are within a controlled and defined vocabulary, and these keywords need to accurately describe the information that will be delivered.

In an environment where classifying content is controlled and where a content provider is unable to find suitable keywords that describe the content of the information it is providing, there are two options:

- request that the classification keywords are extended to include the new categories being covered within the content;
- modify the content to fit with the types of keywords within the classification.

Both strategies can be valid in different situations.

In many cases, it should be up to the organization how much control it exerts over classifying content, and the amount it controls it may depend on the skill levels of those creating and providing the content classifications. It may be assumed that content being classified by those who are highly trained in classification techniques and use tools to work with defined vocabularies can be trusted to add new categories and keywords appropriate to the type of content that is being delivered. Lesser skilled content providers may need a system where new keywords are requested, and a single information architect captures these requests and ultimately decides whether they warrant changes or additions to the defined vocabulary.

Clearly there are advantages and disadvantages to both techniques. As soon as a workflow is introduced that requires intervention by someone else in terms of providing classification information, this will inevitably slow down the publishing process. However, having a trained information architect who is responsible for the correct classification of site information will also increase the likelihood of the user finding that information through any site search facility that is offered or through any site-wide summary views that can be automatically generated.

In most large company websites, the information load is so vast that there needs to be some sort of classification strategy to help users find the information they are looking for. When a user gives up trying to navigate a site and starts to rely on a search mechanism, this will be the last chance the site will have to satisfy the user's goal of trying to find the required page. If the search is then ineffective, the user has no more strategies left to complete this task; they will have no other choice than to find some alternative.

Sites that do not support a good information architecture are usually those that are unusable. Understanding how users classify information and then providing a method by which they can access the information according to their classification model is an important part of any information architecture process.

Providing a method for building automatic navigation paths and different site structures

Having a hierarchical information architecture expressed as a controlled and defined vocabulary, and classifying content according to some predefined rules, means that there exists the opportunity to build automatic navigation paths based on different classification criteria. In the example given above, where foreign news articles were classified by country, they could also have been classified according to a story type, for instance, politics, sport, culture or business. A site could then offer an alternative structure to one that has at the top level UK news and foreign news and offer the same articles organized by the story type.

It is also possible to design a search interface that displays the classification criteria and allows users to build queries based on the scope of the information. For instance, the news site could provide two drop-down lists whereby the user could select a country and a story type to find articles within both categories, i.e. all business stories about Japan. This is far more usable than presenting the user with a blank entry field and asking them to guess how the news site has classified articles.

It is also possible to dynamically define contextual navigation paths based on predefined classification data. For instance, an article to do with an art exhibition at the Tate Gallery in London may dynamically build a related information list by having an embedded query that runs against the news article archives. The query may return the last ten articles to do with art exhibitions in the UK, or may return the last ten articles written about the artist across all story types. The more dynamic the content of a site, the more necessary it becomes for automatic lists to be generated. Manually updating related information lists is a time-consuming exercise and relies on the person doing the job having a good knowledge of all the content that is available to link to. This becomes an impossible task in a site that generates large amounts of material and maintains an active and searchable archive.

An extreme example that proves the point is on a site such as the official website for the Sydney Olympics 2000 (*see* Fig. 8.5). The amount of information that is generated during the 17 days of competition is colossal, with 200 countries taking part in 300 medal events held in 39 competition venues. Such a site is designed to expect at least 634 million hits – the record number received at the Nagano 1998 Winter Olympics.

A site that has to handle such a high level of content generation and move that content very quickly on to the site has to rely on a predefined classification system being in place. This allows dynamic lists to be created that display the most up-to-date results and news stories related to the page being viewed. Building views and lists dynamically is the only achievable way of supporting the presentation of this information due to the high volatility of the site content and the sheer amount that is generated. Under these circumstances, it would be an impossible task to create these kinds of pages manually. Therefore, such a site is designed with this in mind, so that when new content is added, the classification system is in place to automatically build navigation paths, and the view templates are already defined that can automatically flow the content on to the site.

Figure 8.5   IBM e-business solution courtesy of the International Olympic Committee
www.olympics.com/eng/

Although there are not too many examples of sites where the system has to support this amount of changing content, there are still very good reasons why many sites should look at the cost savings that may be gained from a level of automation. Classification is only one side of the story, the advantages of using view templates is covered below.

Supporting the notion of alternative classification hierarchies

It is unlikely that any homepage will be able to provide a classification hierarchy that will automatically be obvious to all the different types of users coming to the site. As part of the user analysis stage, the human factors engineer may have found equally valid ways of grouping information that are quite logical to a significant number of users. In this instance, there is no need for a site to constrain a hierarchy structure so that one entry can only appear within one group.

If it is found that a significant number of people look for a certain piece of information within one category, then that piece of information should appear within that category, irrespective of whether it already exists in another.

Having a controlled classification system that supports the notion of hierarchies can help automatically build these navigation paths, and present this hierarchy to the user. This can have many advantages in allowing the user the ability to access part of the site that is deep within the hierarchy with a single click, without having to work through each main category level.

A good example of how this has been practically achieved on a website without cluttering up the interface is within the Vauxhall homepage that presents the top level hierarchy with a drop-down facility to provide access to further information levels (*see* Fig. 8.6).

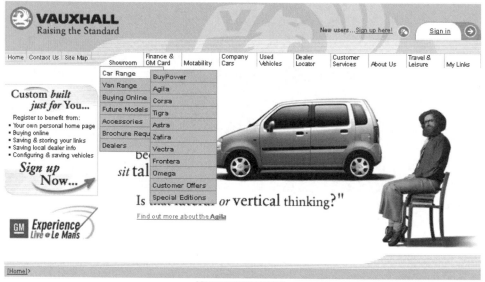

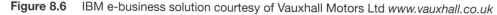

Figure 8.6   IBM e-business solution courtesy of Vauxhall Motors Ltd *www.vauxhall.co.uk*

In addition, this hierarchy supports different user classification models by sometimes including the same option within different groups (*see* Fig. 8.7).

Supporting a business model that includes keyword rental

For certain kinds of sites it is a valid business model to collect revenue by renting out keywords to external companies. Although it is illegal to try passing off as another company, for example adding a competitor's homepage URL within

Figure 8.7   A hierarchy that supports different user classification models

meta-data information, within a search facility on a site, there is nothing wrong with associating a regularly used term with the URL of another site so that this link will appear first within a search results list.

For instance, a site that offers information on where to eat, or where to go out at night, may wish to rent out keywords such as 'Italian restaurant', 'night-club' or 'Irish pub'. When a user searches for any of these terms, a list of matches will be returned and top of the list will be the link to the customer's site.

There will always be a balance to be struck between a site that attempts to be objective and impartial and the necessity to bring in revenue. However, if the business requirement exists, then a classification system will need to be provided that allows the definition of keywords and the ability to associate these keywords with a customer and a customer URL.

Summary

Websites that contain large stores of information should really be thinking of employing a centralized classification scheme. To work effectively, the classification system needs to:

- contain the common keywords that users are familiar with;
- support synonyms, acronyms and common spelling mistakes for these keywords;
- support a hierarchy mechanism whereby content can be found in keywords higher up the tree;
- support a keyword and query facility to allow new keywords to be added that map to more than one keyword that has already been defined;
- support rules to be associated with keywords;
- allow new keywords to be added;

- allow content creators the ability to request that new keywords be added;
- allow contextual relationships to be automatically generated;
- allow site-wide views to be automatically generated;
- allow query analysis reports to be created;
- support keyword rental.

The amount that a website invests in a classification scheme will ultimately depend on the nature of the site and the type and amount of information the site supports. The cue should come from the user requirements captured within the user analysis – requirements that are based on analyzing how users find product and service information today and how they would ultimately like to complete these tasks in the future.

View templates

For medium- to large-sized websites, it is unrealistic to expect a dedicated graphic design team to create individual HTML layouts for each page of content on a site, especially in the situations where it is expected that new content will be created on a regular basis. Therefore it is practical to create some general view templates through which the same types of content can be presented. A good example of when view templates are necessary is within online newspapers and online stores that support a large and changing product catalogue.

In cases such as a free online newspaper, the business model is such that it would be far too expensive to provide individual layouts and designs for each news article. During a user analysis for an online newspaper, it was probably found that the presentation of an article is secondary to the article content and timeliness, and that a free service is more preferable by far to one where the user has to pay, even if the user has to put up with a few flashing adverts.

There are many reasons to justify defining a view template and there it a large percentage of content on the web that could easily be presented in this way. To support view templates, there needs to be a data model that allows the content to be provided in a format so that it can be broken apart into its important parts. These information segments can then be displayed within different areas of the screen within a carefully designed layout defined by the view template.

It would be unusual for every page within a website to be defined in this way. For example, one-off designs make sense for homepages, online registrations and credit card transactions, where there is likely to be only one instance of that type of page on the site. However, when there is a sizable number of instances of the same type of content, it makes good sense to invest in the effort of designing a template that provides the underlying data model for content providers to deliver the content that will be flowed through these views.

Figure 8.8   IBM e-business solution courtesy of Abercrombie & Fitch
www/abercrombie.com/anf/onlinestore/index.html

A common example of where these templates are best utilized is within an online shop that needs to display a catalogue of products. The template allows new products to be flowed on to the site, as well as providing a consistent interface where the user can view and select products to buy (*see* Fig. 8.8).

Providing consistency within the user interface for the user

In many types of web pages, the user is scanning the interface for information relevant to the task they are trying to complete. It might be the cost of a particular service, or the name of the author of a book, or the operating system a piece of software will run on.

Catalogues that offer many instances of the same types of product are ideally suited to being delivered using view templates, because the information about each product usually has the same structure. In these kinds of interfaces, it makes life much easier for users if the price of the product is always situated in the same place on their screen. Users quickly become familiar with the structure of a page and a common layout and will become efficient at scanning the page for the information they are interested in. User interface consistency can increase user satisfaction because it reduces the cognitive load, i.e. they have to think less to achieve the same task.

Specifying a level of content detail

A similar advantage to the user having consistency in interface layout is having pages that provide the same level of detail for the same types of products. This enables users to compare product information quickly and efficiently. From a content creator's point of view defining the sets of fields that need to be provided for a particular type of content clearly defines the level of information that they are required to provide, which can help lead to more structured content and a higher quality of information that will be provided to the user.

Breaking the bottleneck between designer and content provider

When the web development process demands that the layout of a site is controlled by trained graphic designers, this can naturally lead to a bottleneck in delivering new content to a site. Even if an organization is so flush with designers that one is always available at the drop of a hat, they still have to work with the content provider and preferably a usability expert to define a layout that is not only attractive and usable by the end user but applicable to the content they are presenting. This process can be time consuming, and the design approach ultimately is a reactive one to the content provided by a content provider.

A site such as the Sydney Olympics has no choice but to flow content through predefined view templates due to the sheer amount of information that needs to be captured and displayed. It would be impossible to offer such an information service to users if each piece of new content had to be individually laid out and designed by a graphic designer. Therefore the goal of view templates is to remove this graphic design phase from the process of publishing content and to place it within the analysis and design stage of the site. This requires a graphic designer to create a page design that can be used for all content instances of the same type, and this template must be in place before any of the content items are created and published (*see* Fig. 8.9).

Writers generate
the content

Graphic designers design
the visual layout

Developers translate into HTML and move
pages on to web server

Figure 8.9   The HTML development bottleneck

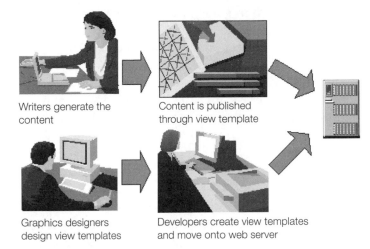

Writers generate the content

Content is published through view template

Graphics designers design view templates

Developers create view templates and move onto web server

Figure 8.10 Breaking the bottleneck by using view templates

Therefore view templates provide a proactive approach, where the design has been based on previous instances of the same types of content. The initial design exercise is done once, and from then on each piece of new content is flowed through the same design. This theoretically means that new content can be added to a website immediately without any extra intervention from a graphic designer or usability expert.

Reducing the cost of delivering new content

Creating one design for each type of content is far cheaper than creating a design for each individual piece of content. A second cost saving could also be realized by reducing the cognitive load on the content provider, thereby making the process of creating new content quicker and the review cycle on that content item shorter. By clearly defining which pieces of information are necessary for a content provider to deliver, it becomes clearer when a piece of work is complete and correct. There are also likely to be other examples of the same types of content available for the content provider to look at and learn from.

Preventing the content author producing their own layout

In the majority of cases, the initial impression of a website is defined by the visual professionalism of the interface. Allowing content providers to define their own layouts can seriously undermine the whole feel of a site, and ignore any style and presentation guidelines that have been carefully considered by professional visual designers.

View templates provide the ability to extract just the content from a content source and independently apply the visual layout for that content. The content provider has no influence over the display. This strongly backs up the roles and responsibilities within a website team, where professional writers provide content and layout is controlled by professional visual designers.

Summary

View templates are a way of defining a single design for a type of content. View templates are used extensively on the web for pages showing news articles or for product sites that support large product catalogues. They are ideally suited for sites that have a number of instances of the same type of information. The main advantages for defining view templates are:

- to provide a level of user interface consistency that allows the same information to appear in the same place;
- to specify a required level of information from the content provider;
- to speed up the publishing process for content writers;
- to reduce the cost of content creation;
- to ensure that the layout of content is controlled by visual designers.

There will always be a place for one-off individual designs, such as the homepage or forms for online registration and ordering product goods. However, every business should consider the cost of maintenance when looking at the different design options, and recognize that any individual design that is created will also have to be individually maintained.

Summary views

For sites that contain large amounts of information, the ability to generate views that span the entire content of a site in a meaningful way to the user can be invaluable.

Site contents

Reference books provide readers with content pages in order to offer a summarized and condensed view of the information contained within the book. Content pages usually group information into related subjects and usually in some sort of serial order that makes sense for the reader. If the reader needs to understand topic A before reading topic B, then the section on B will follow the section on A.

On the web, this progressive revelation is achieved by putting the details behind a hierarchy, so that the hierarchy root or homepage acts as a high-level pointer to the main sections within the site (*see* Fig. 8.11). Many sites adopt a strategy of allowing the user to drop down only one level at a time. If the user has an idea of the level of detail they are looking for, this can be a time-consuming way to get to the information they are after.

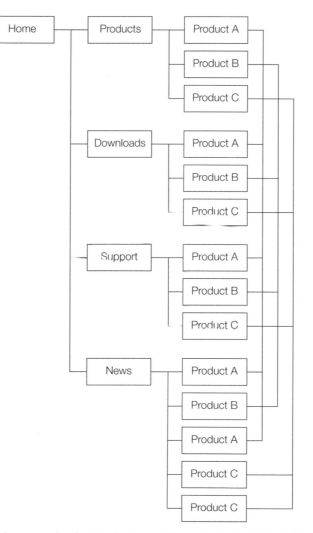

Figure 8.11   Typical model for primary navigation backed up with contextual relationships

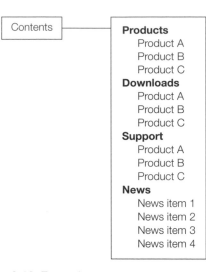

Figure 8.12 Example contents

The equivalent mechanism in a printed form would be for the main contents page to contain only the titles of each chapter, and then at the start of each chapter, another content pages would provide the titles of each section, and then at the start of each section would be another contents page with a list of each major heading, and so on until the hierarchy had been exhausted.

This is not a particularly useful way for a reader to scan the content of a book. It would necessitate someone having to turn to three different pages before finding out that the page did not contain the information they were after, as opposed to a one-page operation, which would be all that was necessary if all the sections and sub-sections were available within a single main contents page.

Many website designs could easily incorporate the same mechanism successfully employed by millions of reference books. This would be to offer a content summary view that attempts to group the contents of the site into a subject-oriented summarized way, showing enough detail of the hierarchy for the user to avoid having to click through progressive hierarchy layers to get to anything useful. Simple indentation quickly conveys a hierarchy of information and well-indented lists are easy for the user to scan and a familiar way to focus in on a particular area of interest (*see* Fig. 8.12).

Figure 8.13 shows an extract of the site map offered by Vauxhall. This provides the user with an overview of the site scope and a quick mechanism to click through to areas of interest.

Site indexes

Indexes offer the reader a way of looking at the coverage of terms within a reference book. This technique addresses the user goal of finding information when they have a pretty good idea of the terms they are interested in. It offers a method for directly accessing that information by providing page numbers where the terms or subjects are covered. Indexes rely on the reader knowing the term and the spelling of the term they are interested in. Some indexes will support a level of synonym support and will redirect the reader to the alternative term that has been used.

Figure 8.13   An extract of the site map offered by Vauxhall

Index pages differ from content pages in their approach to finding information by sorting the subjects or terms in alphabetical order (*see* Fig. 8.14), whereas the terms and subjects within content pages are sorted in a subjective contextual way, according to how the writer of the book perceives the reader should progress logically through the book. Providing both of these methods has proved very successful in allowing the reader to find and access information using two different search strategies.

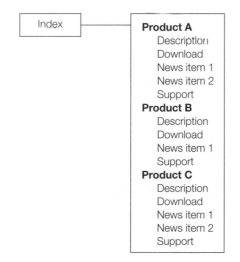

Figure 8.14 Example index

Indexes can be a useful technique to transfer to certain types of websites. When sites offer primary navigation schemes that break content down into main subject areas, they may not offer all the contextual relationships that will help the user find the related information they are looking for. A common scenario for users is to drill down a main hierarchy by recognizing terms that are of interest, and finding that the particular path they have come down does not give them the information they are looking for. When users find themselves in this position, they either have to try another hierarchy path or resort to the site search facility, the problems of which have already been documented.

Therefore the role of a website index should be to try to bridge the gap between the logical organization of the information, which can be seen as a subjective contextual contents page mapping, and an alternative way of accessing the same information in a way that covers the main links for each important term or subject, sorted into alphabetical order. Ideally, the model should try to emulate the results from a search facility that returns only relevant and useful matches. This implies that the entries should map directly to the terms and keywords identified within the user analysis, and should be reviewed and updated as a result of an ongoing query analysis from the site search facility.

Specialized lists

Many books offer specialized lists such as glossaries and bibliographies. In certain circumstances, the ability to provide the user with a single point of reference for a type of information can be very useful. A common example on the web is a page that shows useful links out to other sites placed in some sort of subject-related context, as the BBC website in Fig. 8.15 demonstrates.

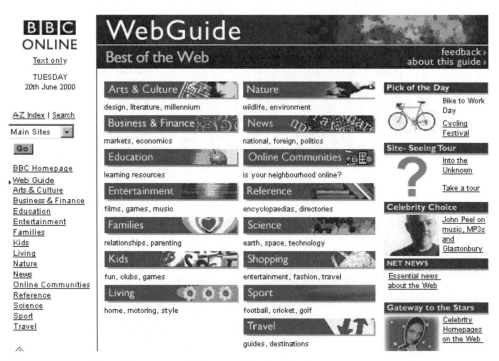

Figure 8.15   Useful links to other sites on *www.bbc.co.uk/webguide/*

However, there can be many other types of lists generated from website content that could provide the user with value-added information. For example, references to printed papers, biographies of referenced individuals, lists and addresses of organizations and businesses could be grouped together within a single reference place and be useful in certain types of web interfaces.

These kinds of lists can be time consuming to create and a nightmare to maintain if a manual approach is taken. With this in mind, if such lists can offer value to the user of the site, a system should be considered that automatically generates these lists from the underlying content, and displays them using a pre-designed view template. To achieve this, the parts that make up the lists need to be analyzed, created and made identifiable in such a way within the underlying data model to generate the view template that pulls together all the necessary information fields into a summarized view. It is possible to create a view template that automatically applies ordering according to some predefined rules and in addition automatically provides the links to the referenced content. It is the process of identifying these objects and their corresponding attributes that forms the main part of the content analysis stage covered in the next chapter.

Combination views

Not only is it possible to define relationships between different content types and content instances, such as relationships between news articles or relationships between different CDs, it is also possible to define relationships between different information within these content types and instances.

In the example of the Winter Olympics 1998 Nagano site created by IBM, the results for each event were entered into a results template and stored in such a way that journalists could easily query which countries were winning which events, and how individual athletes were doing. Details about each competitor within the games were entered into a competitor template and stored in such a way that journalists could look up details about each individual taking part in the Games. However, a view was also created that combined the details from events and the details from competitors into a single view definition. This combined view showed summary details about a competitor and displayed how well they had done in the events in which they had taken part. This was achieved by creating a view template made up from a set of individual view fragments, where each fragment could display the results of an individual query. This is more advanced than having a view template that has a one-to-one association with a content type.

When a development team goes to the trouble of creating data models for different content types it opens up the possibilities of dynamically generating all sorts of different views based on the different models available. One of the more powerful arguments for going down this route is the flexibility it gives to provide new views on existing information, views that at the time of content creation had not even been thought about.

Offering different views on a site

'Adaptive interfaces' is the term that is used within interface design to describe the ability of a screen presentation to change according to some predefined criteria. In website design, there are three different types of circumstance where it makes sense to do this:

- when the site understands who the user is and has different types of content for different types of users;
- when the site wishes to display different visual attributes or view designs that are optimized for different client environments;
- when the site supports content relationships to external factors such as time, for example, supporting the requirements to push or advertise barbecue goods, such as charcoal, hotdogs and burgers during the months of June, July and August.

Targeting adverts

In Chapter 5 we discussed how a business may wish to target adverts at different types of users. A view template could be designed that changes the content of a site to support predefined relationships. Take the homepage example of the online music store, where the homepage view can comfortably display a single advert set aside for CDs that have just been released. In a week in which 20 new CDs are added to the catalogue, a relationship could be created between each user type identified within a classification system and one or more of the CDs that have just been released. When a recognized user comes to the site, the advert for the CD associated with the user type can be displayed. A second visit could prompt a different advert to appear. This kind of target advertising can be very powerful, and could be a lucrative source of advertising revenue if the website has successfully managed to register a high percentage of users, who have also imparted enough information about themselves to be usefully categorized.

Another variation on this theme is linked to the idea of keyword rental discussed earlier, where a site may offer advertising space on a search results page that is linked to the search criteria entered by the user. An example of a site that does this is Yahoo!, where a search for 'laptop' will result in an advert for IBM, whereas a search for curry results in an advert for a speciality foods retailer (*see* Fig. 8.16).

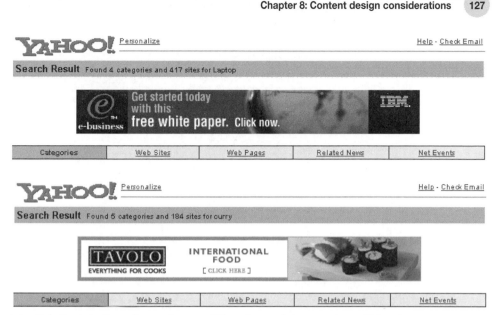

Figure 8.16   Adopting the interface depending on different search keywords on Yahoo!

Cross marketing

Cross marketing in a website context is where links are generated that relate to the content that the user is viewing. The business purpose of these links is to tempt the user to buy more goods from the site. The user's opinion of these kinds of links varies depending on how they perceive the usefulness of the relationship. In most cases they are viewed favourably as adding value to the interface. The idea is for the site to create logical relationships that say, 'If you are interested in this product, you will probably be interested in these other products as well'.

Perhaps the best example of where this service has been offered to users on the web is within the hugely popular Amazon site (*see* Fig. 8.17). When a user views a page showing details about a book, a list is displayed containing links to other books that have been purchased by customers who have also purchased the book that is currently being viewed.

The 'If you like this...' box on the left-hand side of the screen is extremely useful in helping users find the most popular books in the same genre as the one they are currently looking at. This is exactly the kind of subject-related contextual linking that needs to be more common within web interfaces.

Figure 8.17   Amazon offers a good example of cross marketing

Cross-marketing links can also be defined by the same kinds of rules used for targeting adverts. If information about the user is known, the generated list of links can include products that are most likely to appeal to the identified user type. How these generated links are created is the same as the technique used for summary views, where individual view fragments have their own query defined.

Customizing information to the user

In some website environments, there may exist a requirement to change the way that information is presented, depending on a range of criteria. For instance, a site that reviews football matches between different countries may change the description of the game depending on which country the user is coming from. An internal intranet may show only certain pieces of information to certain classifications of employees, and a website navigation scheme may change as a result of recognizing the type of user coming to the site and present a customized set of options applicable to the user type.

As with any of these techniques that require the interface or information to change as a result of attributes or behaviour, there has to be a sound business or usability reason to do it. Adaptive interfaces are not cheap to develop or maintain, so there has to be a cost justification for investing in the development effort.

Providing a customized service to known users

Offering personalized interfaces can be a double-edged sword, and has to be carefully informed by the user analysis. Personalized interfaces adapt to the individual using them. On the web, this is achieved by a website creating a cookie, so that when the user revisits the site, the website can recognize the user. A common example of where personalized interfaces are used is when a site offers a one-click buy option and pre-fills all the purchasing information in readiness for the user to purchase goods. This technique is achieved without users having to explicitly make themselves known to the site through a registration technique.

When viewed from a purely logical standpoint, an interface that adapts to the user seems a highly desirable goal to aim for. However, there are trust and privacy issues to take into account. Most users feel uncomfortable with any business knowing too much about them. No one wants to feel that they may be inundated with junk mail or pushy marketing. Nor do they wish to experience the uneasy feeling that a business may be watching and analyzing their behaviour. Therefore any design that centres on collecting information about an individual user, and then visually feeding back through the interface that they know who the user is, and they know information about them, can seriously threaten the usability of a site and break any trust that has been built up.

For each task, where a personalized interface may seem appropriate, a user analysis needs to take place to ascertain what the feelings are about the proposed technique. Users are generally favourable to personalized interfaces when:

● they save time;

● they pre-fill information within forms that otherwise would be a tedious user task;

● they provide the opportunity to link to additional useful and relevant information;

● they are used on an already trusted site.

Users generally dislike these interfaces when:

● there is a feeling that the site is hiding information;

● the site uses personalized gimmicks that provide no added value, such as a personalized greeting on the homepage; such sites forget that more than one person can use the same computer, and this is likely to be the case when the computer is within the home environment;

● a site is using the information inappropriately and making assumptions on behaviour.

A good example of a personalized interface that saves time is the one-click buying service provided by Amazon (*see* Fig. 8.18). This button provides a fast path for existing customers to purchase goods without having to re-enter any

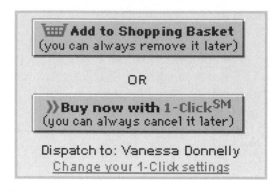

Figure 8.18 1-click buying service from Amazon

personal or payment details. Obviously the first time a user buys goods from the site, they will have to enter all the relevant details to complete the transaction, but after that the site does not require the customer to do this again. It relies on the fact that users have already experienced a safe and reliable buying experience from the first successful transaction. Users, for the most part, will be happy to trust the site with getting the details right the second time as long as they continue to receive a safe and reliable service.

An example of a personalized interface that is likely to irritate users is where a user has previously purchased a printer from the site and returns to the homepage to be reminded that it is probably about time they purchased a new print cartridge. This kind of personalized interface may seem clever, or even usable, but in general users see it as threatening and intrusive, with too much similarity to the feeling that 'Big Brother is watching you'. A far better approach would be to feature or highlight a link to the section on print cartridges, without any indication that this adaptation is linked to any specific knowledge of the individual user. If by luck the user has come to the site to purchase a print cartridge, this link will be useful, if not it can be easily ignored.

Supporting different client environments

Many website teams face a dilemma as to what screen size they should be designing. A user analysis may provide some insight into the most common environment used by the target audience, but there is still likely to be a significant spread among the target users of different screen sizes and resolutions.

Most website designs are optimized for 800 pixel by 600 pixel screens; however, if a site truly wishes to keep everyone happy, it still needs to create designs that will work effectively within a 640 by 480 space, and at the other end of the spectrum be respectful of those users who have more pixels than they know what to do with. The majority of designers feel constrained by this amount of screen real estate, especially when many of these designs do not look particularly good when viewed on high-resolution graphical monitors. The compromise is to create multiple designs optimized for the client environment, so that when the website is accessed, it queries which screen resolution or size the user has and switches in the appropriate view.

Some sites offer alternatives such as a site with frames and one without, or a text only version of a site, although the need for most of these alternatives is diminishing as the percentage of users who have older browsers that do not support frames and the percentage of users accessing the web in text mode only is falling rapidly.

However, there is a significant shift in the number of users who access the internet through hand held-devices. A business will seriously need to consider whether it is appropriate for a site to work within this environment, and if so how it will need to adapt and work within the technology bounds of the device. It may be the case that a system will need to be designed that allows for the interchange of different views and the interchange of different levels of content. A design for a hand-held device would not be able to include large graphics, anything that relies on colour, or long-winded textual descriptions.

View templates will provide the ability to switch in different views depending on the environment, but the underlying data models will also need to be adapted to suit the kind of information applicable to such interfaces. These design considerations need to be taken into account very early on in the design process, as going back and reworking a complete website and all the existing content and individual views will be costly and time consuming. As with all these adaptive interface decisions, the requirement for this work needs to come from the business and be backed up by any user analysis work that has been carried out.

Supporting different languages and cultures

Some websites may wish to change their content to support national characteristics. National language support is always difficult in any development project, and there is a sliding scale of the extent that websites may wish to provide support for different languages and different cultural characteristics. The sliding scale will go from single language and single design right through to translating all the site content into different languages and redesigning the site, view designs and embedded graphics in order to optimize the site for the culture of the target country.

As with most things, national language support should be designed in at the start of the project, and should be driven as a business requirement into the process. The procedures involved in the design of systems to support national languages and any cultural implications that may apply to the visual design of interfaces across countries is too complex to cover in this book. However, there is an opportunity when setting up view templates to identify those fields that are to be externally published and visible to the user. If a website thinks that in future it may wish to translate its site content, going down the view template road will save a lot of time and effort.

Summary

There are many reasons why a business may want to invest in adaptive interfaces for a website. These are:

- to target adverts at different user types or individuals;
- to target related products to different user types or individuals;
- to offer different access to information depending on some information classification;
- to offer different versions of the same information depending on the type of user or geography;
- to provide a more target task-oriented navigation scheme depending on different user types;
- to offer a quick service to known customers;
- to provide different visual designs optimized for different client environments such as screen, browser level and different devices;
- to support different languages and designs for different cultures.

Switching views and switching content as a result of some predefined criteria is all possible, and made easier when a site is built upon a defined content model using view templates to present the underlying information. However, developing and maintaining different versions of a site is difficult and expensive and there needs to be very strong business or usability reasons to do it. The majority of businesses will find it an impossible task because their websites are not structured or managed in any way.

In this kind of environment, suddenly recognizing the business need will necessitate a complete redesign of the content, views and site structure. It will almost be the same as starting a website development project from scratch. If a company finds itself in this position, this will be the right time to adopt a more structured approach to the development of the site, and to consider the options of using content models and view templates.

9 Content analysis

A content analysis defines the characteristics of the different kinds of information that will be published to a website. Some content will easily fit into recognizable and identifiable types, such as a news article or a book definition. Other collections of information will not be so well defined and may have a less rigid structure. However, if an organization wishes to step up to having a content-driven website that will be managed and controlled within a content management system, a level of content analysis will be needed. This will identify the different content types and their attributes and relationships and allow these documents to be created, published and maintained.

Irrespective of the special properties that set apart different content types, there will also be common attributes that will apply to all the content within a site. It is the definition of what these common attributes are, as well as the definition of the specific attributes for an individual type of content, that makes up the main part of a content analysis. The kind of site, and the different content involved in creating it will determine how critical this analysis stage is. Any site that is heavily content based, that will be judged by the quality and timeliness of the information on it, will need to rely on a well-managed and well-integrated publication model. It will also need to rely on automated services that make content easy to create and maintain. In the long term it will be far cheaper in this situation for a company to invest in a level of content analysis.

Content types

Common content types do exist on the web. When looking at news articles on different news sites, and at the similarity between the data attributes and content relationships that have been defined, it is not too big a leap to consider the possibility of defining a single common template that could be used by all of them.

What is apparent is that news sites are different because of:

- the way articles are displayed;
- the way a site organizes and classifies articles;
- the subject matters being written about;
- the writing styles used.

Their similarities are:

- the underlying structure;
- the attributes related to the article type;
- the mechanism to link to related information;
- the way the user navigates, reads and generally interacts with the information.

In all cases a news article has at least a title, a lead paragraph, an author, a publication date and body text.

Identifying the important objects within the system

When starting a content analysis from scratch, the first thing is to identify the different underlying objects within the system that the user perceives as important. Most of this will come from the user analysis, and in particular from the list of user goals and tasks that have been identified. This method of distinguishing important nouns is the first stage within an object-oriented analysis, and exactly the same techniques can be used for a content analysis.

For instance, in the example of the online florist, the user tasks were:

1   Find a florist that can deliver to the required area.
2   Select a bouquet of flowers to send.
3   Provide details of where the flowers should be sent.
4   Add a personal message with the flowers.
5   Pay for the order.

This simple task-list identifies five important objects that need to be captured. Fig. 9.1 is an example of a simple Unified Modelling Language static view. UML is fast becoming the industry standard for depicting object-oriented analysis and design concepts and also a way of describing designs that can then be translated into code. Throughout the rest of the book, these diagrams will be used to convey design ideas and concepts; however, there will also be textual descriptions provided for those who have no desire to interpret the UML notation.

Figure 9.1, therefore, shows the main objects identified within the task-list and the main relationships between these objects.

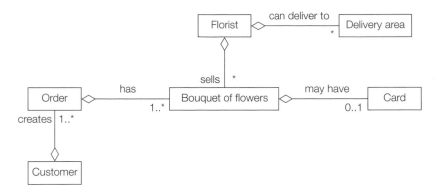

Figure 9.1   A simple object model for an online florist

- A customer creates one or more orders.
- An order contains one or more bouquets of flowers.
- A bouquet may have a card associated with it.
- A florist sells many bouquets.
- A florist can deliver to many areas.

The primary focus of this exercise is to clearly capture the user's model of the site and record that in terms of the main and important objects that they perceive within the system and the main relationships between those objects.

Validating the main objects and their relationships with users

An analysis of the main objects and their relationships can be performed interactively with users, or validated after an initial pass of an analysis has been completed. Either way, it is recommended that the analyst does not openly display the kind of object-oriented analysis diagrams shown above, as this may only cause confusion.

When users do not understand diagrams, they will spend more time trying to figure out what they are trying to say than validating the rules the diagrams are trying to depict. It is far better to simply capture the objects as words on sticky notes that can be pasted on a white board for clarification. Lines can be drawn between the notes to represent the relationships, and each relationship should be created at the same time as the analyst is validating the rule.

For example, during the validation of the above model, the analyst will need to clarify the rules that have been defined between the objects. The relationship between the 'bouquet of flowers' and the 'card' states that 'a bouquet of flowers' may have one card associated with it. The important clarification here is the fact that the relationship states that:

1   The card is optional.

2   The site will allow the user to create only one card.

When the analyst explains this relationship rule, it is possible that a user may query why they are limited to sending only one card. They might provide a valid reason for sending more than one, and describe the situations in which they would like to do so. At this point the analyst should note down the user requirement and the additional background information provided. However, it is not up to the analyst to make a judgement at this point on whether the requirement is valid.

Validating the main objects and their relationships with content experts

The important part of a content analysis is to examine the content information from the viewpoints of everyone who will be involved with it. A user analysis within a software development environment traditionally concentrates on capturing the requirements of end users of the system, i.e. those who will be buying the product and attempting to use it. Within a content-driven web development environment, it is important to examine the requirements of everyone within the system, and this will include those who will be creating and managing the information on the site.

Content providers are those who create the information for a site. They are really the content experts, and their view of the information that will be presented may be different from that of the end user of the website that will be displaying the information. It will be necessary to capture their user model of the main objects and their relationships in order for the user interface designs of the content management system to be created. It should be a goal to make this system as easy to use as possible. If the interfaces that are used to create the site information start to use terminology and definitions that are foreign to the content provider, their productivity will be seriously impacted and this may lead to a deterioration of the quality of information that they provide.

There are likely to be several iterations of this exercise, as the content experts may require that certain types exist that the user does not necessarily perceive as being different. In the example where a site offers reviews of products, content experts may see a difference between software reviews, hardware reviews and benchmark test results (*see* Fig. 9.2). During the user analysis, users may have perceived the existence of only one object, that of a product review.

Both viewpoints are valid. Further examination of the attributes that define each type identified by the content expert will probably substantiate that these types are indeed different, and will need to be created in a different way. However, the user is also right. The interface will need to support the 'product reviews' keyword, as this is the term that the user will be expecting to find.

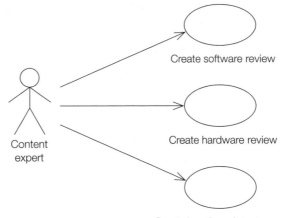

Figure 9.2   A content expert's view of the content on a site

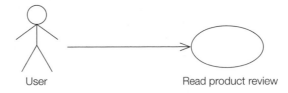

Figure 9.3   An end user's view of the site

A prototype design may take both viewpoints and combine them into a single interface. 'Product review' may be displayed as a category name, and underneath this heading the names of the different types of product reviews may be available as links (*see* Fig. 9.3). A user validation of the classification and terms used within the prototype design will determine whether this is the best approach to organize the underlying information on the site, and whether users can quickly find the kinds of information they are looking for.

Providing scoping information for the main content types

Once the types have been distinguished, the next stage is to provide scoping information for them. Scoping information is a short definition that a content provider can use to decide whether this is the content type they should be creating. It should provide additional information on top of the type name that qualifies its applicability to the site.

For instance, the content type of news article for the IBM Ease-of-Use site could have been: 'Press articles by leading industry publications highlighting the Ease-of-Use of IBM Products'. This definition makes it clear to content providers that this content type is only for:

- news items on IBM products;
- news items that cover ease-of-use issues;
- News items from respected publications.

These definitions can be created during the user analysis stage by involving representatives from the target audience to find out what they would like the scope of the information to be. However, the formal wording of these definitions will need to be reworked at a later stage to ensure that they are clear and easily understandable by those creating the information for the site. Their primary purpose is to clarify to content providers the kinds of information they should be writing, as well as providing a short checklist that allows them to decide whether the content they wish to create fits into the defined scope for the information type.

Content properties

Content types are identifiable because they have a defined set of properties or attributes. The grouping of these properties essentially defines the type. A news article has a title and a lead paragraph; a white paper has a title and an abstract; a product has a product name, description and price.

The next stage within the content analysis is to define the properties that set out the content type.

Validating properties with users

The main content types are derived from the goals and primary tasks identified during the user analysis stage. The important properties for these types can be derived from the critical design features that need to be supported in order for the user to achieve these tasks.

In the example of the online florist, one of the main tasks was the opportunity for the user to 'select a bouquet of flowers to send'. In order for them to complete this task, the following critical design features were identified.

- The list of available bouquets should be sorted by price.
- The price of each bouquet needs to be very clearly displayed.
- A picture needs to be available for each bouquet.
- More detail should be available, giving a clearer picture of each arrangement and information about the types of flowers.
- Users should be able to search for bouquets within a certain price range and colour scheme.
- Users should then be able to select the bouquet they want to order, and provide delivery details.

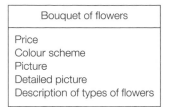

Figure 9.4 Identifying properties of a bouquet of flowers

From this list the following properties can be identified. If the user analyst had identified the most likely price ranges for users to search under, Fig. 9.4 could be extended (*see* Fig. 9.5) to indicate to the site designers:

- the price ranges thought appropriate;
- the wording that users have used to describe these price ranges.

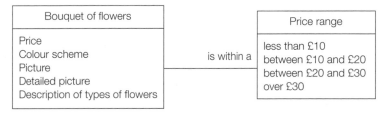

Figure 9.5   Extending the description of a bouquet of flowers

Bringing in the content experts

Within a structured and well-designed focus group environment, users tend to find it easy to describe how they perform a task and what needs to be in place to enable them to perform it. These descriptions are analyzed and captured within a task analysis and then used to identify the primary tasks and familiar task flows needed in the interface for the site to be usable by the target audience.

However, during the user analysis phase, the analyst will also try to capture new ways in which users would like to achieve tasks in future. A brainstorming exercise that attempts to capture new ideas does not judge whether they are achievable. Some interesting thoughts may emerge from users, but for the most part they do not understand the domain well enough to see where different information could be used to achieve a better user experience.

Users do not have the skills to design interfaces, nor the ability to design information architectures or classification systems. Content experts, on the other hand, know the types of information that could be made available to users within a certain domain and are in a much better position to suggest new ways to access that information.

For instance, within the critical design features for selecting a bouquet of flowers to send, the analyst identified two ways for the user to do so:

- by price;
- by colour scheme.

This is hardly surprising when one considers the experience of walking into a high street florist and seeing a selection of bouquets for sale. The first selection criterion that is likely to be used is 'does it look good?'; the second is 'how much does it cost?'. These criteria are only this way round because florists do not usually display their bouquets in price order. This is unlike estate agents, who have recognized that house-hunters come to them with a predefined price range and then start looking for houses they like within it.

What has been created here is a set of critical design features for tasks that users can do today within their familiar world. It is vital to get them right, as the majority of users will come to the website with a traditional model of how the system should work, and will be confused if they cannot follow a familiar task flow. However, there are opportunities on the web to do things in a better way, and the goal of any website development project should be to try to improve upon the traditional methods that users employ to achieve their tasks. A content analysis can help provide better and more efficient ways of doing things by making information more accessible to users.

Task synthesis is the word that is given to the definition of how tasks could be achieved in the future. Performing a similar brain-storming exercise with content experts is much more likely to result in new ideas that will make it easier for users to achieve their goals. This is because they are in a better position to know the scope of information they could provide about any particular type of object.

Take the example of the online florist. A content expert may see the potential of allowing users the ability to search for bouquets that contain a certain type of flower (*see* Fig. 9.6). They might also see value in allowing users to associate their name or the name of the person they are sending the flowers to, with the name of a particular variety of flower – for example, varieties with female names, such as the geranium Josephine. The average user may not know that such names exist, and therefore would not be in a position to suggest that a site support such a feature.

Of course, it is always dangerous to start introducing features to a site just because it is possible to do so. Any of these new ideas would need to be checked with users to see whether they would be of value, and whether they affect the priority of tasks that have already been identified.

Figure 9.6   Searching additional attributes to the user

Naming properties

It will be the content experts or content providers who will need to define the best name that should be associated with a property, as they will be the ones seeing the names within the interfaces to create the content type. A journalist who creates news articles knows that the short paragraph after the news title is referred to as a lead paragraph. This term has a special meaning to journalists in terms of style and content. By contrast, a user or reader of the article may perceive only that there is an overview paragraph that summarizes the text that follows.

For each property, additional scoping information should also be identified. For instance, there may be a house style that limits the length of a lead paragraph to fifty words, defines a reading level, and sets a tone for the writing style.

Creating a pure data model

When performing a content analysis, it is necessary to think of properties that make up a content type as being independent of how they will eventually be displayed within a web page. It is important to try to achieve this so that any interface that is designed does not try to force the information to fit the design. Sometimes a visual designer will try to engineer the situation so that all the keywords within a primary navigation layout are no longer than a certain number of characters, purely because the layout of the web page will look better if all the words are kept short. This approach to designing a website can be disastrous – the layout might look great, but the user may not understand how to navigate the site or find the information they are looking for.

The design of the information and the way that a site organizes it should be handled independently from the visual design of that information. And the process that defines the information structure should be primarily driven by the way the user needs to access the information in order to achieve a task, and the way the content expert needs to understand how to create it.

As this exercise continues it may become apparent that there are strong similarities between one property definition and another within a different content type. It may be tempting to share the definition of an author of a book, with an author of a white paper. And at first glance this seems reasonable. However, at this stage within the process it is safer not to make any assumptions that definitions can be shared. There will need to be an exercise that cross-refers the results of the user analysis specifically with any task analysis or task synthesis requirements to see if it makes sense to share fields – or if the ability for users to undertake the task they wish to perform would be comprised, or problems or confusion would be created for content providers.

XML Standards

XML stands for Extensible Markup Language and is defined by the W3C World Wide Web Consortium (*www.w3.org/XML*). In the context of web design, it complements HTML by providing a mechanism to describe information. When a content analysis has taken place and the object types and properties are well understood, the data structures can be translated into XML so that programs can be written to understand, interpet, manipulate and exchange information and data streams.

XML defines the framework for describing information in a standard way[26], but does not define the names or naming conventions to be used. However, when deciding on property names, it is useful to understand that various standards have been defined to allow data to be shared between businesses. It may be applicable to follow standard naming conventions, if it is anticipated that information will need to be shared and understood programmatically by others outside the company.

Content relationships

Defining the relationships between different objects within the system sets out the underlying rules, abilities and constraints that will eventually be applied within the website design. The task analysis and critical design features will supply the information that will define the essential relationships within the system that must be supported in order for the site to be functional and usable. Validating these main relationships is inextricably linked to validating the main objects within the system and has already been covered. However, there are other relationships that need to be considered. The task analysis or any task synthesis may provide requirements for extra content relationships to be created that will provide access to related information and will make the job of finding information on the site easier and more efficient.

Building in relationships to provide additional capabilities

During the user analysis, the analyst will try to discover user requirements. For instance, an online newspaper may offer a list of links to related news articles on the same subject. A requirement may be for this related information to be more flexible, allowing the user to decide which kind of related information they are interested in. For instance, they might wish to see:

- previous news articles by the same author;
- links about the country covered in the article;
- news articles that refer to the people mentioned in the story.

An expert user may also like to see information on how a news article will be archived, in order to build up an understanding of the archive structure. This information may help the user to browse the news archives in future.

A user analysis that captures these requirements will be able to feed this information into the content analysis. The goal of the content analysis will then be to take these requirements and build a rich data model able to accommodate the kinds of views useful to and usable by the target audience. A content model that deals only with the obvious will ultimately restrict the views and functionality that can be offered by the site. In the long run, it will be quicker, cheaper and more efficient to consider all the data-modelling possibilities and potential relationships up front, rather than trying to retrofit attributes into existing or archived information at a later date.

Therefore, this stage within the content analysis identifies the different relationships that may exist between different object types, and between objects of the same type. There are five different kinds of relationships that should be considered.

- The relationship between content to content.
- The relationship between content and a business priority.
- The relationship between an individual user and content.
- The relationship between user types and content.
- The relationship between content and time.

Content to content relationships

This is the relationship that may exist between different content items. Content to content relationships can be created manually or automatically through queries and rules. They try to provide the user with a subjective opinion on what may also be of interest relative to the content that is being viewed.

In the example of the online florist, a relationship may be added that provides the facility to display the most popular bouquets of the selected colour within the selected price range (*see* Fig. 9.7).

This kind of requirement is typical of the type of related information that can be generated by a query. However, in order for the query to work, the attributes need to be there. The new requirement for the online florist would necessitate the additional attribute of number sold being added to the bouquet of flowers object, so that the query could determine which bouquets were the most popular for each colour scheme. It is often the case that the requirement to add new relationships often means that new attributes will need to be added to the content type to support the kind of query that will need to be run.

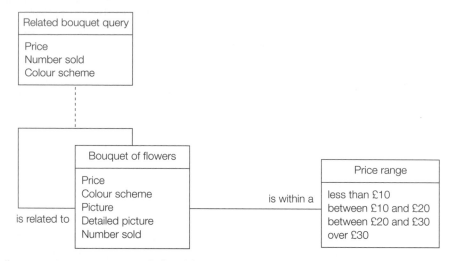

Figure 9.7   Adding a content to content relationship

Related information lists that are defined by queries are by far the better option as far as maintenance is concerned. They allow relationships to be dynamically created at the point when a page is displayed, which means that it is possible for an older content item to display links to information created after the content item was published without anyone updating the original file. This means that a related information list generated by a query has a far better chance of remaining relevant and up-to-date compared to a list that is manually created inside a content item.

Common examples of where related information is generated by queries is the news article that displays related stories, or the CD that displays related CDs. How specific a query is will depend on the content relationship. For example, consider the relationships between CDs and the relationship between one music artiste and another. A specific relationship may be defined between CDs by David Bowie and CDs by Lou Reed, due to the fact that the buying audience for one is likely to be a similar buying audience for the other. This kind of industry-related information would need to be defined as individual query rules, irrespective of whether the rules are defined within individual content items or across the system as a whole within a single classification scheme.

Content to business priority relationships

Another aspect to consider in defining these relationships is that of business requirements that may influence the way that additional information is made available in relation to a content item. A CD store may be 'featuring' a certain artiste, or might have a 'special offer' on certain goods. The words are in quotes because the meaning behind them is usually related to the way that a business would like to push a product for whatever reason. A product that is being pushed may still have a contextual relationship to the current content item. For example, it might be the same category of music, or even be by the same artiste. However, in order to meet the business requirement, the rules for deciding which items appear within the related information list and the order in which they appear might alter according to an external definition of a business priority.

In the example of the online florist, the business may need to shift certain bouquet arrangements for whatever reason. To achieve this, an extra attribute will need to be made available to set the marketing priority for the item (*see* Fig. 9.8). If the underlying data is defined and accessible, queries and views can be designed that will display adverts or links to bouquets that have a high marketing priority.

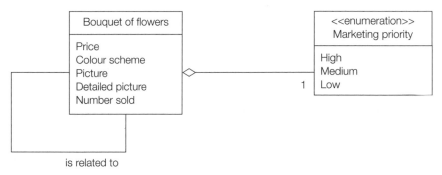

Figure 9.8   Establishing marketing priority

Content to user relationships

When a site manages to sell a product or service to a user, it immediately has the opportunity to not only capture information about that customer, but the ability to record the relationship between the consumer and the content item that has just been purchased.

Any site that has customers should generate a customer database. There will already be a short-term requirement to do this if products need to be sent to a customer address or an order needs to be confirmed via e-mail. However, it is the long-term capabilities of storing this information which are of interest within a content analysis. Many internet stores have seen the benefits that personalization can offer within an interface. One-click shopping, where repeat customers do not have to fill in their personal and credit card details a second time, can be very attractive to the shopper in a rush.

In the florist example, a customer could create many orders for bouquets of flowers over time. Customers pay with a single credit card, but they may change credit cards or have a choice of which to use.

In this case, therefore, the relationship rule between a customer, an order and a credit card (*see* Fig. 9.9) will need to be:

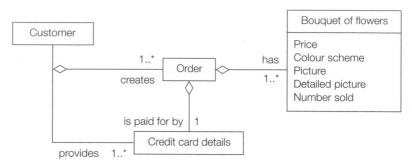

Figure 9.9   The relationship rule between a customer, an order and a credit card

- an order is paid for by one credit card;
- a customer can provide details for more than one credit card;
- a customer can create one or more orders.

Recording customers' credit card details allows a one-click buying experience, which may make purchasing goods online easier. However, it will be the relationship between the order, the customer and the products they buy that will provide the business with data that can be analyzed to understand customers' buying patterns. This relationship is defined by the fact that:

- a customer can create one or more orders;
- an order can contain one or more bouquets of flowers.

If this data is then stored, the system has access to the buying patterns of all the customers who come to the online florist. It will be possible to design views to adapt to that behaviour if this is a business requirement, and if the proposed views and personalized features are acceptable to the target audience.

Maintaining a list of the products that the user has previously bought can offer the opportunity to design additional personalization features that not only improve the users' experience of the site, but let the business understand buying trends and adopt more effective push marketing. For example, a business customer who is a frequent flyer with an airline might have a pattern of buying tickets to a limited number of airports. If an airline has a special offer to a destination the customer uses frequently, the customer can be targeted with this information at an appropriate time. In addition, e-mail can be used if the customer has agreed to additional marketing material being sent to them.

Within the online florist example, the business may recognize another opportunity to generate sales from ordering history information. If the card sent with a bouquet is typed – i.e. it is associated with a recognized event such as birthday or anniversary – then the business has additional information about:

- the person receiving the flowers;
- the reason they are receiving the flowers;
- the date associated with the event.

The business is now in a position to record information about dates important to the customer, and about who is associated with these dates (*see* Fig. 9.10). It would be possible to personalize the interface to remind the customer when one of these dates is coming up and make suggestions as to which bouquet may be appropriate.

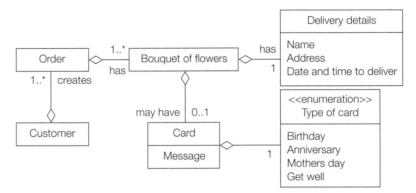

Figure 9.10   Capturing more information about user buying patterns

Of course there are problems with personalization; some users feel uncomfortable if they feel that a site is monitoring everything they do. There are also practical considerations, in that users have to identify themselves for personalization to be effective. User analysis and validation will be able to distinguish between the helpful service and the intrusive one.

Content to user type relationships

Even if a site does not overtly introduce a personalized interface, collecting data about the buying patterns of customers can provide an invaluable source of information to the business analyst, especially if combined with additional lifestyle information that the customer may be persuaded to supply. A useful way to capture this is by providing a free service or an incentive of some sort that requires users to provide additional details about themselves in order to qualify.

Such information might be gender, age range, social and economic factors, hobbies and so on, and can be used in a variety of ways. It can identify buying trends and identify the types of people who are coming to the site. This can then be used to compare against any target audience definitions that have been made. It can also be used to validate existing user group information and to analyze behaviour by gender, age or other significant factors. When patterns can be identified, this can then influence how a site can be adapted to take advantage of particular usage patterns.

For instance, a behaviour analysis might reveal that women are more likely to go for a cheaper delivery option when buying books from an online bookstore. The business analyst can take this information and define strategies that will influence this user type to buy more books. An idea might be to introduce a bundle option for books targeted at women that offers a cheaper delivery deal. The analyst will ensure that the total amount taken in profit will be the same, but the spin or cost saving perception will be different. If the customer does not see the value in delivery cost, this could be reduced and transferred on to the bundle of books.

These kinds of marketing tricks are commonplace, but need a level of consumer behaviour information to be developed effectively. Supermarkets have been adapting their techniques for years to react to customer behaviour analysis information. This is why they waft the smell of fresh bread over customers as soon as they enter the store, and then position the bread as far from the door as possible. They want to generate the impression of freshness as well as creating a demand for fresh bread. They want customers to wander the aisles and browse their product range before they fulfil their goal of getting the fresh bread. They figure that only the most single-minded of customers will be able to resist the temptation of passing something that they hadn't thought of buying and popping it into the trolley.

To support the ability to analyze user behaviour by group, the data model will have to define what the groups are, and what are the important attributes and values that define the members of each group. Initially the business analyst will sort these groups under target audience definitions, and the user analysis will provide profiles to establish the attributes necessary to identify them.

For instance, an important target audience definition for the online florist may be working females in their 30s. The attributes that will need to be collected to support this definition will be gender, age range and salary range.

The term 'working' is interesting; the user analyst would need to discover whether there are any significant economic factors that would influence the acceptance of this user type buying flowers on the web. For instance, would a working female in her 30s have access to the web and if so:

- how often would they use the web?
- under what conditions would they buy flowers through it?
- what sort of price would they pay for flowers?
- how much would they pay for delivery?
- how often would they use such a service?

If a site is able to capture these kinds of attributes (*see* Fig. 9.11), the information can be used to build up a picture of the types of people who are buying flowers from the site, and whether any relationships exist between the type of user and:

- the flowers they buy;
- the amount of money they spend;
- the way they search for the bouquets they are interested in;

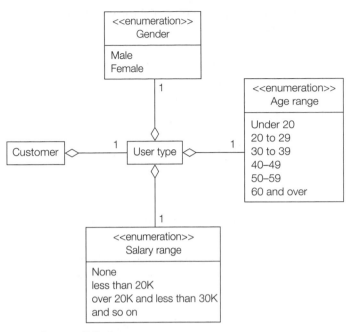

Figure 9.11   Capturing a range of user attributes

- the terms they use to search for this information;
- the criteria that they search on;
- the occasions when they send flowers.

By analyzing buying patterns and behaviour, a business may see the opportunity to use adaptive interfaces to push certain products at an appropriate time. They may also see the opportunity to bring in extra revenue through advertising. It will be the business model that will define the requirements and the user analysis that will determine the acceptability of any proposed design. Only then will the content analysis define the relationships and attributes that will need to be in place to enable any adaptive interfaces to be created.

Temporal relationships

Temporal relationships can apply to both content and visual attributes. They define an association between an object and time, whether that is time defined by actual time such as minutes on the clock, calendar dates, or years, or other measures such as seasons, special dates that move such as Easter, or other business-defined segmentations. One of the ways that an organization can look ahead and try to plan a site that will be adaptable for change is to identify important temporal patterns that affect the business and important temporal associations for its users.

Within a supermarket environment there are obvious temporal buying patterns for customers with regards to food, and there are also temporal constraints on the supermarket being able to offer certain foods at certain times of the year. For instance, soup sells better in the winter and strawberries will be in short supply; ice cream sells better in the summer, but it may be harder to buy mince pies. Due to the global buying patterns of supermarkets, these relationships are less to do with availability and more to do with the buying trends of their users, an obvious example being the sudden appearance of barbecue paraphernalia as soon as the weather starts to warm up.

We have covered how these relationships can be used to target content within the interface; another facet to this is being able to automatically change the visual attributes according to some temporal relationship. The florist shop may wish to look at the possibility of switching the palette between one that uses warm and seasonal colours for winter to one that uses lighter pastel shades for summer. If the visual designer is given the opportunity to design for change up front, then the ability automatically to swap visual attributes in the interface can be built into the system.

The problem with soaring maintenance costs has a lot to do with systems being built and content being provided that have no provision for change apart from someone having to manually edit files and add to the underlying function. Errors are introduced when those making a change are unfamiliar with the files they are editing and with all the associated relationships that might exist with other files on the system. A change made in one place can introduce errors in another, a classic example being the broken link. Therefore, wherever possible, a development team should be looking for opportunities to:

- centralize variables so that changes can be made in one place;
- identify and provide support for those objects that are likely to change over time;
- automatically keep track of the relationships between content items.

Validating content relationships with users

At this point within a content analysis there is no need to restrict the number of relationships that may apply. From the initial user analysis stage, there should be an indication as to the kinds of tasks that users would like to perform. However, during the initial interviews with users, it will have been difficult to anticipate some of the possibilities and scenarios for achieving tasks that may start to be identified during a content analysis. Because of this, user analysis and validation needs to be an ongoing exercise throughout the web development process, and is especially important during these early analysis stages where decisions are being made that will be fundamental in defining how the website will eventually work, and what information will be published to it.

A task synthesis created from the ideas of content experts can be used to walk through suggested task scenarios with representatives of the target audience to establish whether certain information would be useful when viewing a content item or type – for example, when viewing details of a CD within an online CD store whether it would be useful to see:

- other chart-topping CDs from the same year;
- information about the year's biggest-selling singles and the albums in which they feature;
- products related to the artist, such as T-shirts or videos.

A user validation exercise will need to take place in order to gauge the usefulness of this extra information, and the likely acceptability of any proposed design that incorporates these features.

Content classification

The main reasons to provide a classification system are to:

- help build site hierarchies;
- help create dynamically-built contextual relationships through queries;
- support a more advanced site-search function than a simple full text search.

A further benefit of defining a classification system is to constrain the way that content providers describe the information they are creating. This is so that an automated system, such as a search function or a run time query, can rely on the existence of certain attributes being defined within the data, and on finding matches on known values.

Using classified keywords to constrain values

When a system allows content providers the freedom to provide their own values in key fields, there will always be a variation in the words that are used, and a possible variation in the way those words are spelt. To illustrate the point, consider a simple example of a person's title and how an interface could be designed to capture this information (*see* Fig. 9.12).

The first example is a typical entry field that will allow any value to be entered. The content provider has the complete freedom to enter whatever they wish, but they also have no help. This kind of field is not only prone to errors, but can slow down the task of entering data. When the content provider has to stop to think about which value to enter, how to spell it and whether the value that they wish to use is allowed or appropriate, they will need to start concentrat-

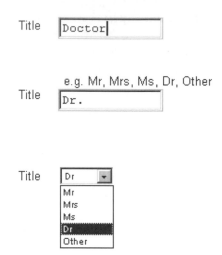

Figure 9.12 Different ways to enter the same information

ing on how the information should be represented rather than on the more important task of creating the information content.

The second example is better because it provides some assistance. However, still relying on a free-form entry field allows typing mistakes, variations and errors. Validating the field is still a viable option, but it can be validated only after the content provider has entered the value. Forcing a content provider to go back and correct errors is time-consuming and can break concentration; far better to provide prompted entries wherever possible and applicable, as in the third example. Prompted entries display all the allowable values, and by selecting a value from the list the content provider does not have to think about how a term should be represented or how it is spelt. There will also be no room for typing mistakes. The biggest problem is when the list is incomplete and does not contain the value that the content provider wants to use. The ability to add values to a classification system is covered later.

Once a classification system is in place that has a set of defined keywords used throughout the content, it will be far easier to generate queries that can run against that content. For instance, a requirement to identify all customers who are doctors can prompt a search on 'Dr' without all the possible alternatives that may have been thought up by content editors.

Providing better query support through classification hierarchies

Most of these points are well known with interface design and common practice for those designing database-driven systems. However, one of the additional advantages of supporting a central classification system, rather than just sharing common fields that have a predefined set of values, is the ability to bring in a level of hierarchy.

Consider the example of a website that sells theatre tickets for performances in the UK. The user analysis may have discovered that the critical information that needs to be in place for users to select a performance covers:

- the details, such as the name of the play, the type of play, when it is on, and who is in it;
- the location of the theatre.

Common user scenarios will be:

- checking local theatres on a regular basis for any plays of interest;
- checking the theatres in other areas, if users will be visiting those areas;
- checking the London theatres to see if there is anything worth going to, irrespective of whether the user will need to travel.

From this information it would be possible to set up two classification schemes, (*see* Figs. 9.13/9.14) one to contain types of plays and one to contain theatre locations. Consider the design of a simple classification system to contain the types of performances that the site can sell tickets for. Part of it may support the following hierarchy.

This classification hierarchy allows *Othello* to be found by five different queries:

Performance	● find a performance
Play	● find a play
Classical	● find a classical play
Shakespeare	● find a Shakespearean play
Othello	● find the play *Othello*.

Figure 9.13 Tracking down *Othello*

UK
England
Midlands
West Midlands
Coventry
Belgrade Theatre

If the location of the theatre is now captured within another hierarchy, theatres can be found in more than one way. The Belgrade Theatre will be returned in a query if a user specifies the location as Coventry, West Midlands, and England or just doesn't set it at all.

Figure 9.14 Finding a theatre location

Having these kinds of systems in place makes the job of the content provider much easier. In the above example, the person putting performances into the system would select which theatre they were putting details in for. The act of selecting the theatre name will automatically provide the additional support for other possible ways in which the user may try to find the theatre.

Having this information in one place allows the keywords and the hierarchy to be controlled and managed. This sort of classification support within a content management system should be the kind of environment that the web development teams are aiming to create.

Obviously the difficult part to having a hierarchical classification system is its design. How best to design classification systems cannot be covered here; however, the best goal to aim for is defining a system that is flexible and easy to change. No classification system is ever likely to be complete and correct, because like a language it will change and evolve over time. In fact it will probably take a few months of content creation for it to settle into something like a stable vocabulary. However, the content analysis can help with the initial design by defining which terms should be classified, useful category names that users understand, and the relationships that need to be captured within the classification system provided.

Classifying the main objects within the system

During the user analysis, the primary tasks should have been firmly defined and any terminology that the user associates with these tasks clearly identified as keywords.

The first classification that is usually created is that of the main objects within the system, and the keywords that users associate with these objects. For instance, CD, tape and video are all keywords for objects within the online music store. The name of the object or the keyword that identifies the type of object needs to be constrained, so that a content provider does not have the ability to freely enter variations on the type name or make any mistakes typing it in.

Supporting the classification of the object types as keywords, understandable and recognizable by users, will enable the sort of queries that start:

- find me all the CDs by…;
- find a video about…;
- find a tape or a CD released before…

A content-heavy site should be aiming to build a search interface around a predefined classification system in order for the search function to be helpful, efficient and usable. The results of such a search query will be complete and correct only if all the site content has been classified in a complete and correct way which means reducing the chance of classification errors or omissions. This can be achieved by:

- requiring that certain attributes must be set by content providers;
- constraining their ability to set these attributes by providing only those options that appear within the classification system;
- having a process that reviews content classification before content is published to a site.

Identifying category names

During the user analysis, it is likely that inadvertently the user provided an indication of the classification hierarchy that they associate with the main objects within the system. For instance, a Bowie CD is a 70s Rock and Pop CD, which is a CD, which is a product the user can buy.

Product
    CD
        Rock and Pop
           70s
              Ziggy Stardust

Figure 9.15 Classification by type

Product
    User type
        New releases
           Most popular

Figure 9.16 Classification by user type

Many standard classifications are already likely to have been defined by the industry or business. Any high street store will have needed some method of sorting the products in order for users to find them. However, a high street store can realistically offer customers only one way to find products. They define a system and then physically put the goods in the right space allocated to that category. On the web it is possible to have many different ways of categorizing information, and to pass these different access mechanisms on to the user (*see* Fig. 9.15). This is where the power of classification comes into its own, and why it is essential to try to find the right mix of attributes that will help make the content of the site more accessible.

The first classification example of the products within an online music store is the traditional categorization by type. This is the method that nearly all CD shops use, and is easily recognizable and understandable by users. This does not mean that it is the only way to find CDs. In some circumstances, there may be a better way for a user to browse a CD catalogue.

An interesting angle may be to offer a classification based on 'who is buying what', or 'who is likely to buy the product' (*see* Fig. 9.16). This could be enormously helpful for anyone who needs to buy a present for someone.

Identifying the different strategies users employ to find information

How the user wishes to find information is the next clue as to what other classification attributes are needed. A scenario that may come out of a user analysis stage is the task of buying a gift for someone and providing details of their user preferences. For example a customer may wish to buy a CD for someone in their 30s who likes David Bowie. Providing an intelligent service for this kind of request requires that the necessary classification fields have been defined and that the underlying content has the appropriate level of information. In this example, a useful classification might be audience, i.e. the user type that is most likely to buy the product, and also a music category or even a hierarchy of music categories that defines 70s rock music as part of an overall category of rock music. There might even be a case for defining a classification for similar artistes where it would be possible to capture the subjective relationship between David Bowie and Lou Reed. With all these fields defined for each CD, it would be possible to generate a reasonable response to such a query that would search for matches based on audience, music category and similar artistes in order to return a list of CDs that might be appropriate as a gift.

It will be through this level of identification of the necessary classification fields and the task of expertly and thoroughly classifying the underlying content against them that will:

- provide the ability to design a search interface that helps users build queries based on the underlying content available on the site;
- help build related information lists that contain links to other sources of information relevant to that being displayed.

The support for underlying subjective relationships provides the user with a value-added service that may differentiate one online store or service from another.

Content measurements

There are a number of measurements that may be applicable for an organization to test the success of the website and the success of any content management system that has been provided. Measurements will give an indication if things are not right but they will not provide the answers to why there might be a problem. This is why any requirement to provide a series of ongoing measurements must also define what happens after the measurements have been taken. Otherwise, the exercise will be a waste of time.

To ensure that a site will constantly improve, user validation and further user analysis techniques must be adopted. Design recommendations that come out of these exercises to improve the usability of the site or content management system should be incorporated at an appropriate time within the development cycle.

Content usage

One of the measurements that is most useful to the site information architect, is the number of times a user visits a piece of content on the site. This can highlight where users find the most interesting information, or highlight areas of information redundancy. If it can be proved that users are not interested in whole sections of content, the information architect has a chance to simplify the site structure and remove the areas of information that are cluttering it up.

However, there might be other reasons why users are not visiting these pages. It might indicate:

- problems with the site structure;
- a badly designed primary navigation mechanism;
- a lack of contextual navigation links;
- a lack of classification data that is stopping users from finding the information;
- inappropriate positioning of the information in relation to the user's task.

Without further investigation, the answer will be unclear.

When a site finds itself in this position, a content analysis has to be undertaken to understand what the purpose of the information is, and what user goal it is supporting. During this exercise it might be discovered that the pages do not support any useful user task and there seems to be no clear purpose in offering the information to users of the site. This is the architect's chance to remove the information and to clean up the site.

However, in the event that the information does serve some purpose and does support a user task, a user validation exercise should be designed to test whether users can achieve the task that this information is supposed to support. This exercise may reveal that users have problems with the interface, and perhaps problems finding the information they need in order to complete the task. At this point, a user analysis should be conducted to identify where the mismatch is between the task model on the site, and the user model of how that task should work. This should lead to a new task-flow design that will be easier to understand and easier to use. It should also solve the problem of users being able to access the original set of information that highlighted the task-flow problem.

If a usability test shows that users have no problems completing the task and can easily find the information needed to do this, there is some indication that the task the information supports is not something the audience of the site wants to do. Again, the analyst will need to go back and perform a user analysis to clarify the user goals, and specifically the tasks that the site should be supporting, in order to understand whether the task in question actually supports anything that the user wishes to do. At this point, it might be found that some design assumptions have been made, and functions have appeared that do not map to any goal that the user has in visiting the site. This will be another opportunity to clear the clutter from the user interface and remove anything from the site that does not support the defined business or user goals.

Site exits

It is possible that there is a problem with the interface at the point where a user exits the site. If the place where they leave is in the middle of a critical task such as a form needed to complete an online order, it will be crucial to take a close look at the design of the task flow and supporting interface. A user validation should be carried out to make sure that users are not being put off completing the task by something within the task-flow or interface design.

If users are leaving a site at a page of supporting information, questions that must be asked within a user analysis are:

- is the information understandable?
- does it provide what users are looking for in relation to the task or goal they are trying to attain?

The user analysis should provide the terminology that the user is familiar with, which will help test whether the interface is understandable. The critical design features defined within the user analysis also provide invaluable pointers to what the content of supporting information needs to be to complete a task. This can again be used to test whether the interface is supporting these critical design features. Without involving users specifically, if this information is available a heuristic evaluation can take place with the current design to see whether it matches the recommendations of the user analysis work.

A content analysis will also be able to determine if the page is a dead-end and does not offer the user any routes to other parts of the site. There may also be a relationship to the query analysis. If the exit point is after a user performed a search query that produced little or no useful matches, there is a strong chance that the user does not think the site supports the information they are looking for. At this point the information architect will need to look at the content queries and decide if there is any problem with the types of content offered on the site.

Content queries and content coverage

When a classification system is set up, there is an expectation that it will provide better support for users when they are trying to find information on a site. With the identification of keywords that the user is familiar with, and allowing for synonyms and common spelling mistakes, a correctly classified piece of information should be easily found with a site search facility. This is part of the justification for investing in a central classification mechanism. To test this assumption, it will be necessary to capture the search queries that users are entering on to the site, and to test whether the content supports the subject coverage that the user is expecting to find.

Analyzing user search queries will test three things:

- whether the terminology within the classification system matches the user's which has been identified during the user analysis stage. This will include missing keywords, missing synonyms and spelling mistakes;
- whether the content has been classified correctly. This will highlight the situation where the classification system is correct but the process to ensure that content is correctly classified is error prone;
- whether the content on the site matches the expectation of the user. This will highlight a mismatch between the user's goals and the information model adopted by the site.

The first case will be expected with any new classification system. User queries can strengthen the vocabulary to support a wider language for more users. The classification vocabulary will be able to grow and evolve over time and with use. This is a healthy feedback mechanism that can be used to good effect to improve the central classification system.

The second case is a little more serious as it highlights a problem within the organizational workflows that have enabled information to appear on the site, without being properly classified. There is little point in having a classification system if it is not applied correctly across the whole content of the site. In this situation, an information architect needs to be involved very closely in the review cycle for new content being published to ensure that the defined classifications are applied consistently.

The last case is very serious as it could mean that the design of the site and the content that appears on it does not correspond to the user's model of what the site should be providing. This is likely to be the case when no user analysis work has been carried out, and the design has been based on assumptions about what users want to be able to see and do.

One of the most important areas of work within a user analysis is the identification of critical pieces of information that need to be in place for users to achieve their goals. If the user is trying to find this information by using or looking for vocabulary they are familiar with, and they are unable to proceed because they cannot find it, they will not be able to complete their tasks. This will mean that the user will have no choice but to give up and go elsewhere.

Whenever a user leaves a site because they were unable to complete a valid task, the site design has failed. The definition of an unusable site is one that is not designed around what the user wants to do, and prevents the user from completing valid user tasks. When a site is in this position, a complete user analysis must be undertaken to go back to the basics of defining what the user goals are and what are the primary tasks the site needs to support in order for these goals to be achieved.

Summary

A content analysis takes the requirements from the business and the user analyzes and defines the content models that will need to be in place in order to meet these requirements. Because a content analysis goes into far more detail about the definition of rules that will need to be in place, this stage requires constant rechecking with those involved with the interfaces to ensure that any design assumptions that are being made are valid and correct.

The main stages involved in the content analysis are:

- defining the main content types and the attributes that define them;
- defining the rules and main relationships that exist between these content types;
- defining the names of the properties that will be used for any interface that allows the creation of these types;
- defining the requirements for contextual relationships between types;
- specifying the control attributes that must be in place to capture additional relationships;
- defining the requirements for content classification and categorization.

The next stage within a content analysis is the definition of the workflows that are needed within the organization. These definitions will create requirements for additional control variables to be added to the content types, and this is covered in detail in the next chapter.

10 Defining workflows

To set up a controlled environment that allows information to be published to a website, an organization will need to invest in the definition and implementation of workflows. A workflow is a definition of the stages that a content item goes through and the rules associated with the work that needs to be done at each stage.

To support a web-publishing environment, workflows will need to be defined that move content from creation through to publication and cover the additional stages needed for content maintenance.

The point of defining workflows and providing a system to support a defined process is to bring a level of control to the way that an organization handles information, by monitoring the status of that information and the progress of those involved in moving the information from one stage to another. The goals will be to:

- improve the efficiency of the publication process;
- to improve the quality of the information that is provided.

To improve the publication process, it will be necessary to create workflows that reflect the best processes within the organization and cut out any redundant steps or unnecessary processes. Workflows need to identify and involve the right people with the appropriate skills and try to mimic the most natural way that information gets moved around an organization. To be in a position to set up an environment that supports the publication of content to a website, it is necessary to define workflows that cover the way content is proposed, created, reviewed, published, updated, archived and finally removed from the site.

Automating workflows as part of a content management system can bring additional efficiency benefits by automatically notifying those within the organization when actions are required to move the content from one stage within the publication cycle to another. A further benefit is the ability to keep a record of the publication history and who within the organization has been responsible for the content item at each of the different publication stages.

To realize the goal of improving both the site and the content quality, it will be necessary to ensure that proper review and change procedures are in place. Because a workflow explicitly defines stages and defines what needs to be achieved at each stage, an organization will need to identify individuals to do certain jobs. The job of assigning an individual to a task and making that person responsible and accountable for completing a task can have the positive effect of improving a process, even without any automated system to back it up.

Analyzing the existing environment

Understanding the organization

The first stage in understanding the processes that are needed to set up the required workflows for a publishing environment is to identify how an organization manages the same kind of information within the current business environment. This can be done by applying user analysis techniques to determine how individuals within the organization create, manage and release information, and who within the organization is responsible for what.

It may be found that different processes are defined for different types of content, or the decision to follow one process over another depends on certain attributes within these content types. A content analysis will need to identify what the underlying rules are that make one content item follow one workflow and a different content item follow another.

There is a tendency to try to simplify a process in order to define a simple and clean workflow. For instance, a clean model for publishing news articles to a website may be that all news articles are created by journalists and are reviewed by a news editor before they get published (*see* Fig. 10.1).

When new workflows and processes are being defined, it can be seen as an opportunity by the organization to simplify the ways things are done, and to set about defining a new way for people within the organization to work. These thoughts and ideas will need to be captured and tested with individuals within the organization, but the job of the analyst at this stage is to capture the way that a job is actually done, rather than how an organization would like it to be done in the future.

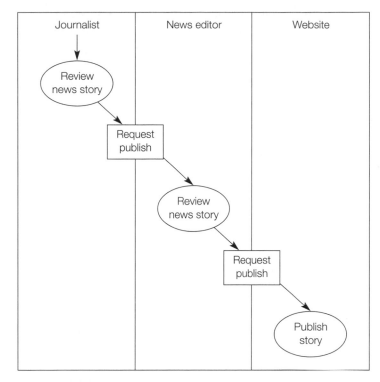

Figure 10.1   A simple model for publishing news articles

The simple workflow in Fig. 10.1 is likely to be an example of how a business might like the process to work, rather than reflecting how news stories really wend their way through the system. It might be possible for an organization to accommodate this workflow, but it may not match the natural or realistic way that people within the organization work and how they really create their articles and get them published to a site.

Therefore the first stage is to:

● understand the current way that people work within the organization;

● understand the life cycles and workflow for each type of content;

● understand the rules that define which workflows are used;

● understand the skills that are needed within each workflow stage.

Only then will it be possible to look at new ways of doing things, because only then will it be clear what is involved and what the requirements and skills are of the people who will be doing the work.

The part of the business that creates printed marketing or product-related material should already have well-defined publishing processes and the skills available to ensure all the information being published is to the required standard. However, it is unusual for this group to wholly own and manage the publication processes for all the content that appears on a company website.

For many of the reasons already covered, content for a site tends to be generated by individuals from every part of the business, and review procedures do not tend to be handled centrally. The type of content that is being created is normally owned by the part of the business responsible for that content type and many websites are visibly fragmented and display inconsistencies because of it. Therefore those responsible for bringing control to an existing website publishing environment, or setting up processes for a new site, will need to understand carefully how the business organizes and publishes its data. The goal should be to make it easy for everyone involved in the process, or for those who should be involved in the process, to follow any required workflows that are created.

Understanding the formal workflow stages

As part of producing a process diagram for the various types of content that will be published to the site, the different workflow stages will need to be identified. Some organizations will require that a proposal is created before a piece of work is undertaken or commissioned. This can be especially useful in those organizations where individuals propose work but do not actually do it themselves. The person responsible for accepting or rejecting proposals can then take the role of a resource manager and assign people to tasks as part of the proposal acceptance stage (*see* Fig. 10.2).

The next major stage to consider is how content is reviewed before it appears on the site, and how many, if any, review procedures are in place. Reviews are usually carried out against a set of review criteria, which will need to be identified and associated with each review process (*see* Fig. 10.3).

Once content is published, the next major consideration is how an organization wishes to manage any changes that need to be made against that content (*see*

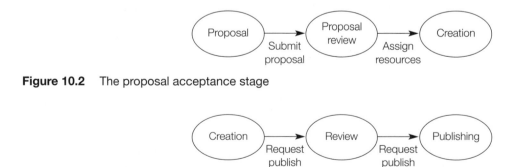

Figure 10.2   The proposal acceptance stage

Figure 10.3   Reviewing content before publication

Fig. 10.4). A workflow stage can be incorporated that sees that changes are proposed so they can be scheduled and assigned to people to fix. This can be a very useful approach for the types of sites with content that will incur many changes and has a more dynamic nature. It might be overkill for sites that rarely change.

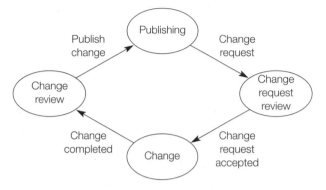

Figure 10.4 Changing content

Within a system that supports version control, this issue is not as great as where content is held outside of a database or content management system. The worst sort of chaos is when different people are trying to change the same piece of information – it's a lottery as to which change will be overwritten and which will make it on to the site.

The last and final stage to consider is how content is moved off the site (*see* Fig. 10.5). An organization may wish to support the archiving of published content, where the information is still available to the user through a search facility, but is removed from the primary and contextual navigation schemes on the site. There will almost always be a requirement to provide a facility that removes content from the site completely and make it unavailable to users.

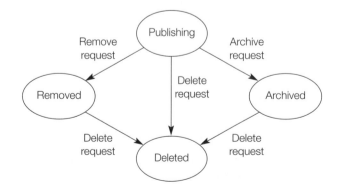

Figure 10.5 Moving content off the site

The removed stage is different to the deleted stage, as it requests the removal of the item only from the site and not from the underlying content management system or database. A removed or unpublished stage allows the item to be republished if necessary. A deleted stage provides the facility for content to be marked for deletion. How an organization handles deletion will be up to the database administrator. Content may be physically deleted, or just moved out of any content management system that is in place. Either way, once an item is deleted, it cannot return to the site.

Understanding roles and responsibilities

Within an organization is it essential to capture who is responsible for what. For instance, a news editor is responsible for reviewing all news articles, a features editor is responsible for reviewing all feature stories, and the overall editor needs to see everything before it gets published.

What the analyst needs to capture is:

- the definition of the role;
- the circumstances whereby the person within the role can start the job;
- what information is needed to do the job;
- what actions are available to the person doing the job;
- what happens if the task is completed successfully;
- what happens if the job fails.

In the case of the news editor, the analyst may capture the following.

- The role of the news editor is to review all the news articles that are due to be published.
- The news editor can start to review a news article when it has been created, completed and passed on by a journalist.
- The news editor reviews the article for writing style, factual accuracy and an appropriate level of references to previous stories.
- A news editor has a number of actions during the review cycle that can be applied to a news story (*see* Fig. 10.6).
  - It can be passed back to the journalist with comments on what needs correcting or adding.
  - It can be passed to the archive expert who can provide more information on related stories.
  - It can be passed to the lawyer to make sure that the story will not cause any legal problems.

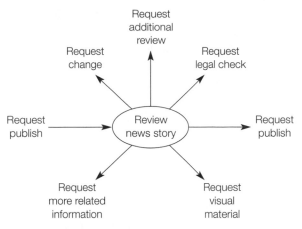

Figure 10.6   Actions available to the news editor

- It can be passed to another journalist for review and comments on factual accuracy and style.
- It can be passed to the artistic editor with a request for supporting visual material.
- If the news story passes the review it gets passed to the editor with a recommendation of where within the publication it should appear.
- If the story does not pass the review criteria, the news editor can request that it be deleted or put on hold.

The actions available to the news editor within this workflow stage are captured in Fig. 10.6.

Understanding informal information flows

Whenever a task analysis is undertaken, it is just as important to understand the informal workflows as much as the formal ones. For instance, individuals within an organization may put their ideas to a manager to get approval first before they start writing an article or document. They might also exchange their ideas with others in the group to get their thoughts and feedback. These are examples of informal processes.

An informal process is something that happens naturally within an organization to help move a process along. What happens, who is involved or what is delivered is not defined by any specific rules. Usually there will be some information flow between individuals about a content item, which enables someone to complete their job.

It is useful to understand informal processes because an automated system may be able to assist with these information flows and help capture any thoughts and feedback associated with different documents within the system. Any additional information could then be permanently kept with the document and provide history information for anyone interested in seeing it. Background information is always useful to keep, especially when ownership of a content item changes, or when content maintenance is required.

Defining new workflows for content management

Defining the ideal workflow rules

Introducing a content management-style system to handle the publishing workflows for a website provides the opportunity for an organization to define far more complex rules about how documents are handled within it.

This is due to a number of reasons.

- The content is in digital format and held in a central place where it can be easily accessed when required.

- Individuals can be notified automatically when they have to do something with a content item.

- Informal information flows and group working can be supported by allowing individuals to pass round documents for comments and additional information.

- Rules about who does what and when can be stored and applied to documents automatically.

- Different rules can apply to different documents based on any combination of attribute values.

- Access control can prevent more than one person changing a document; access control rules can change according to the status of the document.

- Version control can keep a history of changes and a history of who has made them.

- Control variables can record any additional information applicable to the document and added by those involved in the publishing workflows.

So far, the only kinds of associations for workflows that have been mentioned have depended on the type of document being handled; for instance, a new article follows one workflow, a feature article follows another. However, in an automated system it is possible to set up far more complex rules that enable documents to be routed through the organization, depending on a range of different values or settings. The attributes need to be identified that cause documents to be routed differently so that when any information templates are created, these control variables can be added and the attributes can be set appropriately.

Defining the control attributes that will capture the workflow rules

Once individuals and their respective roles within the organization have been identified, a process diagram should be created and any workflow control attributes
identified that will make sure the content item is routed down the correct workflow path. There is a very clear distinction that needs to be made between a
classification system and workflow control attributes. Classification information
will primarily be used and surfaced to the user, either through the creation of a
main navigational path, contextual relationships or search functions on the site,
and through archive material. Workflow control attributes are those settings that
are not seen by the user, but are used to route content through a publication model
within an organization. They should match the inner workings of the company,
something a site should never want to surface to their customers.

An example that can be used to demonstrate the difference is where a news
article is written about a particular country. The news article classification hierarchy might have top-level category labels of headlines, home affairs, foreign affairs
and feature articles. The foreign affairs category might then have each continent
listed, and within that, each country, so that the content provider can provide a
more detailed geographical classification for the news story. It is unlikely that the
main navigation scheme used within the website interface will surface the additional classification information, but the extra detail can provide a more granular
indexing capability for users to search the current stories or news archives.

In contrast, the group that reviews foreign affairs news articles may include
experts on particular countries. Someone might always review articles on China
and Japan, someone else might cover Germany and France, and another person
might get everywhere else.

The process diagram that is created will need to capture these rules, and
clearly show how the document will be routed as a result of these settings.

Figure 10.7 shows that a news article moves to an expert China/Japan review
if the news category attribute is set to 'foreign affairs' and the workflow country
attribute is set to 'China/Japan'. The action that moves the article into this stage
is a 'request publish' action by the person creating the article.

This country split is entirely organizational, and has no meaning to anyone
outside that organization; it may easily change when someone else comes into
the group.

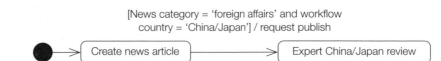

Figure 10.7   Routing to different workflows based on control variables

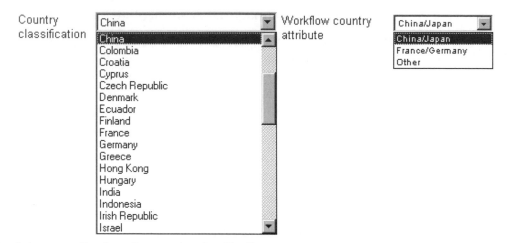

Figure 10.8   Auto-generation from the country classification

The field that contains this data could be auto-generated from the country classification (*see* Fig. 10.8) or it could be a mandatory field that the content provider has to supply. Either way, this information has no purpose other than to route the content item to the role within the organization that will review it, and will never be surfaced to the end user. It is, therefore, very important to distinguish between those attributes destined for the website and those that are used purely to move a content item from one place to another.

Assigning individuals to roles

Content needs to have identified owners within an organization so that a point of contact is available for purposes such as feed-back if the content fails a quality review, or if any clarification is needed should change be required. Content ownership on the web can be a sticky affair. This kind of point-of-contact role really involves the person responsible within the organization for the content, and not necessarily the author or the owner of a piece of work. Therefore the role of content owner is a useful one to have associated with a content item. However, there are many roles that will be created as a result of defining workflows for information destined to be published to a site.

The purpose of defining a role, instead of just identifying individuals who do a certain job, is that support can be provided automatically to back up and cover the job associated with the role. When automated or manual workflows are introduced to an organization that require that certain processes are followed, there is a natural fear that these will slow everything down. This fear can be justified, if backup procedures and controls are not put in place to ensure that documents are not waiting indefinitely on individuals within the process chain. Therefore any job that needs to be completed within a workflow should:

- have a defined amount of time by which the job should be completed;
- be achievable by more than one person within the organization.

This does not mean that a preferred person cannot be identified to do the job. But in the event of that person being on holiday or sick or just busy doing something else, the workflow process is not held up and people are not waiting on that one individual to move the document on to the next stage.

Therefore for each stage of the workflow there needs to be identified:

- primary contacts;
- secondary contacts;
- an allocated time for the job to be done before it is passed on to someone else;
- an allocated time for the job to be done before intervention by the process owner.

Defining the access rules

It is possible to define access rules at a number of different levels. The three main questions to ask for each document type and each property within that document type are:

- who has access?
- what is the level of access?
- when is this access applicable?

For instance, an organization may allow everyone in it to read all the information within a content management system, irrespective of the state the information is in. However, it would be silly to give anyone write access to content that is currently being published especially when there is a controlled change management process in place. It is all well and good having carefully defined workflows that notify individuals when they need to do certain jobs, but if the access controls have not been set up to support that process then there is nothing to stop uncontrolled information appearing on the site.

When defining who has access to certain documents within an organization, it is useful to set up different user groups to hold individuals' names and user identities. These groups can be given levels of access as required, so that a database administrator is not forever maintaining names in multiple access lists whenever someone joins the company, leaves it or changes jobs.

The roles identified during the roles and responsibilities exercise will also become user groups that the access rules can be associated with. When a role has been defined as being responsible for a job within a workflow, this will mean that access to the actions and variables associated with that job have to be restricted to that role. Obvious roles include the content owner, who will always have write access during a content creation stage. As a role can be held by more than one person, there will still be a reliance on a version control system being in place that records changes being made by individuals, and prevents more than one person making changes at any one time.

There will also be a need for a super user or process owner user group – in other words, people within the organization who have the power to intervene whenever documents are stuck within a workflow. These individuals will need to be able to edit or select any action that enables documents to move on to the next stage.

Measuring the workflow process

When automated workflows are introduced to an organization, they are unlikely to run smoothly from day one. Bottlenecks may occur, the workload may be unevenly distributed, and the time it takes for content to reach different stages within the workflow may be unacceptable. Without any measurements, it will be difficult to substantiate any real complaints that people may have, and it will be difficult to identify why certain problems may be happening.

Workflow measurements can test a number of things.

- The number of items that are being created by individuals.
- The time it takes for a content item to be created.
- The number of items being reviewed by individuals.
- The time it takes for a content item to go through a review procedure.
- The time it takes a content item to be published to the site.
- The number of changes that are being made to a content item.
- The time it takes for a change to be completed and moved on to the site.
- The number of times an intervention has been needed to move a content item on to the next stage.

Whenever there seems to be a problem with how long a particular process is taking, there are three things that need to be looked at.

- The amount of time that individuals believe they have to do the job.
- The workload for individuals.
- Whether the number of different stages within the workflow or the number of different people involved within the workflow is excessive and can be reduced without noticeably affecting the quality of the information.

The first problem can be fixed by simply reducing the time allowed for the job to be completed. If this is not enough, additional resources will need to be added to the role, so that it will be likely that at least one individual who has the right level of access and the skill to complete the task can do so in the allotted time. The second problem is a resourcing issue, and will need a resource manager to change the allocation of roles and responsibilities within the organization to be more evenly distributed. The last problem is with the workflow design. There is a tendency in some organizations for everyone and his dog to be involved with review procedures. This is a control issue, where managers feel they need to sign off everything before it appears on the site. In fact, there should be very few people involved in the review procedure. The more people involved, the slower the process will be, and the amount of errors found does not automatically grow in relation to the number of people looking for them.

Summary

To bring a level of control to the way that information is published to a website, an organization will need to define and implement a set of workflows. A successful roll-out of automated workflows within an organization will necessitate that the design of these workflows and the interfaces that enable them to operate must be easily understood and easily used. To achieve this, an organization will need to invest in an amount of user analysis work to understand how the business works today and how users work within this environment. With this information a content analysis will be able to document the different workflows required by identifying:

- the different stages a document goes through;
- any criteria that determines whether a document can move to the next stage;
- the actions available to move a document to the next stage;
- the roles and responsibilities associated with each stage;
- the potential for a super user role for moving documents through the system if a bottleneck occurs;
- the workflow control variables that cause a document to route to different stages;
- the access rules for each document, who has access, the type of access, and when the access is applicable.

All this information will combine to create quite a detailed picture of how the organization operates, and how information is passed between different roles in order for it to be created, published and maintained.

3

Analyzing the requirements of the different contributors to the site

The third section looks at the individual requrements of those people within an organization who will need to interact with a system set up to deliver a website. It provides an overview of the advantages of a content management approach and then, in detail, covers the way that an environment could be provided that makes it easier to deliver a site that contains quality content and is both manageable and maintainable.

chapter

11 Website teams overview

One of the most difficult things to manage in any development organization is the way that a team works together and the way that different opinions and views within a development team are resolved. During the analysis and design phase, there are potentially many ideas on how things ought to be done. When these viewpoints conflict, which is quite common, this can lead to problems that affect how well the web development project will run and ultimately how well the website will be designed and implemented.

For this reason it is very useful to have clearly defined roles and responsibilities laid down up front in relation to how a site will be designed, developed, managed and maintained. That way, everyone will be clear as to what their role is within the team and who is responsible for making which decisions. A good development team will work together to generate ideas and to solve problems. However, a successful team will recognize the need for one person to be in charge of the area they are skilled in and responsible for, and accept that this person will be the final arbiter on any decision within that skill area that needs to be made.

Defining the required roles will also identify the skills needed by those people within the organization who will be performing the role. Identifying the skill and the tasks that need to be done by the roles within the development team is the same as building the user profiles for the target audience of any content management system that is to be provided. The tasks identified for each role will need to be mapped to the functionality that a content management system should support. The critical design features for those tasks will provide input as to what information needs to be available, and what actions the system should support for the individuals within the roles to complete their tasks.

There are at least seven different roles needed within a website development team. For each role it is useful to define:

- what the role is primarily responsible for;
- the skill that is needed by the role;
- the primary tasks that the role needs to perform;
- any deliverables that the role creates.

All the tasks that must be completed by all the roles within a web development environment will be considered in order to define the requirements for any content management system that is put in place.

It will be the combination of all the various skills within the development team that will help to successfully create a website – one used by and useful to its target audience, but one that can also be maintained, managed, redefined and redesigned if necessary without incurring excessive development and maintenance costs.

Team roles

Internet and business analyst

The internet and business analyst role involves the one person or group of people who define the purpose of the site and the primary goals, targets and objectives that must be achieved to satisfy the business investment. These goals should support any business models that justify the return on investment for developing a site, and ideally should define at the highest level the kinds of user tasks the site should support.

Primary responsibility	The business success of the site, be it revenue from online orders, advertising revenue, user subscriptions or promotional marketing
Primary knowledge	Expert knowledge of the business opportunities on the internet or intranet
Primary tasks	To define the business criteria To measure the business success
Deliverables	The set of business requirements created from a business analysis, in particular:

- any business targets that need to be met;
- any organizational constraints such as predefined delivery options, terms and conditions or the list of credit card types that are accepted.

Human factors engineer

The human factors role involves the one person or team who work with the target audience definitions and set down the user profiles for the website. By carrying out user analysis studies such as requirements gathering, task analysis, user scenarios and conceptual interface designs, the human factors engineer defines the critical design and usability features that the site will need to support for it to be an enjoyable experience for the website user.

Primary responsibility	The usability of the site and in particular the task flow design
Primary knowledge	User analysis and user validation techniques
Primary tasks	To define user goals, tasks and task flows
	To define critical design features
	To define user profiles from the audience definitions
	To create user scenarios
	To define usability review criteria
	To measure site usability
Deliverables	The set of usability requirements created from a user analysis, in particular:

- task goals for the site;
- review criteria for content;
- task flow definitions and critical design features;
- any user constraints such as likelihood of paying for expensive delivery options, the need to support certain types of credit cards, and acceptable minimum font sizes for reading.

Information architect

The information architect role identifies the one person or team who define the information architecture or classification and categorization of the information presented through the site. There may exist some formalized information system that is used to categorize documents created by the content providers. This role defines the site maps or information paths that the user will experience within the site, and as such the information architect owns the way that information is defined and organized and how the site presents that organization to the user.

Primary responsibility	The design of the information and information relationships
Primary knowledge	Content analysis, information and classification design
Primary tasks	To define the content types, attributes and relationships that will be used to create content within the system
	To define and maintain any information classification system
	To define the search model
	To define and maintain the site structures
	To review any information classification before publication
	To measure the success of the classification and navigation structure
Deliverables	The set of content requirements created from a content analysis, in particular:

- definition of content types, attributes and relationships;
- definition of content categorizations;
- definition of classification system;
- definition of access rules;
- definition of workflows.

Interface designer

The interface designer role identifies the one person or team who translate the task flows and design requirements from the human factors engineer and maps them into visual layout definitions for a website. This group owns the visual style and defines the layouts for both individually designed pages and view templates that can be used to display the content provided by the content creators.

Primary responsibility	The visual design and style of the site
Primary knowledge	Expert knowledge of visual design techniques and page layouts
Primary tasks	To define site-wide visual attributes
	To design view layouts and templates
	To design individual views such as the homepage
Deliverables	The design of the visual interface, in particular:

- the design of specific individual pages such as the homepage;
- The layout and design of page templates;
- The definition of common visual attributes such as the site colour palette, fonts, banners and footers.

System architect

The system architect role involves the one person or team who create high-level design, and defines the functionality that will support the requirements and tasks identified by the business analyst, the human factors engineer, the information architect and the interface designer. This role designs the information models that will support site-wide views and individual content and view templates.

Primary responsibility	The design of the system that will create the website
Primary knowledge	Expert knowledge of system architecture, data models, technical opportunities and constraints
Primary tasks	The design of data models for document types The design of content relationships The design of content actions The design of content categorization The design of the classification system The design of any back-end integration
Deliverables	High-level design specifications for website design, in particular:

- the designs for the content templates, workflows, classification system and back-end integration.

Content manager

The content manager role identifies the one person or team responsible for controlling resources, defining and maintaining the workflows, and assigning responsibilities. During production, this role approves proposals; reviews published material; monitors status, and performs site analysis. This role is ultimately responsible for the content published to a site and will probably be responsible for commissioning or allocating work to content creators.

Primary responsibility	Publishing processes within the organization, content delivery and site quality
Primary knowledge	Expert knowledge of resource availability, team skills, project planning and organizational workflows
Primary tasks	To define access to the system To define organizational workflows To review content proposals To review content before publication To review change requests To review changes to published material To review archive and delete requests To manage third-party content

To manage resources
To measure the success of the workflow processes
To measure the quality of the site

Deliverables   Definition of the processes to ensure content quality, in particular:

- definition of organization workflows;
- definition of the workflow roles and responsibilities;
- definition of access rule.

Content creator

The content creator role involves the one person or team who create both textual and visual content or arrange for content to be acquired and added to the system. This role has to cross-reference other documents and views, look at other site content, and have content reviewed and published. Content creators are either expert in a certain domain – for instance, writers of subject material – or have certain skills necessary for content creation such as illustrating or graphic designing.

Primary responsibility   Content creation

Primary knowledge   Expert knowledge of content domain or specific knowledge or skill in creating content

Primary tasks   To access content within a content management system
To create content items
To classify content
To make changes to content
To remove content
To provide cross-referencing information
To work with an asset library

Deliverables   The information published to the website, in particular:

- completed content types such as news articles, products and file downloads;
- any supplementary content such as graphics, sounds and video files.

Website developer

The website developer role identifies the one person or team who set up the system to support the publication of a website, and then maintain the system, plug in new views, reorganize the site, provide new document types and maintain links. The team might also provide programming support for visual designers wishing to include more interactive interfaces.

Primary responsibility	The implementation of the website and any supporting content management system
Primary knowledge	Expert knowledge of HTML, XML, Java, JavaScript, database programming, content management design environments
Primary tasks	To create new document types To create content forms, views and queries To define and create website view templates To enable authentication To set up website measurements To deliver any integration to back-end systems
Deliverables	A working website and content management system, in particular:

- The required files, code, forms, and views needed to build the website and content management system.

Summary

The roles included here are common examples found within a web development environment, but the list is not exhaustive, nor is it definitive of what must be in place before a web development project can start. A simple guide as to where an organization should make the investment in the skills needed within a team is to look at the main goals of the site. If a primary goal is ease of use, then a human factors role needs to be involved in the development process very early on. If a primary goal is a superior search capability that can easily query large amounts of information, then an information architect will be key to designing the classification system and putting processes in place to ensure that content is classified correctly. Whatever the goals, the relevant skills must be put in place, and in an ideal web development environment the tools should be available to make it easy for these individuals to do a good job.

The next few chapters look in more detail at some of the roles already defined and the common tasks they perform. Of interest here are the kinds of requirements for a team to create the main components that define the design of the web solution, plus the requirements that need to be met to create, manage and maintain the content to be published to the site. By understanding these requirements it will be possible to start to define common information models that can be used to help design a website and any supporting content management system that is provided.

The roles that pick up this information in order to design and develop the supporting systems are the system architects and website developers. Their requirements are not covered here, as their individual needs must be addressed by development tools for analysis and design, and tools that provide integrated development environments for specific languages. Their requirements are also close to the technology that will be delivered, a subject that has been purposely avoided in this piece of work.

12 Analyzing the requirements of the business analyst

Defining business criteria

The business analyst defines the business criteria for a site (*see* Fig. 12.1) and is responsible for:

- defining site goals and messages;
- defining the business model for the site;
- defining any targets that will measure the success of the site;
- defining the target audience for the site;
- defining the customer role.

Defining the site purpose, goals and messages

The business analyst defines the business aspects of a site and as a priority should clarify the site purpose from a business perspective. The clearest way to do this is to define a set of site goals and messages that the business feels the user should associate with the service offered on the site. An example of a site goal is:

- to offer the customer a safe environment in which to purchase goods.

Site messages that may support this goal could be.

- The company offers a superior returns policy.
- Delivery is guaranteed within the specified time or the delivery charge is waived.
- Credit card transactions are secure.

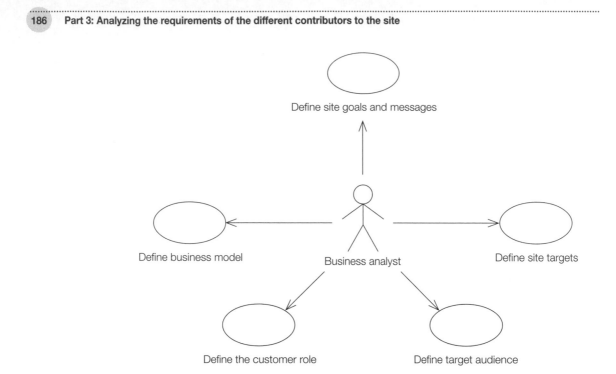

Figure 12.1   Defining business criteria

- Customer details are kept private and are not passed on to other companies.
- All major credit cards are accepted.
- The online receipt can be printed out and used as proof of purchase if any problem occurs.

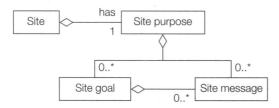
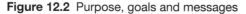

Figure 12.2 Purpose, goals and messages

Therefore, a site should have a purpose that may have one or more goals. A site may have a set of overall business messages, or messages may be associated with a specified goal (*see* Fig. 12.2).

Defining the business model for the site

The business analyst defines what the business model will be for a site. The common business models are:

- commerce; which will involve taking orders for goods or services over the web;
- advertising; which involves displaying adverts for other companies on the pages of the site;

- user subscription; which means setting up a regular payment from customers to give them access to site information;
- promotional; which is used to market an existing business.

It should be possible for a site to contain more than one business model; for instance, a site may wish to support advertising as well as taking online orders.

Commerce, advertising, subscription and promotion are all types of business model (*see* Fig. 12.3).

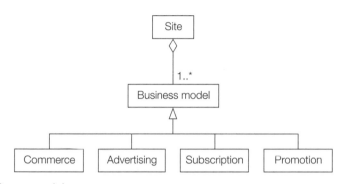

Figure 12.3   Types of business model

Defining the commerce business model

If a site is to support online orders, certain business decisions will have to be made and certain information supplied to the web development team, so they can design the visual interface and develop the code that will allow online ordering.

In defining the business rules, the analyst must supply a terms and conditions statement, one or more payment methods that the site will support – such as Visa or MasterCard – and the delivery options. A delivery option will have a cost, time-scale and area.

Therefore commerce, which is a type of business model, has terms and conditions, a list of payment methods covering one or more card types, and one or more delivery options. A delivery option has a duration, a cost and an area (*see* Fig. 12.4).

Defining the advertising business model

For a site to support advertising, a business analyst must define the different advertising rates available to outside companies. These rates can be complex and may depend on a number of factors such as the type of page the advert will appear on and how big the advert is. There may be different rates, depending on the customer – a regular advertiser may receive a discounted rate. Figure 12.5 is a sample model for capturing some of the combinations that might define an advertising rate.

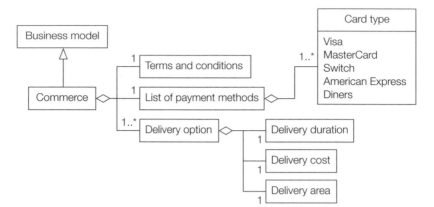

Figure 12.4 Defining a commerce business model

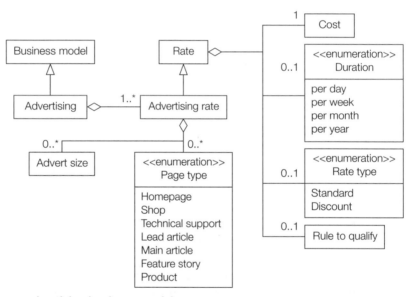

Figure 12.5 Defining an advertising business model

An advertising rate is a specialized type of rate. A generalized rate is defined by having a cost, which in this case would refer to the price that someone would pay for an advert to appear on the site. This cost may also be associated with a duration to which that cost applies, for example per day, per week, or per month. A rate may also have a rate type, for example a standard rate or a discount rate. This allows the definition of different types of rates depending on certain business criteria – defined within the rule-to-qualify attribute – allowing the business analyst the opportunity to create different prices for different circumstances or customers. An advertising rate may be further defined by adding such attributes as:

- The size of the advert;
- The type of page it appears on.

Defining rates for keyword rental

In an advertising business model that wishes to support the rental of keywords from within a search function, (*see* Fig. 12.6), rate cards will need to be devised that define rate charges. This may be based on:

- the number of keywords a company may wish to rent;
- the rental of specific high-value keywords identified for special rates;
- the rental of a number or bundle of keywords based on their usage pattern on the site.

Therefore a keyword rate is a specialized type of rate that is associated with the number of keywords the rate applies to, by the definition of how popular the keywords are, and maybe having a rate specific to high-demand keywords within the system. To support this, a keyword may need to have a usage variable that defines how many times the keyword has been used within a search facility offered on the site.

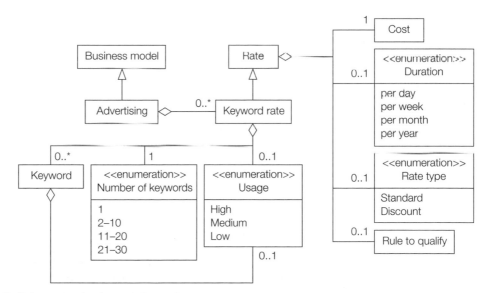

Figure 12.6   Defining rates for keyword rental

Defining sponsorship rates

If a site wishes to include sponsorship as a revenue stream (*see* Fig. 12.7), sponsorships rates will need to be devised to define how much can be charged. These rates may be based on:

- individual high-profile content items published to a site, such as the page containing the headlines on a news site;
- a type of content item such as a newsletter;
- some other content category defined within the classification hierarchy.

To achieve the last criteria, it is important that the categories are within an enumerated list, where the content providers can choose only one category, and that the underlying site content is classified correctly using this scheme.

Sponsorship extends a rate through an optional association to a content item, a content type or some other content category such as newsletters, sports articles or restaurant reviews.

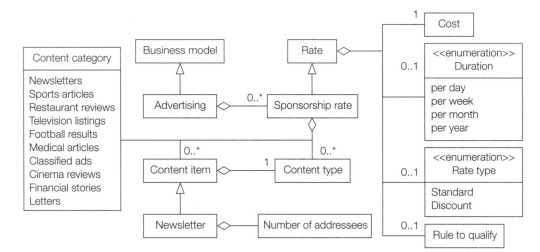

Figure 12.7   Introducing sponsorship rates

Defining the subscription business model

Just as an advertising model may have different rates, a subscription model (*see* Fig. 12.8) may have different subscription options depending on a number of factors.

For instance, a content-heavy site that features different analysis reports in various business sectors may aim to implement a charging model based on the different types of information on the site. They may also like to define a range of charges depending on how long a subscription is taken out. Companies usually provide incentives for users to take out a subscription for longer periods of time, for example 12 months for the price of 10.

A subscription rate is a specialized type of rate that may be further defined by specifying an access category, such as news archives and financial reports. A generalized rate is defined as having a cost and optionally having a duration to which that cost applies. A rate may also have different types defined such as standard and discount, and the rule to qualify attribute allows the business analyst to qualify how the different rates should be applied.

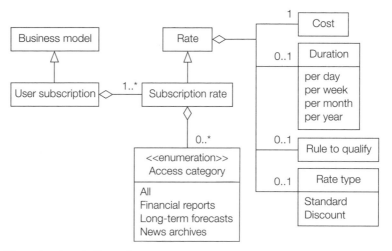

Figure 12.8   Defining different subscription rates

Defining the audience

As part of the business analysis, the business analyst is responsible for defining who the target audience is for a site. This information is critical for marketing purposes, and for providing enough information for the human factors engineer to undertake a useful user analysis.

Each business model has a target audience that has one or more user types (*see* Fig. 12.9). A user type has a name, a description and one or more properties. These properties are defined through a user analysis, in which the human factors engineer clarifies the attributes that define the different types of targeted users.

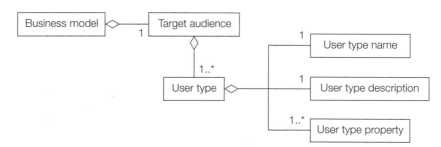

Figure 12.9   Defining the target audience

Defining the customer role

There may be certain information that the business analyst wishes to track with regard to customers, and certain information the customer must provide when ordering goods, buying advertising space or subscribing to an information service. In this instance, the business analyst should define the information the customer must provide during the purchasing process.

A site may have many orders, adverts, keyword rentals, sponsorship deals and subscriptions, each of which has one customer (*see* Fig. 12.10). A customer, however, can be associated with many orders, adverts, keyword rentals, sponsorship deals and site subscriptions. A customer is a type of person and is defined by a customer role and a personal role. A customer role and a personal role are different types of roles. It is likely that when defining the customer role, the business analyst will set down the level of payment information that the company requires an individual to provide before they are able to purchase anything on the site. The personal role is likely to contain personal details about the individual, such as home address and telephone number. (For more detail on defining roles, see the next chapter on modelling requirements for the human factors engineer.)

It is useful to separate the role from the person filling it – a site may wish to keep other information for an individual relating to the role or task they are performing.

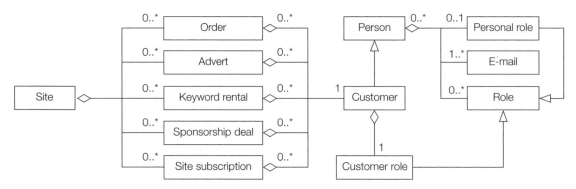

Figure 12.10   The customer role

Defining site targets

A business analyst may wish to define targets against a site to measure how well it is doing. For the different business models there may be any number of targets defined. The common ones will be for revenue and profit over a defined period, and the amount taken, whether that be the number of orders, adverts sold, or subscriptions taken.

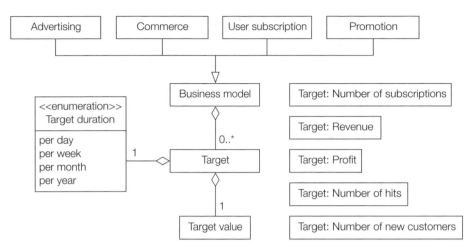

Figure 12.11 Choose your target

A business model may have a number of targets defined (*see* Fig. 12.11). Advertising, commerce, user subscription and promotion are all different types of business models. A target has to be measured against a defined period of time, such as per day, per week, per month or per year. These periods can be selected from a target duration attribute. A target will have a target value that establishes the property to be measured.

Examples of different targets include number of subscriptions, revenue, profit, number of hits, and number of new customers.

Defining marketing priorities on content

A business analyst may need a way of promoting certain content items on the site in order for them to be more visible within the interface. For instance, if a product is not selling and the company wishes to promote it, the business analyst might wish to set a marketing priority attribute so the product starts to appear at the top of related information lists (*see* Fig. 12.12).

There are many different sorts of information that a business analyst might wish to promote, which is why it may be restricting to define a marketing priority for just products or services.

A content item may have a marketing priority of high, medium or low.

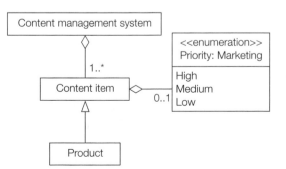

Figure 12.12 Marketing priority

Creating content items and adding them to a content management system

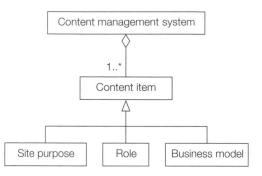

Figure 12.13 Adding information to a content management system

The business analyst will need to create the site purpose document that contains the goals and messages, the business model with any associated targets, and the roles or audience types that will be targeted by the site. All these content items will have to be created and added to an underlying content management system (*see* Fig. 12.13) that will make them accessible to others within the organization, and any defined or typed information made accessible to an automated system that can be programmed to understand the different attribute types.

Measuring business success

The business analyst measures business success (*see* Fig. 12.14) by:

● analyzing the success of the business model against defined targets;

● analyzing the actual site audience against the target audience definitions;

● analyzing page hits to determine the most popular and least popular parts of the site;

● setting up and scheduling reports to analyze the site on an ongoing basis.

Analyzing online orders

It is the responsibility of the business analyst to measure how well a site is performing and specifically how well it is supporting the core business site goals. When the business model for a site is commerce and therefore the main site goal is to generate online orders, the business analyst will need a mechanism that allows online order information to be made available through some predefined business status reports.

To create a summary report on orders taken on the web over a period of time, an order must contain certain pieces of information – the date it was taken, the delivery option with its associated delivery cost, the payment method used, the list of products purchased, and the product options that were selected (*see* Fig. 12.15). Each product option will have an associated product cost. In addition, if a report needs a total of profit rather than revenue, then the report will need to access the underlying profit margin information for each product option that appears on the order. The report will have to compare the actual figures against

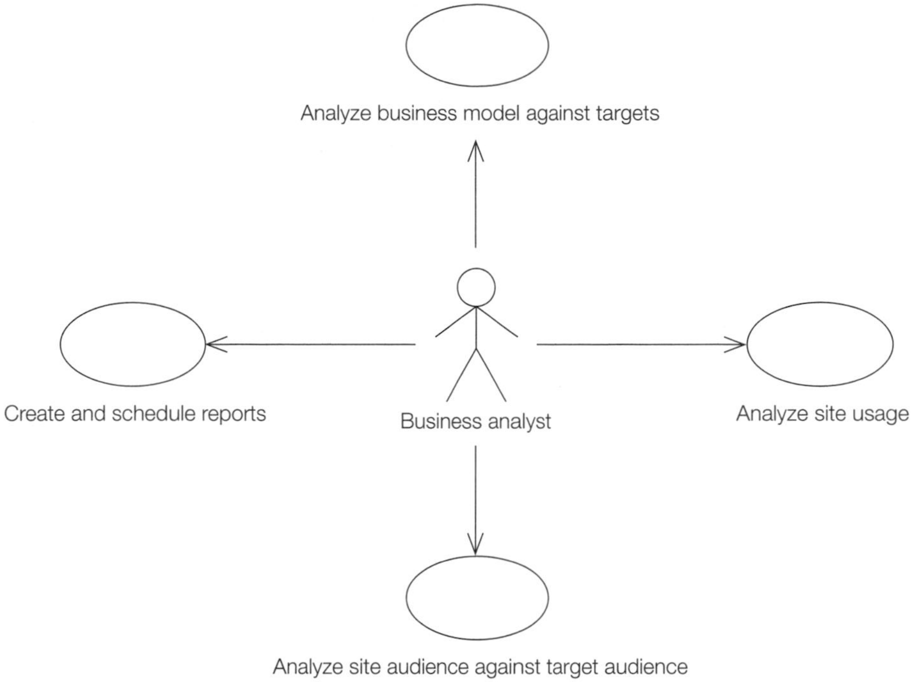

Figure 12.14   Ways to weigh up success

any targets that have been defined as part of the commerce business model. These targets may measure the number of orders taken, the total money received or a total of the overall profit generated.

To support these requirements an order report will need to run against the orders and compare the results against any targets that have been defined. Commerce may have many targets, with a target duration and a target value. Examples of targets that may be set are number of orders, profit and revenue. Each order has a total cost, an order date, a customer, a delivery option, a card and one or more product options. A product option has a product cost, a profit margin and is associated with a product. A card has a card type that appears within the list of payment methods attached to the commerce business model. Delivery options have a delivery cost and are also associated with the commerce business model.

Analyzing advertising revenue

When the business model for a site is advertising and the main goal is to generate revenue from online adverts, the business analyst will need a mechanism that allows online orders for advertising space to be made available through some predefined advertising status reports.

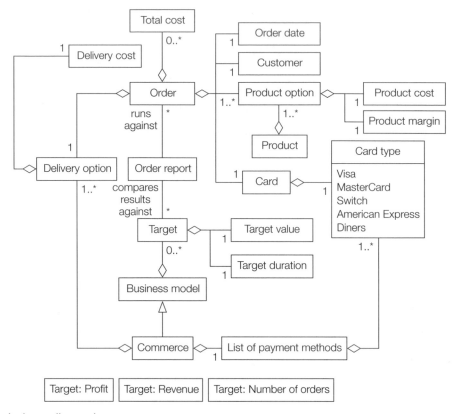

Figure 12.15 Analyzing online orders

To create a summary report on adverts taken on the web over a period of time, an advert will need to contain certain pieces of information – the date the advertising order was taken, the rate used with its associated cost, how the order was paid, and the size of the advert taken out over the duration (*see* Fig. 12.16).

An advertising report has to run against all adverts taken out on the site and compare these against any targets that have been defined for the advertising business model. A target has a target value and a target duration that defines the period the target applies to. Examples of targets that a business analyst might set are the amount of money to be generated by adverts, the number of orders taken for adverts, and the percentage of advertising space taken on the site as a whole. An advertising report runs against adverts to determine cost to customer, duration, and size; it will then compare the adverts against targets for the business model.

An advert will have an order date, a customer, a card used to pay for the order, and a total cost. A card has a card type, such as Visa or MasterCard. These card types appear within the list of payment methods attached to the advertising business model.

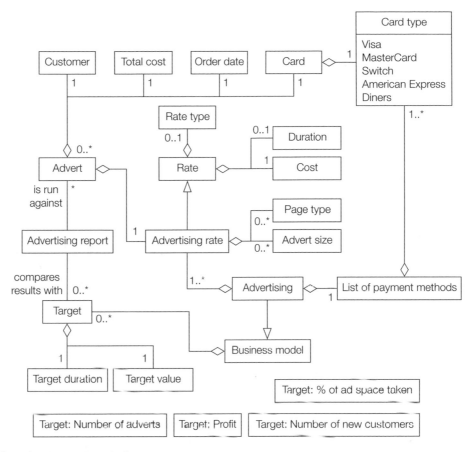

Figure 12.16   The advert report analysis

Analyzing advertising usage

If a site is built on an advertising revenue model, the business analyst needs a way of tracing the usage of adverts within a site (*see* Fig. 12.17). The success of the advertising business model may need to be determined by measuring the number of hits each advert gets. This in turn may determine how much can be charged for advertising on the site in future.

In order to capture this information any page the advert appears in will have to store the number of times a user comes to the page, and the number of times a selection is made within that part of the page displaying the advert.

Each advert must record the total number of hits it receives, for an advertising report to compare this figure with any targets defined for the given advertising rate. An advert appears within an advert layout, which is a type of fragment. A fragment can be described as an area that can be used to lay out user

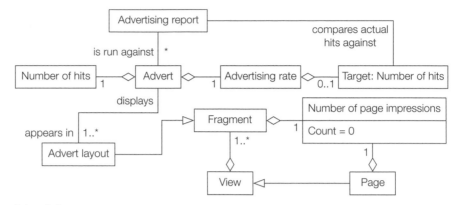

Figure 12.17   Advertising usage

interface objects within a web page. A page can be made up of one or more fragments, and both pages and fragments can keep a count of the number of page impressions they receive. Therefore, recording the hits within each fragment can provide the actual number of hits for each advert.

Querying advertising space

When a customer wishes to place an advert on the site they need to be able to find out the advertising space that is available. The business analyst will have defined the different rates as part of the advertising business model, by way of a number of attributes such as cost, duration and size. Rates may also be set against the type of page the advert will appear in.

Irrespective of the range of rates available, any automated system that publishes a website will have a predefined number of advert layouts available through templates or individual pages (*see* Fig. 12.18). The system will need to query when these slots are available to be filled. To do this, the query will need access to each page on the site that has an advert layout, to see whether the layout has an advert on it. If it does, the query has to determine when the advert will be removed from the site, so that the advertising space can be displayed as available.

To capture these requirements, each advert will have to have a start and remove date and be linked to the advert layout fragment in which it is being displayed. A page may contain more than one advert layout fragment. It is possible for advert fragments to exist that do not currently display an advert. An advert also has a rate, which may have an associated page type for the advert to appear in. Each advert has a customer and a customer may make a query for an advert.

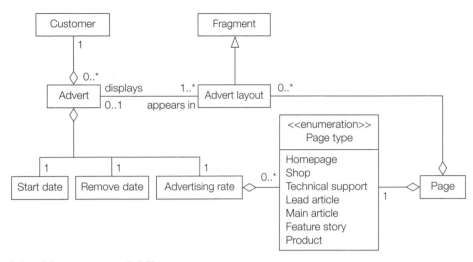

Figure 12.18   Advertising space availability

Analyzing user subscriptions

If a site is built on a user subscription revenue model, the business analyst will need a way of measuring how well the site is performing by reporting on how many subscriptions have been taken out and how much revenue is being generated.

To create a summary report on user subscriptions taken on the web over a period of time, the user subscription must contain certain pieces of information – the date the subscription was taken, the areas of the site it applies to, the date it is to start and when it should stop, the card used to pay for the order, and the total cost to the customer (*see* Fig. 12.19). The user subscription report will need to compare the actual number of subscriptions taken against any targets defined as part of the user subscription business model. Additional targets that may have been defined are those to measure the number of new customers, and those for the actual revenue generated by the user subscriptions.

If a site offers different access categories, it may also be useful to measure the popularity of the different parts of the site in order to look at charges in the future, and whether the balance of site content needs to be changed. If it is found that an access category generates little or no interest, it might be an indication that either the content needs to be extended to be made more appealing, or it may indicate that the category should be removed.

A site subscription needs to be associated with the following attributes – a start date, a total cost, a stop date, an order date, a card that has a card type, a customer, and a subscription rate. The subscription rate is a specialized type of rate and is defined by a cost and a duration – which decides how long the subscription payment will last, and may have a number of access categories the subscription applies to. The subscription report compares the subscriptions taken out on the site against the targets defined for the user subscription business model.

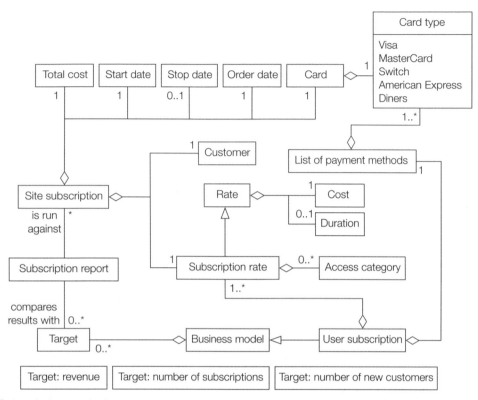

Figure 12.19   Subscription analysis

Analyzing revenue from keyword rental agreements

When keyword rental has been identified as a revenue stream (*see* Fig. 12.20) and rates have been put in place to charge for this mechanism, the business analyst will need a way of measuring how successful this kind of revenue source is through a predefined status report, finding out which keywords are available for rental, or, for keywords that are currently in use, when the rental agreement period ends. To achieve this, each keyword rental agreement will need to store start and remove dates to be applied to each keyword within the agreement, plus a total cost that can be used for reporting purposes. Each keyword rental will also need a web reference that will be used and displayed within the search results list created as a result of the keyword being entered by the user.

A keyword rental has a customer, a web reference, a total cost for the rental, a date when it was ordered, a card that was used to pay for the rental, and a start and remove date, defining when the rental will be in operation.

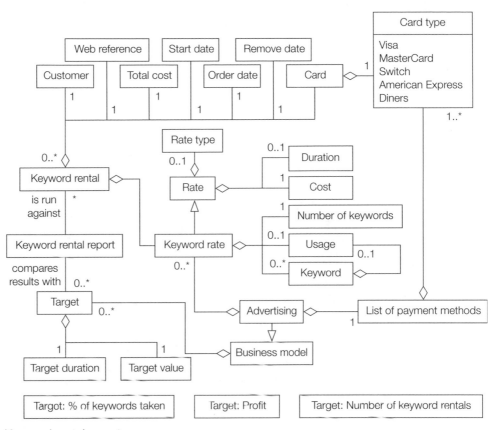

Figure 12.20 Keyword rental report

A keyword rental report is run against keyword rental agreements and compares the results with any targets that have been set for the advertising business model. Example targets that may be set are: the percentage of keywords taken out over a period of time, a target for profit from rental agreements, and the number of keyword rentals that have been paid for.

Analyzing sponsorship deals

In the happy event of a site having many sponsorship deals set up against the content (*see* Fig 12.21), an automated report will need to be generated in order for the business analyst to measure this success against targets that have been defined as part of the business model. A sponsorship deal will have been taken out against a predefined sponsorship rate, and therefore will have an association with either individual content items, items of the same type, or a particular content category that has been defined.

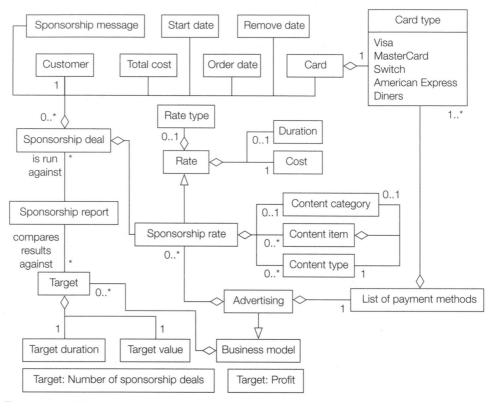

Figure 12.21   The sponsorship deal

A sponsorship deal has a customer, a total cost, an order date, a card that was used to pay for the sponsorship, and a start and remove date defining when the sponsorship message will be in operation.

A sponsorship report is run against sponsorship deals and compares the results with any targets that have been set for the advertising business model. Example targets that may be set are – the target number of sponsorship deals taken out over a period of time, and a target profit.

Analyzing site promotion and usage

When a site has a purely promotional business model, a business analyst may wish to measure how many times the site is accessed. They may also wish to see in more detail the number of times different pages are accessed (*see* Fig. 12.22). This data may be used to decide where on the site different promotional information is placed, and an informed decision can be made to move information important to the business to more popular pages. This information may also be used to determine whether the site structure is working as it should.

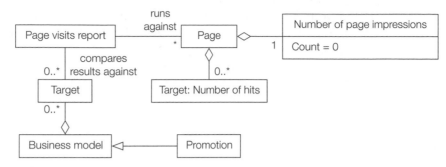

Figure 12.22   Finding the popular spots

To measure this, a page visits report will need to run against each page within the site and access the number of page impressions over a period of time. The report can then compare actual figures with any targets that have been set, for example the target number of hits that may have been defined for a page.

Analyzing the customer

It is the responsibility of the business analyst to define the target audience for a site. As a result, it should also be their responsibility to measure whether the site is attracting the types of users targeted within the business model. In order to discover whether this is the case, the analyst will need to define the types of users who are coming to the site and compare them with the user types detailed as part of the target audience.

If a user is ordering goods, buying advertising space or taking out subscriptions keyword rentals or sponsorship deals, it is possible to collect certain pieces of pertinent data at that time. Once the site knows a customer, it is possible to compare this data with attributes that identify different user types. If there are major differences between the two, then adjustments might need to be made. If the analyst is quite happy with the types and number of customers that the site is attracting, then the target audience definitions should be changed to reflect the new status quo. However, if this exercise highlights problems with the type or number of customers coming to the site, this may signify that changes need to be made to the site or to the way it is marketed. A user analysis will determine if there are problems with the site design with respect to the target audience, which may recommend changes to the site content, the way task flows are designed, or the general site style. However, to be able to recognize that a problem may exist, the necessary system needs to be in place to collect the information and to perform the comparison.

A customer report needs to run against all customers on the site who may have generated an order, taken out a user subscription, rented out a keyword, paid for a sponsorship deal, or bought advertising space (*see* Fig. 12.23). It needs to compare actual customers with the target audience that has been defined as part of the business model. A target audience contains one or more user types. Advertising, commerce, user subscription and promotion are all types of business models.

More detail on how this is achieved is contained in the next chapter, on modelling the requirements of the human factors engineer.

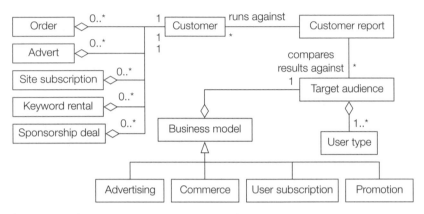

Figure 12.23 The customer report

Creating a report and adding it to the system

The business analyst should be able to define, create and add new reports to an underlying content management system.

A report needs to be a type of content item that is held within a content management system. It is not in the scope of this book to be able to cover all the requirements that an analyst would need with regard to report generation. However, there are a number of common types of report that have been mentioned already that would be useful for the business analyst to have access to such as order reports, advertising reports, subscription reports, keyword rental reports, sponsorship reports and page visits reports (*see* Fig. 12.24).

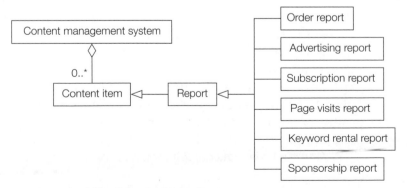

Figure 12.24 Creating reports and adding them to the system

Scheduling when a report is run

The business analyst may wish to set up a report so that it automatically runs at regular intervals. For instance, it might be appropriate for a report against online orders to run every week. To allow this, a mechanism needs to exist whereby a business analyst can specify if a report is to be scheduled and what the time interval should be between runs.

There should be a scheduled report facility that has a schedule run, whereby reports can be generated automatically at intervals (*see* Fig. 12.25).

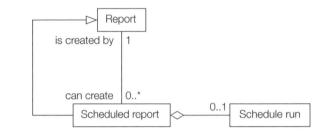

Figure 12.25   Scheduling a report

Analyzing the requirements of the human factors engineer

Defining usability criteria

One of the main deliverables from a user analysis will be the creation of usability criteria that can guide the design of the website itself and any content management system. The human factors engineer is specifically responsible for (*see* Fig. 13.1):

- defining the audience;
- defining the user vocabulary;
- defining usability goals;
- associating usability review criteria with different types of content.

Defining the audience

The human factors engineer takes the initial target audience definitions from the business analyst and uses this information to conduct a user analysis. During this exercise it might become clear that certain types of users have certain characteristics that differentiate them from others. For instance, a working father user type will require any registration interface to collect data on gender, children and salary range. The user type for middle-aged men who play golf will require that data be collected on age range, gender and the sport the user participates in.

It is useful to define a type of property that can be used to identify these attributes so that roles can be created using the same properties wherever possible. This will enable a correlation to be made between a real person providing information on the site, and a user type definition held within the target audience (*see* Fig. 13.2). Why this is desirable is covered later.

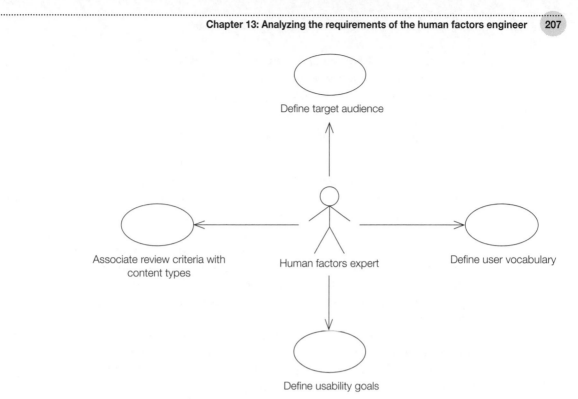

Figure 13.1   Role of the human factors engineer

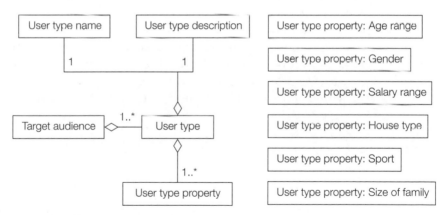

Figure 13.2   User type properties

The definition of a user type needs to contain a name, a description that will initially be defined by the business analyst, and a set of user type properties that will be used to identify the type; examples of which are age range, gender, salary range, size of family, sport and the type of house the person lives in. A business model requires that a target audience is defined and a target audience has one or more user types. It will be up to the business analyst and the human factors engineer to define the additional properties that make up the user type and the range of values for those attributes that are of interest.

Associating audience definitions with content items

Once the different user types have been created, the human factors engineer may wish to associate different audience definitions with particular content items. For instance, all press releases may be targeted at journalists and all documentation for software fixes targeted at computer engineers. The human factors engineer will need the flexibility to provide a scope for target audience information, as individual pieces of content may have a wider or narrower appeal than the majority of content items of the same type. For instance, although press releases will be predominantly aimed at journalists, there may be instances where an individual press release will be aimed at investors, whereas another press release is aimed at a technical community.

In addition, the human factors engineer may wish content providers to supply their own target audience definition of who they think the piece of work is aimed at. To achieve this the audience definitions will need to be selectable when the content item is being edited. This will then allow the content provider to set the target audience for their own piece of work. However, it might still be appropriate for the human factors engineer to review these definitions during a publishing review cycle.

Review criteria need to exist within a content management system that contains many content items (*see* Fig. 13.3). Review criteria are types of content item and have a scope attribute that defines which content items the review criteria apply to. Content items have one or more properties. A user property is associated with a property and has a user editable attribute that defaults to 'no'.

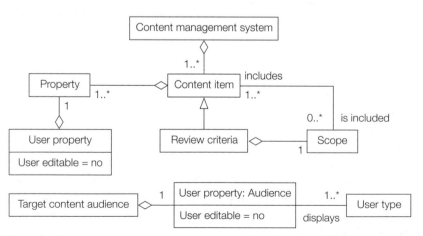

Figure 13.3   The review criteria

An example of review criteria is target audience, which has a user property of audience that displays one or more user types.

Defining the user vocabulary

As part of the user analysis, the human factors engineer needs to capture the user's vocabulary and any synonyms and common spelling mistakes for the main objects within the system that the user understands and expects to work with. For instance, a user expects to find CDs within an online music store; a suitable synonym that needs to be associated with this keyword would be compact disc, and a common spelling mistake may be compact disk (*see* Fig. 13.4).

A keyword is a type of content item that can contain other keywords. A keyword may have a number of associated synonyms and a number of associated common spelling mistakes. Content items are held within a content management system.

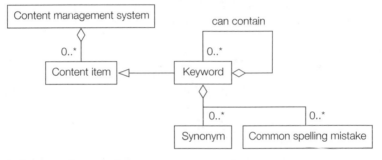

Figure 13.4   Capturing users' vocabulary

Defining usability goals for content items

Information that should be well understood and documented as part of the user analysis stage are the usability goals that need to be achievable by the user of the site. In addition, the analyst should also be in a position to document any usability criteria or targets that apply to these goals; for instance, the time it takes the homepage to load, the minimum font size that should be used for comfortable reading, or the acceptable time it takes a user to find a certain piece of information within a page. These usability goals will need to be captured and associated with the content items or content types to which they apply.

Usability goals may apply to the site as a whole, individual web page or to all pages that are of the same type. For instance, within a site that displays news articles, a usability goal may be to display the title and lead paragraph within three seconds, and the main text within eight. All product pages may have a similar performance goal to display the title, description and cost before displaying the product graphic. All homepages may have a performance goal to display high-level navigation links before anything else is displayed.

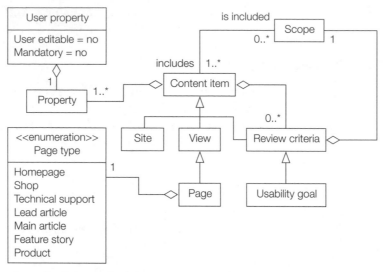

Figure 13.5 Relating review criteria to content items

Identifying a page type provides the added capability of attaching review criteria to all web pages of the same type – in the same way having a content type attached to a content item provides the similar capability at a higher level. For instance, all web pages must undergo a visual design review, and all news articles must contain an archive classification and links to related information.

Because a site and different kinds of views such as a page are all types of content item, review criteria can be associated with them through the scope attribute (*see* Fig. 13.5). Identifying usability goals as a type of review criteria allows them to be identifiable from other types of review criteria. This can be useful when access controls and review workflows are set up at a later stage.

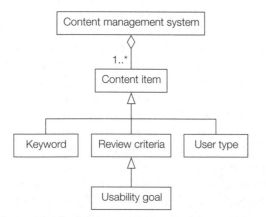

Figure 13.6 Keywords, review criteria and user type

Creating and adding keywords, review criteria and user types

To enable review criteria to be created and reviewed by the human factors engineer, they must be held within an underlying content management system (*see* Fig. 13.6). In addition, the keywords identified during the user analysis also have to be created and added as well as the user types that make up the target audience.

Keywords, review criteria and user type are all types of content items that are held within a content management system. The usability goal is a type of review criteria.

Defining user roles

The business analyst and the human factors engineer define user roles to capture the necessary information from users who are coming to the site to buy products, order services, take out subscriptions or simply register (*see* Fig. 13.7). They are responsible for:

● defining the different types of user roles required by the site;

● defining the core attributes for each person within the system;

● defining the specific attributes for each role and associating these attributes to the user type properties within the target audience definitions.

Define a person   Human factors   Define user roles
                              expert

Figure 13.7   Defining roles to capture information

Defining the different user roles

There may be situations where a site displays different information depending on the type of user viewing the site. There may also be situations where the site requests different information from the user depending on the type of task they are performing. For instance, the information required from a user to buy a product is unlikely to be the same as that needed to register with a site to receive notification of updates. To achieve this the different classes of user, or user roles, will need to be defined.

Two content item types are needed – a person object that represents a real person within the system, and a role that is a collection of additional attributes associated with a person when that person is within a certain state. As one would expect, a person could have many roles, examples of which are employee, business partner, customer and a conference attendee (*see* Fig. 13.8).

Defining the common attributes for a person

The definition of what constitutes the core attributes for all the people or users held within a content management system should be customizable by the human factors engineer (*see* Fig. 13.9). Users of the website must be held within the system in order for any user analysis reports to be created. User information will

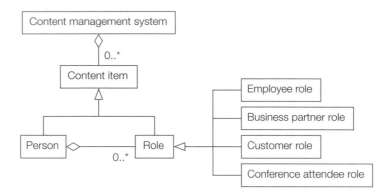

Figure 13.8   A person can have many roles

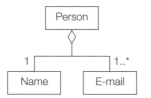

Figure 13.9   Defining a person's core attributes

also be needed to process any tasks that the user has requested from the company. Users of the content management system must also be held on the system in order for the automated workflows to run, and for system administration purposes such as access and version control.

The attributes defined with a person must be the subset of all attributes that apply to everyone within the system. Specific attributes that are relevant only when a person is performing a specific task, or when that person needs to be identified for a specialized purpose, should be defined within a specific role.

In fact it is likely that this subset of core attribute will be very small and in this example, a person is only defined as having a name that can be used to identify the person on the system and an e-mail that can be used for notification.

Defining the specific attributes for different roles

The definition of what constitutes a defined role will need to be customizable by the human factors engineer. However, any role hierarchy that is created must be designed by a system architect so that the optimum combination of attributes can be created to allow roles to be joined together to build up more complex roles. The system architect will be in a better position to organize the attributes into a better reusable scheme for the types of users the system will need to support.

For instance, the core attributes defined for a person in Fig. 13.9 are limited and do not include the types of attributes one would normally expect to find with a person, such as address, date of birth and telephone number. However, these properties are all personal and on a system that provides for instance a work telephone directory are also totally redundant. If a personal role is created to hold all personal details such as home phone number and home address, then addresses and phone numbers can be separated into those pieces of information that are applicable to the employee and those that are not.

A good example of where defining different roles is appropriate is where a site wishes to recognize business partners. Business partnerships are built on a relationship between one company and another. The individual coming to the site in a business partner role is representing the company. Any registration process for business partners should not require the person registering to provide personal information. Therefore, a role attempts to separate out a level of information appropriate to the task in hand, or a level of information applicable to the system being offered. Because the association exists between the core person and roles, it is still possible to access all the information available for a person, while segregating where that information is applicable.

A person can have many roles and an identifiable name and e-mail. Role types include an employee role and a personal role. A personal role may contain such attributes as a home address and a home phone number. An employee role may have a work phone number, a tie line and a job title (*see* Fig. 13.10).

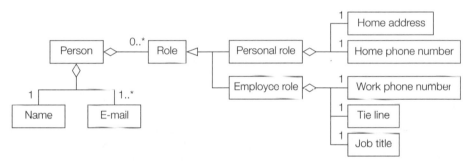

Figure 13.10   Attributes that are applicable to different roles

Relating people to user types

Defining user roles is the mechanism whereby attributes are grouped together to achieve some purpose – for instance, personal details such as a home phone number and a person's address in order to be able to deliver and confirm orders. We can group all payment attributes together, such as credit card details, in order to pay for an online order, and group all employee details together, such as a work phone number and job title, in order to provide an online company telephone book.

These roles relate to the information that the user is viewing and the task that the user is performing. They provide the mechanism for obtaining the relevant information from the user at the appropriate time and provide a way that information can be filtered or presented based on the role of the user coming to the site.

Roles are different to user types, because a user type defines a type of person. User types have a set of attributes and values that distinguish one type of user from another, irrespective of the task that the user has come to the site to perform. It should be possible to analyze the actual website users in relation to the user types if the attributes used within the roles are the same as those used within the user types. It will be a natural requirement for the business analyst to try to capture this information to find out if the users of a site match the target audience definition.

In any interface design that requests information there will have to be some awareness of how acceptable that request will be to the users of the system. The human factors engineer should be in a position to provide an informed opinion as to whether requesting any particular piece of information from the user is appropriate to the task they are engaged in. If the requested information is obviously not needed, then a decision will have to be made as to whether the request will be deemed intrusive or, more seriously, will stop the user from completing the task they are engaged in. Often, incentives are offered to users who are prepared to provide extra information about themselves, and they are given a reason why this information is of interest to the site. Usually, the reason is as bland as: 'So we are able to improve our site as a result of knowing who our users are'.

In any event, to enable actual users to be compared to the user types that have been defined within the target audience definition there needs to exist some glue between the user type and the roles that a person can be. This glue is the user type property.

Both a role and a user type contain user type properties. Examples of these types of properties are gender, age range, salary range, sport, and size of family (*see* Fig. 13.11). A person may have many roles and may be associated with many user types. A person has a method that calculates user types; it does this by analyzing all the roles that are associated with a person and comparing the values of the user type properties within these roles to see if there is a match with the values of the user type properties within a user type definition. If there are matches, then the user type is associated with the person.

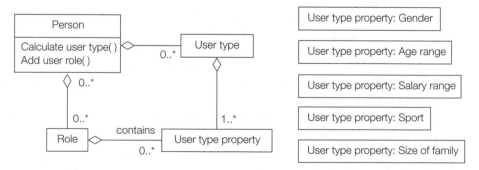

Figure 13.11   User type properties

Defining user tasks

Every site has a set of task flows that users coming to a site will work through. Depending on the functionality of the site, these task flows can range from being simple, such as selecting an article to read and then reading it, to quite complex, such as choosing products to buy, providing credit card details and selecting delivery options. The business goals and user analysis will determine which task flows are critical to the success of the site, and the human factors engineer should also be in a position to provide the critical design features within these task flows that will enable users to complete these tasks easily. There is little point in doing a user analysis if this level of information is not passed on to the site designers and developers; therefore, before any serious design work commences, the human factors engineer should be responsible for:

- defining task goals;
- defining individual tasks and task flows;
- defining critical design features for tasks;
- associating tasks with different user types;
- defining any review criteria for task design (*see* Fig. 13.12).

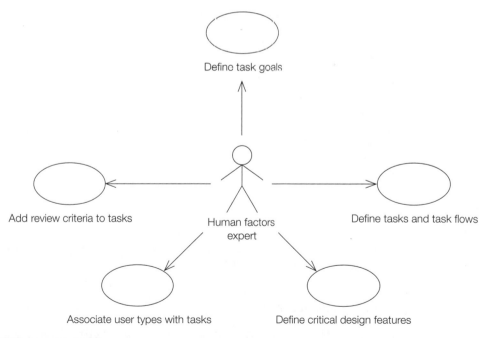

Figure 13.12   Defining user tasks

Defining task goals

A vital part of the user analysis phase is to capture the reasons why users come to a site and what they expect to be able to do once they get there. These are task goals, and the human factors engineer will need to capture this information and assign a priority to indicate how important the goal is to the user. For instance, a user task goal might be to buy a product. This will have a high priority for any site that is based around a commerce business model. However, a goal to find out details about the company might be a very low priority.

When defining what the main task goals are for a site, the human factors engineer needs to assign a user priority to let the site designers know what the emphasis should be within any interface that is created. Therefore, a site may have a number of task goals that have an assigned user priority, which can be high, medium or low (*see* Fig. 13.13).

Figure 13.13   The main task goals

Assigning task flows to task goals

A task goal may have more than one way of being achieved. For instance, in the example of the task goal 'to buy a product', two task flows might be created – one for new customers where the system will need to collect all the necessary payment details for the first time, and one for existing customers who have already provided their payment details to the site. A much quicker buying process can be defined for a customer if the system already has all the necessary payment details to complete an order.

This puts an additional requirement on the design of a task flow that enables the association to be made between the task flow and the user type that it relates to.

To support this, a task goal may have more than one task flow associated with it. A task flow may be associated with a number of user types. A person can be associated with many user types. Examples of user types are unknown user and existing customer (*see* Fig. 13.14).

Defining a task flow

As part of the user analysis stage, the human factors engineer performs a task analysis and may create new task flow designs. As a result, a set of main task goals

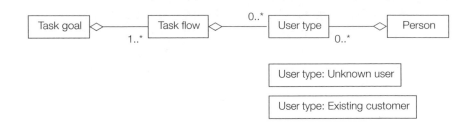

Figure 13.14   Task goals may have more than one task flow

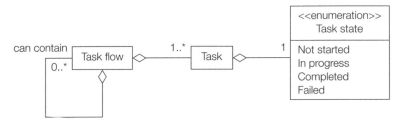

Figure 13.15   The task state

are specified and task flows are created that will enable the user to achieve the goals that have been defined. The human factors engineer will further break down these task flows into smaller task flows and individual tasks, and will need a way of capturing the hierarchical relationships between:

● different task flows;

● different tasks within a task flow.

To support this, a task flow will need the ability to have one or more tasks associated with it, and may have one or more task flows (*see* Fig. 13.15). To determine which task is the current one within a task flow, a task state will determine if a task is not started, in progress or completed. The task state also indicates when a task has failed.

Defining an individual task

As part of the exercise to define task flows, the human factors engineer identifies for each task:

● the information that needs to be present within the interface to allow the user to complete the task;

● the actions that need to be selectable to support the user with the current task and also to move the user on to the next task.

To do this there needs to be a way of defining the available actions that the user can perform when they are at a particular stage of a task, and what the information is that needs to be made available to them to be able to proceed (*see* Fig. 13.16). The human factors engineer will also assign a user priority to this information and the selectable actions to capture the essence of the critical design features that must be in place for the task to succeed. All critical design features will be marked as having a high priority. Other usability criteria may have a lower setting.

Therefore, when user properties and user actions are associated with a task, the human factors engineer will need a way of setting the user priority of the objects within the interface.

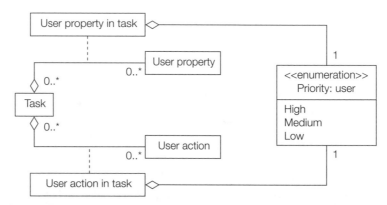

Figure 13.16   Associated properties and actions within a task

Defining the flow of tasks within a task flow

There will be logical paths through a task flow that the human factors engineer will expect the user to follow. These paths will need to be defined by specifying the actions that will allow the user to move from one task to another. When transferred to a visual design, this movement may be a page link, or just a scroll down to another section within the same page. The visual interface designer defines the eventual correlation of a task flow to view layouts as part of the visual design exercise; however, it is the human factors engineer who will need to define the logical task flow path that should be in place.

Therefore, there needs to be a type of action that updates the state of the current task and changes the state of the next task to being in progress (*see* Fig. 13.17). User actions that are associated with a task can contain many actions.

Defining the available information

The available information for a task may relate to other information that has been created within other content items on the system. In this case, it would be useful for the human factors engineer to be able to link to these informational properties from within a task definition so that information is not duplicated, and the information supplied elsewhere is related to the task that it is used within. It should also be possible to add the user priority setting to the property when it is associated with a task.

User properties are associated with properties that are held within content items (*see* Fig. 13.18). A user property may be associated with many tasks and a task may be associated with many user properties. When a user property is associated with a task it can be assigned a user priority of high, medium or low.

Associating review criteria to a task flow and individual tasks

Task flows and individual tasks may have review criteria associated with them. For instance, the human factors engineer may wish to state that the audience to complete a task flow that involves configuring a PC is highly technical, and the tone or style of writing used within a task that involves installing a device driver is also technical. This allows any review procedure to take into account

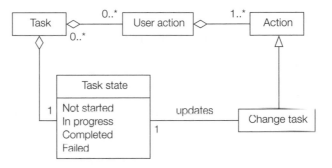

Figure 13.17   Defining the logical task flow

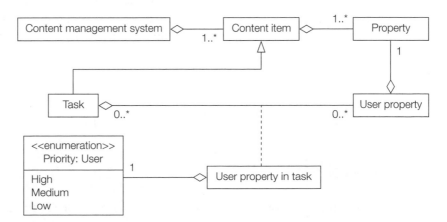

Figure 13.18   User properties

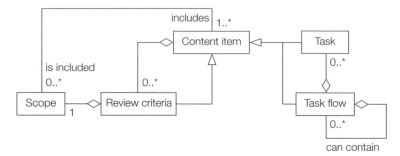

Figure 13.19   Review criteria and tasks

who the task or task flow is aimed at, and therefore how the interface should be written or visualized.

This can be achieved by defining and associating review criteria to tasks and task flows, and defining the scope query attached to a content item, that forms the relationship between the required review criteria and the tasks and task flows to which it applies (*see* Fig. 13.19).

Creating and adding tasks and task flows to the system

The human factors engineer needs to be able to create and add tasks and task flows to the underlying content management system.

As such, the task flow and the task are types of content items that are held within a content management system (*see* Fig. 13.20).

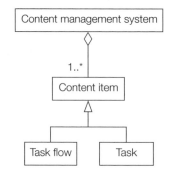

Figure 13.20 Adding tasks and task flows to the system

Sample task flow for buying a product

Figure 13.21 is a sample task flow that defines the process for buying a product from a website. The human factors engineer should translate critical design features into the information and actions that the user needs to be visible within the interface to complete the task. The actions highlighted in bold represent the highest user priority actions that enable the user to move to the next logical stage.

Measuring site usability

The human factors engineer is ultimately responsible for the usability of the website and at some point will need to test how usable it is (*see* Fig. 13.22). Many usability tests involve recruiting a number of subjects that match the profiles

	Available information	Available actions
Select item Select item to buy ↓	Item price Item description	**Select item to buy,** determine T&Cs. return to inventory, compare with similar
Select delivery option Select delivery option ↓	Return policy, guarantee, delivery costs & radius, tax	**Select delivery option,** return to inventory, return to item, determine T&Cs
Select payment method Select payment method ↓	Available payment methods, payment method information	Return to inventory **select payment method,** return to item
Confirm price Accept price ↓	Bottom line price, selected item, selected delivery, selected payment method	Query price, **accept price,** change delivery, change payment method, return to inventory, return to item, return to T&Cs
Make payment Buy ↓	Payment method, bottom line price, payment method information, delivery option	Enter required payment fields, **buy,** query price, change delivery, change payment method, determine T&Cs, return to item, return to inventory
Confirm payment	Exact amount of order	Print invoice, e-mail confirmation, **return to inventory**

*The information included within this task flow sample was created by Ernest Reid in an internal IBM paper on shopping behaviours.

Figure 13.21 Sample task flow for buying products from a website

within the target audience and asking them to complete the main task goals identified during the user analysis. When the human factors engineer has written up the task goals, designed the task flows and ensured that the website design takes note of the critical design features associated with tasks, this kind of usability test should be fairly straightforward and should not throw up too many surprises. Of course, if problems are found it will probably be an indication that the user analysis was not completed successfully, or the design has not followed the task flow specifications.

These kinds of usability tests are useful, but they are still undertaken in a very controlled environment, with the types of people the site expects to attract, performing the types of tasks that the designer expects them to perform. A far better indication of whether usability problems exist is to analyze real data that is collected from the site; when such data is made available the human factors engineer should be responsible for:

- defining online questionnaires;
- analyzing user feedback;
- analyzing the success of task flows;
- analyzing the users coming to the site.

The human factors engineer may also be interested in analyzing search queries, which is covered in the next chapter.

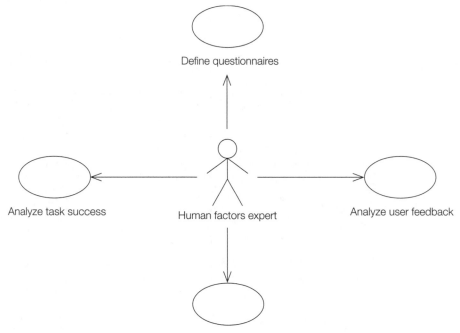

Figure 13.22   Is the site working properly?

Defining usability questionnaires

To measure how well users perceive a site, a human factors engineer may wish to design an online questionnaire for users to answer. The human factors engineer will need to define the level of information they wish the respondent to supply in order to sort the answers into useful categories. These categories will almost always try to match the user types defined within the target audience, and therefore the questionnaire will need to contain the same user type properties in order for this mapping to be made. A questionnaire will also need to support a submit action that displays an acknowledgement when the user completes and sends the form.

A site may have a number of questionnaires (*see* Fig. 13.23). A questionnaire has one or more question and answer objects, which have a user property of a question, which is not editable by the user, and a user property of an answer, which is. There may also be an error object that contains one or more error messages. A questionnaire has one respondent, which is a person that has a respondent role. A person can have one or more roles. A questionnaire also has a submit user action and an acknowledgement, which is a non-editable user property that displays when the user has submitted the form.

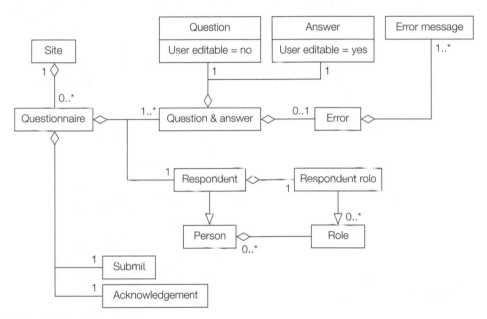

Figure 13.23   Getting feedback from users

Analyzing questionnaire results

When a human factors engineer defines a questionnaire, publishes it and has a number of completed forms returned, there will need to be a way that the results can be summarized and analyzed through a questionnaire analysis report.

A questionnaire has one or more question and answer objects that each have a user property for an answer. A questionnaire summary report (*see* Fig. 13.24) summarizes these answers and organizes the results by user type, comparing the values given within the user type properties to the values defined within the target audience definition. A questionnaire also has a respondent, which is a type of person. A person can be associated with one or more user types.

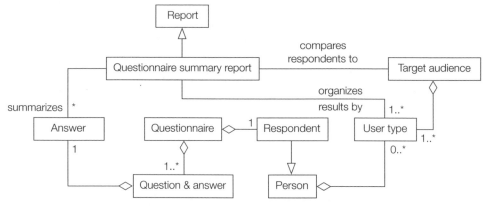

Figure 13.24   Summarizing questionnaire results

Analyzing user feedback

If a site supports feedback from users, this feedback should be tracked by a human factors engineer and perhaps passed on to other members of the web development team.

A site may have a number of feedback forms from users. Feedback is a common example of a questionnaire, and is used extensively on many types of websites (*see* Fig. 13.25).

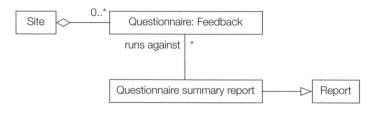

Figure 13.25   Feedback

Analyzing task success

By providing a task model that contains a number of tasks that have a task state (*see* Fig. 13.26), it should be possible to measure the completion success for the overall task flow and the success rate of each individual task within a task flow. This information could be analyzed by a human factors engineer to identify if there are significant numbers of users who are failing to complete tasks on the site. It will also provide enough information to pinpoint where within a task flow users are giving up.

This will help identify problem areas with the site design; however, it will not provide the reason why a particular task is failing or why users are giving up. To determine whether there is a problem with the task flow design, or a problem

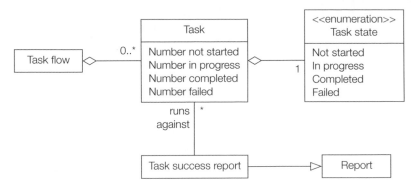

Figure 13.26   Identifying problem areas

with the visual interface that presents this design, the human factors engineer will need to create and run a usability test that covers the problem area.

A task flow can contain other task flows and one or more tasks. A task has a task state and a number of variables that keep a count of:

- the number of times the task was not started within a task flow;
- the number of times the task flow stopped while the task was in progress;
- the number of times the task was completed successfully;
- the number of times the task failed.

A task success report runs against this information for all of the tasks within a task flow.

Analyzing users of the site

When the business analyst goes to the trouble of defining a target audience for the site, and identifying the types of people that the site needs to attract, there is some justification for tracking whether the site is actually bringing in those types of users. Therefore, the human factors engineer will need to run a report against the people registering with the site and compare the attributes that have been supplied by these users with those defined against the user types within the target audience definition.

A user analysis report (*see* Fig. 13.27) needs to be created and run against all the people on the system. By associating different roles with a person, it will be possible to distinguish the different types of people that have been created. For instance, the report may run only against people who have a customer role, or people who have a subscribers' role.

A person has a method that calculates whether the individual falls into one of the predefined user types that make up the target audience for the site. A target audience forms part of a business model, and a user analysis report needs to run

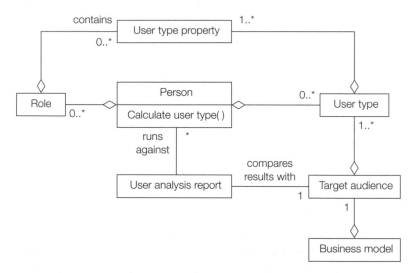

Figure 13.27   Tracking user type

against the required person objects and compare the results with the target audience definition. If enough of the relevant data has been collected against the people of interest, this report will confirm or deny whether the site is attracting the types of users that were expected.

14 Analyzing the requirements of the information architect

Defining different content types

As a result of a content analysis, the information architect should be in a position to define the conceptual design for each content type that will be needed within the system. This will eventually equate to creating a form definition for each content type that allows content providers to create content items of that type and in addition maybe a page view definition that will display the content information within a web page view.

Forms, views and tables will eventually need to be entered into the system. However, this does not mean that the information architect will necessarily be responsible for creating these objects. It is likely that a system architect or developer will create the underlying data structures to store properties within a content item and create the view definitions to display and allow the creation of the content information. However, the information architect should be responsible for defining the attributes that need to be present within content forms and the content relationships that will need to be supported (*see* Fig. 14.1). Therefore, in defining different content types the information architect will be responsible for:

- defining the different content types within the system;
- defining the attributes for each content type;
- defining the attributes to store relationships between different content items.

Defining the different content types within the system

The main user-perceived objects identified within the content analysis will need to be defined as self-contained content types in order to support the creation of these types and the definition of content relationships. In addition, each content

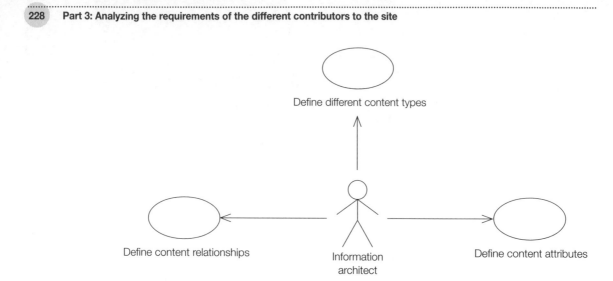

Figure 14.1   The information architect is responsible for defining content types

type will need a scope or content definition that allows content providers to decide whether this is the content type they should be creating, and in particular whether the content that they wish to create falls into the category of information that the site wishes to support. Therefore each content item will have a content type and a content definition. A form template, which is a type of view, is associated with a content type and is used to create instances of this type within a content management system (*see* Fig. 14.2).

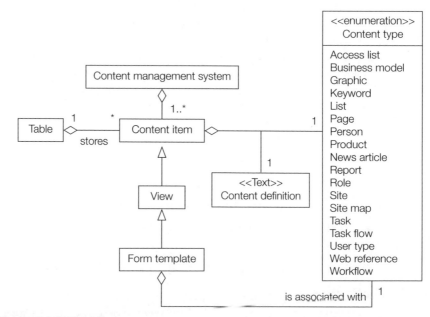

Figure 14.2   Structure of a content item

Defining the attributes for each content type

During the content analysis, each content type should have been broken down into the constituent parts that define the type. This breakdown will need to result in properties being defined for each content type and UI elements associated with these properties to allow content creators the ability to edit these attributes through a form interface, and users the ability to view content information through a page view.

How a property is defined and stored within a table is not of particular interest to the information architect, nor is the way that a property definition can be shared and stored in a common table. The system architect will be responsible for the data model design but will need the information that relates to the context of the property, which the information architect should be providing. For instance, a news article content type will need a form to allow the creation of a lead paragraph, a web reference will need a form to allow the entry of a link description, and a paper will need a form to allow the creation of an abstract. These labels refer to the description of the property that the content provider sees, rather than the field name that will be used to store the property value.

Therefore a content item has many properties, as shown in Fig. 14.3. A property has a field name and may be stored within a table. Views, which are types of content items, have many fragments that display UI elements. A UI element is associated with a user property that in turn is associated with a property. When a UI element is within a fragment, it has a position and it may have a label and a hint. These labels provide the ability to name a property within the context of

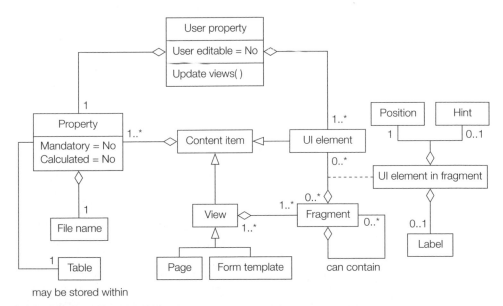

Figure 14.3   Properties of a content item

the view in which it appears. Therefore, a property with a field name of short description could be used to contain an abstract, a lead paragraph, and a link description. Individual hints can also be defined to help content providers with the creation of the property in the context of the view.

Defining the attributes to store relationships between different content items

For any content item type or even content property there may be a requirement to allow content providers the ability to supply related information. The information architect may define the level of related information that is required for a content type, or it may be left to the content provider to define the level that is applicable to the information being provided.

For example, for any particular product, the information architect may predefine a related information query that generates a list of links based on the most popular selling products within the selected product category. However, in a news article content type, the information architect may define a field for related articles and leave the content provider to supply the query, with the assumption that the journalist will be in a better position to define the keywords that will return other news articles that relate to the story that has just been written.

There may also be a requirement to allow individual fields to be associated with related information lists. For instance, an academic paper may have both a subject and an author field. It may be a requirement to display two related infor-

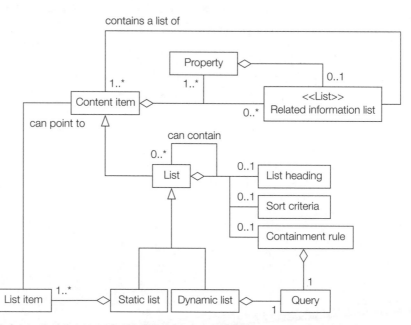

Figure 14.4 Related information lists can be defined for content items and for individual properties

mation lists that are associated with the contents of these fields, a list to display other papers written by the same author, and a list of papers related to the subject being written about.

Therefore related information lists may be associated with a content item and with individual properties within a content item. Related information lists can contain other lists and can be either statically defined by adding links to existing content items on the system, or dynamically defined by specifying a query (*see* Fig. 14.4). A list can have a heading, sort criteria, and a rule that defines the type of content items that the list can contain.

Defining an information classification system

The information architect is responsible for designing the classification system that will be used both within the organization to create content and externally on the website to navigate and search for information. An information architect designs these classification systems by taking the user keywords, synonyms and common spelling mistakes identified during the user analysis and combining this vocabulary with the content types, content attributes and content relationships and requirements identified during the content analysis. The information architect is therefore responsible for:

- defining the classification system;
- maintaining the classification system;
- reviewing keyword requests;
- defining content review criteria (*see* Fig. 14.5).

Defining a central classification system with keyword hierarchies

In most cases, it makes sense to create a separate system to hold classification keywords. This is because designing classification hierarchies and maintaining a controlled vocabulary is a very specialized task. In most cases access to this information will be closely guarded, and usually will be restricted to allow content providers the ability to look up, search and select keywords, but not add, change and delete them.

Keywords provide a mechanism to capture a term and associate other pieces of useful information against that term, exactly as a dictionary would. However, keywords can also capture relationships between terms, and therefore can be organized into hierarchical structures. This is particularly useful when defining navigational hierarchies for a website. Keywords created within a classification system provide the mapping between the classification of content created and published to a website and the vocabulary and content hierarchy that the user expects to see and interact with through the website interface. Getting this mapping right is key to making a website easy to use.

Therefore there needs to be a system to allow an information architect to create keywords and to build keyword hierarchies. A classification system can be defined that is a specialized type of content management system. Keywords can contain other keywords and are types of content items that can be contained within a classification system (*see* Fig. 14.6).

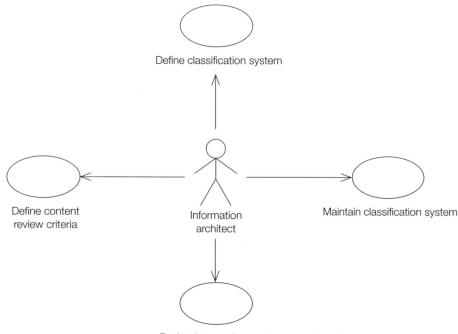

Figure 14.5   Defining the classification system

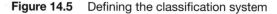

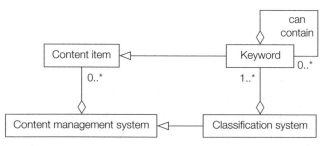

Figure 14.6   Creating a classification system to hold keywords

Adding synonyms and common spelling mistakes

It is unlikely that all those coming to a site will use exactly the same vocabulary. This is especially the case if a site is aiming to produce an English-speaking version aimed at different English-speaking nations such as the UK and US. Therefore, when defining a keyword the information architect will need to define any associated synonyms and common spelling mistakes that exist for that word. This will enable a search mechanism to automatically perform a mapping between the term supplied by the user and the keyword that has been used to classify content. To support this, a keyword needs to be able to be associated with synonyms and common spelling mistakes (*see* Fig. 14.7).

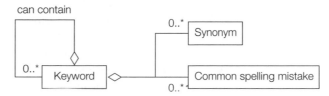

Figure 14.7 Associating a keyword with synonyms and spelling mistakes

Adding a scope attribute to keywords

Once a classification system and keyword hierarchy have been designed, the content classified and the search mechanism and site are up and running, it is likely that users will start to enter terms that are not only missing from the classification hierarchy but that do not easily fit into the classification design. For instance, a site that supports a range of information about animals may have a beautifully crafted classification hierarchy based on standard animal classifications, yet this perfect information design may fail to produce any matches if a user enters a query to search for 'jungle animals'.

If the information architect chooses to try to support such a term, there are a number of ways to proceed. The classification system can somehow be redesigned to include the new term, and in addition, all the relevant content reclassified to use it, or a new keyword can be defined that has the ability to bring together individual keywords from different hierarchy trees. Obviously the second option is a lot better, as the clean classification hierarchy can be maintained and no reclassification exercise is needed.

Supporting such a mechanism can be achieved by providing a facility that allows the definition of a query to be associated with a keyword. Running the query results in a temporary classification hierarchy of associated terms being built that can be used in the same way as the existing hierarchies that have been defined.

Therefore a keyword may have a keyword scope which is a type of query that can be used to link to other keywords within the system (*see* Fig. 14.8).

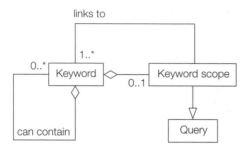

Figure 14.8 A keyword scope

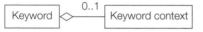

Figure 14.9 A keyword context

Adding a context to a keyword

There may be situations where a classification system has keywords within it that are spelt the same but have different meanings. For instance the word 'orange' can be both a colour and a fruit. If a user searches a classification system for this term, there will need to exist a mechanism whereby they can select which meaning is appropriate to the content they are searching for or classifying. Adding a meaning to a keyword is called disambiguation, and it can be used within an advanced search facility on a website if a user also enters an ambiguous term.

To support this a keyword may have a keyword context that is used to hold a description that clarifies which meaning is meant by the keyword (*see* Fig. 14.9).

Adding attributes to a keyword

For some types of content there might be a requirement to provide more advanced features within a classification system. Complex classification services are more likely to be needed by sites that offer content based on a digital library model, e.g. an image library, a video library, or a CD library. If a site has a large digital catalogue of items that it expects users to search, it will need:

● an advanced search interface that is easy to understand and helps the user build queries based on the underlying classification system;

● a comprehensive classification model that has been applied correctly and consistently to all the items within the library.

The ability to define and add attributes to a keyword is an advanced technique that can be used to describe in more detail the item that is being classified. For instance, a card company that specializes in pictures of animals may wish to describe what the animal looks like and what it is doing: 'The tiger is orange, has black stripes and is sleeping.' Anyone searching for a card with tigers will find this card, but so will anyone searching for a card showing any animals that are asleep.

Another requirement may be to provide an indication of how applicable the keyword is to the item, or indeed how applicable the attribute is to the keyword (*see* Fig. 14.10). This information can then be used for sorting search results into a better relevance order. For example, if someone is looking for a card that has an animal which is asleep, the first links that are returned should be links to cards with animals that are fast asleep, followed by those which just look a little tired. To ensure that attributes on keywords can also be searched by users, they will

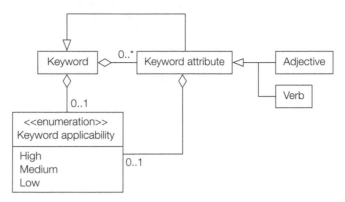

Figure 14.10   Advanced classification techniques

need to be keywords themselves, so that a classifier uses the term 'asleep' rather than an alternative such as 'snoozing'.

To support this feature, a keyword may need to have many keyword attributes. An adjective and verb are types of keyword attributes. A keyword may also have a keyword applicability, which defines how applicable the keyword is to the content item and how applicable the attribute is to the keyword. A keyword attribute is a type of keyword.

Linking the classifications to the content

There is little point in defining a classification system if the keywords cannot be associated with the underlying content that is being published to a site.

Therefore, there needs to exist a mechanism whereby a content item can be classified by a number of keywords and in addition individual user properties within a content item can also be individually classified (*see* Fig. 14.11). This is so that any views that are created that pull together user properties from different content items will still be classified correctly and the relevant page returned as a result of a user search.

Analyzing requests to add keywords or synonyms

It is unlikely that the classification system will contain all the keywords that a content provider will ever want to use. Therefore there needs to exist a mechanism where the person classifying the content can search for keywords and synonyms, and then make a request for a keyword to be added if the term they wish to use is not present.

Therefore, with an edit task there may be a task flow that allows content providers the ability to search for keywords and within that there may exist another task flow that enables them to add a keyword to the classification system if the one they were searching for does not exist (*see* Fig. 14.12).

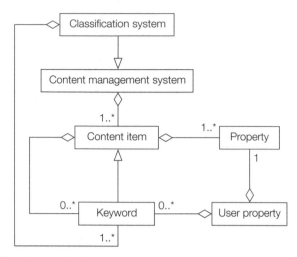

Figure 14.11   Linking classifications to content

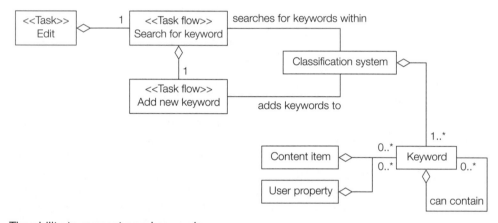

Figure 14.12   The ability to request new keywords

Searching for and adding keywords are task goals for both the content provider and the information architect. However, the task flows that they use to achieve these goals are likely to be different (*see* Fig. 14.13). For instance, the information architect may be able to add keywords without anyone else needing to review the additions. However, a request to add keywords by a content provider might necessitate the information architect reviewing the request and accepting or rejecting the new keyword as appropriate.

As a task goal can have one or more task flows associated with it, it allows different task flows to be created for different user types within the system.

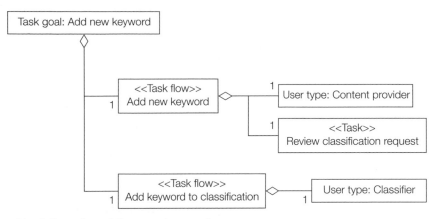

Figure 14.13   Different task flows for adding new keywords

Defining content review criteria

There are potentially other review criteria that an information architect may wish to define that do not relate to any categorizations that the website user sees. Examples may include how documents are classified from the point of view of who within the organization is allowed to read them or the criteria for defining the writing style for a particular type of content item. It should also be possible for the information architect to define whether it is mandatory for an attribute to be provided by a content provider (*see* Fig. 14.14).

Therefore, there should be a type of review criteria that can be used for content review, such as access classification and tone. User properties have a user editable flag, which defaults to 'No' and a mandatory flag, which also defaults to 'No', thus allowing the information architect the ability to set those attributes which must be provided by the content provider.

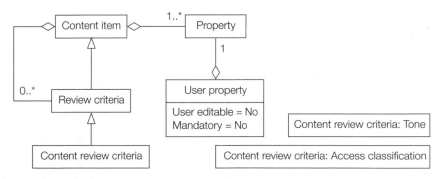

Figure 14.14   Content review criteria

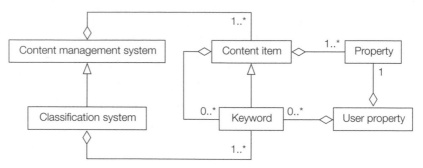

Figure 14.15   Adding keywords and content review criteria

Creating and adding keywords and content review criteria

The information architect needs to be able to add keywords to a classification system and content review criteria to the content management system (*see* Fig. 14.15).

Defining search requirements

The information architect clarifies the search requirement and ensures that the underlying classification system will be able to support the level of search interface required. Specifically, the information architect:

● defines the keywords necessary to support a keyword search;

● promotes certain keywords to facilitate an advanced search results interface;

● defines key web references associated with keywords;

● defines the common structure for a web reference that can be displayed within a search results list (*see* Fig. 14.16).

Supporting keyword search

The advantage of supporting common keywords and associated synonyms is that a keyword search can be provided that searches on the supplied keyword and returns a list of corresponding links. Commonly, the user recognizes the standard quick search entry field within a page and uses this to type in a term they wish to find. This mechanism is the quickest route to information on a site when:

● the user is fairly confident of the terms they are looking for;

● the site has invested some effort in classifying the content on the site using terms that are recognizable to the user;

● there is a level of support for synonyms and common spelling mistakes;

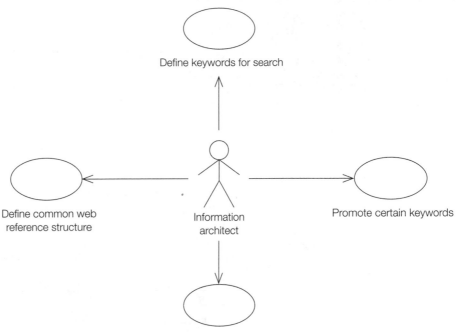

Figure 14.16   The information architect defines the search requirements

- the user is not trying to search a digital library;
- the site tries to offer alternatives if no matches are found;
- the search mechanism tries to offer the results sorted in some kind of relevance order;
- the site regularly removes content clutter and keeps the content correct and up to date.

Example of a keyword search interface

The example screenshot in Fig. 14.17 shows the standard mechanism of returning a list of matches based on a quick keyword search.

Therefore a search results list may contain many web references and is displayed within a search results fragment. Fragments are contained within views and a page is a type of view. Keywords, web references and views are all types of content items, which can have many keywords, which in turn can have many associated synonyms and common spelling mistakes. A content item may have a web reference, which may appear within a search results list (*see* Fig. 14.18).

SEARCH NEWS FOR

Thinkpad | Go |

IBM EASE OF USE NEWS

IN THE NEWS

FEATURE STORIES

PRESS RELEASES

March 1999

The new thinking behind ThinkPad

In less than 12 months, IBM's ThinkPad team has produced the industry's highest-rated notebook -- not once, but twice. According to press reviews, the reason for the overwhelming success is simple: no one else makes a laptop easier to use or easier to choose than the ThinkPad 770 and 600.

Published: *Link to:*

5th Jun 1998   Feature Article - Ease of Use News

IBM preps $1,499 ThinkPad

The ThinkPad look and feel designed with the features and price that consumers want.

Published: *Link to:*

13th Oct 1998   Product Review - CNET news.com

IBM Launches new ThinkPads -- aimed squarely at the consumer

After studying the consumer mobile market, IBM gave the consumers the

Figure 14.17   A list of matches based on a quick keyword search

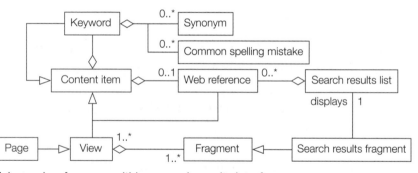

Figure 14.18   Using web references within a search results interface

Promoting certain keywords

Another requirement may be to expand the information around certain keywords, so that a more advanced search results interface can provide extra information about the subject area (*see* Fig. 14.19).

To support this kind of mechanism, a keyword will need to be extended in order to provide all the extra information required to display within the designed search results template, as outlined in Fig. 14.20.

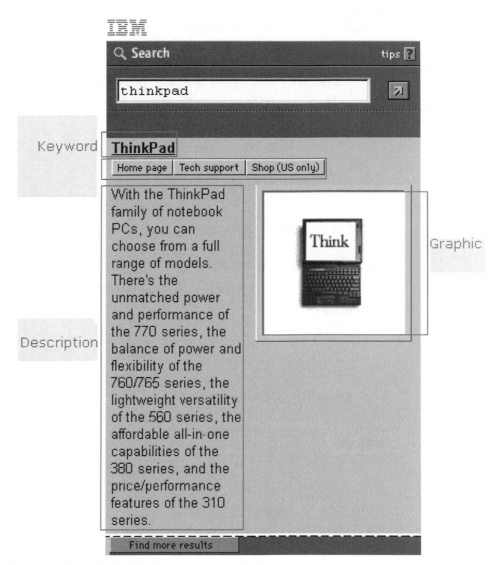

Figure 14.19   Example of an interface that promotes certain keywords

Therefore a subject area object could be defined that extends a keyword and displays within a subject area fragment within a web page. A subject area will have a short description, a link graphic, and a set of key web references such as homepage, shop or technical support. Each key web reference will have a web reference, a link graphic that can be selected to link to the page, and link text which will be a very short label to describe the link. This of course is only an example of an extra level of information defined for a keyword. It may be more applicable to provide more or less.

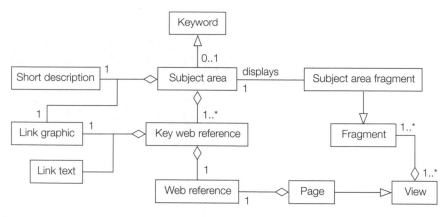

Figure 14.20   Adding more information to a keyword

Defining the key web references for a subject area

When defining key web references in relation to a subject area, the information architect may wish to use the default link attributes or specify new ones that have more meaning to the subject area.

As a web reference represents a page, and a page has a page type, a graphic can be associated with the type that can be used as a default for the link graphic (*see* Fig. 14.21). The page type name can also be used as a default for the link text that appears within the template. However, it should be possible for these defaults to be changed if required to be more applicable to the keyword with which they are being associated.

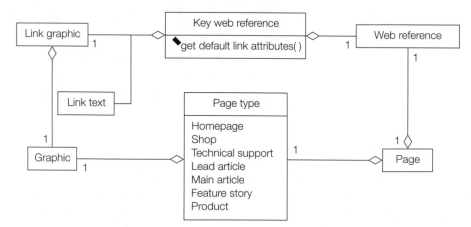

Figure 14.21   Defining key web references

Providing a common way to display web references for search results

When search results are displayed or even just references to other web pages within related information lists, it will be necessary to support a common level of

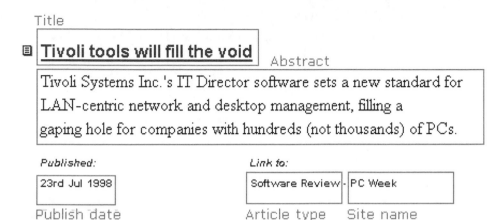

Figure 14.22   Example of a web reference template

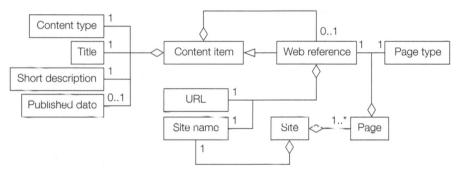

Figure 14.23   Defining a web reference

information that represents a web page link. Lists of related references can then be displayed within a fragment, and offer additional information about the link to the website user (*see* Fig. 14.22).

Therefore a web reference has a URL and a site name and is a type of content item. A content item has a title, a short description, and a published date. A web reference represents a page and a site contains many pages. A page has a page type and a content item has a content type, as illustrated in Fig. 14.23.

Defining site structure

The information architect designs the structure of the site and the main navigation paths that link different pages of information, and is responsible for:

- defining site maps;
- defining the structure of a site map;

- defining navigation lists;
- defining different types of links (*see* Fig. 14.24).

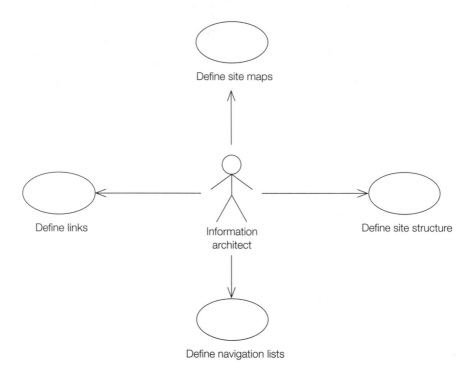

Figure 14.24   The information architect's role in designing the structure of the site

Defining different site maps

The information architect needs the ability to define a default site map, but in addition should be able to define alternative site maps if required. This is to satisfy the requirement of offering different versions of a site depending on certain criteria, for instance supporting an internal version of the site for company employees (*see* Fig. 14.25).

Therefore a site may have more than one site map, in which case it will need a method to determine which map to use. A site map has a site map type, exam-

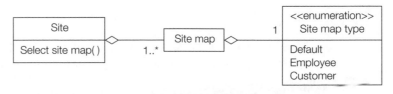

Figure 14.25   Defining alternative site maps

ples of which are default, employee and customer. If the only criteria used to alternate between different site maps is the type of user that is coming to the site, a site map may be associated with a user type instead (*see* Fig. 14.26).

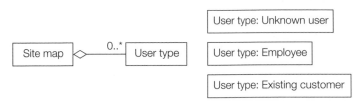

Figure 14.26   Associating a site map with a user type

Defining the structure of a site map

The information architect will need a way of defining the information structure for each site map that is required (*see* Fig. 14.27). This will include the structure of the main navigation paths and the definition of any contextual navigation lists that are offered within different pages.

Therefore every site map will have a homepage, which is a page that has a page type of homepage. Any page can contain one or more navigation lists, which are lists, and may have many web references. A navigation list contains one or more web references. A navigation list fragment, which is a type of fragment, displays a navigation list and contains one or more links, which are used to display a web reference. A web reference represents a page. Pages are specialized types of views that can have one or more fragments within them.

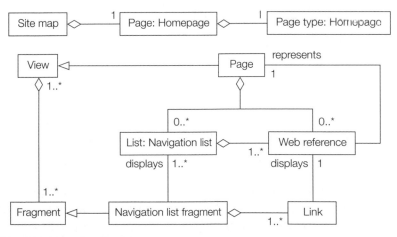

Figure 14.27   Information structure of a site map

Defining the contents of a navigation list

As part of the process of defining the structure of a site map, the information architect needs to define the links that will appear within a navigation list and the order in which they will appear. It should be possible to define these lists both statically and dynamically, i.e. be able to explicitly create a list of required links or to define a query that will automatically create a list of links at publish or run time.

Therefore a general list object may have a list heading, sort criteria and a containment rule that defines the types of objects that are allowed within the list (*see* Fig. 14.28). A list can also contain other lists. A static list is a type of list that has one or more list items. A dynamic list is a type of list that has a query.

A navigation list is a list that has a containment rule that states that the content type has to be a web reference.

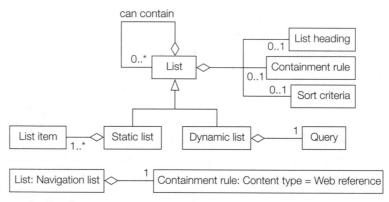

Figure 14.28   Defining a navigation list

Specifying the different types of links

Views on a site or a site map view allow the user to understand the structure of a site and to quickly jump to different parts of the site. The site hierarchy is usually shown by drawing lines between different pages to show that the two pages are linked. To stand any reasonable chance of this view reflecting the true site structure at any particular point in time, the drawing of the site map really needs to be created automatically. This structure should be determined from the structure of the site map and the relationships created as a result of the links that exist within individual pages.

Any large site may wish to filter the relationships lines that are drawn within a site map view in order to reduce the number of lines that the user sees. To support this there will need to exist a type attribute associated with a link that allows any automated process to select which relationship types to display. For instance, if all pages have a link to a homepage, a shop and a feedback form, the site map view may wish to ignore drawing these relationships as they may cause the view to be too overcrowded with lines.

To support this, a web reference will need to have an attribute that describes the type of link it is. Link type examples are global, internal content and external. This link attribute determines how the site map view, which is a fragment, will draw the link relationships (*see* Fig. 14.29).

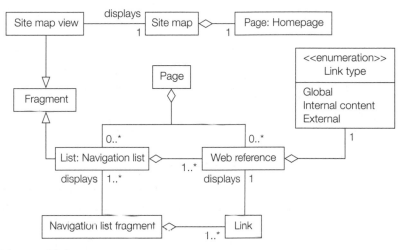

Figure 14.29 Different types of links

Adding a site map to the system

The information architect needs the ability to create and add site map definitions and lists such as navigation lists to the underlying content management system (*see* Fig. 14.30).

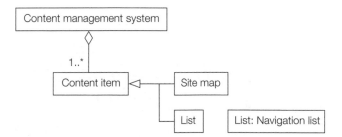

Figure 14.30 Adding a site map to the content management system

Reviewing content and content classifications

As part of any process to ensure information quality, the information architect should review the content that has been created before it is published to the site. This should include:

- reviewing how content has been classified;
- reviewing the content against any predefined criteria (*see* Fig. 14.31).

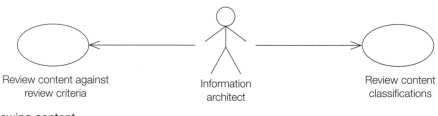

Review content against review criteria   Information architect   Review content classifications

Figure 14.31   Reviewing content

Reviewing content classifications

There are potentially two requirements to enable an information architect to review content classifications before the content is published to a site. The first is having a classification review process that takes place before a content item is published for the first time. The second is having a classification review process after a content item has been changed during a maintenance exercise (*see* Fig. 14.32). This review is likely to fall into a generalized change review process. Reviewing classification information within a content item allows the information architect to ensure that the item will be returned correctly from within a search function on the site, and also such a review may check that the correct level of content relationships have been provided as well as archive classifications if required.

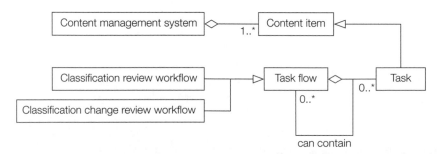

Figure 14.32   Reviewing content classifications

Therefore two task flows need to be created: a classification review workflow and a classification change review workflow. Task flows are types of content items that can contain other task flows and tasks.

Reviewing content

In a similar way to content classification reviews, reviewing the content against content review criteria should take place before a content item is published and again after an item has been changed as part of a change review process. Reviewing content against content review criteria allows the information architect to ensure that the item has met any rules that have been defined to increase content quality and in some cases control content access.

Therefore two further task flows will be needed: a content review workflow and a content change review workflow (*see* Fig 14.33).

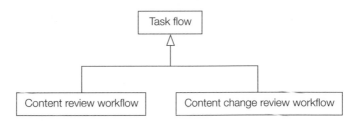

Figure 14.33   Adding task flows

Measuring the success of the classification and navigation structure

To understand whether users manage to find the information they are looking for on a site, the information architect will need to measure the success of the classification and navigation structure and will need to:

● analyze search queries;
● analyze content usage (*see* Fig. 14.34).

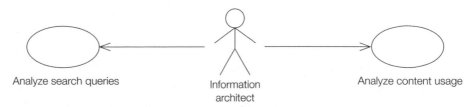

Figure 14.34   Measuring the success of the classification and navigation structure

Analyzing user search queries against site content

The information architect should analyze the search queries that users are entering as it may reveal problems with the site. When terms are being searched for that are not found, it may indicate that either content is missing, it has been incorrectly classified, or there are misleading messages within the interface. In other words the user is expecting to find certain pieces of information on the site that the site has no intention of offering. Alternatively, if users are searching for important terms that should be found easily, it may indicate problems with the navigation structure, causing users to resort to a search function to find information that should be easily accessible through obvious or prominent links.

Therefore a search query report will need to summarize the query keywords entered through a search query and compare them against the content items stored within the content management system to see if the level of matches found is acceptable (*see* Fig. 14.35). There should also be an exception flagged when a user types in a search query that receives no matches. Ideally, this should automatically generate a notification to the information architect as soon as it happens.

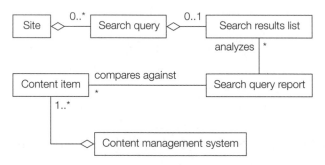

Figure 14.35   Search query report

Analyzing user search queries against keywords

As it is unlikely that all synonyms and keyword variations that users enter within a search facility will be present within the classification system, it would be useful to track the keyword queries that the end user is typing in. This way, the information architect can detect missing keywords, missing synonyms, or common spelling errors.

Therefore a keyword search report summarizes the keywords that have been entered within a search query and compares them against the keywords that appear within the classification system (*see* Fig. 14.36).

In addition if the site is renting out keywords, there will need to exist a mechanism of measuring which keywords are creating the most user queries, so that any rental rates can be related to real data being collected on the site (*see* Fig. 14.37).

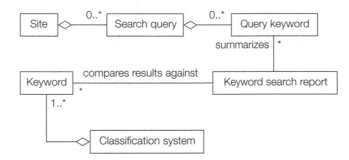

Figure 14.36   Tracking keyword queries

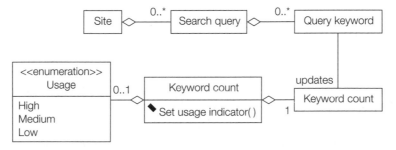

Figure 14.37   Measuring which keywords are creating the most user queries

Analyzing content usage

There are a number of interesting measurements that can be taken to analyze content usage. Pages that receive little to no hits may indicate that the navigation structure is not working as well as it should. Pages that receive the most hits may indicate popular and useful content that may be worth increasing, or alternatively it may indicate that users are getting lost on the site and keep ending up at the wrong page. Something else worth measuring are the hits on pages which are deemed critical to the success of the site (*see* Fig. 14.38). If these pages are not attracting a significant percentage of user hits, it may be time to review the navigation structure and design.

Figure 14.38   Measuring hits on pages

15 Analyzing the requirements of the content manager

System access

The content manager decides who within the organization has access to which documents or content items, and when that access is applicable. When defining system access, the content manager is responsible for:

- defining default access levels;
- define the different access roles within the system;
- defining access control lists for a content type;
- defining access control lists for individual content items;
- defining access control lists for task flows and tasks;
- defining access control lists for individual properties;
- defining access control lists for individual actions;
- managing different content versions (*see* Fig. 15.1).

Defining default access levels

One of the common approaches to setting up system access for a content management system is to define a set defaults that can be used as a base for all the content items held within the system. There are four different types of access:

- readers, who are authorized to read only the contents of documents;
- editors, who can create content and edit existing documents;

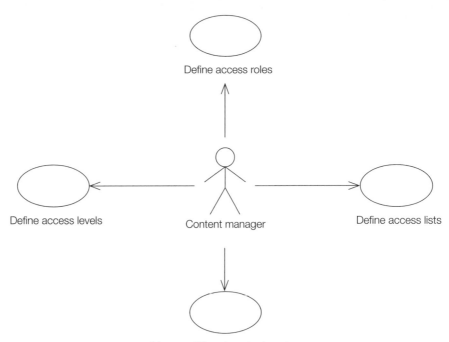

Figure 15.1   The content manager defines system access rules

- designers, who can add and modify the structure of the underlying content types;
- content administrators, who have the control to add and modify content access levels.

By setting up a default set of access control lists for the system, it enables the system administrator or content manager to add alternative access control lists only when required to either override the default lists or add to them as necessary. There will also be a requirement to be able to set up access groups that hold lists of people. Access groups provide a simple mechanism to group people together so that access levels can be applied to the group as a whole rather than having to define access levels for each individual within the system (*see* Fig. 15.2). Access groups can also be shared between different access lists.

Therefore an access list has an access level that can be a content administrator, designer, editor or reader, and can contain many roles and many people. A person can have many roles.

In addition, a content management system has four default access lists. The default content administrators' access list has an access level of content administrator. the default designers' access list has an access level of designer. The default editors' access list has an access level of editor, and the default readers' access list has a default access level of reader (*see* Fig. 15.3).

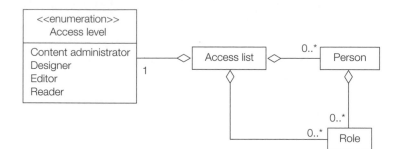

Figure 15.2   Access groups

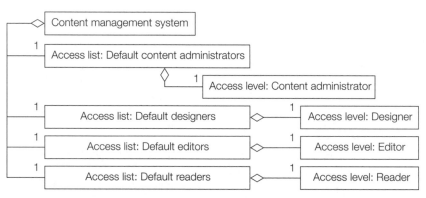

Figure 15.3   Default access lists

Defining different access roles

During the workflow analysis for the organization, the analyst identifies the necessary roles and responsibilities for each workflow. Example of roles within an online newspaper are journalist, news editor and editor. The content manager will need a mechanism to create these roles on the system and to assign individual people to fulfil the role (*see* Fig. 15.4).

Therefore an access list can contain both roles and person objects, and roles can contain other roles and a person can have many roles. Access lists, roles and person objects are all types of content items.

An example of roles within a role hierarchy is displayed in Fig. 15.5 where a person can be associated with a number of different roles. In more detail it shows a content provider role containing a journalist and a feature writer role, a content owner role, and a further role of a content reviewer. A content reviewer role contains three roles: a news editor, a legal advisor role and a classification reviewer. The person, John Smith, has three roles, that of journalist, content owner and classification reviewer.

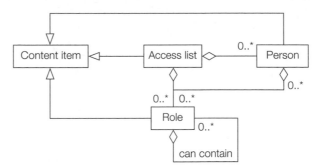

Figure 15.4   Creating roles

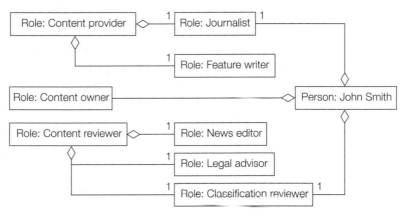

Figure 15.5   Roles within a role hierarchy

Defining a user group through a query

It is likely that for most default access control lists, the system administrator will not wish to individually add people or user roles into the system. This would be too time consuming for many types of systems that are used by a changing workforce. For instance, the system administrator may wish to allow anyone who has access to the system to read content on that system, otherwise there would be little point in having access in the first place. In this case, there will be a requirement for user groups to be created that are defined by a query. A query could be defined to create a dynamic list based on attributes of people held on the system.

Therefore an access list will need to be associated with a user group, which is a type of dynamic list. A dynamic list has a query and is a type of list. A list may have a containment rule that restricts the types of items that can be within the list. User groups have a containment rule that restricts the query to items of type person or role (*see* Fig. 15.6).

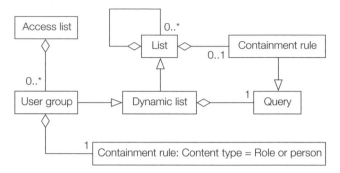

Figure 15.6   Using a dynamic list to create an access list

Defining access control lists for a content type

In some cases it makes sense to apply different access rights for different types of content held on the system. For instance, content managers are likely to want to control how many people have the authority to change workflow documents. Workflows control the way that content gets moved around the organization and will include the definition of how content is reviewed before it is published. Any change that mistakenly wipes out a publication review process may have serious consequences on the information quality published to the site. Likewise, a content manager is unlikely to want anyone apart from graphic designers and developers tinkering with view template definitions, irrespective of how good their intentions are.

Another requirement for those defining access control lists is the ability to specify whether any new list replaces the one that is being used or just appends to it. The append option will allow the administrator to build up a series of access controls on top of each other and allow smaller lists to be reused in different circumstances.

Therefore an access list may be associated with many different content types, such as workflow, keyword, and web reference, and has an access level that can be content administrator, designer, editor or reader. An access list has a 'replace existing' flag, which indicates whether the list replaces other lists defined or whether the new list is appended to an existing list. An access list can contain many roles and many person objects (*see* Fig. 15.7).

Defining access control lists for individual content items

There may be situations in which an organization needs to define individual access control lists for individual content items. For example, the business plan for a site may be an instance of a document on the system that can be edited by a very small number of people. Reports that look at the success rate of workflows,

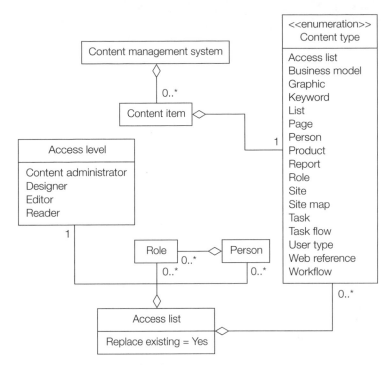

Figure 15.7   Defining access at a context type level

for example a report showing items that need the most changes or content items that have taken a long time to create, may be viewable only by content managers. So there needs to exist a mechanism whereby content managers can protect the access to individual content items if required (*see* Fig. 15.8).

Therefore an access list that can have an access level of content administrator, designer, editor or reader can be associated with one or more content items.

Defining access control lists for individual task flows and tasks

There may also be a requirement to define at a task flow and individual task level what the access is at any particular point within an overall workflow. For instance, each content item defined by a type will be associated with a creation workflow that has within it a 'create new task'. Defining and associating an access list that has an access level of editor for that individual task will define who is able to create content items of that type (*see* Fig. 15.9).

Therefore an access list that can have an access level of content administrator, designer, editor or reader can be associated with task flows and tasks (*see* Fig. 15.9).

Another common example of where this level of access control is applicable is during a proposal workflow when a content creator has submitted a proposal

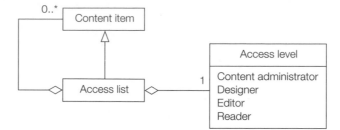

Figure 15.8 Defining access at a content item level

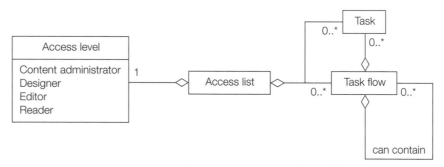

Figure 15.9 Defining access at a task flow and task level

for a new content item. While the proposal is under review by a content reviewer, the access rules may change to allow the content item to be edited only by the person responsible for reviewing the proposal. This will disable any further editing or changes to be made to the proposal while it is undergoing a review.

Defining access control lists for individual properties

Following on from the above example, the content manager may also wish to protect certain properties from being edited while a task is being performed and may also wish to explicitly establish who within the organization has authority to set certain properties. For example, a person reviewing a proposal may not have the authority to decide who within the team will do the work if the proposal is approved. A content owner field may only be edited by a resource manager after a proposal has been approved.

Another common requirement is to have the ability to hide sensitive fields such as an employee's salary. Employee details may be openly read by everyone on the system, but certain properties within these details may be protected and viewable only by those people with the correct level of access. To support this, there will be a requirement to override or append existing access lists at an individual property level.

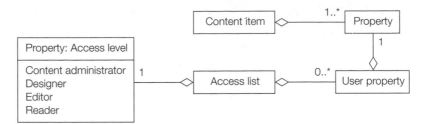

Figure 15.10   Defining access at a property level

Therefore an access list that has an access level of either content administrator, designer, editor or reader can be associated with many user properties. A user property is associated with a property that is contained within a content item (*see* Fig. 15.10).

Defining access control lists for task actions

There may be a further requirement to provide access on the actions that are available within a task. For instance, a user action that approves the publication of a content item may be viewable and selectable only by a final reviewer of the content.

Therefore, in addition to being able to associate access lists to user properties, there may be a requirement to associate them to user actions that appear within tasks (*see* Fig. 15.11).

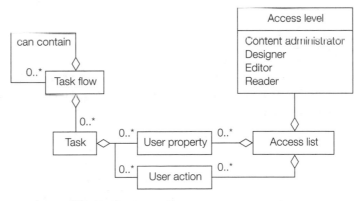

Figure 15.11   Defining access at an action level

Managing different versions of content items

There will be a requirement for a content management system to support version control so that changes can be rolled back if necessary and so that changes to published material can be verified before they are put back on the site. Version control also allows for a history to be maintained of who is making which changes, and safeguards against changes being overwritten.

Each content item will need a content owner that represents who will be the main contact point for any changes that are requested. This may be different to the person who creates the item or different again from the person who creates the different versions. Ownership is important to put in place as it is hoped it will instil some sense of responsibility and accountability for the quality of the content item.

Therefore a content item has a name, an initial version, a content owner that defaults to the person who created the initial version, and a short description that also defaults to the description supplied for the initial version (*see* Fig. 15.12). Each version of the content item has a 'created by', a created date, and may have a description.

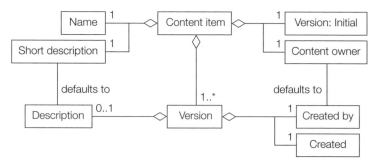

Figure 15.12   Supporting different versions of a content item

Defining workflows

The content manager decides what the workflows will be with respect to publishing information on to the website. When establishing these workflows the content manager is responsible for:

- defining the main stages;
- defining the different workflows within a stage;
- defining the tasks within each workflow;
- defining when a workflow can be started;
- defining whether task notification is needed;
- defining the required levels of approval;
- defining what happens when a request is rejected within a notification action;
- defining acceptable time limits for task completion;
- associating workflows with content;
- creating tasks and task flows and adding them to the system (*see* Fig. 15.13).

Define workflow stages   Define workflow tasks

Associate workflows with
content

Define workflow
preconditions

Content manager

Define levels of approval

Define task notifications

Define acceptable task
completion times

Figure 15.13   Determining workflows

Defining the main workflow stages

A workflow may group together a set of smaller workflows to form a logical stage
within a content item's life cycle. For example, a preparation workflow could be
created that groups together all the smaller workflows needed to move a content
item through from creation to publication. Another main workflow might be a
maintenance stage, which groups together all the workflows involved in maintaining published content.

A workflow that is used to describe the stages of work within an organization
to achieve some goal is barely different in concept to the task flows that are used
to model the way that users wish to achieve their task goals on the site. The only
difference is the target audience and maybe the system that the task flow will be
delivered on. Therefore the definition of the different stages within a workflow
and the requirements needed to support transitions between these stages are
exactly the same as how tasks and task flows are defined.

Therefore a preparation workflow and a maintenance workflow are examples
of task flows that can contain other task flows and tasks (*see* Fig. 15.14).

Figure 15.14 Defining work flow stages

Defining the different task flows within a workflow stage

When setting up the workflows for different types of content, it should be possible to define the combination of stages that make up each overall workflow, for instance, whether for a certain type of content there exists a proposal stage or whether a change request process is necessary to make updates to currently published material (*see* Fig. 15.15).

There will need to be many different types of standard workflows predefined such as a change review workflow, a publish workflow and a proposal workflow. The content manager should be in a position to group together different instances of these workflows and associate them with different types of content.

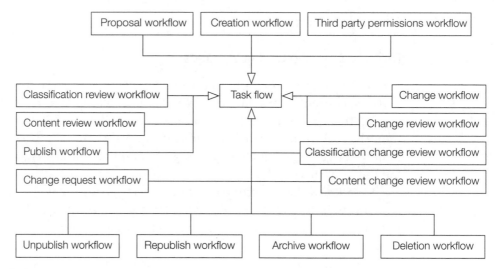

Figure 15.15 Defining types of workflow

Defining the tasks within each workflow

Even though standard workflows might be provided, it may be necessary for the content manager to edit these workflows, to add new task flows and tasks, or edit the ones provided. In this instance, a requirement would exist to define what happens within a workflow by defining the tasks and flow of tasks within any task-flow process.

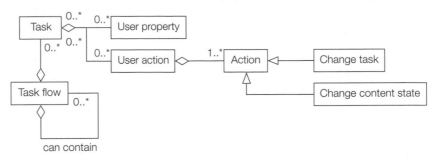

Figure 15.16   Defining the flow of tasks

Therefore a task that is part of a task flow can have many user actions, which in turn can trigger one or more actions. 'Change task' is an action that updates the task state and 'change content state' is an action that updates the current state of the content item (*see* Fig. 15.16). A task also has user properties defined.

Defining when a workflow can be started

When creating a workflow, the content manager will need a way of defining the states that a content item must be in before the workflow can begin. For instance, a proposal workflow may be applicable only when a content item has a current state of new, whereas a removal or deletion workflow may be available when a content item has a current state of publishing, archived or in review. When there is more than one content state when a workflow can be started, the workflow will need to remember the current state of the content item at the time the workflow process was started. This allows the state of the content item to be reinstated if the workflow process does not complete successfully. An example of this might be where a content item is currently publishing and a request is made to delete it from the site. The person responsible for reviewing delete requests may reject this request, in which case the content item would need to be reset to the state it was in before the delete request was made.

Therefore a task flow will need to have a list of start states that define that list of states that the content item must be in before the workflow is made available. This list has a containment rule where the content type has to be a state. A content item has a current state which is a state, and may have a saved state, which is also a state (*see* Fig. 15.17).

Defining the start actions for a workflow

To set up a system that supports automated workflows, each workflow will need to be provided with enough information for it to know when it should be available and visible within the interface. There are two types of triggers that can

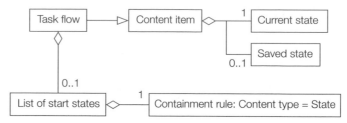

Figure 15.17   A list of start states within a task flow

occur. The first and most common is a user-invoked request such as a user select-ing an option to publish the content item. This option may be made available through the interface in the form of a push button and upon selection a content review workflow may be triggered.

Secondly, there might be instances where a workflow is triggered by a con-tent item being in a certain state or condition. Start conditions or start queries may be defined within a workflow, so that when a content item matches the start condition, the workflow will be automatically triggered against the content item. For example, it could be a policy to review all currently publishing material after a certain time to ensure that the content is still relevant and up to date. To achieve this, a publish review date property may be added to the content item. When this date is the current date, a content review workflow may be automati-cally triggered to decide whether the content item should be archived or removed from the site. To set up these automatic triggers, the content manager will need to create start queries within the workflow that allow it to be started when con-tent items are within the required state.

Therefore the first decision the content manager will need to make is, will the workflow be automatically triggered? If the answer is yes, the conditions that will trigger the workflow need to be defined as a start query and associated with the workflow. If the workflow will be triggered by a user action, the content manager needs to define the action that the user selects to start the workflow, for instance a publish push button and secondly, when this action is visible within the inter-face and available to be selected. This can be achieved in two ways, either based on the current state of the content item and therefore use the start states as defined earlier, or the task flow can be contained within a task and therefore the start actions will be available while the task is being performed.

Therefore a task flow may have a list of start actions that has a containment rule stating that the list can only contain user actions (*see* Fig. 15.18). It may also have a start query. Task flows contain tasks, but a task can also contain a task flow.

Defining whether task notification is needed

One of the things that a content manager will need to do is to define the roles responsible for moving content through a workflow and the notifications that are sent out to inform these individuals that an action is required.

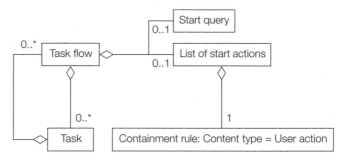

Figure 15.18   A list of start actions within a task flow

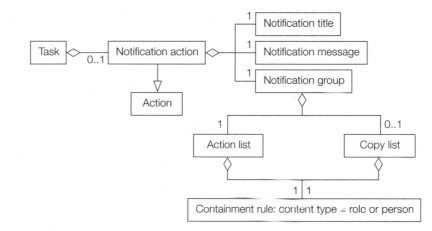

Figure 15.19   Task notification

To support this a task may have a notification action, which is a type of action. A notification action will have a title, a notification message and a notification group. A notification group has an action list, which is used to define the list of people responsible for completing the task, and may have a copy list, which is used to copy people for information only. Both the action list and the copy list have a containment rule of only containing content items of type role or person (*see* Fig. 15.19).

Defining the required levels of approval

When defining a notification group there may exist a requirement to define the required approval level when a notification is sent out. For instance, the level of approval may require that everyone within the action list needs to approve the content item. This method would require a notification being sent to the first person in the group, and only when that person gives an approval does the notification get sent to the next person in the list. The other method is where only one person within the action list needs to approve the content item, but it does

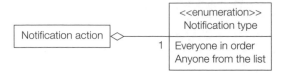

Figure 15.20 Notification types

not matter which person it is. This method requires that a shared mail queue exists between the people within the list, so that when one person reads the notification, the notification mail item is removed from the incoming mail for the others within the list.

Therefore the content manager has the ability to set a notification type for a notification action, which can be either everyone in order from within the action list, or anyone from the list (*see* Fig. 15.20).

Defining what happens when a request is rejected within a notification action

When a content item is under review and is being sent around a list of people in sequence, there will be times when someone within the list rejects the item. In this situation, the content manager will need to decide whether everyone within the list should review a content item that is resubmitted for review after a rejection, or whether it can bypass those who had originally accepted it and restart the review at the point where it was rejected.

To support this requirement, there will need to exist an option that defines the rule for repeating a review cycle. The two choices will be that the content item should be resent to everyone within the list or it should be re-reviewed from the point within the list where it was rejected (*see* Fig. 15.21).

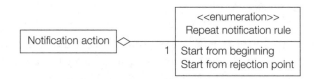

Figure 15.21   Rule for repeating a review cycle

Defining acceptable time limits for task completion

At any stage during a workflow process, content may be held up in the system because those required to move the item on to the next stage do not do so. In order to avoid this situation there needs to be a mechanism in place that allows the definition of super approvers that have the authority to step in and move content items through to the next stage or divert content items along another workflow path. As well as defining who these approvers are, there needs to be an elapsed time set (e.g. one day) that is used as a time limit for normal approval before triggering a super approval process.

As well as having a default approval backup mechanism for all content within a content management system, there might also be a requirement to be able to set these limits at an individual notification action level. For example, in a real-time news publishing environment, there might be a requirement to complete a publishing review of news articles within 60 minutes in order to meet publishing deadlines.

To support this, a content management system will need to have an action monitor that has a default completion time for all notification actions within all workflows. However, each individual notification action may also have an action monitor. The monitor notification action group within the monitor notification action has an action list that has a containment rule where the contents of the list can only contain super user roles (*see* Fig. 15.22).

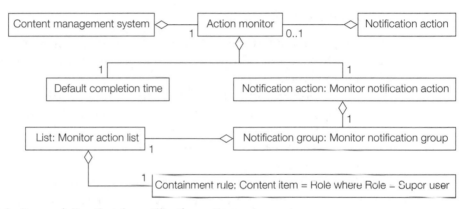

Figure 15.22   Default completion time for notification actions

Associating workflows with content

Defining the association between the content items within a content management system and the different workflows that may exist can be achieved by outlining a list of association rules that link an individual workflow to a content item instance. The list will need to contain a number of workflow conditions in a priority order. If none of the conditions are true, the default workflow will be used.

A workflow condition could have many conditional states, such as content type = 'news article' and content owner = 'John Smith'. This example defines a workflow for news articles written by John Smith. If another workflow were defined for news articles with a lower priority, this would be used for all news articles not written by John Smith.

Therefore a content management system will need to support a workflow association list that is used to hold a set of queries in a priority order. This list is used to associate individual workflow instances with content item instances; if no association is made, the default workflow is applied. A workflow association list has a containment rule where the content type has to be a query (*see* Fig. 15.23).

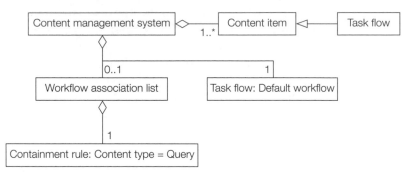

Figure 15.23   Defining the association between content items and workflows

Tracking the workflow history

To track the actions of a workflow on a content item, there needs to exist a mechanism whereby a workflow history is logged against and held with the content item it applies to.

A workflow history will need to keep a track of all the workflow actions that are made against the content item, the dates when the actions were performed, and the person responsible for performing the action. This information can then be used to analyze the progress of content items through the various workflows within the system.

Therefore a content item should contain a workflow history, which is a list that contains one or more workflow entries (*see* Fig. 15.24). A workflow entry is defined by having a who, that records the person committing the action, a what,

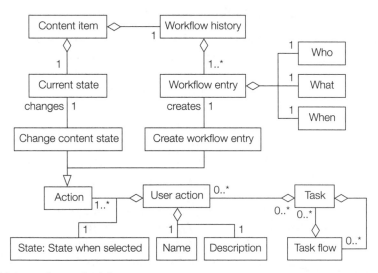

Figure 15.24   Workflow history of a content item

that describes the action that was committed, and a when, that records the date and time the action was completed. 'Create workflow entry', which is a type of action, creates workflow entries and the 'change content state' action changes the current state of the content item. Tasks can have many user actions, which have a name, description and a state when selected. This information will be used to create the what field within the workflow entry when the user action is selected.

Setting up a proposal workflow

The content manager is responsible for setting up the different workflows and associating them with the content items that should follow them (*see* Fig. 15.25). When setting up the proposal workflow, the content manager is responsible for:

- defining the proposal forms and proposal workflows;
- adding a content proposal workflow to an overall preparation workflow;
- defining the start states and start user actions for a proposal workflow;
- defining who is responsible for reviewing proposals;
- defining how the review notification is handled;

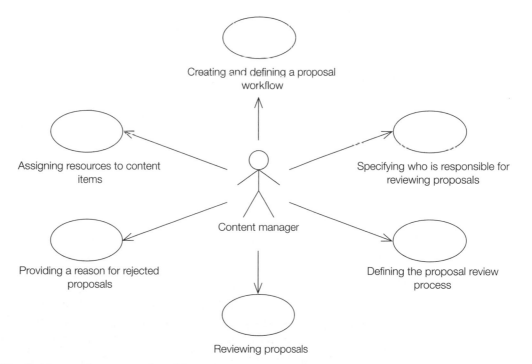

Figure 15.25 Setting up the proposal workflow

- accepting or rejecting content proposals;
- providing a reason why proposals are rejected;
- assigning resources to content items.

Creating proposals and a proposal workflow

The person responsible for setting up a proposal workflow should only need to edit a predefined template that exists and add in the information and rules that are specific to the organization. In addition, there should be a default proposal form that allows proposals to be created for different types of content items within the content management system. The default proposal workflow will then be used to move the proposals through a review cycle.

Therefore a proposal workflow is a type of task flow that acts upon a proposal. A proposal is used to propose one or more content types and each content item has a content type. Examples of content types are reports, news articles, products and web references (*see* Fig. 15.26).

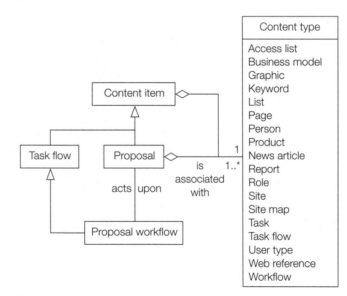

Figure 15.26   Proposal workflow

Default proposal states

The proposal workflow moves a proposal document through a default set of states. The proposal workflow provides the user actions that allow those responsible for moving the content item through the workflow to select the actions that they wish to invoke upon the proposal document (*see* Fig. 15.27).

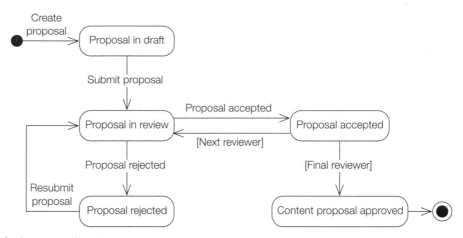

Figure 15.27   Default proposal states

Adding a content proposal workflow to an overall preparation workflow

For some types of content it might be applicable for new content ideas to be proposed before they are commissioned or resourced within an organization. As such it should be possible to define or modify a proposal workflow process as part of an overall content preparation workflow.

Therefore a proposal workflow may form part of a preparation workflow. There are three tasks within a standard proposal workflow: create new proposal, edit existing proposal, and review proposal (*see* Fig. 15.28). Task flows contain tasks and a task may contain a task flow. A proposal workflow is a type of task flow.

Defining the start states and start user actions for a proposal workflow

A standard proposal workflow will have a set of user actions that will start the process. It will also have a default set of start states that a content item or content management system will need to be in before the start user actions will appear. The content manager will need the flexibility to refine this list and modify it as necessary to cover other processes that an organization may wish to add.

Therefore a proposal workflow will have two start actions within the list of start actions: new proposal and open existing proposal (*see* Fig. 15.29). As a start state is not defined, these actions will always be available, irrespective of the state of the content management system or any open or selected content item.

Defining those responsible for approving proposals

When a proposal workflow is defined, the content manager will be responsible for deciding whose job it is to review proposals within the organization. As such,

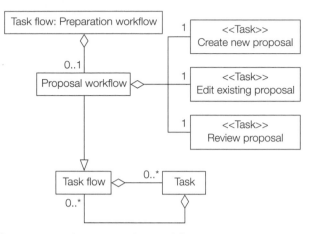

Figure 15.28   A proposal workflow as part of a preparation workflow

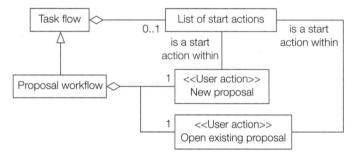

Figure 15.29   List of start actions in a proposal workflow

there will need to be a mechanism whereby these names are added to the system and the notification message set up so that those receiving a notification to review a proposal understand what is required of them.

Therefore a review proposal task has a notification action, where the content manager can specify the title and message of the notification and who the notification is sent to. The different lists are the action list to contain the people or roles responsible for reviewing the proposal, and, optionally, a copy list to define people or roles who will get a copy of the notification but are not responsible for doing anything. The content manager will also need to specify whether the proposal needs to be reviewed by everyone in the list or just one person from the list (*see* Fig. 15.30).

Accepting or rejecting new content proposals

The proposal workflow process will need a mechanism whereby those reviewing proposals can accept or reject the proposal.

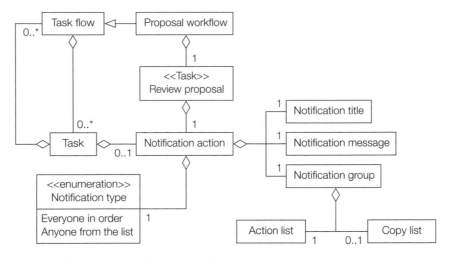

Figure 15.30 Specifying notification in a review proposal task

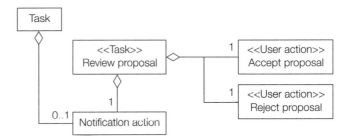

Figure 15.31 User actions in a review proposal task

Therefore the review proposal task will have two user actions: accept proposal and reject proposal (*see* Fig. 15.31).

Providing a reason why a proposal is rejected

When a proposal is rejected, there needs to be a mechanism whereby the person rejecting the proposal can provide a reason why the decision has been made.

A review proposal task will have a reject proposal user action, which will have a feedback action. A feedback action is a standard type of action that allows a message to be sent back to the content owner. The feedback title will be set to be a proposal rejection, but the message will be open so that the person creating the feedback can explain why the rejection has been made (*see* Fig. 15.32).

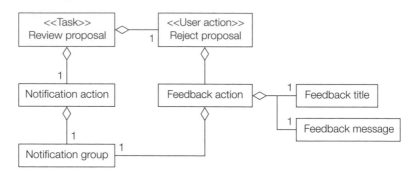

Figure 15.32   Feedback action within a reject proposal user action

Assigning resources to content items

When a proposal has been created and submitted for review, there might exist a requirement for those reviewing the proposals to assign ownership to the piece of work and maybe the definition of a creation team which should contribute to the content item.

Therefore a content item will have one person identified as the content owner, which defaults to the person who created the first version. However, this field can be edited by a resource manager along with the creation team, to allow the definition of who will be working on the project (*see* Fig. 15.33).

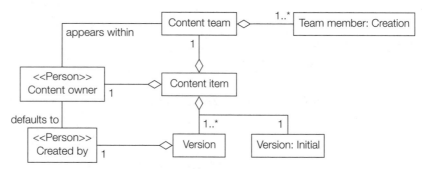

Figure 15.33   Defining who is working on a project

Arranging permissions for content use

An organization may wish to include pieces of content on its website that it does not own. In this instance the content manager may be responsible for putting in place a process for gaining permissions to use content that is owned elsewhere. In defining such a process, the content manager will be responsible for:

- creating publishing agreements and a third party permissions workflow;
- adding a third party permissions workflow to an overall preparation and maintenance workflow;
- defining the start states and start user actions for a third party permissions workflow;
- defining who is responsible for handling requests for using external content;
- defining who is responsible for reviewing publishing agreements;
- defining how the review notification is handled;
- accepting or rejecting requests for using external content;
- providing a reason why a request to use external content is rejected;
- accepting or rejecting publishing agreements;
- providing a reason why publishing agreements are rejected (*see* Fig. 15.34).

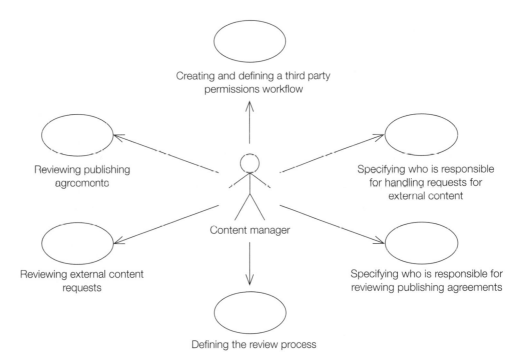

Figure 15.34 Gaining permission for content use

Creating publishing agreements and a third party permissions workflow

The person responsible for setting up a third party permissions workflow should need only to edit a predefined template and add in the information and rules that are specific to the organization. In addition, there should be a default publishing agreement form that allows publishing agreements to be created. The default third party permission workflow will then be used to move the publishing agreement document through a review cycle.

Therefore a content item may be associated with many publishing agreements and a third party permissions workflow, which is a type of task flow, controls the process for how publishing agreements are created, reviewed and approved (*see* Fig 15.35).

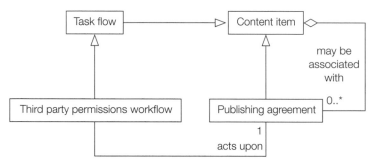

Figure 15.35   Establishing publishing agreements

Adding a third party permissions workflow to an overall preparation and maintenance workflow

When it is necessary to organize permission for third party content, a publishing agreement will need to be put in place before the content item is published. Therefore it should be possible for the content manager to define or modify a third party permission workflow process as part of an overall content preparation workflow

In addition, in the event where it is found that a publishing agreement should have been arranged for content that is already publishing, such a workflow will need to be made available as part of an overall maintenance workflow (*see* Fig. 15.36).

Therefore a third party permission workflow may be part of both a preparation workflow and a maintenance workflow. The default third party permissions workflow has four tasks within it: a review request to use third party content task, a create new publishing agreement task, an edit existing publishing agreement task, and a review publishing agreement task.

Default publishing agreement states

The third party permission workflow has two distinct stages. The first is the request for external content to be used; this would probably come from the

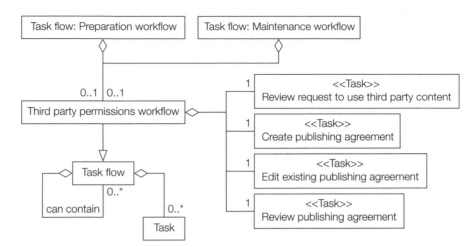

Figure 15.36 Third party permission workflow process as part of an overall content preparation workflow

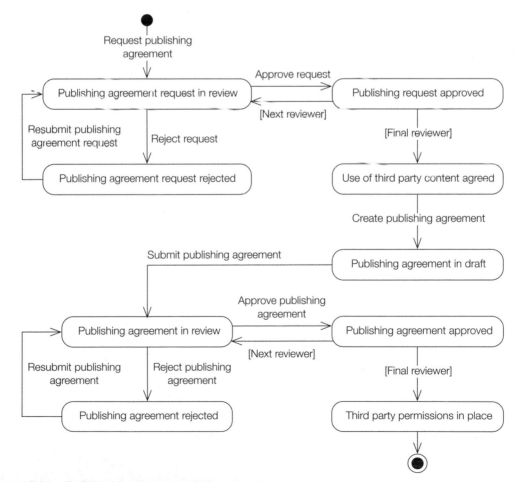

Figure 15.37 Default third party permission states

person creating the content item. The second is the creation of a publishing agreement document that contains the formal agreement to use the third party content on the site (*see* Fig. 15.37). Both of these stages by default need a review process.

Defining the start states and start user actions for the third party permissions workflow

The default third party permission workflow will have a set of user actions that will invoke the workflow process to begin. It will also have a default set of start states that a content item or the content management system will need to be in before the user actions will appear. The content manager will need the flexibility to modify the list as required to cover other processes or actions that an organization might wish to add.

Therefore a third party permissions workflow may have four states within a list of start states which define when it can be started. These are when a content item is in draft, when a publishing request has been rejected, when a content item is currently publishing, and when a content item is being changed within a maintenance cycle (*see* Fig. 15.38). The start action that appears when the content item is within any of these states is a request publishing agreement user action, which starts the workflow when it is selected.

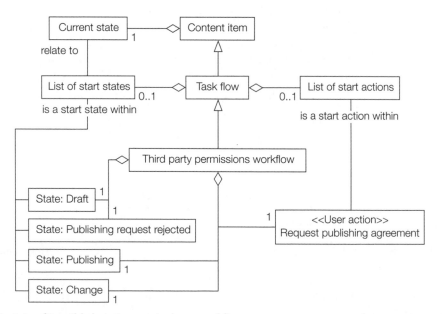

Figure 15.38   Start states for a third party permissions workflow

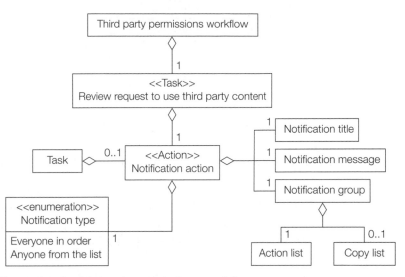

Figure 15.39   Notification action for third party permissions workflow

Defining those responsible for approving requests to use third party content

When setting up a third party permissions workflow process there will need to be a mechanism whereby those responsible for approving the use of third party content within the organization can be added to the workflow process.

Therefore the task to review requests to use third party content will need a notification action that can be used to define the list of people within the organization who are needed to review the request and the list of people within a copy list who simply get notified that the request has been made. The notification that is sent out will need a title and a message to let those people know what they are supposed to be doing, and the content manager will be able to determine whether everyone on the list is needed to review and approve the request or just one person from the list (*see* Fig. 15.39).

Defining who is responsible for reviewing completed publishing agreements

Once a request to use third party content has been approved, the publishing agreement will need to be created and also approved. Thus it will be necessary to define who is responsible within the organization for reviewing completed publishing agreements.

Therefore the task to review publishing agreements will also need a notification action (*see* Fig. 15.40).

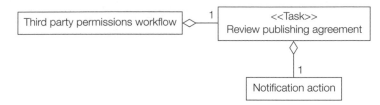

Figure 15.40   Notification action for reviewing a publishing agreement

Accepting or rejecting requests for using external content

The third party permissions workflow process will need a mechanism whereby those reviewing the request to use third party content can accept or reject the request.

Therefore the review request to use third party content task will need to display two user actions: an accept request action and a reject request action (*see* Fig. 15.41).

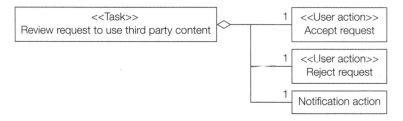

Figure 15.41   User actions for review request to use third party content task

Providing a reason why a request for external content use is rejected

When a request to use third party content is rejected, there needs to be a mechanism whereby the person rejecting the request can provide a reason why the decision has been made.

Therefore the reject request user action within the review request to use third party content task will need a feedback action that allows the person rejecting the request to send a feedback message to the content owner and the person submitting the request (if they differ) with the reason why the request has been rejected (see Fig. 15.42).

Accepting or rejecting publishing agreements

The third party permissions workflow process will need a mechanism whereby those reviewing publishing agreements can accept or reject them.

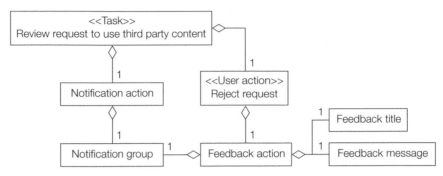

Figure 15.42   Feedback action for reject request user action

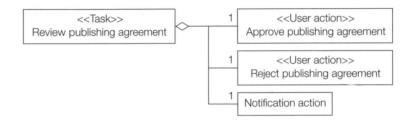

Figure 15.43   Approving or rejecting the publishing agreement request

Therefore the review publishing agreement task will need to display two user actions that allow the reviewer to either approve the publishing agreement request or reject it (*see* Fig. 15.43).

Providing a reason why a publishing agreement has been rejected

When a third party publishing agreement is rejected, there needs to be a mechanism whereby the person reviewing it can provide a reason why the decision has been made.

Therefore the reject publishing agreement user action will need a feedback action that allows a message to be sent back to the content owner or person sending the request (if they differ) with the reason why the publishing agreement has been rejected (*see* Fig. 15.44).

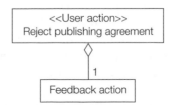

Figure 15.44   Feedback action for rejecting a publishing agreement

Setting up a content review workflow

The content manager is responsible for setting up any content review workflows that are needed to review new items before they are published to the site. When setting up a content review workflow, the content manager is responsible for:

- creating a content review workflow;
- adding a content review workflow to an overall preparation workflow;
- defining the start states and start user actions for a content review workflow;
- defining who is responsible for reviewing new content before it is published;
- defining how the content review notification is handled;
- accepting or rejecting new content items;
- providing a reason why a content item has been rejected (*see* Fig. 15.45).

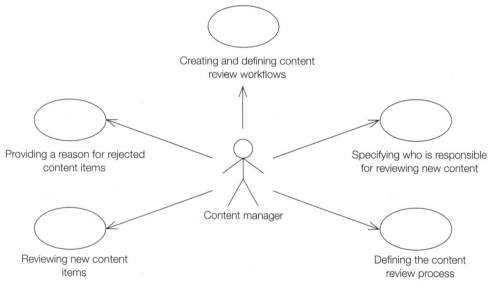

Creating and defining content
review worktlows

Providing a reason for rejected
content items

Specifying who is responsible
for reviewing new content

Content manager

Reviewing new content
items

Defining the content
review process

Figure 15.45   Setting up a content review workflow

Creating a content review workflow

The person responsible for setting up any content review workflows should only need to edit a predefined template and add in the information and rules that are specific to the organization. The default content review workflow should be modifiable to allow content items to move through to publication on the site.

Because a task flow can contain other task flows, it is quite likely that an overall content review workflow will contain other content review workflows, for example, a content review workflow for reviewing news articles before they are published to a news site. An overall content review workflow may contain three separate review stages:

- a news editor review may check for the accuracy and news style of an article;
- a legal content review may check whether the story will cause any legal problems;
- a classification review may check how the article has been classified to make sure that it will be correctly archived and linked to within any automatically generated related article lists (*see* Fig. 15.46).

Only after all three reviews have been successfully completed and approved will the news article be published to the site.

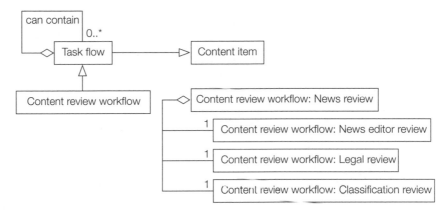

Figure 15.46   Example content review workflow for news articles

Default content review states

A content review workflow has a set of default states that allow a content item to be checked before it is published. It provides those reviewing the item two user actions to approve or reject the publication request (*see* Fig. 15.47).

Adding a content review workflow to an overall preparation workflow

It is likely that an organization will want to put in place some sort of review process before new content gets published to a site. As such it should be possible for a content manager to work with a content review workflow template and modify it as required. It should also be possible to add content review workflows to an overall content preparation workflow. Therefore a content review workflow that has a review content item task may be included within a preparation workflow (*see* Fig. 15.48).

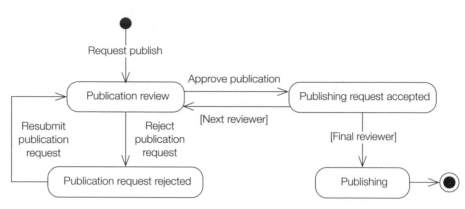

Figure 15.47 Review states

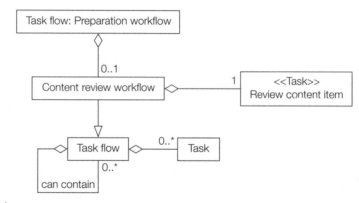

Figure 15.48 Content review process

Defining the start states and start user actions for a content review workflow

The default content review workflow will have a start user action that allows a content provider to request that a content item be published to the site. If the overall preparation workflow that is associated with the content item includes a content review workflow, the selection of this action will start the review process going. The request publish user action appears when the content item is within a certain state, defined in the list of start states associated with content review workflow. The content manager will need the flexibility to refine this list and modify it as necessary to cover other processes that the organization may wish to add.

Therefore the default content review workflow is available when a content item is in a state of draft, when a publishing request is rejected, when a publishing agreement request is rejected, and when third party permissions are in place (*see* Fig. 15.49). The start user action that appears when a content item is in any of these four states is request publish and when this is selected, the content review workflow is kicked off.

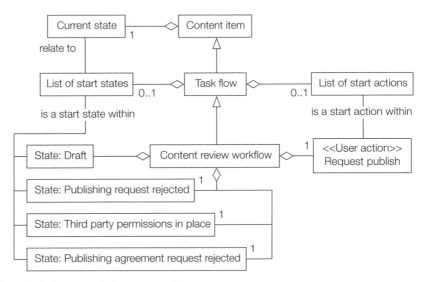

Figure 15.49 Defining start states and start user actions

Defining who is responsible for reviewing new content before it is published

When setting up a content review workflow process there will need to be a mechanism whereby those responsible for approving the publication of new content within the organization can be added to the workflow process.

Therefore the review content item task, within the content review workflow, will need to have a notification action that can be set up by a content manager (*see* Fig. 15.50). A notification action is used to send a message to a list of people requesting them to complete a requested action, the details of which are given within the notification message field. The content manager is able to specify who the notification is sent to by adding people to the action list, which will be used

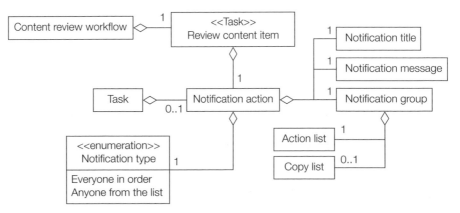

Figure 15.50 Notification action

to contain those people or roles responsible for reviewing the content item, and optionally adding people to a copy list of those who get a copy of the notification but are not responsible for doing anything. The content manager will also specify whether the content item needs to be reviewed by everyone in the action list or just one person from the list.

Accepting or rejecting new content items

The content review workflow process should provide a mechanism whereby those deciding whether the content item should be published have a mechanism that allows them to accept or reject the publish request.

Therefore the review content item task will have two user actions available for selection: an accept publication and a reject publication (*see* Fig. 15.51).

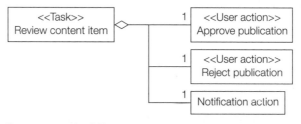

Figure 15.51   Accepting or rejecting new content items

Providing a reason why a content item has been rejected

When a request to publish is rejected, there needs to be a mechanism whereby the person rejecting the publication can provide a reason for their decision.

Therefore a reject publication user action has a feedback action that allows the person making the rejection to provide and send back the reason (*see* Fig. 15.52).

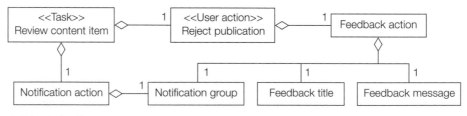

Figure 15.52   Explaining rejections

Setting up a change request workflow

For large sites that require a significant level of maintenance to content being published, it is often a good idea to put in place a change request process to manage when changes are being made and who is making them. In setting up a change request workflow, the content manager will be responsible for:

- defining the level of information required within a submitted change request;
- defining a change request workflow;
- adding a change request workflow to an overall maintenance workflow;
- defining the start states and start user actions for a change request workflow;
- defining who is responsible for reviewing change requests;
- defining how the review notification is handled;
- accepting or rejecting change requests;
- providing a reason why change requests are rejected;
- scheduling when a change can happen;
- assigning resources to content items in order for the change to be completed (*see* Fig. 15.53).

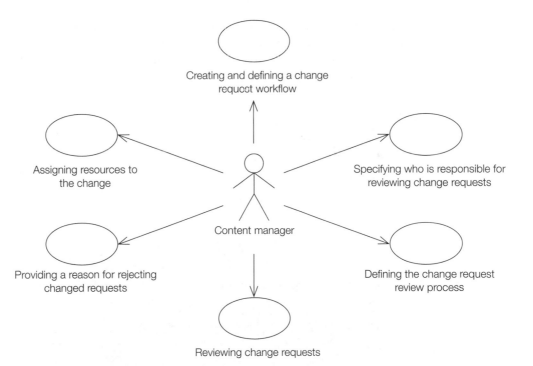

Figure 15.53 Setting up a change request workflow

Creating change requests and a change request workflow

The person responsible for setting up a change request workflow should only need to edit a predefined template and add in the information and rules that are specific to the organization. In addition, there should be a default change request form that allows change requests to be created for different types of content items within the content management system. The default change request workflow can then be used to move change request documents through a review cycle.

Therefore a change request workflow acts upon a change request, which is a type of content item, and a content item may be associated with many change requests (*see* Fig. 15.54).

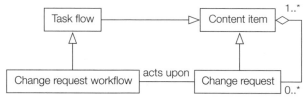

Figure 15.54 The change request workflow

Default change request states

The change request workflow moves a change request document through a default set of states. The change request workflow provides the user actions that allow those responsible for moving the document through the workflow to select the actions they wish to invoke upon the change request document (see Fig. 15.55).

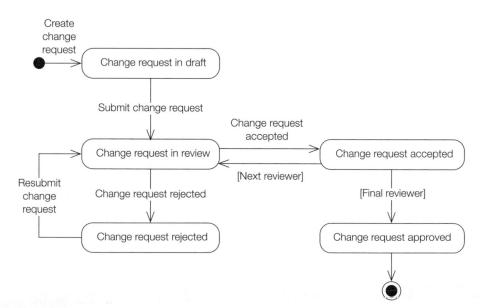

Figure 15.55 Default change request states

Adding a change request workflow to an overall maintenance workflow

If the content manager requires a change request process to be put in place for all or some of the content publishing on the site, it should be possible to define or modify a default change request workflow process and add it to an overall content maintenance workflow.

Therefore a maintenance workflow may contain a change request workflow. A default change request workflow has three tasks: create change request, edit existing change request, and a review change request task (*see* Fig. 15.56).

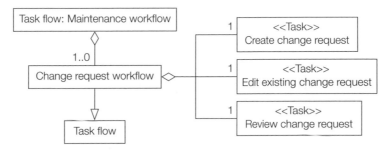

Figure 15.56   Adding a change request to a maintenance workflow

Defining the start states and start user actions for a change request workflow

The default change request workflow will have a set of user actions that will invoke the change request workflow process to begin. It will also have a default set of start states that a content item or content management system will need to be in before the user actions will appear. The content manager will need the flexibility to refine this list and modify it as necessary to cover other processes that an organization may wish to add.

Therefore a default change request workflow has three states within the list of start states, which define when the process can be started: when the content item is publishing, archived or removed. The start action that is used to kick off the change request workflow is a request change user action (*see* Fig. 15.57).

Defining who is responsible for reviewing change requests

When setting up a change request workflow process there will need to be a mechanism whereby those responsible for approving change requests within the organization can be added to the workflow process (*see* Fig. 15.58).

Therefore the review change request task has a notification action, where the content manager can specify the title and message of the notification and who the notification is sent to. The different lists are the action list to contain the people or roles responsible for reviewing the change request, and optionally a copy list to define people or roles who will get a copy of the notification but are not responsible for doing anything. The content manager will also need to

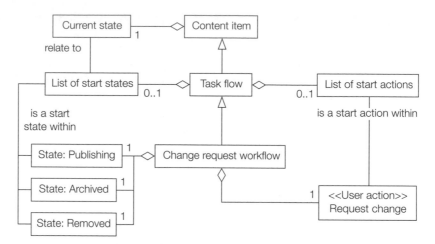
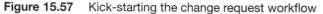

Figure 15.57 Kick-starting the change request workflow

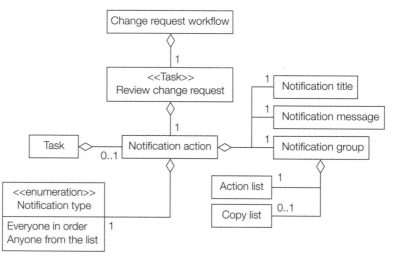
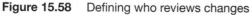

Figure 15.58 Defining who reviews changes

specify whether the change request needs to be reviewed by everyone in the list or just one person from the action list.

Accepting or rejecting change requests

The change request workflow process will need a mechanism whereby those reviewing change requests can accept or reject the proposed change.

Therefore the review change request task will need two user actions that can be selected by the person reviewing the change request: accept change request or reject change request (*see* Fig. 15.59).

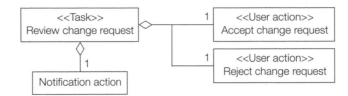

Figure 15.59   User actions to accept or reject a change request

Providing a reason why change requests are rejected

When a change request is rejected, there needs to be a mechanism whereby the person rejecting the request can provide a reason why the decision has been made.

Therefore a review change request task has a reject change request user action, which has a feedback action that allows the person making the rejection to provide the reason why the change request has been rejected (*see* Fig. 15.60).

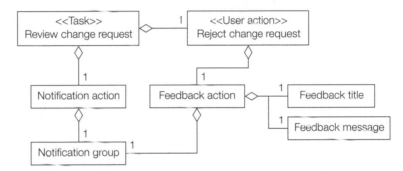

Figure 15.60   Giving the reasons for rejecting a change request

Assigning resources to content items in order for the change to be completed

When a change request has been created and submitted for review, there might exist a requirement for those reviewing the request to establish who will be involved in implementing the change for the content item.

Therefore a content item that has a content owner may also have a change team. A change team has one or more change team members. A team member contains a person, which is itself a content item. A person can have one or more roles and a role can contain other roles. A role is also a content item. A content item has one or more versions and always has an initial version. The content owner defaults to the person who created it (*see* Fig. 15.61).

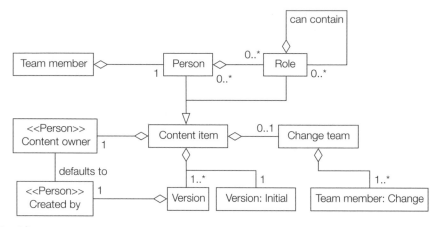

Figure 15.61   Content item resources

Scheduling a change

When a change is approved, it might be applicable to schedule it to take place during a certain time period. For example, if the traffic to a site is high during the week, a change may need to be scheduled over the weekend. As such the content manager may wish to fix a schedule start and end date to the change request.

If more granularity is needed for defining when a change should take place, for instance disabling an online ordering function while a fix takes place, the content manager may wish to schedule such a serious change to take place overnight. In this case the content manager may also wish to specify time parameters.

Therefore creation dates that are associated with a content item can be used to schedule when a change should take place. Creation dates include a scheduled start and a scheduled end, both of which are types of date and time (*see* Fig. 15.62). As a change request is a type of content item, these dates can be used to schedule a change.

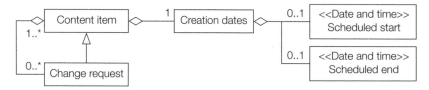

Figure 15.62   Scheduling a change

Setting up a change review workflow

The content manager is responsible for setting up any change review process that is needed and may opt to use the same workflow used to review content before it is published. The default change review workflow follows exactly the same pattern as a content review workflow and the content manager is responsible for the same kinds of tasks. These are:

- creating a change review workflow;
- adding a change review workflow to an overall maintenance workflow;
- defining the start states and start user actions for a change review workflow;
- defining who is responsible for reviewing changes before they are published;
- defining how the change review notification is handled;
- accepting or rejecting changes to content items;
- providing a reason why a change has been rejected (*see* Fig. 15.63).

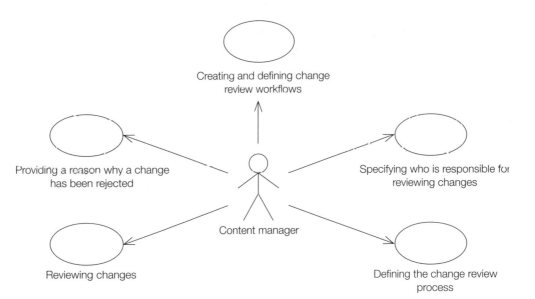

Creating and defining change review workflows

Providing a reason why a change has been rejected

Specifying who is responsible for reviewing changes

Content manager

Reviewing changes

Defining the change review process

Figure 15.63   Setting up the change review process

Default states within a change review

The change review workflow has a set of default states that allow any changes that have been made to a content item to be checked before it is published. It provides those reviewing the item two user actions: to approve or reject the change before publication (*see* Fig. 15.64.)

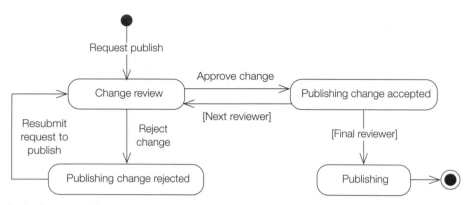

Figure 15.64   Default change review states

Defining the change review workflow in the same way that the content manager set up a content review workflow process, the same process will need to be followed to set up the change review workflow.

Therefore a maintenance workflow may contain a change review workflow (*see* Fig. 15.65). A change review workflow has one start action which is a publish changes user action and has two start states that a content item will need to be in for this action to appear: change and publishing change rejected. The change review workflow has a single task, which is review changes. This task has a notifi-

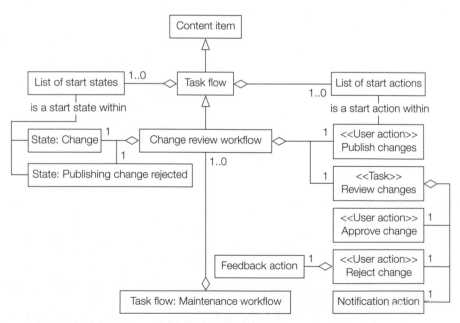

Figure 15.65   Change review workflow

cation action that allows the content manager to define who is responsible for reviewing the changes. The review change task has two user actions: approve change and reject change. The reject change user action has a feedback action that allows the person rejecting the change to provide a reason for doing so.

Adapting the change review workflow to a republish workflow

If an organization wishes to implement a simple unpublish and republish set of workflows, the republish option will probably need some sort of review process before the changed content item is republished to the site. Unpublish and republish are often used to take content items off the site temporarily while a quick or serious change is being made. The important difference between an unpublish workflow and a change workflow is that the unpublish action removes the content item from the site. A request to do this might be linked to fixing a problem or it might be to just remove a content item temporarily, for instance, if a product item is out of stock. In contrast, a change workflow is normally set up so that the old version of the content item remains publishing while changes are made to a new version. Visual design changes will almost always follow a change request workflow. Whatever the reason, a republish workflow may need a republish review, the states and actions of which, are very similar to the content review and the change review processes (*see* Fig. 15.66).

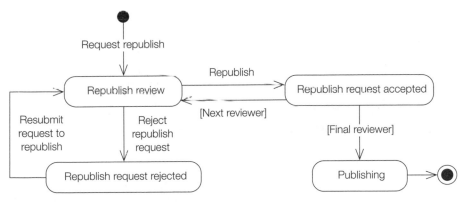

Figure 15.66   Default states for a republish workflow

Setting up processes to remove content from the site

An organization may wish to provide three ways to remove content from a site. An archive workflow can be used to take content off the main site, but make the content still available to users through a search mechanism. An unpublish workflow can be used to completely remove a content item from a site or archive and leave it in a state of unpublished until a republish workflow is used to put it back. A deletion workflow can be used to not only remove a content item from a site if it is currently publishing, but also to delete the content item from the underlying content management system.

All three workflows follow the same model, firstly that a request is made to delete, archive or unpublish, and secondly that a review cycle takes place before the action is undertaken. The content manager, when setting up these workflows will need to:

- create workflows that enable content to be removed or placed in an archive;
- add removal workflows to any overall preparation or maintenance workflows;
- define the start states and start user actions for removal workflows;
- define who is responsible for reviewing archive, deletion and unpublished requests;
- define how review notification is handled;
- accept or reject removal requests;
- provide a reason why a removal request is rejected (*see* Fig. 15.67).

The default states for the process are shown in Figs 15.68 to 15.70.

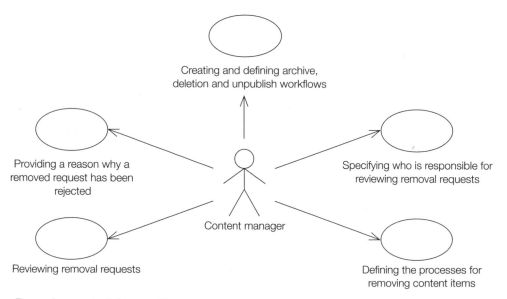

Creating and defining archive, deletion and unpublish workflows

Providing a reason why a removed request has been rejected

Specifying who is responsible for reviewing removal requests

Content manager

Reviewing removal requests

Defining the processes for removing content items

Figure 15.67   Removing content from a site

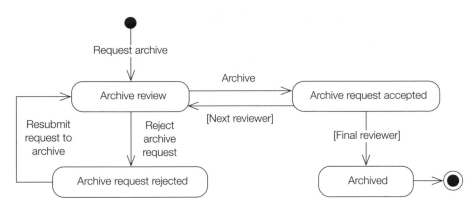

Figure 15.68 Default archive states

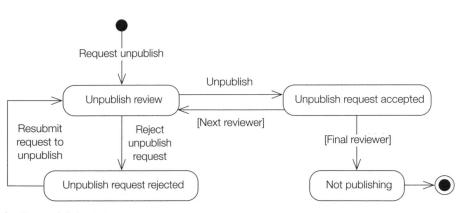

Figure 15.69 Default deletion states

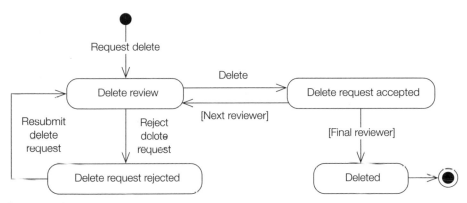

Figure 15.70 Default unpublish states

Setting up an archive workflow

In the same way that the content manager set up a content review workflow process, the same process will need to be followed to set up an archive workflow (*see* Fig. 15.71).

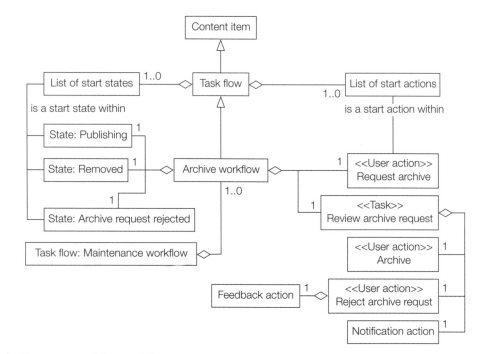

Figure 15.71   Setting up an archive workflow

Therefore a maintenance workflow may contain an archive workflow. An archive workflow has one start action, which is a request archive user action, and has three start states that a content item will need to be in for this action to appear. The three start states are publishing, removed and archive request rejected. The archive workflow has a single task, which is review archive request. This task has a notification action, which allows the content manager to define who is responsible for reviewing archive requests. The review archive request task has two user actions: archive and reject archive request. The reject archive request user action has a feedback action that allows the person rejecting the request to provide a reason why the archive request has been rejected.

Setting up a deletion workflow

A deletion workflow is similar to an archive workflow in as much as the states and actions are virtually identical. The only main difference is that a content manager may decide a deletion review is required for all items before they are deleted within a content management system or, on the other hand, that a review is necessary only when a content item is within a certain state such as publishing or archived (*see* Fig. 15.72).

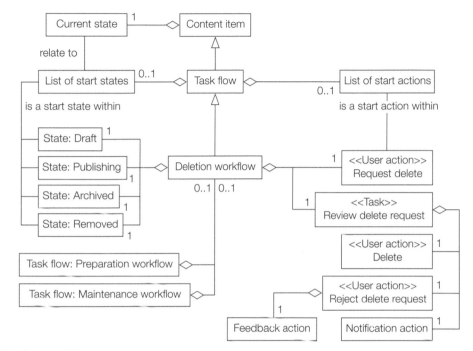

Figure 15.72   Deletion workflow

Therefore both a preparation and a maintenance workflow may contain a deletion workflow. A deletion workflow has one start action which is a request delete user action and by default may have four start states that a content item will need to be in for this action to appear. The four states are draft, publishing, archived and removed. The deletion workflow has a single task, which is review delete request. This task has a notification action, which allows the content manager to define who is responsible for reviewing delete requests. The review delete request task has two user actions; delete and reject delete request. The reject delete request user action has a feedback action that allows the person rejecting the request to provide a reason why the delete request has been rejected.

Determining what the effect will be if a content item is removed

When a removal request is made, it would be useful before the removal is approved, for the content manager to be able to first determine what the effect will be on the site. To this end, it should be possible for a reviewer to see all the views that will be effected if a removal or a change is made to one of the properties that is currently publishing (*see* Fig. 15.73).

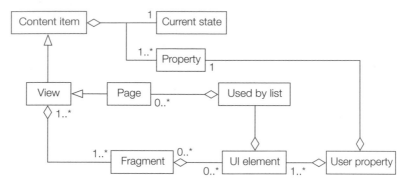

Figure 15.73   Assessing the effects of a removal

To achieve this every UI element that represents a user property needs to maintain a used by list that keeps a record of the pages that the UI element is displayed within. A UI element can appear in more than one fragment, which appears in views, of which a page is a type. A content item is made up of many properties, each of which may be represented by a user property. Each content item has a current state. Therefore because a page through inheritance will also have a current state that defines whether it is currently publishing or not, by removing a content item it will be possible to determine whether the content item, or more specifically the properties within the content item that is being removed, will affect pages available on the site.

Managing third party content

As well as having a workflow in place for requesting and arranging permission to use third party content, the content manager will need to define the information that needs to be provided by those setting up these agreements. When managing and tracking the use of third party material, the content manager is responsible for:

● providing arrangement details for third party content;

● keeping a track of when and where third party content is published;

● setting up automatic removals;

● tracking the cost of third party content;

● managing the use of third party content across different versions of the site (*see* Fig. 15.74).

Providing arrangement details for third party content

If a piece of content is not owned by the organization, it may be necessary to record details about any arrangements that have been made with the owners of

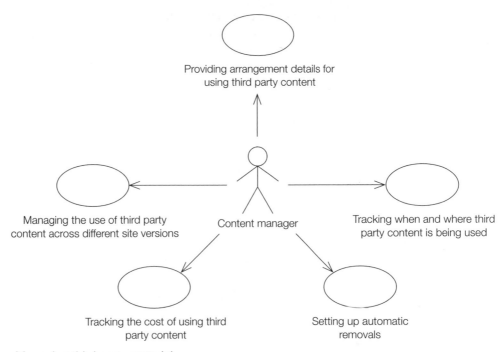

Figure 15.74   Managing third party material

the content. It may also be necessary to keep an audit trail of who within the organization was responsible for setting up the permission. Other information that can be useful is the provision of a required removal date field that can be used within an automated workflow process to automatically trigger a review of the third party content, and whether the agreement to republish has any restrictions on the languages, or sites, that the content can be published to (*see* Fig. 15.75).

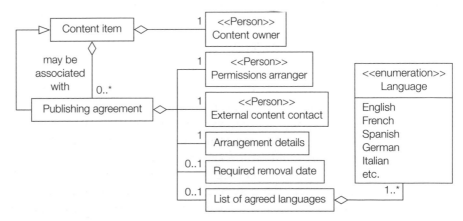

Figure 15.75   Publishing agreements

Therefore a publishing agreement that is a type of content item may be associated with one or more content items and has a content owner, a permissions arranger, an external content contact, and arrangement details. It may also have a required removal date and a list of agreed languages to hold the languages that the content can be displayed in.

Keeping a track of when and where content is published

There may be a legal requirement to keep a track of when and where content items are published on a site. To that end it may be necessary to keep a publishing history of the content items within the content management system. There might also exist a requirement to keep a publishing history at an individual property level, if views have been set up that only reference individual properties within a content item.

To support this there may need to be a publishing history maintained for each content item and even each property within a content item. A publishing history may contain many publishing periods, which keep a track of:

● the site that the item was published to;

● the language that the item was published in;

● the site URL;

● the title of the page;

● the date the item was published;

● optionally, the date the item was archived and the date the item was removed (*see* Fig. 15.76).

Properties within a content item are represented as user properties that may have one or more UI elements. A UI element is displayed within a fragment that appears within a view, of which a page is a type.

Setting up automatic removals

If a required removal date has been specified as part of the third party content agreement, there should exist a mechanism whereby the system can detect when that date has been reached and trigger an unpublish workflow process. There might exist a requirement to specify removal dates at an individual property level if this constraint applies only to single properties rather than all the fields within the content item.

Therefore a publishing agreement may specify a required removal date, which may apply to all the properties within a content item or at an individual property level. A service that may be offered by the content management system is the idea of an action that checks both the required removal date, the current state of the content item, and the current date on the system. If a required removal date

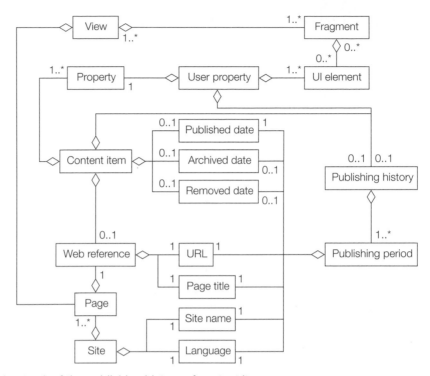

Figure 15.76 Keeping track of the publishing history of content items

has been reached and the item is currently publishing, the system request removal action may automatically trigger an unpublish workflow process, thereby forcing a review of the content item in question (*see* Fig. 15.77).

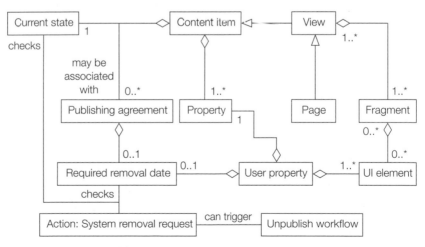

Figure 15.77 Triggering an unpublish workflow process

Tracking the cost of third party content

Some arrangements may be one-off payments, others may incur weekly, monthly or yearly charges. To keep a track of the costs of third party content, the content manager may have a requirement to generate regular reports that track the details of content items currently being charged, and how much these content items are costing.

Therefore a publishing agreement, which has arrangement details, may have a rate associated with it. A rate has a cost and may have a duration specified for that cost. A third party content charges report runs against these rates for content items that are currently publishing in order to track the cost of using third party content on the site (*see* Fig. 15.78).

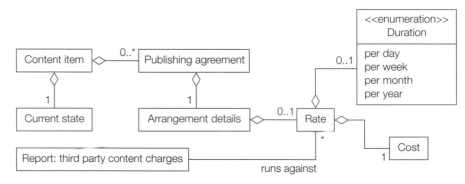

Figure 15.78   Tracking the cost of third party content

Managing the use of third party content across different languages

When supporting different languages it may be useful to signal when content is being used that has no agreement in place to be published to a certain language view or site. In most cases, a third party agreement will not restrict the publishing languages, but in the case where it has been specifically defined, there needs to be a mechanism whereby those reviewing content for publication and those adding content into pages are made aware that this restriction is in place (*see* Fig. 15.79).

Therefore content items that have many properties may have a publishing agreement associated within them that define a list of agreed languages. A site is defined by being in a single language. Therefore it will be possible to flag an exception if pages are added to a site that contain UI elements that represent user properties containing properties from within a content item with a language restriction assigned.

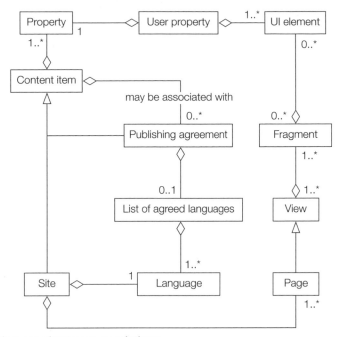

Figure 15.79   Triggering an alert over language restrictions

Managing resources

One of the main responsibilities a content manager will have will be to manage the resources within a team so that proposed work can be completed effectively and efficiently with the right people being involved at the right time. In order to do this, there will need to exist a number of control variables that will enable the content manager to allocate resources, track progress, and understand resource allocation across a website project. The content manager's main tasks will involve:

● allocating resources to create and maintain content items;

● defining the priority of work;

● tracking the progress of content items;

● tracking the progress of individual activities;

● tracking resource utilization across projects (*see* Fig. 15.80).

Allocating resources to create and maintain content items

To track when work on content items has been started and is completed, there may exist a requirement for the person responsible for a content item to provide proposed start and end dates and actual start and end dates when work has in

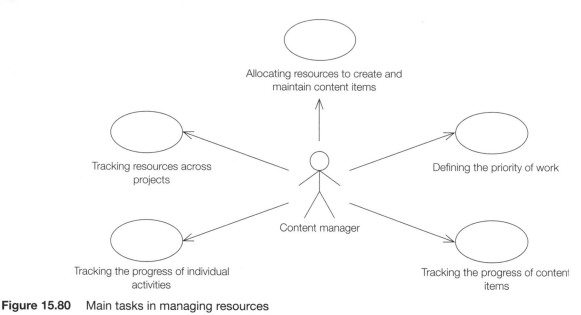

Figure 15.80   Main tasks in managing resources

fact started and been completed. There might also be a requirement to do this for changes to content items as part of a managed change workflow, where the content manager agrees that a change should take place and schedules it to be started or completed by a certain date. Keeping track of start and end dates enables the resource manager to better understand the resource requirements for a piece of work and the resource utilization across the project as a whole.

Therefore a content item will support a set of creation dates that include a proposed start, a proposed end, a scheduled start, a scheduled end and an actual start and actual end. A change request is a type of content item and therefore when these dates are associated with a change request they can be used to both schedule changes and track how long a change is taking (*see* Fig. 15.81).

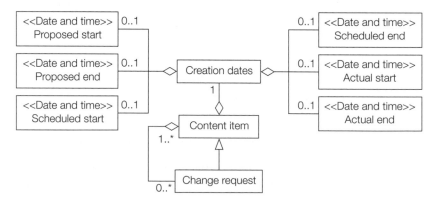

Figure 15.81   Dates associated with a change request

Defining creation teams

When a content item is being created or changed, there might exist a requirement to define who will be working on that content item and how much of their time will be needed to complete the task. This information will help the resource manager to understand the resource requirements for a content item, as well as how current resource requirements will influence the decision to proceed with other content items being proposed or created.

Therefore a content item will have a creation team and may have a change team. A team member has an attribute for the percentage of time needed and is associated with a person. A creation team has one or more team members and includes the content owner. The change team also may have many team members within it (*see* Fig. 15.82).

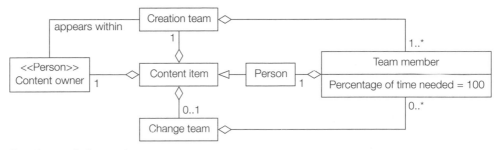

Figure 15.82   Creation and change teams

Defining the priority of work

A content manager may wish to assign a priority to a content item (*see* Fig. 15.83). This is especially applicable to change requests. This priority rating can then be used to make decisions about resource allocation or when work on content items will be scheduled.

Therefore a content item has a development priority that can either be high, medium or low.

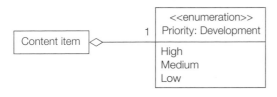

Figure 15.83   Assigning a development priority to a content item

Defining control information at an individual work item level

With the creation of large content items, such as white papers or feature articles, it may be useful to break down the work involved in creating the item into separate work items and have a person responsible and team defined for each stage. Each work item may have its own set of dates to indicate when work is supposed to be started or completed and the dates when the item was actually started and finished. In addition, each individual work item may have a development priority and status. By breaking down the work that needs to be completed into smaller, more manageable pieces, it is easier for the content manager to see a clearer picture of the resource requirements needed to complete the content item. It is also easier to understand the resource requirements and actual usage across the web project as a whole. It is unusual for all the people needed to complete a content item to be required for 100 per cent of their time.

This level of project management tracking is usually enough for even a large website development project. However, if more sophisticated resource planning and scheduling is required, a project management package will need to be used. It will also be necessary to have on board a competent project manager who understands the complexities of time analysis and resource allocations, and who will be able to create the necessary relationships between work items in order for the time lines to reflect the realities of the project.

In most cases, having the ability to define scheduled start and end dates is enough to manage the constraints on content creation and maintenance that a content manager may need to apply. For instance, a change must be completed by a certain date; a content item must start on this date in order for it to be completed by another date. Most content managers only have a need for this level of project management rather than the complexities of full-scale resource allocation with all the necessary relationships and dependencies filled in. In some cases all that will be required will be the ability to create a colourful Gantt chart that is flexible enough to display a favourable end date to senior managers.

Therefore a content item has a development priority and a set of creation dates (*see* Fig. 15.84). Creation dates may contain a proposed start date, a proposed end date, a scheduled start date, a scheduled end date, an actual start date, and an actual end date. A content item may also have a number of work items defined. A work item also has a development priority and some work item dates that may also contain a proposed start date, a proposed end date, a scheduled start date, a scheduled end date, an actual start date, an actual end date. It also has a work item status that can be not started, in progress or completed. A work item has a work item team that can contain many team members. A team member forms the relationship between a person required for a piece of work and the percentage of time they will be needed.

Tracking the progress of content items

Having a set of status dates for a content item and status dates for the individual work items within the content item allows the content manager to track the status of different activities and when these activities are likely to finish. It is also useful for the content manager to be able to see any early warning signs of content items missing their dates. This is equally applicable whether the piece of work is a change or the creation of a content item for the website. An indicator that a content item is likely to miss a completion date is when the individual work items within the

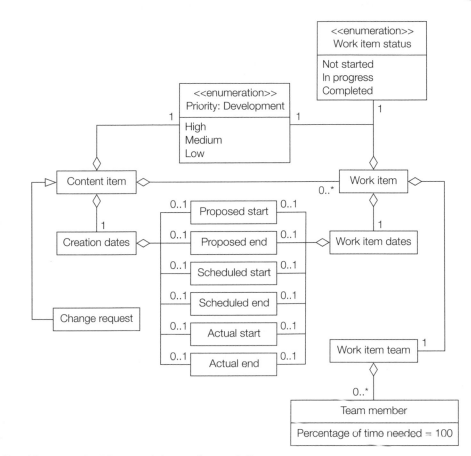

Figure 15.84   Breaking a content item up into smaller work items

content item start to miss their actual dates. A status report will be able to iterate through proposed and actual dates and highlight where there might be problems.

Therefore a status report can run against content items and compare proposed and scheduled dates against actual dates for the creation dates for a content item and for individual work items within a content item (*see* Fig. 15.85). As a change request is a type of content item, these dates can also be used to track changes being made against content items.

Tracking resources across projects

In a situation where many content items are being created and modified, the resource manager should be able to understand who is working on what, and when they can be freed up to work on something else. To support this, there needs to exist a mechanism whereby a report can be generated that looks at all the available team members and summarizes their usage and availability across content items (*see* Fig. 15.86).

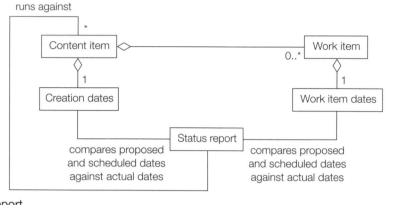

Figure 15.85 Status report

Figure 15.86 Resource usage

A report on resource usage runs against all the team members on the website project and looks at the relationships between the proposed, scheduled and actual start and end dates and how much time that person has been allocated to work on the item (*see* Fig. 15.87). A team member can be within a creation team, a change team and a work item team. A content item has creation dates and a creation team; it may also have a change team. A work item which is associated

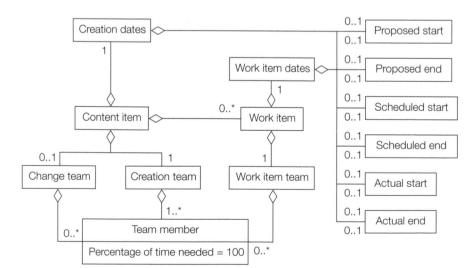

Figure 15.87 Relationship between dates and people

with a content item may have a work item team and some work item dates. A resource usage report will need to look at the involvement of all the team members against the piece of work they are assigned to and calculate the availability of individual team members against the dates that they are assigned work.

Tracking progress

In order for a content manager to be able to define reports that will track the progress of content items through the various stages of publication, each measurable stage should be logged and added to a workflow history attached to the content item to which it relates. These workflow entries should describe the stage that has just been passed, who has changed the state of the content item, and when they did it.

By knowing the list of workflow entry types, exception reports can be created that highlight when stages are taking too long to complete, for instance, the time it takes after a proposal is submitted to when it is either accepted or rejected. By running these exception reports, the content manager will be able to understand where within the publishing process bottlenecks may be occurring and also who within the organization is slowing the process down.

To show the kinds of entries that can be created within a workflow, the proposal workflow is expanded below to show the applicable entries that could be logged within a workflow history file as a proposal moves from creation to approval or rejection.

Tracking proposals

A default proposal workflow is a simple chain of events that provides a mechanism for content creators to develop a proposal and submit it for review. The review process within the workflow allows reviewers to either accept or reject the proposal. When rejecting a proposal, a reviewer provides a reason why the proposal has been rejected. Accepting a proposal passes the proposal on to the next reviewer, or if the reviewer is the last or only reviewer in the cycle, changes the state of the proposal to be approved.

To track the progress of how long it takes for proposals to be created, submitted and reviewed there needs to exist a mechanism whereby workflow entries are created to log when a proposal is created, when it is submitted for review, and when it is either accepted or rejected. With this information, an exception report could be generated to measure how long certain processes are taking, such as the time it takes for proposals to go through a review cycle, or how long a proposal takes to create. Other useful information that a content manager may wish to analyze is where the content proposals are coming from within the organization and how many proposals are being generated at any particular time.

The proposal workflow

A proposal workflow acts upon a proposal, which is a type of content item. Each content item has a workflow history, which is a static list that contains many workflow entries. A workflow entry has a who field, a what field and a when field.

A proposal workflow has two user actions that are within the list of start actions. This means that these actions are available within some kind of visual interface to allow users to start the proposal workflow. The new proposal user action starts a proposal workflow going by creating a proposal and an open proposal user action starts the workflow by opening an existing proposal that is stored on the system (*see* Fig. 15.88).

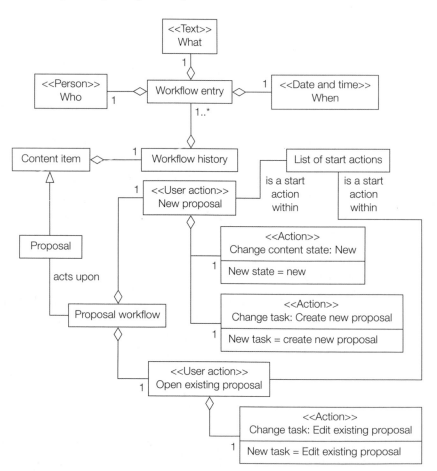

Figure 15.88   Proposal workflow

The new proposal user action triggers two actions upon selection. The first changes the current state of the content item to new and the second changes the task to create new proposal. The open proposal user action triggers a single action, which changes the task to edit existing proposal.

Creating proposals

The create new proposal task within the proposal workflow has two user actions: save and submit proposal (*see* Fig. 15.89).

Figure 15.89   The create new proposal task

The save user action triggers two actions depending on the state of the content item. If the content item current state is new, the save new action is activated which changes the current state of the content item to draft and creates a workflow entry for when the content item was created. The save existing action is activated when the state of the content item is not equal to new. This action creates a workflow entry for when the content item was last edited (*see* Fig. 15.90).

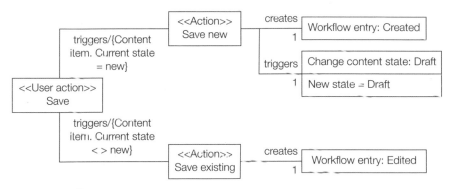

Figure 15.90   The save user action

The submit proposal user action also triggers the save actions and performs a save when selected. If the state of the content item is new, the save new action is activated, otherwise the save existing action is used. Submit proposal changes the current state of the content item to in review, changes the task to review proposal, and creates a workflow entry to indicate when the content item was submitted for review (*see* Fig. 15.91).

Editing existing proposals

The edit existing task within the proposal workflow also has the two user actions save and submit proposal, which work exactly in the same way as outlined above.

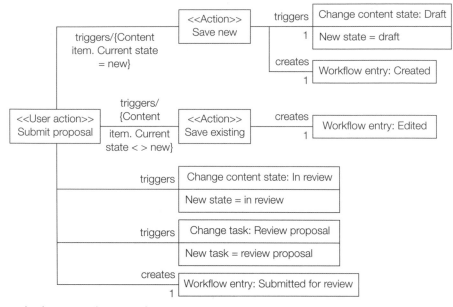

Figure 15.91   The submit proposal user action

The main difference is that the submit proposal user action appears only when the current state of the content item is either draft or rejected (*see* Fig. 15.92).

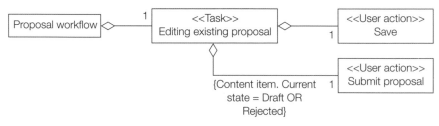

Figure 15.92   The edit task

Reviewing proposals

The reviewing proposals task within the proposal workflow has a notification action that has a notification group, which means that the task notifies people specified within the group that an action is required of them. The task also has two user actions: accept proposal and reject proposal (*see* Fig. 15.93).

The accept proposal user action checks the notification group to see whether the reviewer is the last reviewer in the list. If it is not, the user action creates a work-flow entry of accepted and changes the current state of the content item to accepted. It then triggers the notification action associated with the review proposal task. If the reviewer is the last reviewer, it creates a workflow entry of approved and changes the current state of the content item to approved (*see* Fig. 15.94).

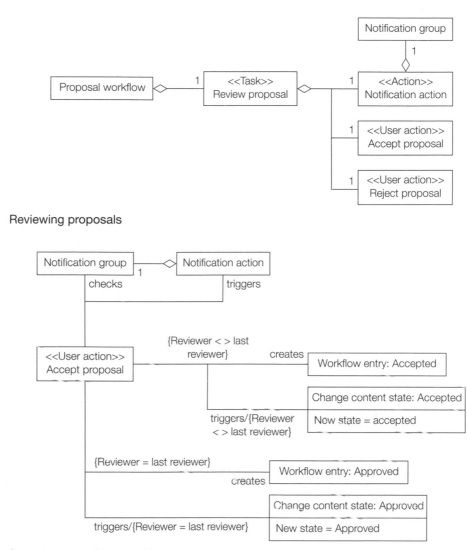

Figure 15.93 Reviewing proposals

Figure 15.94 Accept proposal user action

The reject proposal user action has a feedback action that allows the person responsible for rejecting the proposal to record the reason for the rejection. The user action changes the current state of the content item to rejected and creates a workflow entry of rejected. The reject proposal user action will also need to notify the notification action that the review cycle has failed (*see* Fig. 15.95).

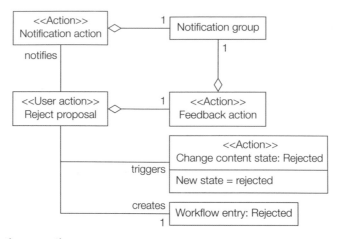

Figure 15.95   Reject proposal user action

Example of the workflow history log that is created

The following table shows an example of the kind of data that will be recorded as a result of creating workflow entries at each stage along the workflow. Such data can then be used to understand any bottlenecks that may exist, any resource problems such as work overload, or any delays which may need further investigation.

What	When	Who
Created	10/4/99	John Smith
Edited	11/4/99	John Smith
Submitted for review	12/4/99	John Smith
Accepted	13/4/99	Paul Jones
Rejected	15/4/99	Gill Black
Submitted for review	16/4/99	John Smith
Approved	17/4/99	Gill Black

Measuring the quality of the site

The content manager will almost always wish to see metrics that show how the site is performing (*see* Fig. 15.96). Many of these measurements will be being analyzed already by others within the team. However, reports may be needed to provide summarized information that will allow the content manager to:

● Analyze workflow progress	Covered earlier in this chapter
● Analyze business model against targets	Covered in the chapter on
● Analyze site audience against target audience	modelling requirements of the
● Analyze site usage	business analyst
● Analyze user feedback	Covered in the chapter on
● Analyze task success	modelling the requirements of
● Analyze users coming to the site	the human factors engineer
● Analyze search queries	Covered in the chapter on
● Analyze content usage	modelling the requirements of
	the information architect

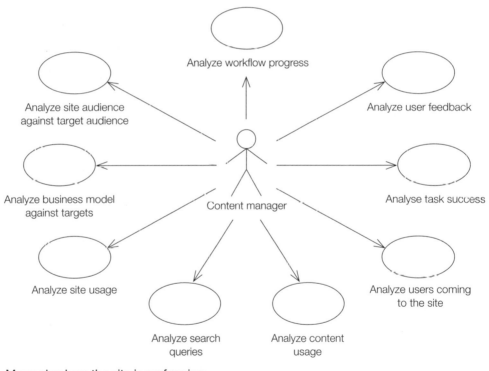

Figure 15.96   Measuring how the site is performing

16 Analyzing the requirements of the visual designer

The visual or interface designer is responsible for translating the tasks flows and design requirements from the business analyst, human factors engineer and information architect and mapping them into visual layout definitions for the website and content management system. The designer owns the visual style and defines the layouts for both individually designed pages and view templates that can be used to display content provided by the content creators.

When analyzing the requirements of the visual designer, those requirements that deal with the creation of visual images, page designs or other interface media such as sound are outside the scope of this book. However, what is of interest are the factors that involve integrating these designs with the underlying site content and how media assets can be better managed using an asset library-type approach.

View templates

It is unlikely that any content management tool will ever replace the standard graphic tools that allow visual designers to create high-quality graphics and design visual layouts. However, once these designs and graphics have been created, a visual assembler should be able to translate these layouts into a form that can integrate with the underlying website content. For example, a template that has been designed to display a set of products within a product database will eventually need to be created to display the details of a product on demand. This integration with the site content means that view templates will need to be created using the product field names that are defined within the underlying database. In addition, any requirement to create summary views will need common fields to be defined for all the types of objects that are required to appear within those views.

For any content or database-driven website, the ability to easily create view templates can be the deciding factor for which tool set to use. There are many very good database products available and there are many professionals who specialize in database design and system access. However, a website solution that uses a database back-end needs the mechanism that allows this data to be accessible to the end user on selection. And the visual designer, who is unlikely to talk the same language as a database designer, needs to be able to understand the structure of that data in order to design the screens that display this information to the user.

In the ideal world, the sequence of events for designing an interface would be as follows.

1   The business analyst would define the required business information.

2   The human factors engineer would define the necessary user information and task flows.

3   Then the database designer would design the information structures as a result of both sets of requirements.

4   Finally, the visual designer would lay out the information on a screen according to the various priorities defined by the human factors engineer and the business analyst.

In reality, this is rarely the way it works. In many cases, data structures already exist and are in use by other back-end systems. For instance, a website team may not have the luxury of redefining the product database from scratch, due to the fact that other back-end systems are already operational and are running against this data for applications such as stock control and distribution. Therefore, in any system that offers the ability to create view templates there needs to be an awareness that those required to create visual interfaces are unlikely to feel at ease working with database structures and data types. In the long run it will be far less expensive to invest the time in setting up a system that makes this data accessible and easy to understand to those having to design the visual interfaces. It will always be preferable for designers to do the job themselves rather than requesting the help of a technical developer to translate designs into convoluted code within the system.

When defining view templates, the visual designer is likely to want to do the following:

● define and lay out fragments within a view;

● add behaviour to fragments;

● associate data with a fragment;

● define properties that appear within a fragment;

● add task information to fragments;

● lay out visual attributes within fragments;

● preview the page with sample data (*see* Fig. 16.1).

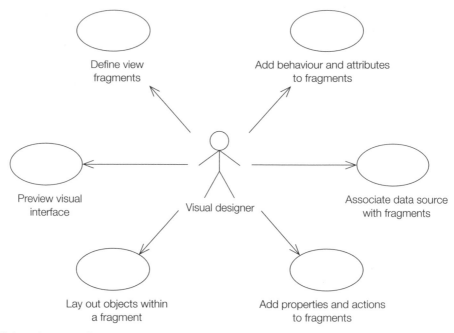

Figure 16.1   Defining view templates

Defining view fragments

In most cases any particular web page design and layout is broken up into different informational areas. For instance, a page may have an area on the left-hand side that is used entirely for navigation. There might be a main content area in the middle, an area that is used for advertising at the top, and a section at the bottom reserved for related information in the form of hypertext links. Traditionally, web designers and developers have had to resort to defining HTML tables to achieve the precise alignment and zoning of areas within a page, which with a complicated layout can be quite a difficult job.

When a visual designer segments a page into different informational areas, each separate area can be designed and laid out independently from the other parts of the page. This independent visual entity can be referred to as a view fragment. Assembling pages from view fragments can be a useful approach if the information within these fragments changes frequently. In the event that a change is made within a fragment, the change will be isolated and affect only the area dedicated to the fragment and will have no impact on other parts of the layout.

In addition, if a fragment can appear in more than one page, a content change can be made once and then applied consistently across the site. An example of this would be a footer area reserved at the bottom of each page to direct users to a privacy statement, legal information or contact page (*see* Fig. 16.2). If a change was needed to this kind of global information that appears on each page

Figure 16.2 Example of a shared view fragment containing footer information

within the site, it is far better to make the change once within a shared view fragment, rather than having to go into each HTML page and make the change manually, a process that is so tedious it will almost always introduce errors.

Banners, footers and adverts are all candidates for sharing across multiple pages. However, there is another use to defining a shared fragment, which is to define common style attributes that can be adopted by fragments of the same type, for instance, defining a default navigation fragment independently of the navigation details that will appear within the fragment. For large sites, defining common styles can save an enormous amount of time when layout changes are needed. It is also a quick way of applying visual changes across a site if a quick visual revamp is required.

Having a recognizable label associated with a fragment can also be useful, especially if a specialized print option is provided. Many users, when they wish to print a web page, will not be interested in printing off navigational text or adverts that are being displayed alongside the main content areas. By typing the different fragments within a page, a print function could be provided that printed only the information areas of interest to the user.

Therefore there needs to be an association where any view can contain one or more fragments and where a fragment may contain many other fragments. Each fragment may be associated with a fragment type, examples of which are navigation, content, related links and advert. A page also has a type, examples of which are home page, lead article and product. A page has a web reference, which in turn has a page title and URL (*see* Fig. 16.3).

Laying out fragments on a page

In defining a page, the visual designer needs to make a decision on what the behaviour will be when the page appears in different sizes and also what happens to the size of fragments when the screen is resized by the user. In most cases, the designer will wish to specify that the main content areas will grow to fill the available space within the window. This will enable a user with a large screen to see more information within it rather than being restricted to a layout designed for the lowest common denominator screen size.

The rules that govern the stretching of fragments may not be as simple as stretching all fragments to all the available space on the screen. For instance, sometimes text is difficult to read when the line length is very long, and if a user resizes a window into a small rectangle, it might be inappropriate for textual areas to try to wrap around into a very long and thin narrow area. Therefore in defining the size and behaviour of fragments within a web page, the visual designer may have a set of parameters that need to be defined for each fragment.

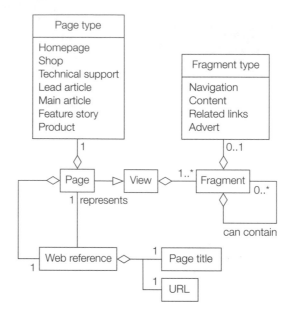

Figure 16.3

Therefore a fragment will need a number of variables associated within it that define what will happen when a page is resized. Each fragment will have an initial size, may have a type associated with it, have a position, an alignment variable, and may have stretch variables. Stretch variables allow the definition of minimum and maximum sizes for X and Y and the definition of a relative size for X and Y based on the relative size and position of the fragment within the page or fragment that it resides within. In addition, a site will have default visual attributes that include a default page, and will contain many pages that may also inherit attributes from a default page. A default page may contain many default fragments. A fragment can contain other fragments, and may inherit attributes from a default (*see* Fig. 16.4).

Associating data with fragments

The point of having a view template is to define a single visual design that can be applied to different rows of data from within a data table. That relationship may be a simple 'one to one' association, for instance a product view template that displays details of an individual product from within a product database, or it may be a more complex view based on a query against many different tables. An example of a complex association based on a series of queries maybe a page that displays the details of athletes who have won medals at the Olympics, plus any links to press articles about those races, and also a summary table of medals won

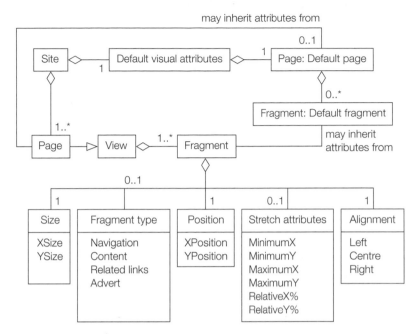

Figure 16.4   Layout variables within a fragment

by the athletes' home country. Such a page may require a query against a race results table, with a join to an athlete's details, plus a further query against the race results table to find medal results by country, where the country is equal to the country of the selected athlete.

When defining such as relationship, it should be possible to set up the main data association for the main fragment within the page, and then, if required, individual queries or associations for any fragments contained within. These secondary associations may be linked to properties of the page at the time of display such as the current date and time or a value that the user has selected within the page.

Therefore each fragment may be associated with a data table, or may have a data source query that creates a temporary table. A fragment may also have an order defined for how the data source will be loaded (*see* Fig. 16.5).

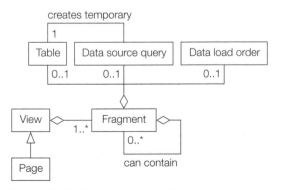

Figure 16.5 Fragment associations

Defining properties within a fragment

Fragments allow a visual designer to group attributes and attach visual behaviour to the group, such as rules for resize and alignment. Once a data source has been set up, the designer needs access to those properties that need to be

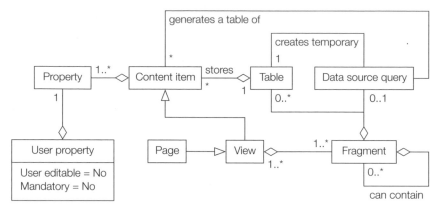

Figure 16.6   Properties within fragments

displayed as a result of the data association in order to create the relationship between the property and the fragment in which it will appear.

Content items contain many properties and are stored within tables. A fragment can be associated with a table or it can have a data source query that generates a table of content items and creates a temporary table (*see* Fig. 16.6).

Adding task information to a fragment

If a web page is in support of a user task that has been defined as part of a task flow, it is to be hoped that the human factors engineer has defined the user properties and user actions that must be present within the interface for the task to complete successfully.

For instance, a task flow to purchase goods online will have such actions as 'Add to shopping cart' or 'Display delivery details'. Actions that the user can select are an important part of the interface and the visual designer will need to include them as part of the design. In addition, a task flow that has been completed by a human factors engineer should have user priorities defined for the properties and actions associated with the task. The visual designer will need access to this information in order to map the task model successfully to the interface and, more importantly, to create an interface that makes the task easy to complete by the user.

Therefore a task may have a number of user properties and user actions. User properties have a property and user actions have one or more actions. When user properties and user actions are associated with a task, they will be assigned a user priority of high, medium or low. Both user properties and user actions are associated within one or more UI elements that are used to display them within a user interface. Fragments can contain many UI elements and views can have one or more fragments within them. Views can be defined as being in support of many tasks. A page is a type of view (*see* Fig. 16.7).

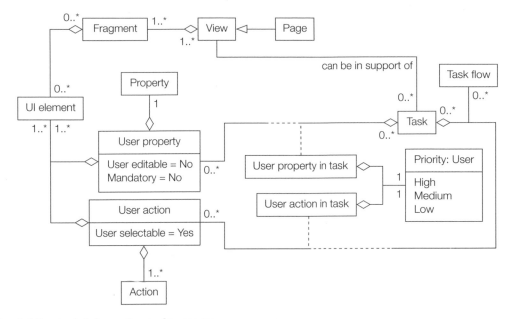

Figure 16.7 Adding task information to fragments

Laying out visual attributes within a fragment

Once the visual designer has associated the properties and actions within a fragment, each UI element that is associated with the property or action will need to be positioned within the fragment area. This will require each object within the fragment to maintain an X and Y position relative to the position of the fragment within which they are contained.

Therefore each UI element that appears within a fragment will have a position for both X and Y (*see* Fig. 16.8).

Previewing the page against content data

One of the most useful functions that a good content management system can offer is an accurate preview facility that allows the visual designer to run a view template against the underlying content data in order to see the view as it will be seen by those using the site.

Therefore a page will need to support a preview page function that allows the person wishing to preview the view to run any query that may be associated with fragments within the page and then to select the row from either the temporary table that is created or the table that is actually storing content items on the system. In addition, if a site has more than one site map defined, there will need to be an operation to select the site map required (*see* Fig. 16.9).

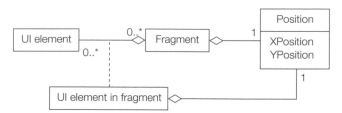

Figure 16.8   Adding layout information

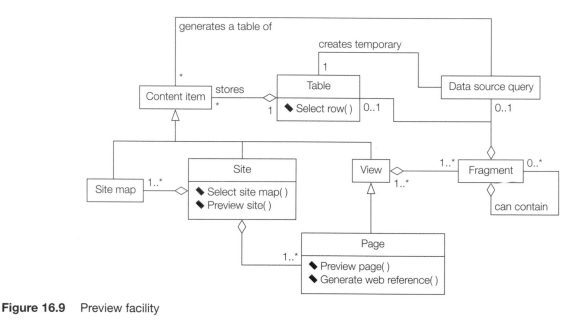

Figure 16.9   Preview facility

Visual styles

When creating website designs, a visual designer usually defines an overall style for the site that includes the fonts that will be used for text within the interface and a definition of a palette that specifies the colours to be used within pages and within any graphical images displayed within those pages. Reducing the number of colours that are used by a website greatly improves the performance of downloading pages and images. It is also a useful technique to apply when a large site is being developed by a number of graphic designers.

Agreeing a site palette up front increases the chances of the graphical work being complementary rather than reflecting the individual visual tastes of each designer. As such, many of the functions offered by word processors and graphical products need to be made available through a site designer function within a content management system.

When specifying visual styles, the designer is likely to want to do the following:

- define a visual style;
- define a style precedence;
- associate a style (*see* Fig. 16.10).

Defining a visual style

When defining a style, it is far easier to create by example rather than to set attributes in isolation. Therefore, a preferable way for a visual designer to establish a style is to create a default page or set of pages that have default parts or fragments. This will necessitate setting a default page size, and a default background colour, and setting up individual fragments to contain banners or navigational areas.

Defining a colour palette within a style allows the use of colours to be restricted to the palette within the style, which can be useful when defining default fonts and background colours. A style will also need to contain default named text styles such as a Heading 1 or Body. A content management tool may offer a function that allows these to be defined with the default page so that the designer will be able to see these text fields within the style of the page in which they will appear.

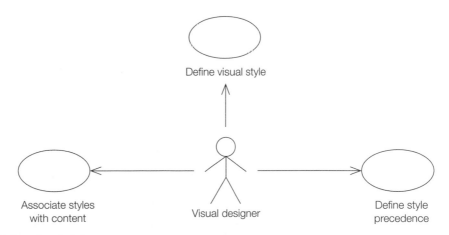

Figure 16.10   Defining visual styles

Defining a default page is the same as defining an overall page template without having to set any data source information. It should be possible to define any number of page templates that can be shared across sites and used individually within a single site.

Therefore, it may be useful to define a default visual attributes object that contains a default colour palette that has one or more colours within it, a default page, and optionally a set of named text styles. A named text style will support a text style that has attributes such as font name and font size and a paragraph style that has attributes such as alignment and line spacing. A text style will also have a foreground colour and a background colour, both of which should be within the default colour palette. A default page will have a default page size and will have one or more default fragments. A default page also has a default page background colour that should be within the default colour palette (*see* Fig. 16.11).

Associating a style

Once a style has been defined, a visual designer will need to specify the scope of that style. For instance, should the style be applied by default to all pages within a site, or to just the product type pages? Maybe an individual style will be applied to certain individual page types such as registration or subscription-type forms. It

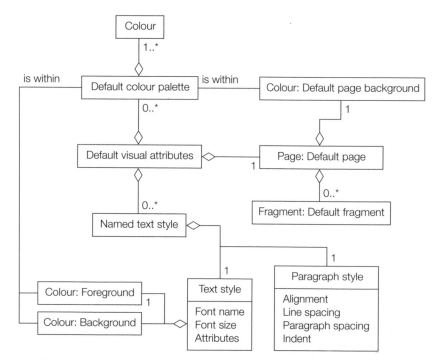

Figure 16.11   Default visual attributes

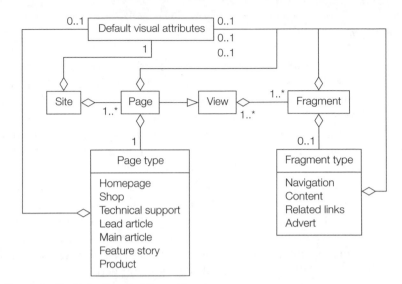

Figure 16.12 Associating default attributes at different levels

might also be a requirement to define a style for a fragment type or even at an individual fragment level. For instance, a style may be created for all navigational areas or for a single related information section within a particular page.

Therefore a site may have a default set of attributes, but so might a page, a page type, a fragment, or a fragment type (*see* Fig. 16.12).

Defining the style precedence

When there are many default styles that have been associated with a number of different levels of display area, a visual designer may wish to set a precedence that governs which style takes priority when a conflict occurs. The most natural order is an inside-out approach, meaning the smallest unit takes precedence over the larger one. For example, an individual fragment style would take precedence over a fragment-type style, which would take precedence over an individual page style, which would take precedence over a page-type style that takes precedence over a style defined for the whole site style. However, this rule may not always apply to any individual site. Therefore there might be a case for defining the priority order of styles to make sure that the designer has the flexibility to define exactly what is required.

Therefore the default visual attributes object will need access to a static list that defines the precedence order for styles. The precedence list contains one or more default visual attributes (*see* Fig. 16.13).

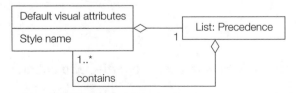

Figure 16.13 Precedence list

Asset library

Visual and new media designers are also usually responsible for controlling the media files that are used on a website. Because there are generally far fewer designers than content creators, there is a tendency for these files to be kept apart from other types of content. At best the designer takes responsibility for backing up these files and at worst, and in many cases, the source of these files is kept locally on the designer's machine. This is not an ideal situation, and can lead to the same problems identified earlier with files that are not held within a system that controls changes and access. Therefore, an answer could be to provide an asset library-type system that is used to manage any media files destined for a website. Such a system would offer the same file controls as a normal content management system, but would offer other useful features such as the ability to query where different media are currently being used on the site and what the effect on the site will be if they are changed.

Apart from the kinds of content management requirements that have already been covered, such as access and version control, the additional requirements on an asset library are likely to be the following:

● associating different media representations with user properties and actions;

● determining the usage of different UI elements;

● adding a classification to UI elements within the library (*see* Fig. 16.14).

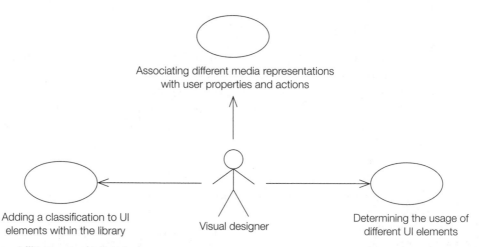

Figure 16.14   Asset library requirements

Associating different media representations with user properties and actions

There are a number of reasons why a site design may require more than one media representation for a property or action interface. For instance, a site may wish to offer a text-only version or may even try to offer a single design that can be used for both a standard PC interface and a small screen device such as a PDA (personal digital assistant). A design may also be ambitious enough to try to cover a non-visual interface such as a telephone. These kinds of design decisions will need to be made fairly early on in the analysis process to ensure that an interface is designed with enough flexibility for the media designer to offer suitable alternatives that will work on the required set of interfaces.

Most pages will be designed around the standard controls that are part of the HTML language. Ideally an asset library should be able to treat controls within a page as being objects that can be reused, classified and indexed in the same way as other assets that are being created. If this were the case, then the idea of switching the styles and attributes on the entire interface would be far easier to achieve. It could be the case that a tool treats these controls as objects within a design interface and then deals with all the HTML generation under the covers. This has to be the ideal situation for designers, as long as they can trust the HTML generator to accurately reproduce the designs created on the screen in a clean and efficient way.

Therefore the requirement would be to have the ability to group all interface elements together in a single library and be able to associate them with the underlying data properties that they represent.

In the same way that document types undergo review processes and work-flows that deal with third party permissions, it may be the case that this also applies to media such as graphics or sound, a common example being the use of music on a site. A design team may wish to keep these workflows separate from the main content and set them up within a library dedicated to user interface objects. Making an asset library a type of content management system ensures all the same levels of access and version control, plus the added features of setting up any additional workflows that may be required.

Therefore an asset library could be created that is a type of content management system that can have one or more UI elements (*see* Fig. 16.15). A UI element is a type of content item and is used to display user properties and user actions that may be associated with a task within a task flow. User properties are associated with a property within a content item.

Determining the usage of different UI elements

Keeping a handle on where all the different user interface files or controls are being used within an active site can be quite difficult, especially if these elements are being reused in different pages. Making a change could be quite risky if it is not clear what the total effect of that change will be on the site. With smaller

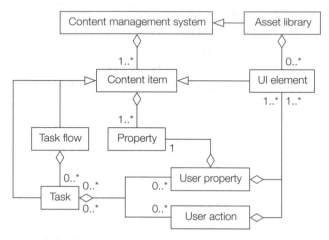

Figure 16.15 Asset library as a specialized content management system

sites, this can be quite manageable, as the designer is likely to have an intimate knowledge of all the pages that are being displayed and the media that are in use. When a site starts to have thousands or even millions of pages, and the media for the site is being supplied from many different sources, a good content management solution will become necessary to bring some control to the change process.

Therefore a UI element will have a function to display where it is used that looks at the relationships where it is contained within a fragment or attached to a page event (*see* Fig. 16.16).

Adding classification to UI elements within an asset library

The larger the number of media files, the more useful a classification system will be for designers to order views and search for files within the system. In addition, having a classification system that is used to define the purpose of the media files and when and where these files should be used can help create a system that allows different sites to be established based on different criteria. For instance, the specification of a classification for a display device could differentiate between user interface alternatives depending on which device is being used to display the site.

Therefore a UI element held within an asset library is a type of content item and therefore can contain many keywords. A control and a media file are types of UI elements, and a media file has a media type, examples of which are graphic, audio, video and animation. A control can be used to provide an interface for a media file (*see* Fig. 16.17).

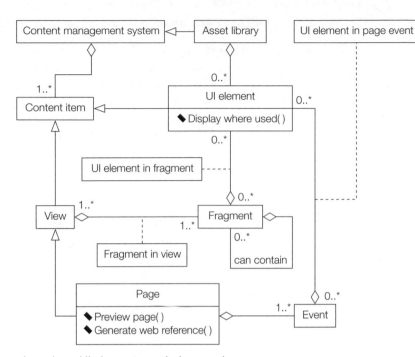

Figure 16.16   Discovering where UI elements are being used

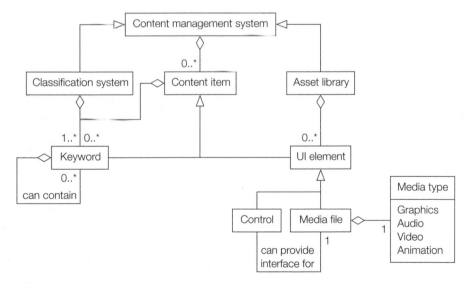

Figure 16.17   Classifying UI elements

Providing an optimized performance version of a UI element

In certain circumstances it may be desirable to create a version of a UI element that can be used to load quickly to allow expert users to assimilate and click through an interface in the shortest amount of time. The quick functional version of the UI element can be replaced by a superior graphical version after the initial load has completed. The most likely use for this is to provide links in a textual format first for power users, followed by a pretty graphical version for everyone else.

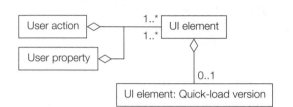

Figure 16.18 Offering a quick alternative for expert users

To support this, a UI element may be associated with another UI element that is to be displayed first before the proper UI element is displayed.

Analyzing the requirements of the content creator

There are many requirements that a content creator has with respect to the tools that are needed to edit data, and save and retrieve files. These kinds of requirements are outside the scope of this book, but those that are of interest are the processes needed to move content from inception to publication and from maintenance back to publication or removal, plus the types of form templates that will allow different content types to be created and maintained.

Creating content types

The content creator uses a content management system as a tool that enables content destined for a site to be input, stored, reviewed and eventually published. The task of creating a content item needs to be a simple and seamless operation. It is usually fair to say that content creators are experts within their content domain and not experts in figuring out how computer systems work. This is why the process involved in designing forms for content creation needs to incorporate a rigorous task analysis as part of an overall user analysis, to ensure that any interface that is provided is easy to understand for all those required to do the job. It should also be a goal to try to automate as many of the manual processes involved in creating the item as makes sense and is useful.

A common set of requirements that a content creator will have is the ability to:

- create content types using a form template;
- define creation teams in order to request input from different contributors;
- signal that a publishing agreement is needed or create a publishing agreement;

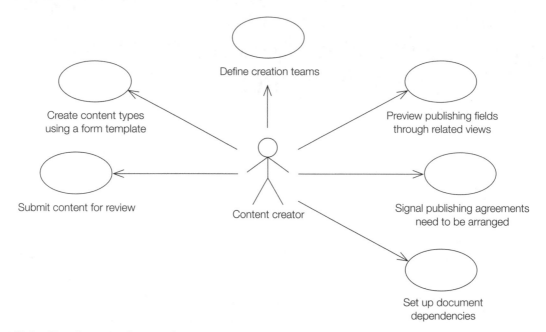

Figure 17.1   Requirements for creating content

- preview publishing fields through related views;
- submit content for review;
- set up a dependency between different document types (*see* Fig. 17.1).

Create content types using a form template

There will exist a requirement for content creators to be able to specify the type of content item that they wish to create and then be presented with an input form to enter the properties defined for that type. Therefore for each content type there should exist a form template that contains user-editable properties that allow the content creator to enter the content information into the system.

Therefore a form template needs to be made available that can be associated with a content type (*see* Fig. 17.2). A form template and a page are different types of views and a view is a type of content item within a content management system. A UI element is also a type of content item. A form template being a specialized view has the ability to contain one or more fragments. A fragment can contain other fragments and potentially has many UI elements within it. A UI element may be associated with a user property or it may be associated with a user action. A user property has one or more UI elements and also has a property. A user action also has one or more UI elements and may also contain many actions. UI elements may be associated with many fragments; therefore an object exists to define a particular UI element within a fragment.

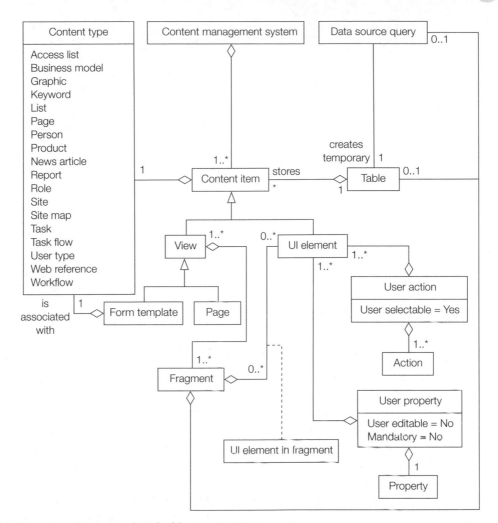

Figure 17.2 Form template associated with a content type

Define creation teams to request input from different contributors

For larger content items, the content creator or person responsible for pulling together a content item may have a requirement to define a content creation team in order to send notifications to individual members requesting their contribution during a content preparation phase.

Therefore a content item has a creation team that always contains the content owner. Task flows and tasks are both types of content items. Task flows can contain other task flows and can have many tasks. A task can have many user properties and many user actions. The creation workflow is a default task flow to create a content item; it has an open new task, an open existing task and an edit task. The edit task has two user actions: to define a creation team, and request contribution (*see* Fig. 17.3).

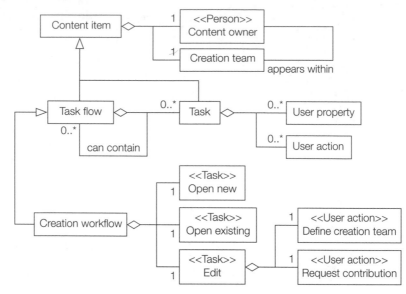

Figure 17.3   Defining a creative team

Signal that a publishing agreement is needed or create a publishing agreement

Whether a specific third party agreement workflow is in place or not, there may exist a requirement within an organization for content creators to signal that some or all of the content needs to have an agreement in place with a third party organization. The agreement might refer to any type of content that can be created and published to a website. However, it will be an access control issue as to who within the organization can create publishing agreements and who is responsible for approving them before publication.

Therefore a default creation workflow to create content items will have an edit task that may contain a third party permissions workflow. A default task flow for third party permissions will have an action to request a publishing agreement and two tasks that enable the content provider to create a publishing agreement or to edit an existing one. A third party permissions workflow acts upon a publishing agreement that may be associated with a content item or a single user property. User properties are associated with properties that have one or more UI elements. A content item may contain a user property to allow a content creator to request permission to use the whole content item, or request permission to use a user property (*see* Fig. 17.4).

Preview publishing fields through related views

When a content creator is creating a content item, there may be a requirement to provide a default published view of the content. This will give the content

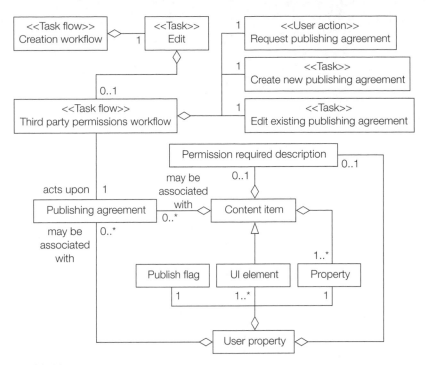

Figure 17.4   Request publishing agreement

provider an indication of how the content item will eventually look once it has been published. It will also provide a better way to proofread the content by presenting it in the same way as the end user will view it.

Therefore a content item has a preview facility that allows the content provider to see the published fields within a page view. The content type for a content item may already have default attributes associated within, including a default page. If this is the case, this is the page definition that is used. If an association does not exist, the content item can generate a temporary page view of the user properties contained within (*see* Fig. 17.5).

Submit content for review

In the case where content is being prepared for publication to a site, the content creator needs to be able to signal that a content item is complete and ready for publication.

Therefore the edit task within a creation workflow may contain a content review workflow. The start action for a content review is request publish; therefore when the content creator selects this action, the content review workflow will be invoked (*see* Fig. 17.6).

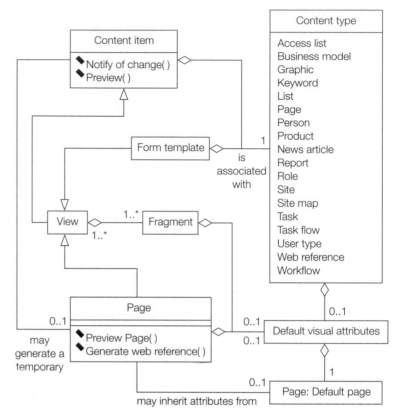

Figure 17.5   Preview page facility for a content item

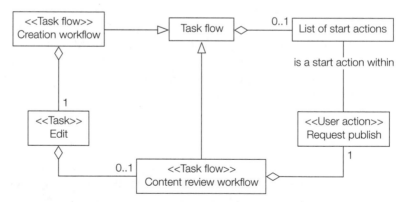

Figure 17.6   Edit task that may have a content review workflow

Setting up a dependency between different document types

There might be a situation whereby the modification of one content item needs to force a review of another. For instance, if a page has been designed to allow the download of software files, and a developer makes a change to the file, anyone

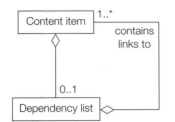

Figure 17.7 Dependencies between content items

responsible for checking that the change has been made successfully will need to try to download the new file from the existing page. In this case, the content creator should be able to specify dependency relationships between different files, so that a change or modification of one signals that other content items also need to be checked.

Therefore a content item may have a static dependency list that holds links to other content items (*see* Fig. 17.7). This list is used to signal that there is a change dependency in place, so that if the content item is modified, a workflow will automatically be invoked to review the other content items within the list.

Classifying content and building content relationships

One of the most powerful aspects of the web is the ability for users to find information. To do this effectively, there are a number of strategies that the user employs. Surfing or browsing involves moving from page to page by selecting links that look interesting or likely to hold relevant information. Searching for specific information relies on a search mechanism being in place, working effectively and being supported by the underlying site content. Either way, finding information on the web and within a site is a primary task of internet users and therefore it is wise for a site design and content creation team to effectively support this task in the best way possible.

The simplest way to do this is to invest time in defining appropriate content relationships to support browsing and define correct and complete content classification to support the act of searching. It should also be an objective to put in place processes that check the accuracy and timeliness of information that is already being published. Leaving content to just fester will eventually affect the usefulness of the site and impair the effectiveness of any search facility that is offered. It also reflects badly on the company.

To effectively provide content classification and related content information, and support content maintenance, the content provider is likely to have the following requirements:

- classify documents according to a single classification mechanism;
- create related information lists by referring to documents and web references;
- create related information by defining a query that resolves at a later stage;
- provide review criteria settings and request that new ones be added;
- register interest in new content that is created within the system;
- define automatic archive and removal dates.

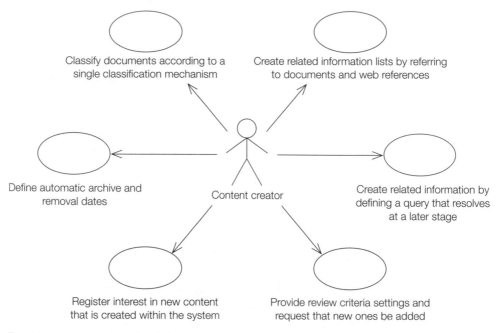

Figure 17.8   Providing content classification

Classify documents according to a single classification mechanism

When a content provider needs to define the keywords that will accurately describe the type of content that is being created, it is far simpler to have access to a central classification system that provides a predefined vocabulary. It is also preferable to have a system that provides a search facility with a good level of synonym support, so that the content provider can enter the term they think is appropriate and the system returns the term that should be used. There should also be a facility whereby content providers can request new terms to be added, or send a query to the owner of the classification system for extra help.

Therefore an edit task within a content creation workflow may have a classify content workflow. The user actions within the list of start actions that allow a content creator to invoke the workflow are add new keywords and edit existing keywords. The tasks that are part of a default classify content workflow include add new keyword, edit existing keywords, search classification database, request to add a keyword, and send a query to the classification owner (*see* Fig. 17.9).

Create a related information list by referring to documents and web references

When a content provider needs to define a list of related documents, it would be useful to define that list by referring to the documents or references within the

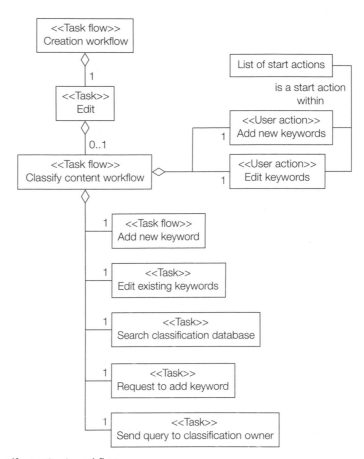

Figure 17.9   Default classify content workflow

system, rather than URLs that reference external locations on a web server. This is a far safer way to reference content, and it also forces web reference content items to be created for all required external links. This will ensure that the additional information about a link is provided, such as the title and description of what the page contains, thus allowing view templates to be created that can display all links within a site irrespective of whether the content is being held internally within the content management system or externally on the web.

Therefore a content item may have many related information lists that are types of lists (*see* Fig. 17.10). A user property is associated with a property and may have one or more UI elements that can display the property within an interface. A property may also be associated with a related information list. A content item may have an associated web reference that represents a page. Web references also exist as content items and a page always has a web reference. Fragments within pages display UI elements.

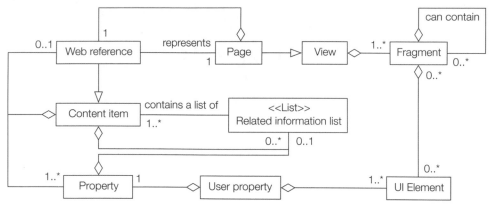

Figure 17.10   Related information list

Create related information by defining a query that resolves at a later stage

When a content provider needs to define a list of related documents, it should be possible to define that list by either selecting relevant content items from the database or by defining a query that resolves at publish time or run time. This would have the benefit of being able to reference content that is created after the content item is published.

Therefore a related information list is a type of list that can either be defined statically to include a number of list items, or defined dynamically by specifying a query. Because a list can contain other lists, it should also be possible to create a related information list that is a combination of both static and dynamic information (*see* Fig. 17.11).

Provide review criteria settings and request that new ones be added

When a content provider needs to provide information against which a content item will be reviewed, such as the tone of the writing or other types of classification attributes, these criteria settings need to form part of the underlying content information. It is also a requirement that the content provider is able to request that new review categories are added.

Content items may have many review criteria fields, examples of which are the target audience that the content item is aimed at, and the tone in which the content item should be written (*see* Fig. 17.12).

Therefore an edit task within a content creation workflow may have a task flow to request additional review criteria. The user action that starts this task flow is a request new review criteria user action. The three tasks that make up the task flow are send review criteria request, review request that has accept and reject request user actions, and an add new review criteria task (*see* Fig. 17.13).

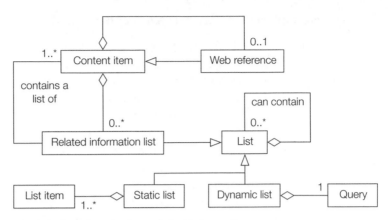

Figure 17.11   Dynamic and static lists for creating related information

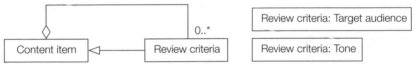

Figure 17.12   Review criteria

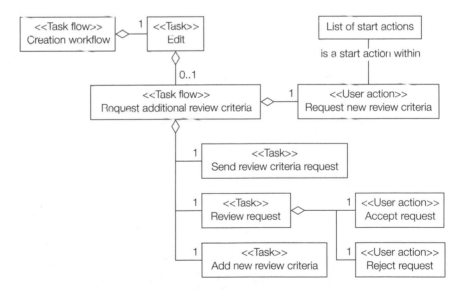

Figure 17.13   Task flow to request additional review criteria

Register interest in new content that is created within the system

When new content is being created on a regular basis with many content creators who may be geographically dispersed, it may be difficult for the content creator to keep a track of items that are being added to the system. In this case, there may be advantages in setting up an automatic notification system that enables anyone within the organization to register interest in certain types of content and be informed when new ones are added. Indeed, there is no need to limit the automatic notification to a content type. It might be quite applicable for individuals to track new content being created by a certain person within the organization. It might also be applicable to extend the automatic notification facility to include situations where an existing content item changes state, for example when a content is accepted for publication, or when a currently publishing content item is about to be archived.

Therefore a person may have a content subscription that contains a query. A content subscription registers with a subscription monitor that is attached to the content management system. When a content item changes, it notifies the subscription monitor that in turn notifies subscribers who have registered interest. Attributes that a person may include in the subscription query are the content type and the current state (*see* Fig. 17.14).

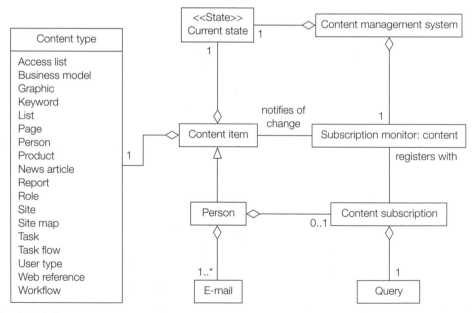

Figure 17.14   A subscription query

Define automatic archive and removal dates

To help keep a site current it is useful to define dates in the future when a content item should be automatically archived or removed. This will force a content review to take place to decide whether the item should be removed from the site. If during the review it is decided that the item should remain on the site for the present time, the automatic dates will need to be reset to new dates in the future.

Therefore there should exist a facility that allows a content creator to provide dates when the content item should be removed or archived, with the expectation that someone will at least assess at that time whether the content item should remain where it is (*see* Fig. 17.15). When it is a legal obligation to remove a content item on a specified date, the required removal dates would be part of a publishing agreement attached to the content item.

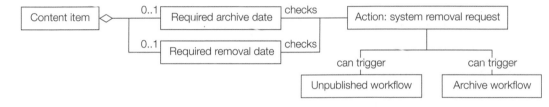

Figure 17.15   Triggering an automatic review of a content item

Signal that a content item should be highlighted

There are some pieces of content that are so important or significant to the company that they deserve to be highlighted on a main page within a site. Such content items might be a product announcement, a marketing coup or an important news story. When such content items are created, there should exist a mechanism whereby they can be flagged and reviewed with this highlight requirement in mind. It will be up to the organization how it wishes to include such highlighted items. A homepage view could be created that automatically embeds all links to content items that have been marked for highlight. However, it is more likely that a designer will wish to manually lay out these links with a layout as important as a homepage. Either way, someone will need to provide the necessary highlight information and flag that the item has been approved to appear as a highlighted item.

Therefore a content item may have a highlight information that has a highlight title and may have a highlight text, some highlight graphics, a date when the item was highlighted, and a date when the highlight was removed (*see* Fig. 17.16). These dates may be added to the publishing history with the URL of the page that they were contained within.

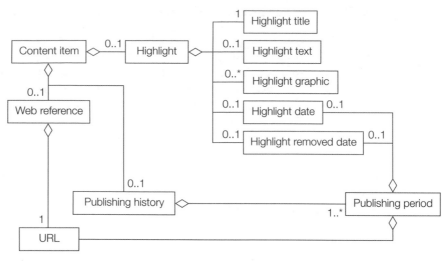

Figure 17.16   Highlighting information

Maintaining content items

Once a content item is publishing, any further work or actions that need to be applied to it should really be controlled within a managed maintenance cycle. This may mean a content creator following a change request process before a change can be made, or it may just mean that any changes that are made undergo a change review before the change is published. Any action to remove a content item from the site should also be viewed as a change. The removal of a page may impact other content on the site, or the way that the user is able to access site information.

Therefore a content provider will have further requirements once a content item is publishing and is likely to want to do the following:

- request a change;
- make a change;
- define a change team in order to request input from different contributors;
- request that a change is published;
- understand the impact of removing a content item;
- request that an item is archived or removed (*see* Fig. 17.17).

Request a change

The content manager is in the position of deciding how much control should be exerted over the process for changing content items once they are within a cer-

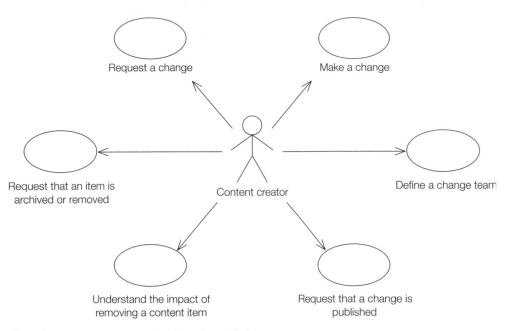

Figure 17.17   Requirements once a content item is publishing

tain state. It is likely that any content item that is publishing will follow some sort of change management process, but it is less clear whether the same level of control will need to be exerted over content items that are archived, removed, or unpublished.

The content manager may have made a decision to restrict write access on certain types of content items to people he knows to be capable and competent to make error-free changes. In this instance, the change management process may be very light and will rely on the competence of those making the change to get it right. However, making available an option to request a change on all content items that are within a 'finished' state provides a mechanism whereby anyone on the system can signal that the item contains an error, irrespective of whether they have any intention of making the change themselves.

Therefore a content item may have many change requests associated with it. A change request has a change request type, examples of which are broken link, legal problem, graphic missing, etc. The default change request workflow acts upon a change request and has a start user action to request a change. This user action will appear when the content item is publishing or archived as the change request workflow has these two states within the list of start states. The change request workflow has two tasks that allow the content provider to create a new change request or edit an existing one. Both these tasks have a user action to submit the change request for review (*see* Fig. 17.18).

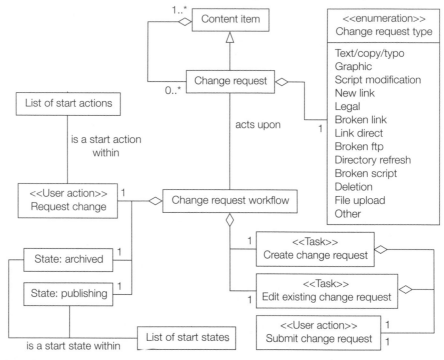

Figure 17.18   Change requests

Make a change

When a change request has been agreed and ownership for the change defined by the content manager, the person responsible for making the change will need to fix the problems identified within the change request.

Therefore a default change workflow will have a user action to invoke the workflow called make change and in addition will support tasks to open an existing content item, edit it, save it and close it without saving (*see* Fig. 17.19).

Defining a change team in order to request input from different contributors

In the same way that a content item may have a creation team defined, a large change may require that a team be put in place to complete it. Defining a team with a content item lets others know who is working on the item and lets the team pass the item around the group in order to add information or review a change that has been made.

Therefore a content item has a content owner and may also have a change team. The edit task within a change workflow that acts upon a content item has a user action to request contribution from team members (*see* Fig. 17.20).

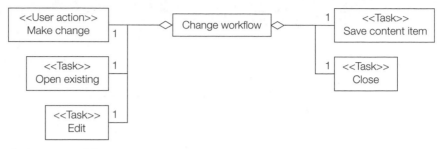

Figure 17.19   Default change workflow

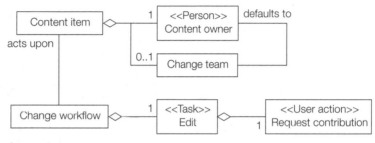

Figure 17.20   Defining a change team

Request that a change is published

Once a change has been made, the content creator will need to request that the new version of the content item is published to the site. If a content change review process is in place, this will necessitate the content item undergoing a review before the change is approved and before it can be moved and published to the site.

Therefore an edit task within a change workflow may contain a change review workflow that will be invoked if the content creator selects the option to publish changes (*see* Fig. 17.21).

Request that an item is archived or removed

As well as setting automatic dates to review a content item for archive or removal, the content creator will need to be able to request that a content item is either removed from the site or put into an archive. This could be achieved by creating a change request. However, a request to remove content should be fairly commonplace within a content-driven site that changes frequently. Therefore in some cases it makes sense to provide a fast-path mechanism to remove content and to assign a role such as a site editor who is responsible for making these removal decisions (*see* Fig. 17.22).

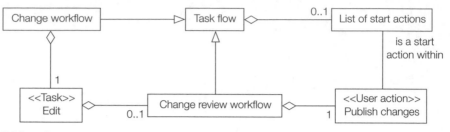

Figure 17.21   Publishing changes

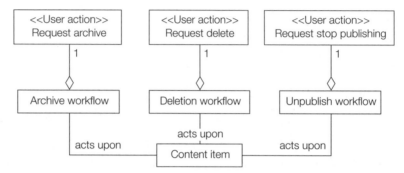

Figure 17.22   Requesting that an item is archived or removed

Therefore for each workflow that removes content from a site, a user action exists to invoke the process.

Sample forms to create different content types

As a result of performing a content analysis of different types of content items that exist on the web today, it is possible to specify some sample templates that define the attributes that make up different content types.

When defining these template definitions, the process that should be followed is to:

- define the complete set of attributes that make up a content type as identified during a content analysis;

- specify the best user interface elements to display within the form that allow content providers to create and edit these attributes.

The definition of such a form brings together all the attributes that are needed to create the content type irrespective of how the properties are actually stored within data tables. The design of these forms is as important as the design of the web pages on the site, and appropriate UI elements will need to be created that enable the content creator to easily provide the information needed.

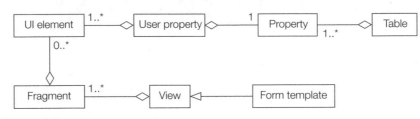

Figure 17.23   Sample templates

The process of analyzing content in relation to the requirements of all the different contributors to the site is likely to throw up the need to define common properties that span all the different content types. This requirement is likely to be driven by the need to support common views, such as a search results list, site map or specialized index pages. However, a form that is created for content providers to input a content type should make no distinction between specialized properties and shared ones. The terms that a content provider sees need to be relevant to the task that they are undertaking, and how the data mapping is achieved between attributes seen within the interface and properties held within a data table should be of no interest to the content provider.

This process of identifying common attributes and designing an underlying data model is covered in the next chapter, where a system architect takes the different data elements and defines the underlying data structures that can be used to support the required information. These information models can then be translated into data definitions within a supporting database to hold the underlying site content.

A form view that is created for content providers needs to group all the required fields within a simple editable interface that enables them to create the content item. It is also important that all the fields within the templates use labels that are familiar to the content provider and appropriate for the information being requested. For example, a news article may have a user property for a lead paragraph. The journalist has little interest in whether the underlying property or field name stored within the table is short description. Using different names within a database and providing a mapping to different labels within a view is sometimes necessary and is covered in the next chapter.

Below are a few samples of common form definitions that may be created as a result of a content analysis.

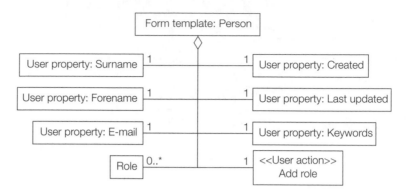

Figure 17.24 Person

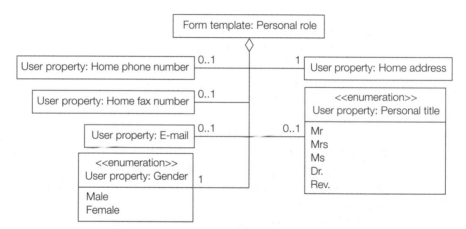

Figure 17.25 Personal role

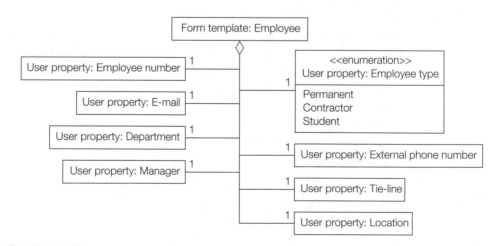

Figure 17.26 Employee role

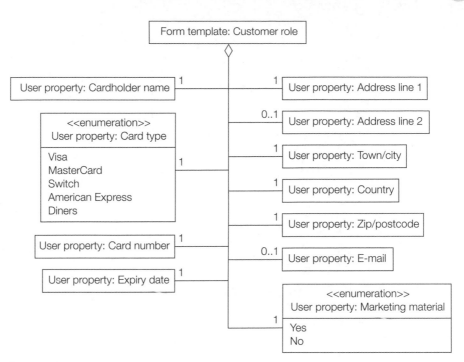

Figure 17.27   Customer role

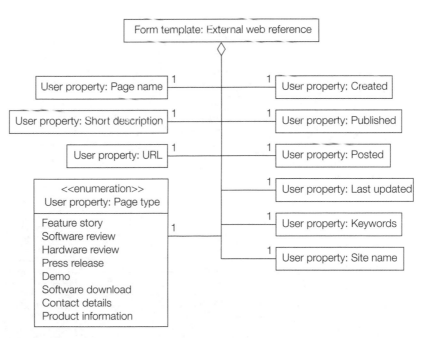

Figure 17.28   External web reference

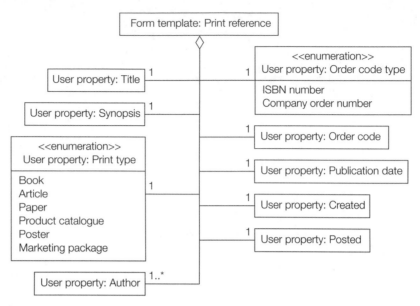

Figure 17.29 Print reference

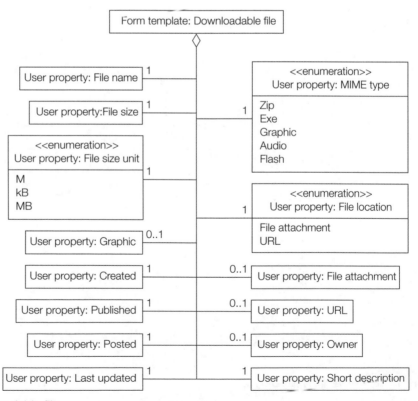

Figure 17.30 Downloadable file

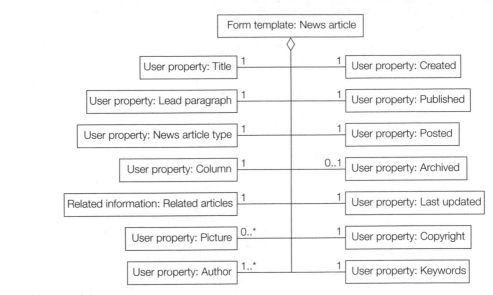

Figure 17.31   News article

part 4

Translating requirements into information models

The final set of chapters looks at how information models can be used to translate requirements into formalized website and content management design specification. This part also provides an extensive number of common information models that have been derived from studying many different kinds of websites and which include and combine require-ments for website content management.

18 Information modelling

Bridging the gap between analysis and design

The objective of any web development team should be to create a quality website whether they are improving an existing design or starting from scratch. The process to achieve this is covered in detail in Part 2, but below is a summary of the key points that a website development team should be aiming to achieve:

- fulfilling the goals and supporting the directions and messages of the business;
- fulfilling the goals and supporting the tasks of the user;
- providing the level of information to support both the site goals and the user's expectations;
- mapping the user model to the concepts and organization presented within the site so that they are familiar;
- providing an obvious and uncomplicated interface to increase user confidence and initial impressions;
- using writing styles that map to the user's vocabulary and level of understanding;
- providing consistent terminology and interaction techniques;
- being efficient, reliable and well integrated (e.g. not having broken links).

Along the way, the analysis stages should have identified the key requirements that the system should meet in order to achieve the above criteria. An information model can provide a single reference point that sums up all of these requirements and translates them into a form that can be used by the system and visual designers to create a design. In a way, an information model should bridge the gap between the two key development stages of analysis and design.

As covered in detail earlier, the analysis stage breaks down into four main work items: the business analysis, the user analysis, the content analysis, and the system analysis. Each of these stages has a direct influence over the next stage undertaken. The system requirements that are derived from a system analysis, although not covered within this book, play a vital role in defining the abstract design of a site, however they must not be the overriding consideration. There is little point in having an expensive infrastructure that supports a million customers if the site is incapable of attracting users through marketing or if the site does not support the goals that the user comes to the site to achieve.

Each stage of analysis places requirements on the solution that is provided. However, the system analysis is slightly different as it places requirements on the underlying technology that will be used to build the system and deliver that system to the users. It is the first three analysis stages that will be used to define the eventual layouts and information that the user sees. Therefore the conceptual design of a site and any supporting content management system is really driven by these stages, where there exists a logical sequence of events in defining what the overall system should be. In the simplest terms, that sequence can be described in Fig. 18.1.

The business analysis should start the ball rolling by defining the site's purpose and the audience that the business wishes to attract. These business goals, such as 'sell as many books on the website as possible' or 'attract users to subscribe to the news service', provide the main development priorities. As a result the user analysis can concentrate on the core task flows needed to fulfil these goals, and analyze the best ways for the target audience to achieve them. Out of this exercise, task flows and task definitions are created, together with the user model of the target audience and the vocabulary that they use.

The content analysis can then take this information and break it down further. Tasks identify the information that needs to be available and the actions that users need in order to fulfil the task. Task flows can be identified for both the web-

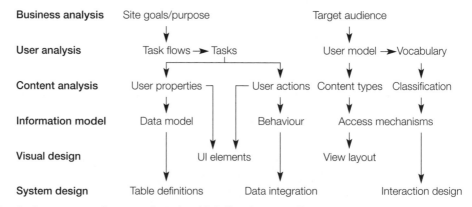

Figure 18.1   Logical sequence of events that should define the overall system

site and the content management system. 'Creating a news article' is as much of a task as 'buying a product'; however, how much effort is invested in the analysis of each task will ultimately be a business prioritization decision. Therefore, a content analysis identifies the different content types that map to the user's model, such as news article, CD, order, shopping basket, etc. and the properties that make up these types. It also identifies attributes from the user vocabulary that can be used to classify documents. This information can be used to create a single classification system to be applied across the entire site content.

From this an information model can be derived. An information model in its broadest definition allows behaviour to be added to a data model and defines the access mechanisms to that data (*see* Fig. 18.2).

The data model can be derived from the content types and properties identified during the content analysis. Behaviour is identified as a result of the requirement for task flows and the actions that move a user from one task to another. For instance, a task to buy a product will almost certainly have a user action of 'buy'. With any workflow requirements that have been identified, behaviour will manifest itself in such actions as the need for users to 'submit proposals', 'request publication' or 'reject a change'. Task flows also identify the need for access mechanisms or views.

An information model does not define the layout of access mechanisms – that is part of the visual design stage – nor does it involve itself with the definition of user interface elements or other media within types of views. Views can be thought of as having their own data model and behaviour, as well as a layout. An information model will define which elements appear in views, but not how these elements are visualized. That is the job of a visual designer.

Figure 18.2   The components of an information model

The visual design stage can take these view definitions and create layouts. User properties and user actions both need user interface elements – the visual designer can create these and add them into views. In theory, all views that are created should support the task flows and tasks with which they are associated. In theory, no view should exist without being in support of a defined task. In practice, the investment in time to analyze and create tasks for every situation on a website would be too onerous, so it will always be the case that the investment in time is given to the priority tasks, and the other less significant ones left to judgement or copycat techniques.

Finally, the system design can derive the table designs from the data model. The system design phase defines how that data is accessed from the required behaviour defined within the information model. It also identifies and designs any interaction logic that is needed within the view definitions and any actions that need to be supported within the interface.

Defining an information model

Creating the data model

The core of an information model is the data model, and the core information to create the data model is derived from the definition of the required document types as identified during the content analysis. The information modelling stage creates a data model that satisfies the storage of all the required data properties across the system using standard normalization techniques, and in addition factors in any requirement for site-wide views.

Normalization is a process first defined by Codd in the early 1970s[27] to help design table structures. It describes a process that reduces the risk of data duplication and wasted space by building extra relationships between different rows of data in different tables. This process is used extensively when designing data models; the web data model, however, can also be influenced by the requirement for site-wide views. A site-wide view requires that a template can be created that displays useful reference information for all the content within a site. The easiest way to achieve this is to make sure that certain fields are standard across all the different content types that are created.

Once these common fields have been identified and the standard normalization process has been completed to create a data model, this can be used to define the table definitions to store all the underlying content that will be used to create the website. In theory, the names of fields within data tables are irrelevant. Obviously, from a maintenance point of view it makes some sense to have a name that bears a relationship to the values that are held within the field. But it is the property name within a view that is important. The labels attached to the properties displayed within views are the attributes identified and described within a content analysis. Therefore a view needs to be able to contain properties that have user-recognizable labels, but that also know the relationship to the real field name that stores the data for that property.

An example of this is a form that allows journalists to edit news articles. Such a form may contain user-friendly labels such as heading, lead paragraph and column. The corresponding field names within the data table may be title, short description and body; however, these field names may never have to be made known to the journalists. It may also be the case that the title and short description fields are held in one table, while the bulk of the article, the column, is held elsewhere (*see* Fig. 18.3). How the actual data is stored should be totally transparent to the users or creators of that data. These are data design issues.

The labels or terms that are used within views should initially be identified during the user analysis and then formalized during a thorough content analysis. Creating the data model within the information model captures these terms by defining the label to be used within a view and the relationship to the data source. The journalists therefore only ever get to see the terms that they feel happy with.

In the same way, a form designed to capture links to external web references can use the same common fields of title and short description, but can present the labels in terms of the task of creating a web reference (*see* Fig. 18.4). It may be decided that the logical mapping to a title is the web page name. Either way, if an index view is created to show all the content on the site, news articles can be listed alongside web references, and the view can display the values within the title and short description fields.

As a content item may have a web reference, which in turn has a URL, the website user will be able to select and link to each item from the single web page view.

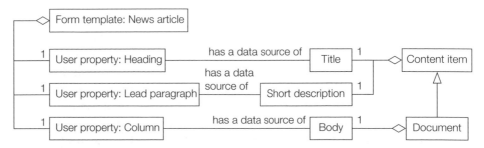

Figure 18.3 Labels used within views may be different to the underlying property name

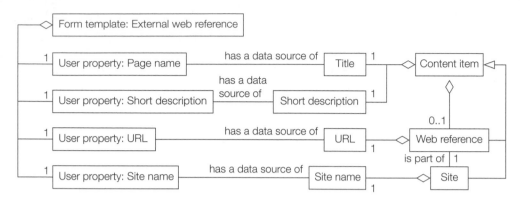

Figure 18.4   Labels differ for creating a web reference

Setting up the classification attributes

Not only is there a data model for different document types, there will also be a requirement to define any classification attributes that need to be in place to create these content types. Ideally, the classification hierarchy should be designed and available before any content is created or added to the system. If it arrives part-way through the content creation process, all the existing content items will have to be re-edited to add the necessary classification information – a job that could be quite time consuming.

Creating view definitions and identifying required behaviour

Once content types have been defined, access to these types needs to be provided through views. A user of the content management system needs two levels of view (*see* Fig. 18.5). At one level, views need to be created to find content items and display different collections of content items based on some predefined criteria. The second access level is a form interface that allows the creation and editing of a content type.

As mentioned earlier, view definitions should be based on task flows that have been created. Therefore there should be mechanism so that a view can be linked to a task flow or a set of tasks for there to be a correlation between the definition of user actions and properties and their defined prioritization, and the user interface elements that are embedded within a view (*see* Fig. 18.6).

Once a task flow is identified, the information model can start to introduce behaviour and state. User actions identify the potential start of a change of state, and state transition diagrams can be created to determine the number of states that are needed to support a flow of events. For instance, workflows, which are types of task flows, in the most part are responsible for changing the state of the content items within the system. When defining common workflows it is useful to identify all the states that a content item may go through while the workflow is operational. It can also be useful to understand these states, so that the user

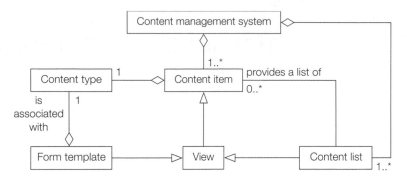

Figure 18.5   Levels of view in a content management system

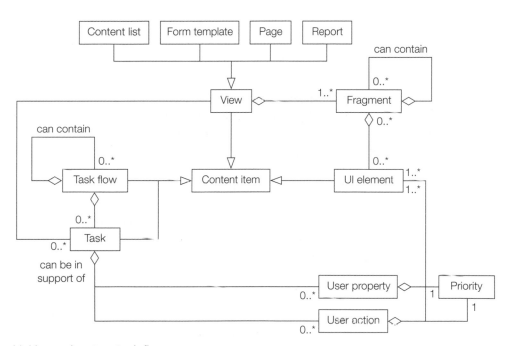

Figure 18.6   Linking a view to a task flow

actions that initiate a workflow can be added automatically into a view when the item is within a certain state. For example, a user action to 'request archive' may be available only when the current state of a content item is 'publishing'.

Detailed state modelling will be part of the system design, and a single information model will never be able to cover the types of design scenarios that cover all eventualities and error situations. However, it is the identification of the essential states and actions that need to be included, so that the essence of the system is captured within a single relationship diagram. It will then be up to the designers to break this down into further detail in order to design the eventual solution.

19 Common information models

This chapter brings together all the requirements from the roles defined within Part 2 and provides the common models that would need to be in place in order to create a system that would support these requirements.

Common model overview

Figure 19.1 provides an overview of the main constituent parts that should be in place to create content based websites.

Ignoring the example content types shown at the top of the diagram, this model could be adapted to form the basis of any content management system that supports the publication of content to a website. The main parts to the model are:

- *content system –*   defines those objects and attributes that can be shared and aggregated on to different content types, ensuring that common attributes are defined across all the different types of content and that common services are available for new content types when they are added to the system;

- *content types –*   some standard content types that are generally applicable to most sites, such as document, person, user types and roles. In addition, there are some examples of specific content types that reflect the user model and the business purpose of the site that is being created;

- *site and views –* defines those objects that enable a site to be created from underlying page definitions, and the types of views that need to be available to create content, analyze the site, and access content items within a content management system;
- *containers –* common services for creating different types of lists;
- *task flows –* objects that provide the ability to define task flows and the actions and properties within tasks;
- *workflow types –* a standard set of workflows to enable the creation, publication and maintenance of content within a supporting content management system.

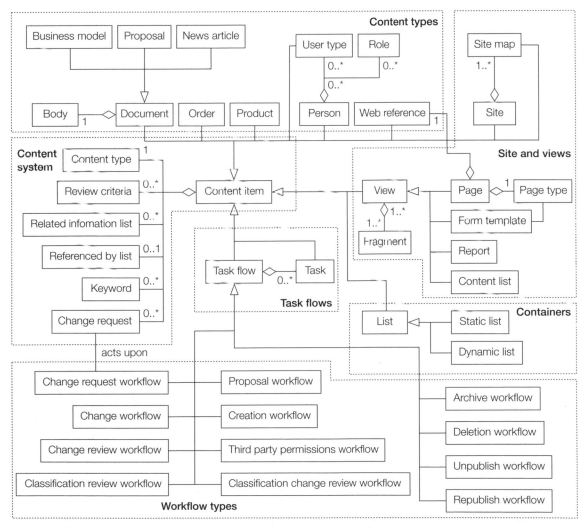

Figure 19.1 The main constituent parts in a content-based website

Overview of how a site is created from different content sources

Figure 19.2 gives an overview of how these main objects within the information model are brought together to create a website. It shows the separation between a task model and how it is depicted, and a view model and how the user interface elements are defined within a layout.

The important aspects of this approach are:

- *content classification –* by associating keywords with whole content items and at an individual property level, classification support at a view level can be automatically built from keywords associated with the displayed content;

- *task flows –* Separating the way a task is completed by defining the properties that the user must be able to see and the actions that need to be available allows different visual or auditory representations to be associated with a single task definition;

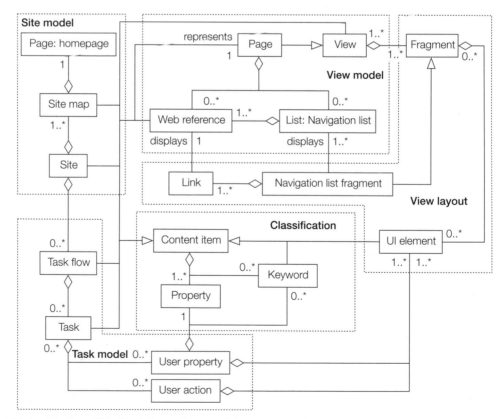

Figure 19.2 Main objects within the information model

- *alternative site maps and hierachies –*

  providing a way of building many different site maps with different views and navigation lists, allows alternative versions of the site to be created and associated with a single site without affecting any underlying content;

- *alternative visual representations of properties –*

  Separating what the property value is from the way that the property is visualized allows different visual or auditory representations to be associated with the same property value;

- *alternative visual representations of actions –*

  in addition, separating what the action does from how the action is visualized allows different visual or auditory representations to be associated with the same action logic.

Note

The common information models that are presented below are meant only to provide ideas and examples on how a specific system could be built using an information model approach. They are not meant to be complete, and certainly would not be able to be developed into a working system without a considerable amount of additional system design work. The idea is more to reflect how the requirements outlined in Part 3 of this book come together to define a set of models that could be used to define the requirements for a web publishing solution.

It is the author's belief that a different object model exists at each stage of the development process. The analysis process creates a model of the required system; a designer then uses this model to create a model to reflect the required high-level design. A programmer's model will again be different to the designer's model and will reflect implementation issues; it is also likely to be different to the model defined by the underlying object-oriented language or class library that is used.

The header used to describe each object uses the CRC method, which describes the class, the responsibilities of the class, and the objects within the system that the class collaborates with. This technique was originally described by Ward Cunningham of Wyatt Software Services and Ken Beck of Apple Computers at the 1989 OOPSLA Conference.[28]

As one may appreciate, defining information models for all the different requirements of all the different websites is a task that has no end. It is hoped that the models included here reflect common requirements for a majority of sites. And it is hoped that they can act as a springboard for any specific website that needs to be developed.

Content management system

Class	*Content management system*
Responsibilities	Management of content items within the system
	Management of content views to access content items within the system
	Management of access control to the content items held within the system
	Association of workflows to content items
	Management of default completion times for workflow actions
	Management of notification to content subscribers
Collaboration	Content item, access list, action monitor, subscription monitor, list

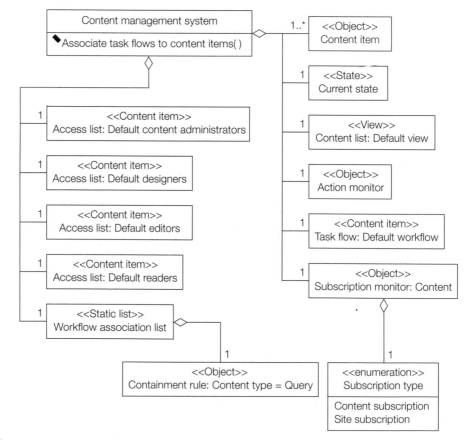

Figure 19.3   Content management system

Class   *Access list*
Responsibilities Provides the ability to define different access lists and associate them with content items, content types, user actions, user properties or states
                 Provides the ability to define an access level
                 Provides the ability to add objects to the access list, such as person, role and user group
Collaboration   Content item, person, role, user group, user property, user action, state

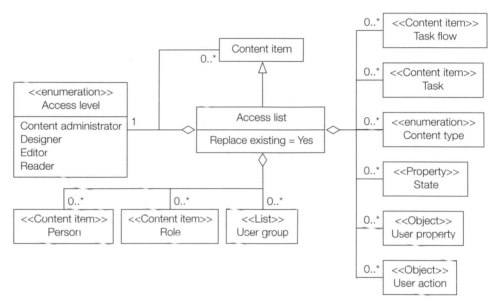

Figure 19.4 Access list

Class   *Subscription monitor*
Responsibilities Manages subscriptions that have been registered against content or against a site
                 Manages the notification messages to subscribers when the requested conditions are met
Collaboration   Content management system, content subscription, site, site subscription

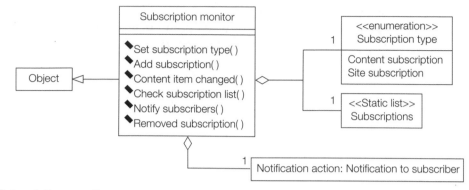

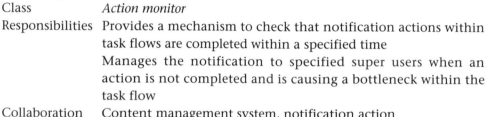

Figure 19.5   Subscription monitor

Class	*Action monitor*
Responsibilities	Provides a mechanism to check that notification actions within task flows are completed within a specified time
	Manages the notification to specified super users when an action is not completed and is causing a bottleneck within the task flow
Collaboration	Content management system, notification action

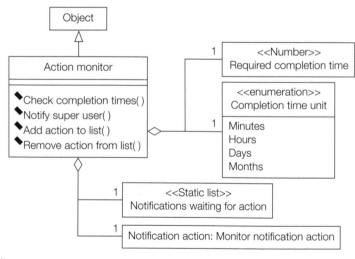

Figure 19.6   Action monitor

Content item

Class	*Content item*
Responsibilities	Provides a mechanism to define common attributes and services for all content items within the system
	Provides a way of defining relationships between different content items
	Provides a way of associating review criteria to a content item
	Provides a way of managing the state of content items
	Provides a common way to associate classification keywords
	Provides a mechanism to maintain a publishing and workflow history
	Provides the management of different versions of the same content item
	Provides the definition of ownership and the teams for creating the item and maintaining it
	Provides the mechanism to associate change requests and publishing agreements with the content item
	Provides the ability to flag that a content item needs a publishing agreement
	Provides the ability to break a content item down into smaller work items
	Provides the mechanism to keep a track of where the content item is being referenced by other content items
	Provides the ability to flag that the content item should be highlighted on the site when it is published
	Provides the ability to define a priority to the content item and in addition a marketing priority that may influence where the content item appears in any generated contextual list
	Provides the ability to flag that dependencies exist between content items, so that if one item is changed there will be a need for the other content items to be reviewed as well
Collaboration	Content management system, review criteria, web reference, keyword, highlight, work item, subscription monitor, publishing agreement, change request, task flow

Content item attributes

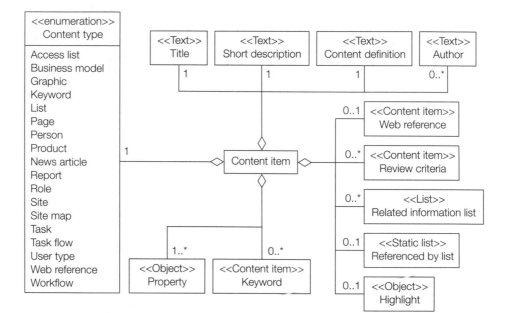

Figure 19.7 Content item attributes (i)

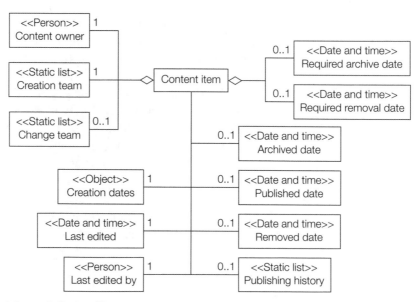

Figure 19.8 Content item attributes (ii)

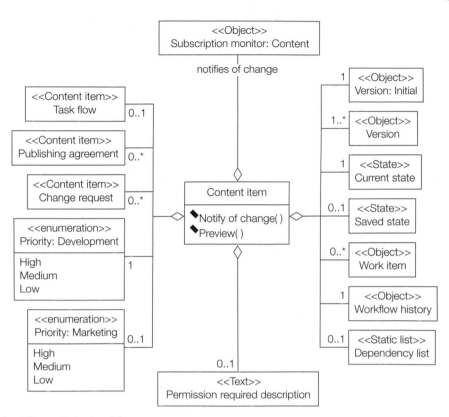

Figure 19.9   Content item attributes (iii)

Class   *Version*
Responsibilities   Manages different versions of content items
Collaboration   Content item

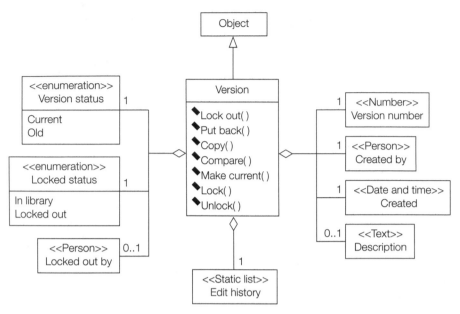

Figure 19.10 Version

Class   *Edit history*
Responsibilities Provides a common way to create a version history of a content
                 item
Collaboration   Version, content item

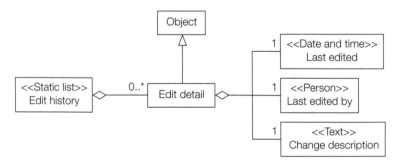

Figure 19.11 Edit history

Class   *Creation dates*
Responsibilities Provides a common way to define the set of dates associated
                 with creating a content item
Collaboration   Content item

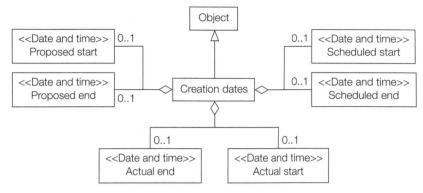

Figure 19.12   Creation dates

Class   *Review criteria*
Responsibilities Provides the ability for content that is intended to be reviewed,
                 to hold attributes which can be used during the review process
                 Provides the ability to define a hierarchical list of site goals and
                 messages
                 Provides the ability to define critical design features and usabil-
                 ity goals
                 Provides the ability for additional review criteria to be added and
                 allows the specification of whether the property is a mandatory field
                 Provides the ability for content providers to request that new
                 categories be added
Collaboration   Content item

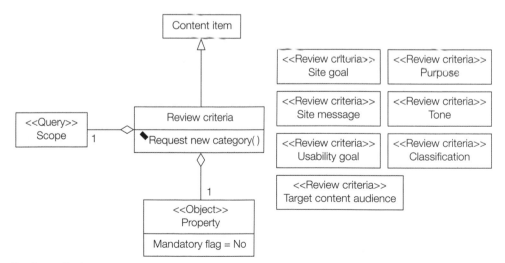

Figure 19.13   Review criteria

Class   *Work item*
Responsibilities   Provides a common way to break down the task of creating or
                   changing a content item into smaller measurable pieces
                   Provides a common way to define the dates that can be used to
                   measure progress
Collaboration   Content item

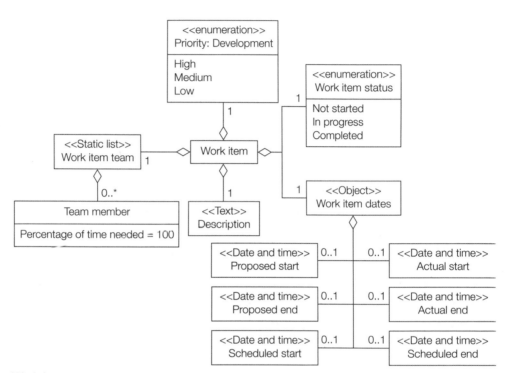

Figure 19.14   Work item

Class   *Highlight*
Responsibilities   Provides a common way to specify that a content item should
                   be highlighted if it is published
                   Provides a set of common attributes that can be used within a
                   view to display a highlighted link
Collaboration   Content item

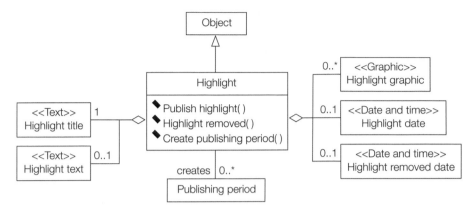

Figure 19.15   Highlight

Class   *Publishing period*
Responsibilities   Provides a common way to build up a publishing history of a content item
                Provides a set of common fields that can be used to provide the details of when, where and how the content item was published
Collaboration   Content item

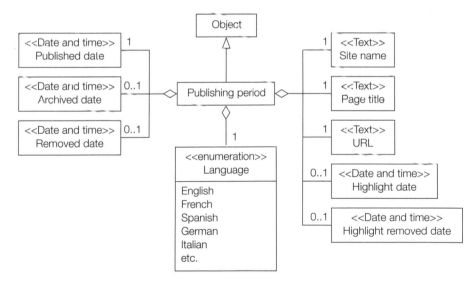

Figure 19.16   Publishing period

Class   *Property*
Responsibilities Provides a base class for all property types within the system
                  Defines whether a property is mandatory or not
Collaboration Content item, user property

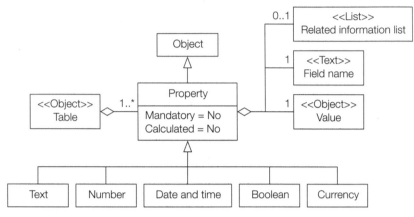

Figure 19.17 Property

Class   *Action*
Responsibilities Provides a common way to define an executable piece of code
                  that is initiated by a user action
                  Provides a base class for different types of actions within the
                  system
Collaboration User action

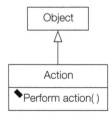

Figure 19.18 Action

Containers

Class   *List*
Responsibilities Provides a common way to define lists within the system
                  Manages the types of objects that can be contained within the list
                  Manages how the list is sorted

Allows a heading to be associated with a list, and as a list can contain other lists, provides a mechanism for building up a hierarchy tree structure

Collaboration   Static list, dynamic list, query

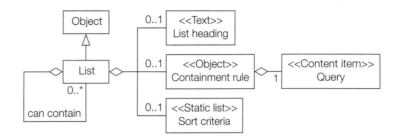

Figure 19.19   List

Class   *Sort criteria*
Responsibilities Provides the means to define how a list should be sorted
Collaboration   List, static list, dynamic list

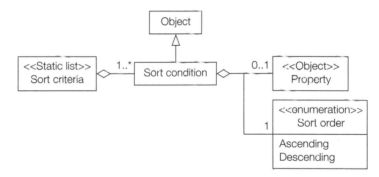

Figure 19.20   Sort criteria

Class   *Static list*
Responsibilities Provides a common way to define a static list that contains a set of list items
                  Manages the addition and removal of list items
Collaboration   List, static list, dynamic list

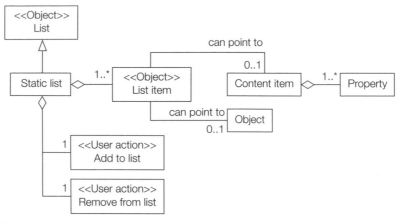

Figure 19.21 Static list

Class   *Dynamic list*
Responsibilities   Provides a common way to create a list by defining a query
                        Provides a mechanism to define how often the query is run
Collaboration   List, static list, query

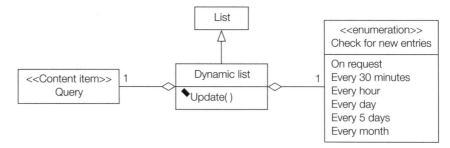

Figure 19.22 Dynamic list

Content types

Class   *Business model*
Responsibilities   Defines a template for the information required to define a business model for a website
                        Defines a common way to establish measurable targets
                        Defines a common way to establish the target audience
Collaboration   Content item, user type

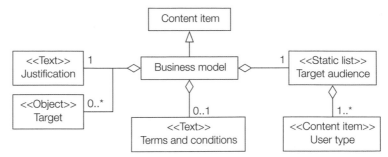

Figure 19.23 Business model

Class   *Target*
Responsibilities Provides a mechanism for defining measurable targets for a website
Collaboration   Business model

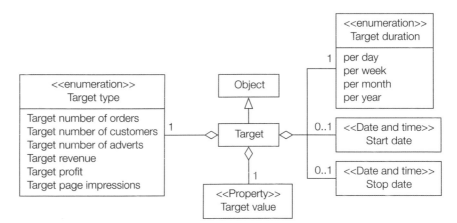

Figure 19.24 Target

Class   *Commerce business model*
Responsibilities Provides a template that can be used to specify the attributes
                 needed to define a commerce website
                 Defines how money can be accepted over the website
                 Defines the available delivery options and the terms and conditions
Collaboration   Business model, target, delivery option, card

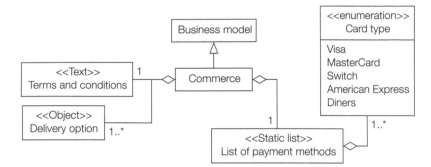

Figure 19.25   Commerce business model

Class   *Card*
Responsibilities Provides a common way to define a credit card
Collaboration   Commerce business model

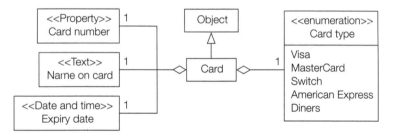

Figure 19.26   Card

Class   *Delivery option*
Responsibilities Provides a common way of specifying different delivery options
Collaboration   Commerce business model

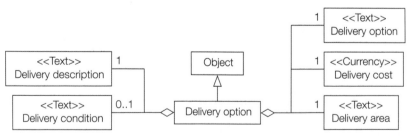

Figure 19.27   Delivery option

Class   *Advertising business model*

Responsibilities   Provides a template that can be used to specify the attributes needed to define an advertising business model

Provides a mechanism to specify different advertising rates

Collaboration   Advertising rate, keyword rate, sponsorship rate, rate, business model

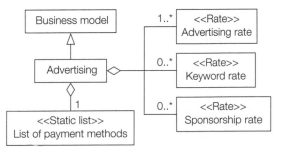

Figure 19.28   Advertising business model

Class   *Rate*

Responsibilities   Provides a common way to define a rate card

Collaboration   Advertising rate, keyword rate, sponsorship rate, advertising business model

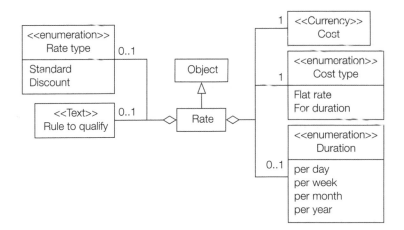

Figure 19.29   Rate

Class   *Advertising rate*

Responsibilities   Provides a common way to define an advertising rate card

Collaboration   Rate, advertising business model, advert

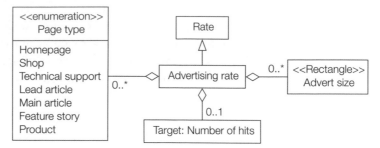

Figure 19.30 Advertising rate

Class   *Keyword rate*
Responsibilities Provides a common way to define a keyword rental rate card
Collaboration   Rate, keyword, keyword rental, advertising business model

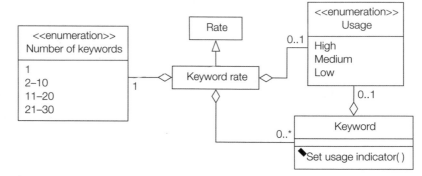

Figure 19.31 Keyword rate

Class   *Sponsorship rate*
Responsibilities Provides a common way to define a sponsorship rate card
Collaboration   Rate, advertising business model, sponsorship deal

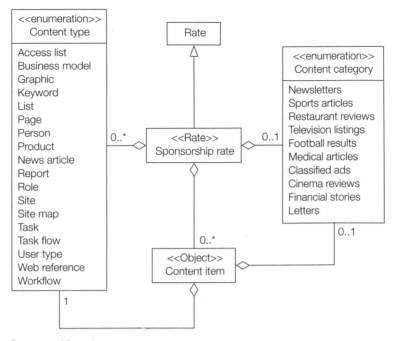

Figure 19.32 Sponsorship rate

Class	*Subscription business model*
Responsibilities	Provides a template that can be used to specify the attributes needed to define a subscription business model
Collaboration	Site subscription, business model, subscription option

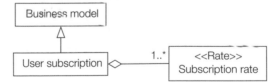

Figure 19.33 Subscription business model

Class	*Subscription rate*
Responsibilities	Provides a mechanism to define different subscription rates that may be associated with different access to the site
Collaboration	Subscription business model

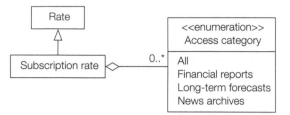

Figure 19.34   Subscription rate

Class	*Order*
Responsibilities	Provides a common class that can be used to define an order
Collaboration	Content item, card, customer, delivery option, product option

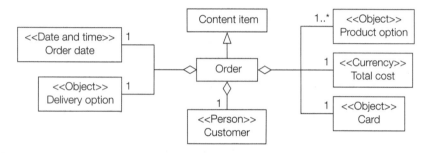

Figure 19.35   Order

Class	*Advert*
Responsibilities	Provides a common way to define an advert that has been taken out on the site
	Provides a way to keep a history of the click-through rate that the advert achieves
	Manages the automatic notification to remove the item once the remove date has been reached
Collaboration	Content item, customer, advertising rate

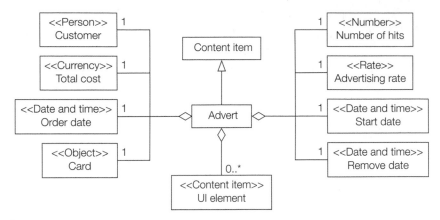

Figure 19.36 Advert

Class	*Keyword rental*
Responsibilities	Provides a common way to define a keyword rental that has been taken out on the site
	Provides a way to keep a history of the usage any particular key word receives on the site
	Manages the automatic notification to remove the keyword association once the remove date has been reached
Collaboration	Content item, customer, advertising rate, keyword, keyword rate

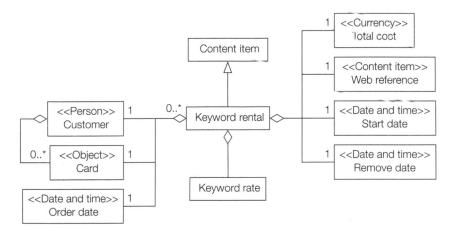

Figure 19.37 Keyword rental

Class   *Sponsorship deal*

Responsibilities   Provides a common way to define a sponsorship deal that has been taken out on the site

Provides a way to keep a history of the content usage where the sponsorship message is displayed

Manages the automatic notification to remove the sponsorship association and message once the remove date has been reached

Collaboration   Content item, customer, advertising rate, sponsorship rate

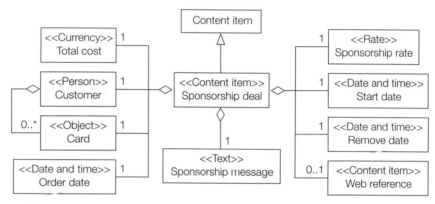

Figure 19.38   Sponsorship deal

Class   *Site subscription*

Responsibilities   Provides a common way to define a subscription request from a user that allows automatic notification when something gets added or changed on the site

Collaboration   Site, subscription monitor, content item

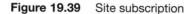

Figure 19.39   Site subscription

Class   *Content subscription*

Responsibilities   Provides a common way to define a subscription request from a user that allows automatic notification when something gets added or changed within the content management system

Collaboration   Content management system, subscription monitor, content item

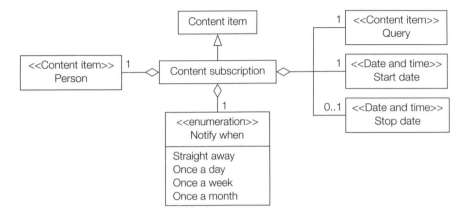

Figure 19.40   Content subscription

Class   *Questionnaire*

Responsibilities   Provides a common way to define a questionnaire for a site

Provides a mechanism to define the acknowledgement text for when a user submits the form

Provides a way of linking a questionnaire to the user types that have been defined as part of the target audience

Collaboration   Content item, user type

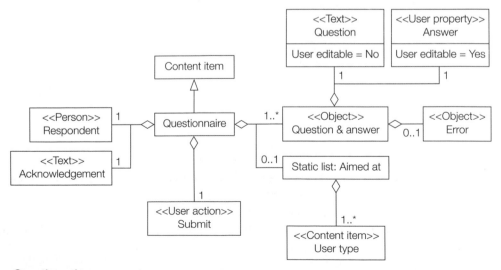

Figure 19.41   Questionnaire

Class   *Web reference*
Responsibilities   Provides a common way to represent a web reference
                   Provides the ability to define a template to show the results of a
                   keyword or full text site search
Collaboration   Content item, page

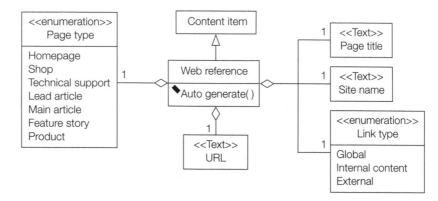

Figure 19.42   Web reference

Class   *Print reference*
Responsibilities   Provides the ability to define the fields to represent a reference
                   that has only been published in printed form
Collaboration   Content item

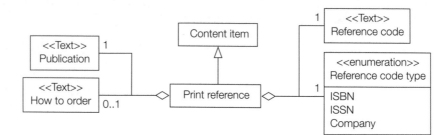

Figure 19.43   Print reference

Class   *Publishing agreement*
Responsibilities   Provides a form that contains the attributes necessary to define
                   a publishing agreement that may be needed to publish certain
                   pieces of information to a site
Collaboration   Content item, third party permissions workflow, role

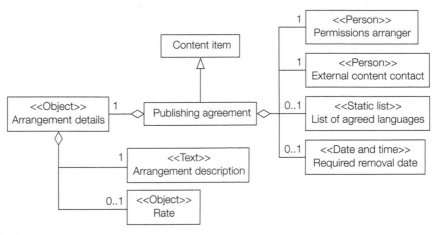

Figure 19.44   Publishing agreement

Class   *Proposal*
Responsibilities Provides a form that can be used to create a proposal to create
                new content items
Collaboration   Content item, proposal workflow, team member

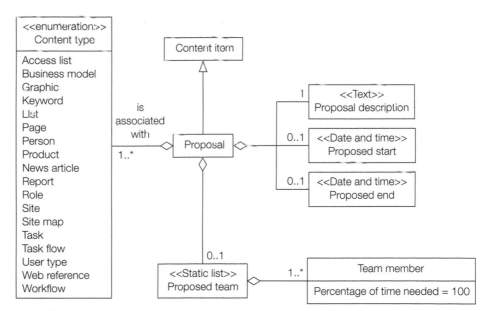

Figure 19.45   Proposal

Class   *Change request*
Responsibilities   Provides the ability to propose a change to a currently publishing document
                       Manages the relationship between the change request form, the content item, and the change request workflow
Collaboration   Content item, change request workflow

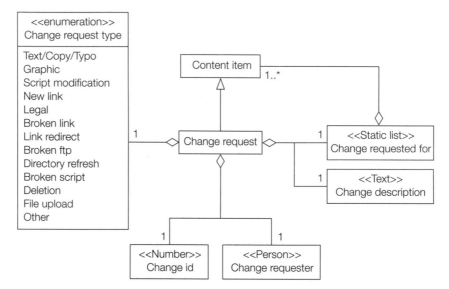

Figure 19.46   Change request

Class   *Downloadable file*
Responsibilities   Provides a common way to define a file that can be downloaded from a web page
                       Manages whether the file is held within the database or externally
Collaboration   Content item

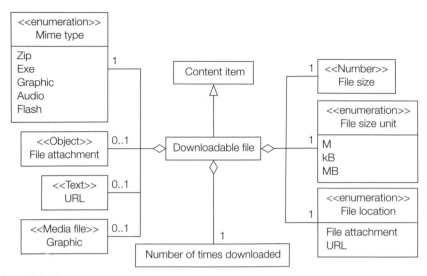

Figure 19.47   Downloadable file

Task flows

Class	*Task goal*
Responsibilities	Provides a way of defining the task goals for a site and associating task flows to these goals
	Provides a mechanism for setting a priority on a task goal of high, medium or low
Collaboration	Content item, task flow

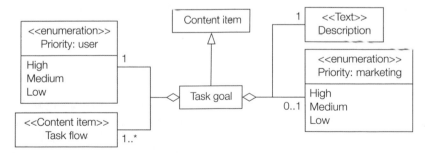

Figure 19.48   Task goal

Class   *Task flow*

Responsibilities Management and definition of workflow for content items within the system

      Management of the tasks and other task flows that a task flow is made up from

      Association of a task flow to a user type

      Definition of the acceptable states that a content item must be in before the task flow can be started

      Definition of the user actions that are displayed that set the task flow in motion

      Definition of any start condition that needs to be met for the task flow to be available

Collaboration Task goal, content item, task, user type

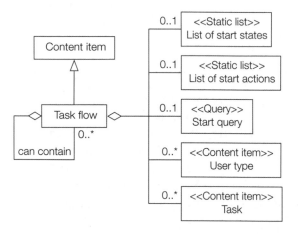

Figure 19.49 Task flow

Class   *Task*

Responsibilities Provides the ability to define a task that is part of any overall task flow

      Provides a mechanism for measuring task success

      Provides the ability to notify users within the system that a task requires action

      Provides the ability to define the information and actions that need to be available for the user to complete the task

Collaboration Task flow, notification action, user property, user action

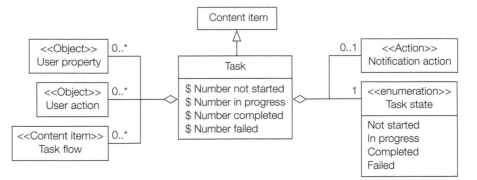

Figure 19.50   Task

Class   *User property in task*
Responsibilities   Provides the ability to set the priority of the user property in
                   relation to the task that is being defined
Collaboration   Task, user property

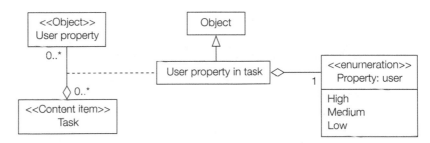

Figure 19.51   User property in task

Class   *User action in task*
Responsibilities   Provides the ability to set the priority of the user action in rela-
                   tion to the task that is being defined
Collaboration   Task, user action

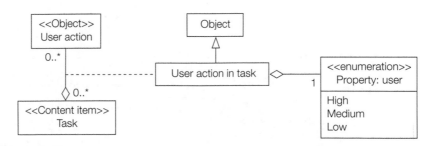

Figure 19.52   User action in task

Class   *User property*
Responsibilities Provides a mechanism to link together a user interface element
                 such as a graphic string or entry field and the underlying prop-
                 erty that the UI element represents
                 Provides a way for multiple views on properties to be kept syn-
                 chronized
Collaboration   Task, property, UI element, keyword, publishing agreement, user
                 action

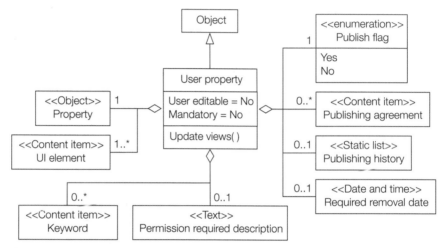

Figure 19.53   User property

Class   *User action*
Responsibilities Provides a mechanism to link together a user interface element
                 such as a button and the underlying executable piece of code
                 that is activated when the element is activated
                 Provides a way for multiple views of an action to be kept syn-
                 chronized
Collaboration   Task, action, UI element, user property

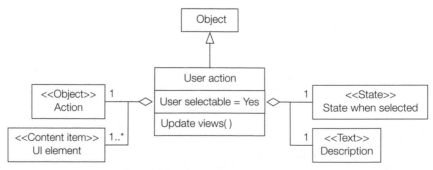

Figure 19.54   User action

Class   *Notification action*
Responsibilities Provides a way to notify users when an action is required
                 Provides a common mechanism to set up the list of users who
                 get notified
                 Provides a common way to define the notification message that
                 is sent
                 Provides a mechanism to define the required approval level from
                 the users within the notification group
                 Allows the definition of individual action monitors to be associ-
                 ated with notification actions, in order to define the required
                 action completion time. If this is not set, the default action
                 monitor is used
Collaboration   Notification group, action monitor

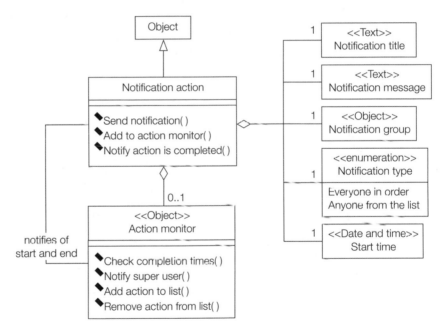

Figure 19.55   Notification action

Class   *Notification group*
Responsibilities Provides a way of defining who gets notified of a notification
                 action
                 Provides a mechanism to define primary contacts and those
                 users who are copied for information only
Collaboration   Notification action, list

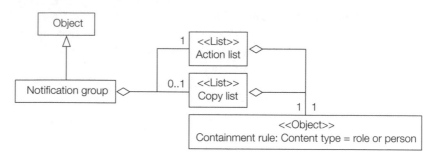

Figure 19.56 Notification group

Class   *Feedback action*
Responsibilities Provides a way to define an action that allows users to provide
feedback as a result of a notification action
Provides a standard way to define the message that is sent, and
who the message goes to
Collaboration   Notification action, notification group, task

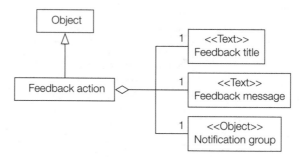

Figure 19.57 Feedback action

Class   *Workflow entry*
Responsibilities Provides a common structure to create a workflow history
Defines the attributes that record the person responsible for
changing the state of a content item, what the action was and
when the change took place
Collaboration   Content item

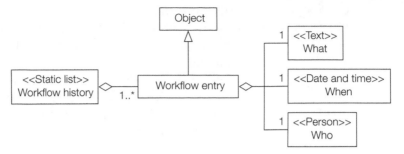

Figure 19.58   Workflow entry

Workflow types

Class	*Proposal workflow*
Responsibilities	Allows the definition of a proposal workflow that can be used as part of a larger workflow that is associated with different content items
	Allows those authorized to create workflows to define what the process should be for the proposal stage of a content item
	Manages the state of the task model and provides the actions for automatically notifying users within the system during the proposal stage of the content item
Collaboration	Proposal, content item, task flow, task, user action

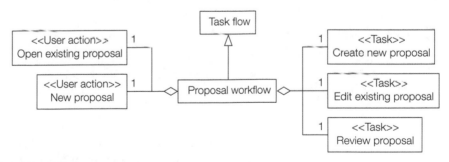

Figure 19.59   Proposal workflow

Class   *Creation workflow*

Responsibilities Allows the definition of a creation workflow that can be used as part of a larger workflow that is associated with different content items

Allows the owner of a content item to define what the workflow should be for the creation stage of a document life cycle

Allows the definition of a creation team

Allows those within the creation team to pass the content item around to others in order to request their input

Manages the state of the task model and provides the actions for automatically notifying users within the system during the creation stage of the document

Collaboration   Content item, task flow, task, user action

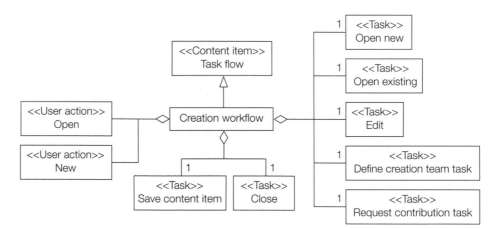

Figure 19.60   Creation workflow

Class   *Third party permissions workflow*

Responsibilities Allows the definition of a third party permissions workflow that can be used as part of a larger workflow that is associated with different content items

Allows those authorized to create workflows to define what the process should be for setting up publishing agreements

Manages the state of the task model and provides the actions for automatically notifying users within the system during the process to set up a publishing agreement for a content item

Collaboration   Content item, publishing agreement

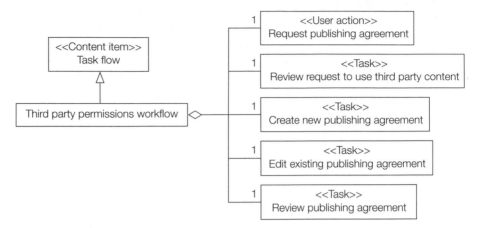

Figure 19.61   Third party permissions workflow

Class   *Content review workflow*
Responsibilities Allows the definition of a content review workflow that can be
                 used as part of a larger workflow that is associated with different
                 content items
                 Allows those authorized to create workflows to define the
                 process for reviewing content before it is published to a site
                 Manages the state of the task model and provides the actions for
                 automatically notifying users within the system during the
                 review cycle of a content item
Collaboration   Content item, review criteria, task flow, task, user action

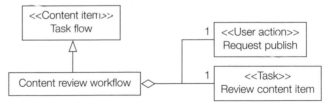

Figure 19.62   Content review workflow

Class   *Publish workflow*
Responsibilities Allows the definition of a publish workflow that can be used as
                 part of a larger workflow that is associated with different con-
                 tent items

Allows those authorized to create workflows to define the process for publishing content to a site

Manages the state of the task model and provides the actions for automatically notifying users within the system during the publication stage of a content item

Collaboration   Content item, task flow, task, user action

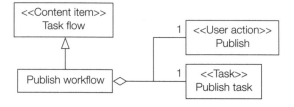

Figure 19.63   Publish workflow

Class   *Change request workflow*

Responsibilities Allows the definition of a change request workflow that can be used as part of a larger workflow that is associated with different content items

Manages the state of the change request task model and provides the actions for automatically notifying users within the system during the change request stage of a currently publishing content item

Collaboration   Content item, change request, task flow, task, user action

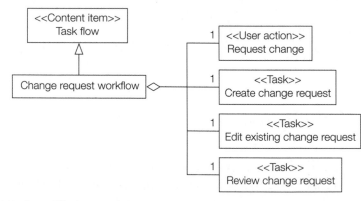

Figure 19.64   Change request workflow

Class   *Change workflow*

Responsibilities Allows the definition of a change workflow that can be used as part of a larger workflow that is associated with different content items

Allows those authorized to define what the workflow should be for adding updates to a currently published content item

Manages the state of the task model and provides the actions for automatically notifying users within the system during the updating of a currently publishing content item

Allows those authorized to define who within the organization is able to make the changes to the content item

Provides a mechanism for requesting that others within a change team make modifications to the content item

Collaboration   Content item, task flow, task, user action

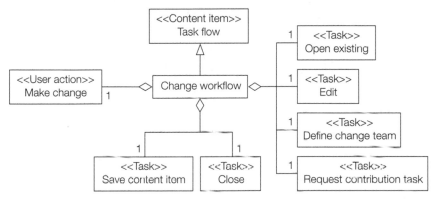

Figure 19.65   Change workflow

Class   *Change review workflow*

Responsibilities Allows the definition of a change review workflow that can be used as part of a larger workflow that is associated with different content items

Allows those authorized to create workflows to define the process for reviewing updates to content items before they are republished to the site

Manages the state of the task model and provides the actions for automatically notifying users within the system during the change review stage of a content item

Collaboration   Content item, review criteria, task flow, task, user action

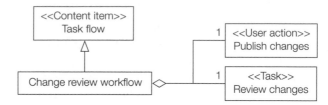

Figure 19.66 Change review workflow

Class   *Archive workflow*
Responsibilities Allows the definition of an archive workflow that can be used as part of a larger workflow that is associated with different content items
Manages the state of the archive task model and provides the actions for automatically notifying users within the system during the archiving stage of a publishing content item
Collaboration Task flow, task

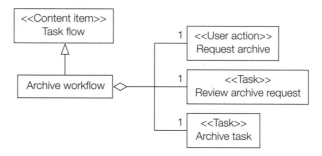

Figure 19.67 Archive workflow

Class   *Deletion workflow*
Responsibilities Allows the definition of a deletion workflow that can be used as part of a larger workflow that is associated with different content items
Allows those authorized to create workflows to define what the process should be for deleting content items. There may be more than one deletion workflow within the system to cover relatively innocuous delete requests as well as those which might have a more serious impact, such as items that are currently being published to the website.
Manages the state of the task model and provides the actions for automatically notifying users within the system during the deletion stage of a content item
Collaboration Content item, task flow, task, user action

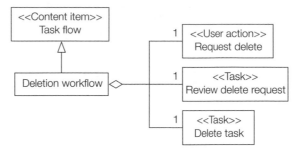

Figure 19.68 Deletion workflow

Class | *Unpublish workflow*
Responsibilities | Allows the definition of an unpublish workflow that can be used as part of a larger workflow that is associated with different content items
 | Allows those authorized to create workflows to define what the process should be for removing published items from the site.
 | Manages the state of the task model and provides the actions for automatically notifying users within the system during an unpublish stage of a content item
Collaboration | Task flow, task, user action

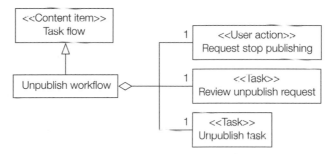

Figure 19.69 Unpublish workflow

Class | *Republish workflow*
Responsibilities | Allows the definition of a republish workflow that can be used as part of a larger workflow that is associated with different content items
 | Allows those authorized to create workflows to define what the process should be to republish removed items to the site.
 | Manages the state of the task model and provides the actions for automatically notifying users within the system during the republish stage of a content item
Collaboration | Task flow, task, user action

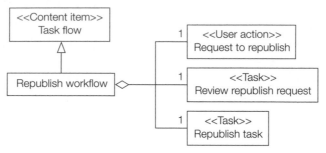

Figure 19.70 Republish workflow

Site and views

Class	*Site*
Responsibilities	Management of the publishing of the site to an external source
	Management of the site-wide feedback and subscriptions from external web users
	Management of the search queries generated on the site
	Management of the adverts included on the site
	Management of any orders taken on the site
	Management of alternative site maps
	Provides a mechanism to define a set of task goals
	Provides a mechanism to define default visual attributes
	Provides a way to define the site purpose
	Provides a way to define the language that is used on the site
	Provides services to allow content providers to preview the site
	Allows the association to be made between page objects and the site
	Allows the association between a business model and a site, and therefore any measurable targets that have been set within the business model
Collaboration	Content item, site map, site purpose, search query, question-naire, advert, order, subscription, business model, task goal, task flow, page, default visual attributes, subscription monitor

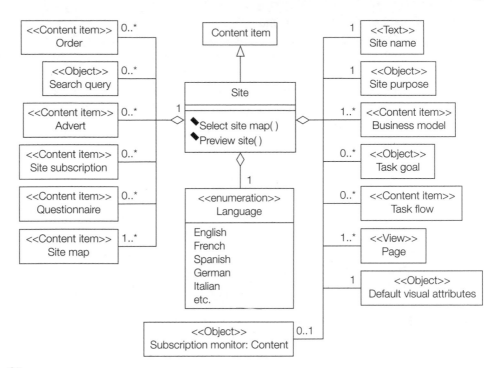

Figure 19.71   Site

Class   *Site purpose*
Responsibilities   Allows the definition of site-wide attributes that can be used within a review process
Collaboration   Site, review criteria

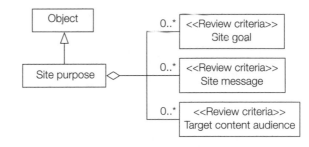

Figure 19.72   Site purpose

Class   *Site map*

Responsibilities Allows the definition of a site content hierarchy or primary navigation scheme by enabling a site to have alternative homepages

Allows user types to be associated with a site map and for a site map to be defined by a type

Collaboration   Site, user type, page

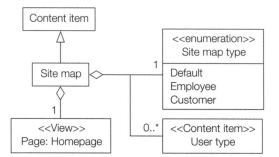

Figure 19.73   Site map

Class   *View*

Responsibilities Provides a common base class that can be used by different view types

Provides a mechanism to create a layout based on the arrangment of fragments within the view

Collaboration   Content item, fragment

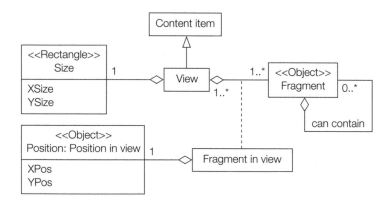

Figure 19.74   View

Class   *Fragment*

Responsibilities   Provides a common way to build up a layout based on visual building blocks or partitions of a view

Manages the position of UI elements within a layout

Manages the resize behaviour of individual parts of the view

Manages the order in which data attributes are loaded and displayed

Provides the ability to set default visual attributes with a part of the view

Provides the ability to define a type and associate it with part of a view, in order to perform intelligent printing if required

Provides the ability to count the number of times the fragment is accessed within the view

Collaboration   View, UI element, default visual attributes

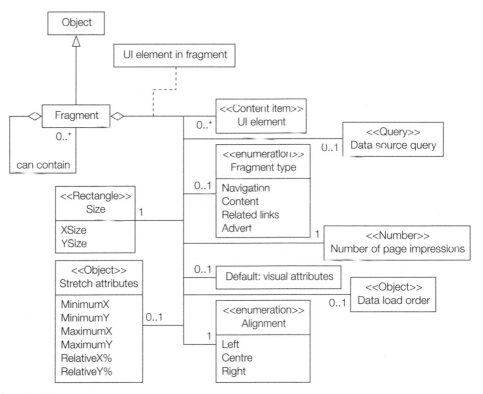

Figure 19.75   Fragment

Class   *UI element in fragment*

Responsibilities Provides a common way to add attributes to a UI element that are related to when the UI Element is within a certain view or fragment

Collaboration   View, fragment

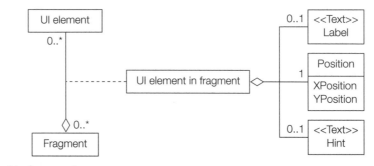

Figure 19.76   UI element in fragment

Class   *Page*

Responsibilities Provides a common template that can be used to define a page or a page template that generate pages from a data source

Manages the automatic generation of a web reference when a page is generated from a data source

Provides the ability to set default visual attributes for the page

Manages the association between a page and page events

Provides the ability to count the number of times the page is accessed within the site

Provides a mechanism to create navigation lists to other pages on the site

Provides the ability to define a page type which can be used with a site search function

Collaboration   View, web reference

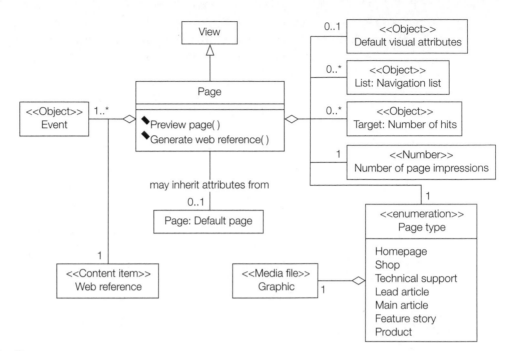

Figure 19.77   Page

Class   *Default visual attributes*
Responsibilities   Provides a mechanism to define a set of default visual attributes
Collaboration   View, page, fragment

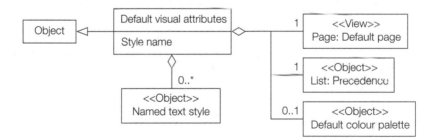

Figure 19.78   Default visual attributes

Class   *Search query*
Responsibilities Provides the ability to store search queries entered by the user through a web search interface
Collaboration   Query, keyword

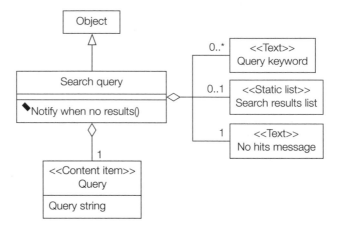

Figure 19.79   Search query

Class   *Content list*
Responsibilities Provides a template to create a view that displays columns of attributes belonging to a collection of content items
Provides the mechanism to define the display criteria of the group of content items that are displayed within the list
Collaboration   View, fragment, content item, content management system

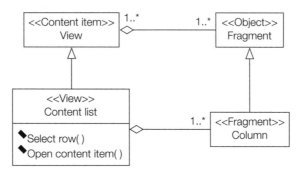

Figure 19.80   Content list

Class   *Form template*
Responsibilities Provides the ability to define a layout that allows attributes to be entered into the system
Collaboration   View, content type, content item

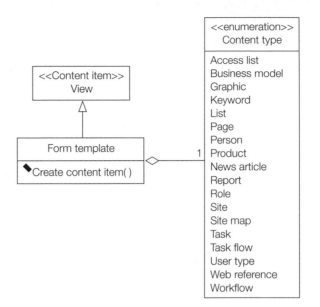

Figure 19.81 Form template

Classification

Class	*Keyword*
Responsibilities	Provides a mechanism to represent the terms and vocabulary that will be presented to the user within the web interface
	Provides the ability to define the user vocabulary through either keywords or an associated list of synonyms
	Provides the ability to define a hierarchical categorization scheme that can be used within a keyword search facility that can also support associated synonyms
	Holds the common categorizations to be used by content providers and provides the ability to search the keyword lists and request that new keywords be added
Collaboration	Content item, subject area, list

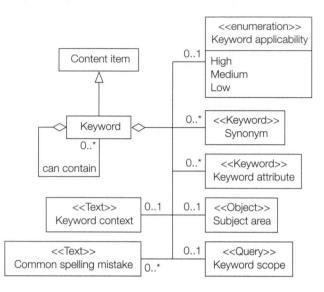

Figure 19.82   Keyword

Class   *Subject area*
Responsibilities Provides the ability to extend certain keywords to have extra information associated with them so that a common UI can be created for a search facility
Collaboration   Keyword, web reference, key web references

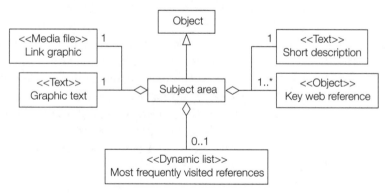

Figure 19.83   Subject area

Class   *Key web reference*
Responsibilities Provides the ability to create a list of key web references associated with a subject matter
                Provides the ability to maintain a list of the most frequently visited links associated with a subject matter
Collaboration   Keyword, subject matter, list

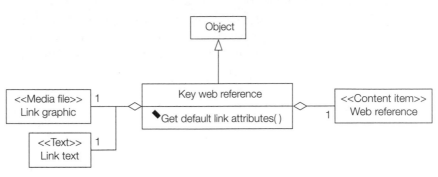

Figure 19.84   Key web reference

People and roles

Class   *Person*

Responsibilities Provides a common base set of attributes to define a person within a system. Person objects can be aggregated with any number of role objects in order to define a more complex object or to complete an object. In this way different combinations of attributes can be created to build up the kind of person required

Collaboration   Content item, role, user type, content subscription

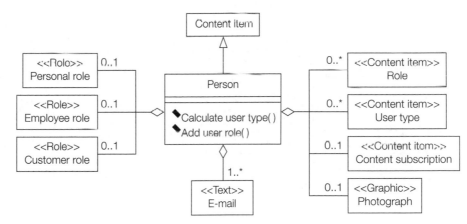

Figure 19.85   Person

Class   *Role*

Responsibilities Provides the ability to define a role that can be aggregated on to a person object

Roles allow a generic person object to be enhanced by associating attributes that define the different roles that a person may have. A person may have different roles, and an object may query a person to see if they contain a specific role

Provides the ability for a person object to be customized to suit a particular purpose within a site or organization, without losing the ability to work within the workflow scheme

Collaboration   Person

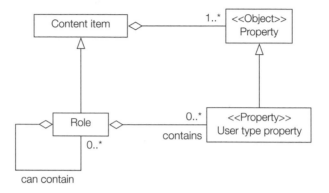

Figure 19.86   Role

Class   *Personal role*

Responsibilities   Provides a specific role to provide personal details such as a home address and telephone number for a person object

Collaboration   Person, role

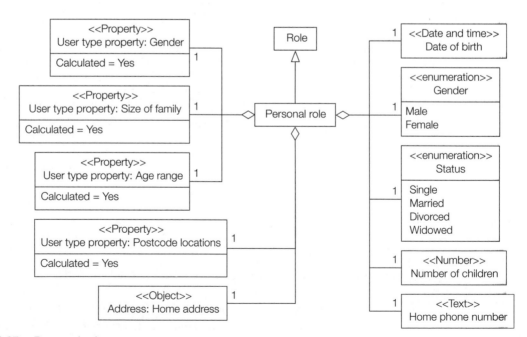

Figure 19.87   Personal role

Class   *Address*
Responsibilities Provides a common way to define different addresses, such as a
                 home, delivery and work address
Collaboration   Personal role, employee role, customer role

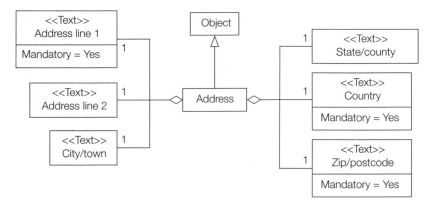

Figure 19.88 Address

Class   *Employee role*
Responsibilities Provides a specific role to provide employee details such as a
                 work location, job title and manager for a person object
Collaboration   Person, role

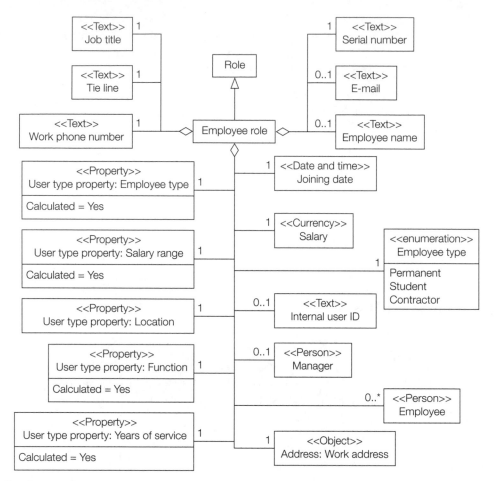

Figure 19.89 Employee role

Class	*Customer role*
Responsibilities	Provides a specific role to give customer details such as credit card information, history of orders, and customer login for a person object
Collaboration	Person, role

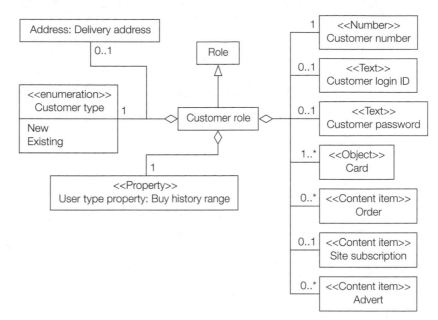

Figure 19.90   Customer role

Class   *User type*
Responsibilities Provides the ability to define a type of user by defining a set of
                 specific properties to distinguish one type from another
Collaboration   User type properties, person

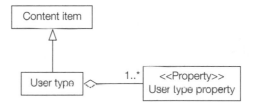

Figure 19.91   User type

Class   *Team member*
Responsibilities Provides the ability to associate a person with the amount of
                 time they will be needed. This variable can then be used to spe-
                 cify resource requirements for creating or maintaining content
                 items and work items
Collaboration   Person, content item, work item

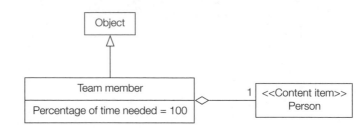

Figure 19.92   Team member

Class   *User group*
Responsibilities Provides the ability to define a dynamic list of people or roles
                 which meet a set of selection criteria
Collaboration   Person, role, notification group, user type, access list

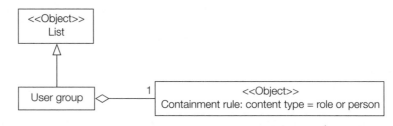

Figure 19.93   User group

20 Content management overview

There is a sliding scale of how much a company may wish to introduce processes that control the creation, publication and maintenance of website content. This ranges from no processes whatsoever right through to installing large document management systems with version control, workflow management and more functionality than you can shake a stick at.

Ideally, an organization should set up a content management solution that provides the appropriate level of functionality to suit the type of content that is being created, and more importantly should provide tools that people will be able to use. Getting the right balance can be difficult. A content management environment that does not support any kind of process for content review before publication could lead to quality control problems. However, any system that enforces too many rules and introduces unnecessary barriers to getting content published will cause major frustration within the organization and lead content providers to look for workarounds to beat the system.

Deciding on the right level of functionality a tool offers should also be dictated by an analysis of the primary tasks of those who need to use it. It is not always a correct assumption that the tool that offers the most functionality is the best one to buy. While it is correct to assume that not enough automated tool support can introduce errors and slow down content creation, too much function can also slow down content creation because content providers do not understand how to use the tool to complete their tasks. They may become bogged down with learning the task model as defined by the tool rather than concentrating their efforts on doing the job that they are being paid to do.

In addition, any tool that is confusing to use – which has nothing to do with how much functionality it offers – will end up dominating the content publishing process. Either content providers will refuse to use it and find ways to bypass the system, or if they are forced to use it they will demand a level of support from the technical community who will then be forced to devote more time supporting and maintaining the tool than is reasonably justified.

With this in mind it is perhaps wise to take some time to understand the major components of a content management environment.

Core services

● **Access control** Defining default access lists across the whole system provides the simplest model to support the roles and responsibilities within a website team. However, if more complex relationships are needed it should be possible to define alternative lists to control access at a content-type level, at an individual content item level, at a task level, and even at an individual property level.

● **Version control** Version control provides the mechanism to safeguard against changes being lost as a result of more than one person trying to change the same file at the same time. It also provides the ability to carry on publishing a version of the content while a new version is being created. In some cases it will allow complex changes to the site that involve multiple files to be synchronized.

An important advantage of maintaining different versions of the same content is the ability to back out changes. Any change management process that supports a review process will need to offer the person reviewing the change the ability to reject changes that have been made. To fully support this, the system will need the ability to return the content item to the state it was in before the change was made. A version control system will be able to support this process.

By maintaining a master work file, the version control system can also support a history log that provides details of all the changes that have been made to the content item and by whom.

● **Workflows** A system should provide a default workflow that can be applied to any content item within the system. As workflows can contain other workflows, the default provided should contain a very simple model for publishing new content and maintaining it. If additional workflows are

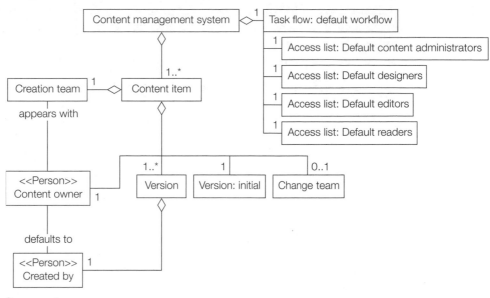

Figure 20.1   Core services

required for more complex patterns of behaviour, it should be possible to define alternative workflows and associate them with different content types or make an association based on other content attributes by defining a query. It should also be possible to set up a precedence list of these queries to deal with any conflicts that may exist.

● **Ownership**   To support the various stages of workflow, it is necessary to assign ownership to files within the system in order to support automatic notification when any feedback is necessary. In this sense ownership is not the person who actually owns the item but the person within the organization who is responsible for it. A content management system needs to support this kind of ownership and be flexible enough for the field to default to the person creating the file, but also be editable by anyone who has authority to assign the role.

Organizing content into different management systems

For a large site with many different types of content that has a large information store and archive, an organization may wish to look at how to partition the content into different management systems. This makes sense when the types of information stored within a system require services specific to that content type, or if it is logical to split out certain content types for access reasons. There also becomes a point when a system is so crowded with files and documents that it is unmanageable and difficult to use.

A logical separation of content an organization might consider is:

- **document management system** – a repository for storing all the different types of documents, such as proposals, news articles, case studies, reports, and different type of references such as web references and print references;

- **site management system** – a repository for all the site and site map definitions, pages, fragments, forms and task flow definitions;

- **classification system** – a repository for all the keywords and keyword hierarchies that can be used to classify content;

- **directory** – a repository for all the people needed and used within the system and the roles that are defined for these people;

- **asset library** – a repository for all assets and UI elements, including controls and asset files, such as graphics, exe and zip files;

- **change management system** – a repository for storing all the change requests within the system.

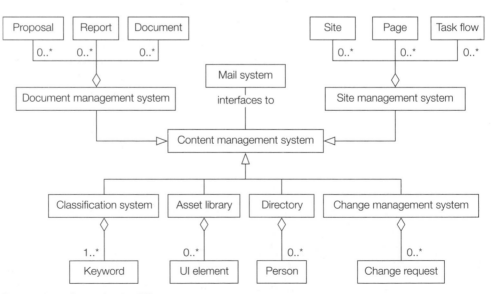

Figure 20.2   Separation of content in different management systems

Summary

When a team starts the process of defining how they are going to deliver a website for a company, much effort is invested in the creative and fun jobs, such as the visual style of the site, how real-world metaphors can be translated to a web page, and how certain pieces of cool technology could be used. Not many web teams get too excited about defining workflows or relish the prospect of getting users involved with the development process.

Unfortunately these jobs can be critical to the success of the overall solution that is delivered. It is a sad fact for visual designers that many users do not care about how the site looks as long as it does what they want it to do. It is the process of trying to find out what users want to do and how they want to do it, and translating these user models into a system design, that will ultimately create an easy-to-use interface. If a company also wishes to create a successful online business, the priorities of the business will also need to be integrated into the design.

Having a clear understanding of the user tasks that must be supported and usability objectives that must be met need not compromise the process of creativity. Having such criteria defined before any visual design work begins provides justifiable constraints that should ultimately create a better solution for the company than one that is created within a vacuum.

Development groups understand the constraints that the technology brings, but can still enjoy a level of creativity in the way that a site is developed. There is a general consensus among software engineers, especially those who have worked with 'creative' people who like making changes along the way, that to have any reasonable chance of producing a good site they really need to be given a clear specification of what is required very early on. Anyone who wishes to change the goalposts half-way through should understand what the implications will be on the development schedules, and the person making the decision to go with the change should also take responsibility for any extension that may be needed to the project end date as a result.

Introducing a structured process for developing websites can improve the time it takes to deliver a good solution and can improve the quality of the site that is delivered. However, it will always rely on the managers responsible for the project putting the required processes and skills in place. It is to be hoped that there will be enough incentive to get the website right so that the momentum will be there to do the right thing. Successful sites are rarely created through luck, and not every business can rely on having a web genius that instinctively knows what will work within the web environment. The majority of teams have to rely on following a process that will work for them. This book will help define what that process should be.

Bibliography

Cooper, Alan (1995) *About Face: The Essentials of User Interface Design*, Idg Books Worldwide.

Diaper, Dan ((1989) *Task Analysis for Human-Computer Interaction*, Prentice Hall.

Nielsen, Jakob (1999) *Designing Web Usability: The Practice of Simplicity*, New Riders.

Nielsen, Jakob and Del Galdo, Elisa M. (eds) (1996) *International User Interfaces*, John Wiley & Sons Inc.

Norman, Donald A. (1998) *The Design of Everyday Things*, The MIT Press.

Preece, Jenny (1994) *Human Computer Interaction*, Addison-Wesley.

Pressman, R. S. (1992) *Software Engineering: A Practitioner's Approach*, McGraw Hill.

Rosenfeld, Louis and Morville, Peter (1997) *Information Architecture for the World Wide Web*, O'Reilly UK.

Rumbaugh, James, Jacobson, Ivar and Booch, Grady (1999) *Unified Modelling Language Reference Manual*, Addison Wesley Longman Publishing Co.

Shneiderman, Ben (1998) *Designing the User Interface*, Addison Wesley Longman.

References

[1] Jakob Neilson, *Failure of Corporate Web Sites*
www.useit.com/alertbox/981018.html

[2] Harley Manning, John C. McCarthy and Randy K. Souza, *Why Most Web Sites Fail* Interactive Technology Series, Volume 3, Number 7, Forrester Research

[3] *How Users Find out About WWW Pages*, GVU's 10th WWW User Survey
www.gvu.gatech.edu/user_surveys/survey-1998-10/graphs/use/q52.htm

[4] Jakob Neilson, *Why People Shop on the Web*
www.useit.com/alertbox/990207.html

[5] Jakob Neilson, *Fighting LinkRot*
www.useit.com/alertbox/980614.html

[6] *Problems using the Web*, GVU's 9th WWW User Survey,
www.gvu.gatech.edu/user_surveys/survey-1998-04/reports/1998-04-Use.html

[7] Andrew Sears, Julie A. Jacko and Michael S. Borella , *Internet Delay Effects: How Users Perceive Quality, Organization, and Ease of Use of Information*, CHI 97 Electronic Publications: Late-Breaking/Short Talks
www.acm.org/sigchi/chi97/proceedings/short-talk/als2.htm

[8] Jakob Nielson, 'Response Times: The Three Important Limits', Excerpt from Chapter 5 of *Usability Engineering*
www.useit.com:80/papers/responsetime.html

[9] Peter Bickford, *Human Interface Online: Worth the Wait?*
developer.netscape.com/viewsource/bickford_wait.htm

[10] Jakob Neilson, *The Need for Speed*
www.useit.com/alertbox/9703a.html

[11] Jakob Neilson, *How Users Read on the Web*
www.useit.com/alertbox/9710a.html

[12] Jakob Neilson, *Concise, SCANNABLE, and Objective: How to Write for the Web*
www.useit.com/papers/webwriting/writing.html

[13] Jon Meads, *Usability is not Graphic Design*
developer.netscape.com/viewsource/meads_usb.htm

[14] Jakob Neilson, *'Top Ten Mistakes' Revisited Three Years Later*
www.useit.com/alertbox/990502.html

[15] Jennifer Fleming, *Designing Web Navigation – Five tips for planning your space*
www.ahref.com/guides/design/199808/0831jef.html

[16] Annabel Pollock, Andrew Hockley, *What's Wrong with Internet Searching,*
www.dlib.org/dlib/march97/bt/03pollock.html

[17] Jakob Neilson, *Electronic Books – a bad idea*
www.useit.com/alertbox/980726.html

[18] Pamela Susan Mullan, *Chapter 4 On-screen reading*
www.users.redcreek.net/mullanp/Fr_thesis/chap4.htm

[19] Daniel Will-Harris, *The best faces for the screen*
www.will-harris.com/typoscrn.htm

[20] Eric Goetze, *Making Web Text Easy on the Eyes*
www.avatarmag.com/columns/ui/default.htm

[21] Melinda McAdams, *Driving a Newspaper On the Data Highway*
www.well.com/user/mmcadams/on-line.newspapers.html

[22] *Ameritech Web Page User Interface and Design Guidelines*
www.ameritech.com/corporate/testtown/library/standard/Web_guidelines/   naviga-tion.html

[23] Jakob Neilson, *The Increasing Conservatism of Web Users*
www.useit.com/alertbox/980322.html

[24] Jakob Neilson, *Inverted Pyramids in Cyberspace*
www.useit.com/alertbox/9606.html

[25] Jakob Neilson, *Applying Writing Guidelines to Web Pages*
www.useit.com/papers/webwriting/rewriting.html

[26] Extensible Markup Language (XML) 1.0, W3C Recommendation 10-February-1998
www.w3.org/TR/REC-xml

[27] Papers on Relational databases and normalisation techniques
E. F. Codd: A Relational Model of Data for Large Shared Data Banks. CACM 13(6): 377-387(1970)
E. F. Codd: Further Normalization of the Data Base Relational Model. IBM Research Report RJ 909, San Jose, California: (1971)
E. F. Codd, C. J. Date: Interactive Support For Non-Programmers: The Relational and Network Approaches. SIGMOD Workshop, Vol. 2 1974: 11-41
For more information on Papers by E. F. Codd see a list of publications from the DBLP Bibliography Server
www.informatik.uni-trier.de/~ley/db/indices/a-tree/c/Codd:E=_F=.html

[28] References for the CRC Method

A Diagram for Object-oriented Programs
Cunningham W. and Beck K.
OOPSLA –86 Proceedings, October 1986

A Laboratory for Teaching Object-oriented Thinking
Beck K. and Cunningham W.
OOPSLA –89 Proceedings, October 1989
Addison-Wesley Publishing ISBN 0-201-52249-7

Object-oriented Design: A Responsibility-Driven Approach
Wirfs-Brock R. and Wilkerson B.
OOPSLA –89 Proceedings, October 1989
Addison-Wesley Publishing ISBN 0-201-52249-7

Designing Object Oriented Software
Wirfs-Brock, Wilkerson and Wiener
Prentice Hall ISBN 0-13-629825-7

Appendix A – IBM Global Services

Many of the examples used within Chapter 8 covering content design considerations were captured from external customer websites created by IBM Global Services.

About IBM as an e-business

Much of what IBM has learned about e-business comes directly from the company's experience in transforming itself into one of the world's largest e-businesses. In 1999 IBM generated $14.8 billion in e-commerce revenue. In addition, it procured $13 billion in goods and services over the web, saving more than $270 million. IBM also web-enabled more than 12,000 suppliers. More than 42 million technical self-service enquiries were handled on ibm.com, resulting in more than $750 million in cost avoidance and productivity gains. Of these enquiries, 6 million were IBM Y2K web-based customer service transactions. Since Q4 1998, 58 per cent of IBM's customer self-service transactions have been done via the web. For more information, visit *www.ibm.com/e-business*

About IBM Global Services

IBM Global Services is the world's largest information technology services provider, with 1999 revenues of approximately $32.2 billion. Services is the fastest growing part of IBM, with more than 138,000 professionals operating in 160 countries. IBM Global Services integrates all of IBM's capabilities – services, hardware, software and research – to help companies of all sizes realize the full value of information technology. For more information, visit *www.ibm.com/services*

About IBM Ease of Use Services

IBM's focus on ease of use has led to technology breakthroughs and advances in design research, as well as vital contributions to the user-centred design process itself. IBM provides development teams with professional assistance in all aspects of product development including assessments, requirements gathering, task analysis, design and prototyping, user studies, laboratory usability testing and product implementations. For more information, visit *www.ibm.com/easy/services*

Appendix B – Overview of the UML notation used within this book

Classes and the 'has a' relationship

Most of the diagrams within the book rely on understanding the relationship between one class and another. For example, this diagram describes the statement 'A Bouquet of flowers may have one Card'.

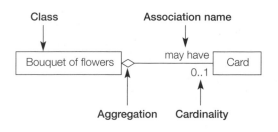

UML uses a rectangle to represent a Class, a line between two classes to represent a relationship and a diamond on the line to represent aggregation, which can be more easily described as a 'has a' relationship. The Cardinality attribute specifies how many instances of that class can be associated with a single instance of the other class.

In this example a single Bouquet of flowers may have 'zero or one' Cards. The '0..' notation shows the number following is conditional, and when a '*' is used, it represents 'many'. So '1..*' would translate to 'one to many', and '0..*' would translate to 'can have many'.

Attributes and operations

When a class is described in more detail, the rectangle or class description can be expanded into sections that can provide a list of attributes for each class and the operations that the class can perform.

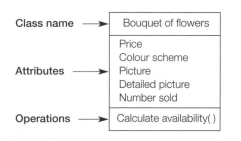

For example, a Bouquet of flowers can have a Price, a Colour scheme, a Picture, a Detailed picture and store the Number that has been sold. It may have an operation that provides the ability to calculate the availability for that Bouquet.

Enumerated types

It may be applicable for some types of attributes to show that the value for that attribute is restricted to a value from within a predefined list. This is extremely useful when providing a method for data input, as it can reduce errors and ensure that standard terminology is used. This amounts to providing a way of classifying information, which can later be used for categorization and keyword search. In this example, it states that a Card has one Type of Card, the value of which can be either Birthday, Anniversary, Mothers day or Get well.

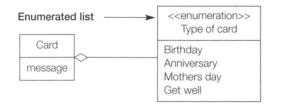

If all Cards are categorized in this way, it allows views to be designed that provide the ability to display content items that match certain criteria. For instance a view could display the entire set of cards available for Mothers day.

Specialized types or generalization

One of the best ideas about Object Oriented techniques is the idea of reusing or sharing small containable objects through aggression or generalization. Generalization is the idea of defining a subclass that shares the structure or behaviour that is defined within one or more super classes. In this example, Roses and Carnations are Types of Flowers.

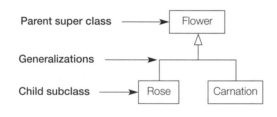

In design terms, generalization is only useful, when the specialized types add new attributes or operations to the class that they generalize, otherwise, an enumerated type attribute as shown above would be preferable and much more efficient.

Use cases

When trying to define the requirements for a system, it can be useful to express these requirements in a way that maps to the understanding or perception of the system by those who are expected to use it. To achieve this, UML provides a way of expressing the types of people who will be trying to use the system (Actors) and a way of succinctly describing the user goal or perceive function that they wish to achieve (Use case). Within this book, use cases are used purely to describe the highest level of requirements that each person within the system may have.

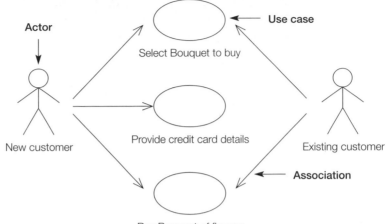

Therefore in this simple example, a New customer may wish to Select a Bouquet of flowers to buy, Provide credit card details and Buy the Bouquet. Whereas an Existing customer may have no need to Provide credit card details, because they are already stored in the system.

State diagrams

State machine diagrams provide a way of showing what happens to a class when events occur both internally and externally. Within the book, they are used to describe the different stages that a content item will go through when associated with a workflow, and the actions and events that move a content item from one stage to another.

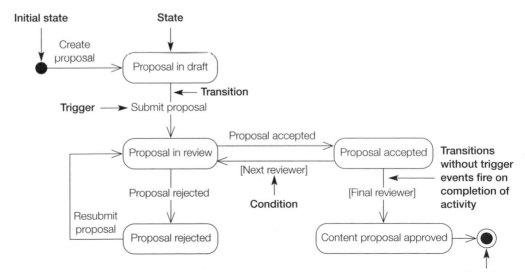

Therefore this example shows a number of states that a proposal may go through when it is associated with a default proposal workflow. The initial trigger for the workflow is a Create proposal, which puts the proposal in a state of 'Proposal in draft'. When a proposal is accepted, this changes the state of the proposal to Proposal accepted, where there are two conditions to test that will change the state automatically. If there is another reviewer to review the proposal, the state reverts back to 'Proposal in review', however if the person who accepted the proposal was the final reviewer then the state automatically fires to a 'Content proposal approved', which is a Final state.

Appendix C – Websphere Advanced CD Bundle

About IBM Software

IBM Software has the industry's leading portfolio of middleware products. Software is where the e-business discussion starts and the questions and answers usually revolve around software. Using the internet to link to legacy applications, making a business available to customers 24 hours a day, transacting with customers, suppliers and partners over the web and having a collaborative network among all the stakeholders requires software that is highly available, provides strong performance and scales as fast as the organization. Software that can deploy new applications as fast as a business evolves on web time and integrates across a business is the software that IBM makes. For more information visit *www.ibm.com/software*

About the IBM Websphere platform

The IBM Websphere software platform for e-business is a comprehensive set of award-winning, integrated e-business solutions. It's a software platform based on industry standards – like Java, XML and J2EE technologies – making it flexible and pluggable, allowing you to adapt on-the-fly as markets shift and business goals change.

IBM WebSphere can help you get to market quickly by allowing you to build, test and depoy e-business applications faster. You can rapidly develop new applications without learning new skills because a lot of the Java code is automatically generated.

With IBM WebSphere Application Server, Advanced Edition, create and deploy business logic using Enterprise JavaBeans (EJB) Technology.

With IBM WebSphere Homepage Builder, create and deploy web pages with web authoring and design software using ready-to-use templates.

With IBM VisualAge for Java, create scaleable, high-performance e-business applications using advanced, easy-to-use functions to build, test and deploy Java technology-based applications, JavaBeans components, servlets and applets.

Note:

VisualAge, IBM, WebSphere are trademarks of International Business Machines Corporation in the United States, other countries, or both.

Java, all Java-based trademarks and logos and Solaris are trademarks of Sun Microsystems, Inc. in the United States, other countries, or both.

For more information visit: *www.ibm.com/websphere*

About your CD

Just place the CD into the drive and from there follow the instructions.

Index